Writers and Missionaries

Verso is pleased to be working with the *London Review of Books* on an occasional series of volumes that draw on writing that first appeared in the paper.

The *LRB* is Europe's leading journal of culture and ideas. Subscribers can read all of Adam Shatz's pieces, and every article ever published by the magazine, at lrb.co.uk/archive

Writers and Missionaries

Essays on the
Radical Imagination

Adam Shatz

VERSO
London • New York

First published by Verso 2023

© Adam Shatz 2023

The author and publisher would like to express their gratitude to the following publications in which these essays originally appeared: the *London Review of Books* (chs. 3, 4, 5, 6, 8, 9, 11, 12, 13, 14, and 15); the *Nation* (chs. 1 and 16); the *New York Review* (ch. 10); the *New Yorker* (epilogue); and the *New York Times Magazine* (ch. 2).

1 3 5 7 9 10 8 6 4 2

Verso

UK: 6 Meard Street, London W1F 0EG

US: 388 Atlantic Avenue, Brooklyn, NY 11217

versobooks.com

Verso is the imprint of New Left Books

ISBN-13: 978-1-80429-059-0

ISBN-13: 978-1-80429-064-4 (US EBK)

ISBN-13: 978-1-80429-063-7 (UK EBK)

British Library Cataloguing in Publication Data

A catalogue record for this book is available from the British Library

Library of Congress Cataloging-in-Publication Data

Names: Shatz, Adam, author.

Title: Writers and missionaries : essays on the radical imagination / Adam Shatz.

Description: London ; New York : Verso, 2023. | Includes index.

Identifiers: LCCN 2022058208 (print) | LCCN 2022058209 (ebook) | ISBN 9781804290590 (hardback) | ISBN 9781804290644 (ebook)

Subjects: LCSH: Intellectuals. | Philosophers. | Authorship—Political aspects—History. | Intellectual life—History. | Criticism. | Radicalism. | Loneliness. | LCGFT: Essays.

Classification: LCC HM728 .S435 2023 (print) | LCC HM728 (ebook) | DDC 305.5/52—dc23/eng/20230110

LC record available at https://lccn.loc.gov/2022058208

LC ebook record available at https://lccn.loc.gov/2022058209

Typeset in Sabon by MJ & N Gavan, Truro, Cornwall

Printed and bound by CPI Group (UK) Ltd, Croydon, CR0 4YY

Contents

Introduction

In 1990, I arrived in New York City to attend Columbia University, with a vague and yet passionately held idea of becoming a writer. A novelist, a journalist, a literary critic? I didn't know, but the uncertainty in no way dampened my hope that, one day, I might be known as an *author*—of something.

Imagine, then, my reaction when, in a class on contemporary French thought, I read Roland Barthes's 1967 essay, "The Death of the Author": "It is language which speaks, not the author . . . To give a text an Author is to impose a limit on that text, to furnish it with a final signified, to close the writing." The "birth of the reader," Barthes went on, "must be at the cost of the death of the Author."

Nor was he alone, I learned, in seeing the author and his or her intentions as an obstacle to the reader's interpretation of a text —even to the reader's freedom. Two years after Barthes's essay was published, Michel Foucault defined the author as "the principle of thrift in the proliferation of meaning," and as a figure of unearned privilege. "What difference," he declared, "does it make who is speaking?"

Quite a lot, you might reply. And had someone else published these obituaries, I'm not sure how much attention I would have paid them.* The allure and, indeed, authority of Barthes and Foucault were only enhanced by their dramatic disavowals of the value of authorship.

---

* Today, of course, the idea that an author's identity is irrelevant to an understanding of their work would be unfathomable to young people who are increasingly taught that an author's identity is almost all that matters; but back then it exerted a considerable aura, at least in critical theory.

But if the author was dead, what was the point of becoming one? Wouldn't it be better for writers—above all, writers on the left, as I already thought of myself—to renounce the narcissistic practice of signing their works, and to become as secretive about their identities as underground revolutionaries, and thereby contribute to (in Foucault's words) the subversive "proliferation of meaning"?

I was fascinated by the program that Barthes and Foucault were proposing, and by the philosophical "antihumanism" they espoused. Their writings were dense and often elusive, but they were also elegant, seductively counterintuitive and even sexy. Barthes, in particular, was a writer of rare literary gifts—an *author*, in spite of himself.

Yet I could never bring myself to join the antihumanist club, for all its temptations, or contemplate with equanimity the death of the author. It mattered to me then (and matters to me still) that Frederick Douglass published his autobiographies under his own name, seizing the power of authorship in a society where the enslaved were forbidden to read. That Antonio Gramsci's notes and letters had been written in one of Mussolini's jails also struck me as proof that authorship could be liberating: you could imprison the man, but not his mind. Knowledge of author's lives and struggles, it seemed to me, could enhance and expand, rather than limit, our understanding of their work. As Jean-Paul Sartre reminded us in his 1948 essay, *What Is Literature?*, "Writers are alive before they are dead." I agreed with Sartre, even though admitting this to some of my more theoretical peers would have been like confessing to a love of Brahms at the Darmstadt school of experimental music.

The leader of postwar French existentialism, Sartre was the philosopher Barthes, Foucault and their peers were determined to overthrow. He was an incorrigible humanist, a stubborn believer in the obsolete category of "man": the opposite of sexy. His major works, *Being and Nothingness* and *The Critique of Dialectical Reason*, were ridiculed by younger philosophers as quaint relics of nineteenth-century thought.

There was some truth in the accusation. The anthropocentric

thrust of Sartre's existential humanism seems even more dated in the Anthropocene. But I was attracted to Sartre less for his systematic tomes (which, to be honest, I couldn't get through) than for his riveting portraits of other writers, from Baudelaire and Genet to Nizan, Merleau-Ponty and Fanon. I loved the way he burrowed his way into their voices, exploring the political and ethical dilemmas they confronted in what he called "situations," the settings of conflict and crisis in which they created their work. He made dead writers, and their intellectual dramas, seem alive and urgent.

To be sure, Sartre tried to enlist these writers for his own ends, usually as an illustration of his philosophical ideas. Yet there was also a humility beneath his bravado, a willingness to give himself over to the work and imagination of other writers, as well a moving sense of the challenges his subjects faced. And he captured the desire for freedom that, as he saw it, lies behind all forms of creative writing. Freedom, he insisted, is "at the origin" of writing, since "no one is obliged to choose himself as a writer." Writing, therefore, "is a certain way of wanting freedom; once you have begun, you are committed."

By "commitment," Sartre meant dedication to a project— intellectual, moral, political, aesthetic or some combination. When we write, we bind ourselves to the project that our work embodies; in the act of commitment, life and work fuse in pursuit of a common goal. In his portraits, Sartre chronicled the efforts of writers and artists to respond to the problems of the world they'd inherited, the "worked matter" left by previous generations that stood in the way of a different future. "To write for one's age," he observed, "is not to reflect it passively; it is to want to maintain or to change it, thus to go beyond it toward the future, and it is this effort to change it that places us most deeply within it."

It is easy, of course, to be cynical about writing, particularly if you make your living from it. The shop talk of writers might lead you to assume that they're mostly concerned about their reputa- tions, or that of other writers, or awards they haven't received, or editors who held or killed their pieces, or about what other, only apparently less fortunate people do for a living. But when writers are back at their desks, most are engaged in a game of higher stakes: describing the world as they see it, and, nearly as often, as they hope to change it. (Even the most pessimistic writers are closet idealists, since they still hold out the hope of being heard.)

Although I'm too old to call myself a Sartrean existentialist, I continue to believe that the adventure of writing and criticism is inseparable from the lived experiences of writers. I do not mean that it is *reducible* to those experiences, the conviction underlying contemporary "identitarianism," which would have us believe that writing is whipped out of collective trauma just as butter is from cream. It is not so much the background and history of writers that determine the shape of their work as how they choose to interpret their past, and how they incorporate this understanding into their project: these choices, these visions, represent, in Sartre's words, their "way of wanting freedom."

The essays in this book are portraits of writers, novelists, filmmakers, and philosophers of various commitments: structuralists (Claude Lévi-Strauss) and deconstructionists (Jacques Derrida), Marxists (Sartre) and black internationalists (Richard Wright, William Gardner Smith), Palestinian nationalists (Edward Said) and Arab liberals (Kamel Daoud), Zionists (Claude Lanzmann) and anti-Zionists (Juliano Mer-Khamis), nihilists (Michel Houellebecq) and sadomasochists (Alain Robbe-Grillet). Although only a few—Houellebecq, Robbe-Grillet, Daoud, the filmmaker Jean-Pierre Melville and indeed Sartre himself—are creators of works of the imagination, all of them share what I would call an artistic impulse: Barthes, Derrida, Lévi-Strauss and Said were novelists *manqués*; Lanzmann described his monumental cinematic essay on the Holocaust, *Shoah*, not as a documentary but rather as a "fiction of the real." Both Said and his chief antagonist, the intellectual historian Fouad Ajami, drew inspiration from Joseph Conrad. And while I write extensively about their political choices, I am just as interested in their aesthetic commitments, the sensibilities and obsessions that give their work its power, its character, and what Barthes would have called its "grain," without which their work would not be worth considering today. Some of the incidents and personalities in one essay recur in another—Sartre's ill-fated trip to the Middle East, for instance, or Derrida's feud with Lévi-Strauss—but these repetitions are more like ritornellos in a symphony, variations on subjects and themes that have preoccupied me as a writer: the politics of France and the Arab world; the problem of the "color line"; and, to lift a phrase from the historian Enzo Traverso, "the end of Jewish modernity" since the creation of the state of Israel. Intellectual portraiture is also self-portraiture, though often in some hidden sense. And sometimes not so hidden: the epilogue of this book is a short memoir of my earliest intellectual commitment: cooking, the childhood passion that awakened my interest in France, and, by an unexpected and twisted path, led me to my work as a writer.

A few years before his death, the historian Tony Judt told me that if you choose the life of an intellectual, you must resign yourself to being lonely. By declaring that Israel would ultimately have to become a single, binational state, Judt had provoked the wrath of an establishment that had long celebrated him. But he stuck to his guns and seemed to exult in his lonely stance, which had left him a free man. Several of the figures in this book, such as Richard Wright and Melville, were self-conscious loners, but even they were familiar with what Said described as the dialectic, in an intellectual's life, of "loneliness and alignment": Wright had been a longtime member of the Communist Party, Melville a veteran of the Resistance. Chester Himes, the subject of another chapter, led the loneliest of writer's lives, seething in defiant exile with (entirely justified) fury at America and its racism. Yet his novels were an act of alignment, or realignment at a distance, with black Americans back home. To write is often—even, some would say, by definition—to write one's way out of loneliness, and into vicarious dialogue with others. (Even the loneliest of writers dream of readers who share their commitments.)

The proud loneliness of Himes, Wright and Melville represents, of course, a certain style of *masculine* solitude (not unlike Bogart's). And here it should be acknowledged that, aside from the extraordinary Egyptian feminist Arwa Salih, who eloquently dissected the vanities and hypocrisies of her male comrades on the Arab left, before taking her own life, the subjects of this book are all men. Some were guilty of what we now call "toxic" behavior, and I make no secret of it. But in my accounts of men like Himes (who brutalized his female companions) and Alain Robbe-Grillet (who fantasized in his fiction about brutalizing women), my purpose is less to indict than to draw a complete and unflinching portrait. Somewhat unfashionably, I still believe that to explain is not to excuse, and that readers can be trusted to reach their own conclusions. To lift a phrase from Hannah Arendt, these are portraits of "men in dark times" who forged their paths amid war, occupation, colonialism, segregation and political exile. Some had the humiliating experience of being treated as subhuman; others had personal encounters with cruelty, mostly as victims, but sometimes as perpetrators.

Men (and women) in dark times often reflect the darkness of their times. I do not believe in fairy-tale heroes, and you will not find any in this book. What you will find are *acts* of heroism —above all the works of prose and filmmaking they brought into being, sometimes at considerable personal risk, and which continue to illuminate our own intellectual universe. It is hard to imagine twentieth-century intellectual life without Wright's novel *Native Son*; Lévi-Strauss's travel memoir *Tristes Tropiques*; Derrida's essays on Western philosophy in *Of Grammatology*; Barthes's rumination on photography, *Camera Lucida*; Said's critical geneaology of Western attitudes toward the Arab and Islamic world, *Orientalism*; or Lanzmann's *Shoah*. These works have not changed the world, to be sure, but they have changed the way we think about it.

In this book, I try to describe how such works came into being: their position in intellectual history, but also their place in the lives of their creators. I make no attempt to present their authors as models for contemporary emulation or social media branding. The nobility of the work does not mean the nobility of its author; brilliance is not immune to bad character. The essays here are sometimes stories of trauma, but seldom of redemption; they investigate obsessions that remain largely unmastered and leave their subjects' contradictions unresolved. The road to creation, like the road to freedom, is long, messy and mostly unhappy—except for those of us who benefit, much later, as the audience. One of the more curious developments in American intellectual life in recent years has been the celebration of radical figures in the pages of mainstream glossies, which now provide us with consoling, tweetable fables of abolitionists, feminists and anti-racist warriors. We are told that this is part of "doing the work," the literary expression of the "Reckoning," but all too often, the people we read about are scrubbed of complexity, fallibility and therefore, in some sense, of humanity—much like the black characters in the "protest novels" that James Baldwin, a figure more sanctified than understood, famously deplored.

The flaws that I describe may, for some, call into question the value of my subjects' achievements. That is not my view. It is impossible to study intellectual history without suffering heartbreak from time to time. (Just think of Arendt on Little Rock, Chomsky on Cambodia, Foucault on Iran, Angela Davis on East Germany, Sartre on Israel, Malcolm X on gender, or any number of writers on Stalinism.) But, for a reader, disappointed love is still love. The purpose of these essays is not to establish a moral balance sheet but rather to explore the difficult and some-times perilous practice of the engaged intellectual: the wrenching demands that the world imposes on the mind as it seeks to liberate itself from various forms of captivity.

I grew up reading essays. In my teens and twenties, I was dazzled by Sontag's imperious judgments on filmmakers and writers, electrified by Amiri Baraka's musings on jazz and black revolution, and enthralled by the swagger of Pauline Kael, whose film reviews turned criticism into the "erotics" of interpretation that Sontag talked about but never succeeded in practicing herself. Later, in the pages of the *London Review of Books*, whose staff I would join in 2007, I discovered the more intellectually rare-fied essays of writers like Perry Anderson, Jeremy Harding and Jacqueline Rose. What I found in these writers was not so much a model as a toolkit; I learned that you could and indeed had to be attentive to the work *and* the life, the formal *and* the ethical, the cerebral and the sensuous. (And they taught this lesson in a much more visceral manner than Sartre.)

Essays spoke to me instinctively, much as jazz did, and, I suspect, for similar reasons: they were responses to, and in a sense improvisations upon, pre-existing material (a book, a painting, a film, an experience); they were relatively short but dense in ideas and full of risk-taking. At their best, they aspired, as Coltrane did, to a transcendence of the form, turning moments into *events*. The frisson of those events is still with me: Sontag, mourning the death of cinephilia in the *New York Times Magazine*; Edward Said, declaring the Oslo Accords a Palestinian "Versailles" in the *London Review of Books*; Judt, announcing the end of the two-state solution in the *New York Review of Books*; Stanley Crouch, trying to exorcise the ghost of Miles Davis in the *New Republic*.

The essays in this book—most of which appeared in the *London Review of Books*—were written between 2003 and 2021, between the launching of America's "war on terror" and the intensification of America's domestic wars: in Washington, on the streets, on campus, and between the "red" and "blue" parts of every state in the republic. The only American figures here are three black writers—Wright, Himes and Smith—who fled to Paris and never returned home: refugees from the long-running war that white America has waged against its black fellow citizens. Most of the reporting that I did in those years was from parts of the Arab world and from France, regions that feature prominently in this book. Some of my strongest "affiliations," to use a word that Said often invoked, are with intellectuals and writers far from the United States.

Nonetheless, I am an American, based in New York, and this book reflects the concerns of an American witness to his country's descent—or rather, further descent—into cruelty, vindictiveness and paranoid rage. This turn of events is, of course, rooted in the uglier aspects of this country's short history: settler colonialism, slavery, white supremacy and Cold War militarism, among others. But Trump's followers are not the only Americans gripped by madness, or seduced by simple solutions to complex problems. Although writing these essays provided me with a welcome distraction from America's crisis (as well as an opportunity to revisit literature and films that I admire), it also led me to reflect upon some of the ills that bedevil us today, and not only in the United States, especially the recrudescence of tribalist thinking, and the decline of solidarity as a political principle. As Sartre would have said, writers can protest their "situation," but they cannot escape it.

Most of the figures in this book are on the political left. But in referring to the "radical imagination," I do not mean an affiliation with the left, so much as a style of thinking that seeks to penetrate the root of a problem and expose "what is fundamental," to borrow a phrase of the composer Julius Eastman. Houellebecq is a reactionary nihilist, or at least a cynic whose thinking happens to converge with the anti-immigrant right in France; Jean-Pierre Melville, for his part, described himself as "an anarchist of the right." But few have examined the malaise and disaffection in contemporary France as acutely as Houellebecq. And in his mesmerizing gangster films, Melville drew upon his Resistance past to explore the question of brotherhood—the very French theme of *fraternité*. The audacity and intransigence of imagination on display in their work surely deserves the adjective "radical," even if neither of them would ever turn up on the barricades.

Fouad Ajami, the subject of the first essay, was certainly no radical, but he started out as a perceptive critic of American (and Israeli) power, even as he raised tough, and still pertinent, questions about the failings of Arab politicians and intellectuals. By the time I profiled him for the *Nation*, in 2003, he had become an apologist for the American invasion of Iraq, earning the praise of Dick Cheney, and was understandably reviled by his former comrades on the Arab left. Yet the story seemed to me tragic, since, in his early and best work, Ajami, who died in 2014, had written about the Arab world with panache, insight and compassion. Ideological conversion has always fascinated me, since it is almost never merely a matter of ideas, much less some lightning-bolt epiphany, but rather of a more complex, slow-burning interplay between conviction, psychology, ambition and political calculation.* In Ajami's gradual turn to the right, I found a troubling parable about belonging, ambition and the temptations of power, set against America's deepening political and military involvement in the Middle East. Some of the "liberal" American intellectuals I knew had made similar adjustments to their principles, under noticeably less demanding circumstances, when they supported the Iraq War as a "humanitarian" intervention.

Some would argue that Ajami's failure was that he stopped "speaking truth to power." This is partly true, of course. And in my own work as a journalist—reporting from Palestine and Algeria, or writing on the Black Lives Matter protests sparked by George Floyd's assassination—I have sought to highlight the abuses of the powerful, and to never forget the asymmetries in any political struggle. But speaking truth to power, and aligning oneself with the oppressed, is less straightforward than it seems. Truth is not singular; neither (as Foucault reminds us) is power. What is more, yesterday's oppressed can become tomorrow's oppressors. Lanzmann made an astonishing film about the destruction of European Jewry, only to help turn the Holocaust into a symbolic Iron Dome, insulating the state of Israel from any criticism of its occupation and apartheid policies. The black expatriate writer William Gardner Smith discovered that his black friends in Paris had no interest in coming to the defense of Algerians fighting for their independence, since France had offered them a comfortable sanctuary where they were (relatively) free from antiblack racism. Neither collective memory nor racial solidarity is a recipe for liberation: each can underwrite someone else's persecution.

Nor is an admirable outlook an adequate guide to changing the world for the better. Take, for example, the case of Juliano Mer-Khamis, an actor, director and activist whose assassination, in 2011, is the subject of another chapter. The son of a Palestinian

---

*   One of my earliest pieces of reporting, for the *American Prospect*, was a profile of Abigail and Stephan Thernstrom, civil rights liberals who evolved into neoconservative opponents of affirmative action.

father and an Israeli-Jewish mother, Mer-Khamis attempted to fight, at one and the same time, Israel's occupation and what he called the "cultural occupation" imposed by social conservatives in the West Bank town of Jenin, where he established a theater for young Palestinians. He imagined that, by his efforts with young people in Jenin's refugee camp, he was waging a form of artistic resistance to both Israel and the Palestinian Authority, thus helping to build the binational future for Israel-Palestine— a future that he felt he personally embodied, as a man who was "one hundred percent Arab, and one hundred percent Jewish." He was a dashing and charismatic man who believed in his ideas, and in the force of his personality. But the "resistance" he led was confined to a small theater funded by foreign donors, and the weapons of truth-telling could not protect the dreamer from his illusions, or defend him against his assassins, who had real weapons and saw Mer-Khamis as an outsider—and a threat—in the insular town of Jenin.

John Berger wrote somewhere that subtlety is a luxury of the privileged, but I am not so sure. It seems to me that subtlety and nuance are indispensable tools of criticism—not least for groups of people (so-called minorities, for example) who have been seen, and often vilified, as monoliths. Irony, skepticism, doubt and detachment are increasingly treated as expressions of elitism or privilege, but I have always found them to be necessary instruments of radical critique—and, indeed, a moral compass, in an age in which social media posturing has often come to substitute for sustained, patient engagement with ideas, and the attention to distinctions and ambiguities that this effort requires.

Mary-Kay Wilmers, who edited many of these pieces for the *London Review of Books*, once told me she did not publish a certain writer I admired because he wrote to have the last word on a topic, rather than to open it up. A good essay, she said, should make room for another one on the same subject. With her guidance, I learned to resist the temptation to have the last word. I also discovered a passion for nuance that has never left me, although I remain fascinated, if at times somewhat fright-ened, by those whose passion runs in the opposite direction, and whom I call "missionaries" in the last essay in the book. The title of the essay, "Writers or Missionaries?," refers to a conversation I had with the late novelist and reporter V. S. Naipaul, shortly after he won the Nobel Prize in literature. Naipaul told me that a writer had a choice: you could be a writer, or you could be a missionary, but you couldn't be both. Naipaul was a visionary writer of prose, but he had a predilection for stark binaries. This was one of them.

At the time, I was wrestling with Naipaul's remark, which spoke to my growing exasperation with polemical writing, and my conviction that ideologically driven writers usually ended up in bad places, whether they were defending Bashar al-Assad as a bulwark against American imperialism, or (like Naipaul himself) the Modi regime in India. But, of course, the line between description and advocacy is more porous than we think. Nearly every description we give is infused, in some way, with our sense of reality, our moods, and our hopes. We are always, whether we realize it or not, trying to move the needle. And even those writers who don't think of themselves as political are driven by a sense of commitment: commitment to their work, which is, of course, the writer's original commitment, the one that gets them off the sofa and to their writing desk. The writers in this book are also missionaries, sometimes for a cause, sometimes for a way of seeing. All of them have pushed the needle forward, mostly for better, sometimes for worse. *Writers and Missionaries* is my attempt to explain how they did it, and why they still matter.

I

Native Sons

1

Fouad Ajami:
The Native Informant

In late August 2002, at a reunion of Korean War veterans in San Antonio, Texas, Dick Cheney tried to assuage concerns that a unilateral, preemptive war against Iraq might "cause even greater troubles in that part of the world." He cited a well-known Arab authority: "As for the reaction of the Arab street, the Middle East expert Professor Fouad Ajami predicts that after liberation in Basra and Baghdad, the streets are sure to erupt in joy." As the bombs fell over Baghdad, just before American troops began to encounter fierce Iraqi resistance, Ajami could scarcely conceal his glee. "We are now coming into acquisition of Iraq," he announced on CBS News the morning of March 22. "It's an amazing performance."

If Hollywood ever makes a film about Gulf War II, a supporting role should be reserved for Ajami, the director of Middle East Studies at the School of Advanced International Studies (SAIS) at Johns Hopkins University. His is a classic American success story. Born in 1945 to Shia parents in the remote southern Lebanese village of Arnoun and now a proud naturalized American, Ajami has become the most politically influential Arab intellectual of his generation in the United States. Condoleezza Rice often summons him to the White House for advice, and Deputy Secretary of Defense Paul Wolfowitz, a friend and former colleague, has paid tribute to him in several recent speeches on Iraq. Despite the relative slenderness of his scholarly output, Ajami is a regular guest on CBS News, *Charlie Rose* and the *NewsHour with Jim Lehrer*, and a frequent contributor to the editorial pages of the

Wall Street Journal and the *New York Times*. His ideas are also widely recycled by acolytes like Thomas Friedman and Judith Miller of the *Times*.

Ajami's unique role in American political life has been to unpack the unfathomable mysteries of the Arab and Muslim world and to help sell America's wars in the region. A diminutive, balding man with a dramatic beard, stylish clothes and a charming, almost flirtatious manner, he has played his part brilliantly. On television, he radiates above-the-frayness, speaking with the wry, jaded authority that men in power admire, especially in men who have risen from humble roots. Unlike the other Arabs, he appears to have no ax to grind. He is one of us; he is the good Arab.

Ajami's admirers paint him as a courageous gadfly who has risen above the tribal hatreds of the Arabs, a Middle Eastern Spinoza whose honesty has earned him the scorn of his brethren. *Commentary* editor-at-large Norman Podhoretz, one of his many right-wing American Jewish fans, writes that Ajami "has been virtually alone in telling the truth about the attitude toward Israel of the people from whom he stems." The people from whom Ajami "stems" are, of course, the Arabs, and Ajami's ethnicity is not incidental to his celebrity. It lends him an air of authority not enjoyed by non-Arab polemicists like Martin Kramer and Daniel Pipes.

But Ajami is no gadfly. He is, in fact, almost entirely a creature of the American establishment. His once-luminous writing, increasingly a blend of Naipaulean clichés about Muslim pathologies and Churchillian rhetoric about the burdens of empire, is saturated with hostility toward Sunni Arabs in general (save for pro-Western Gulf Arabs, toward whom he is notably indulgent), and to Palestinians in particular. He invites comparison with Henry Kissinger, another émigré intellectual to achieve extraordinary prominence as a champion of American empire. Like Kissinger, Ajami has a suave television demeanor, a gravitas-lending accent, an instinctive solicitude for the imperatives of power and a cool disdain for the weak. And just as Kissinger cozied up to Nelson Rockefeller and Nixon, so has

Ajami attached himself to such powerful patrons as Laurence Tisch, former chairman of CBS; Mort Zuckerman, the owner of *US News and World Report*; Martin Peretz, a co-owner of the *New Republic*; and Leslie Gelb, head of the Council on Foreign Relations.

Despite his training in political science, Ajami often sounds like a pop psychologist in his writing about the Arab world or, as he variously calls it, "the world of Araby," "that Arab world" and "those Arab lands." According to Ajami, that world is "gripped in a poisonous rage" and "wedded to a worldview of victimology," bad habits reinforced by its leaders, "megalomaniacs who never tell their people what can and cannot be had in the world of nations." There is, to be sure, a grain of truth in Ajami's grim assessment. Progressive Arab thinkers from the Syrian Marxist philosopher Sadiq al-Azm to the Syrian-Lebanese poet Adonis have issued equally bleak indictments of Arab political culture, lambasting the dearth of self-criticism and the constant search for external scapegoats. Unlike these writers, however, Ajami has little sympathy for the people of the region, unless they happen to live within the borders of "rogue states" like Iraq, in which case they must be "liberated" by American force. The corrupt regimes that rule the Arab world, he has suggested, are more or less faithful reflections of the "Arab psyche": "Despots always work with a culture's yearnings . . . After all, a *hadith*, a saying attributed to the Prophet Muhammad, maintains 'You will get the rulers you deserve.'" His own taste in regimes runs to monarchies like Kuwait. The Jews of Israel, it seems, are not just the only people in the region who enjoy the fruits of democracy; they are the only ones who deserve them.

Once upon a time, Ajami was an articulate and judicious critic both of Arab society and of the West, a defender of Palestinian rights and an advocate of decent government in the Arab world. Though he remains a shrewd guide to the hypocrisies of Arab leaders, his views on foreign policy now scarcely diverge from those of pro-Israel hawks in the Bush administration. "Since the Gulf War, Fouad has taken leave of his analytic perspective to play to his elite constituency," said Augustus Richard Norton, a Middle East scholar at Boston University. "It's very unfortunate because he could have made an astonishingly important contribution."

Seeking to understand the causes of Ajami's transformation, I spoke to more than two dozen of his friends and acquaintances over the past several months. (Ajami did not return my phone calls or e-mails.) These men and women depicted a man at once ambitious and insecure, torn between his irascible intellectual independence and his even stronger desire to belong to something larger than himself. On the one hand, he is an intellectual dandy who, as Sayres Rudy, a former student, puts it, "doesn't like groups and thinks people who join them are mediocre." On the other, as a Shia among Sunnis, and as an émigré in America, he has always felt the outsider's anxiety to please, and has adjusted his convictions to fit his surroundings. As a young man eager to assimilate into the urbane Sunni world of Muslim Beirut, he embraced pan-Arabism. Received with open arms by the American Jewish establishment in New York and Washington, he became an ardent Zionist. An informal adviser to both Bush administrations, he is now a cheerleader for the American empire.

The man from Arnoun appears to be living the American dream. He has a prestigious job and the ear of the president. Yet the price of power has been higher in his case than in Kissinger's. Kissinger, after all, is a figure of renown among the self-appointed leaders of "the people from whom he stems" and a frequent speaker at Jewish charity galas, whereas Ajami is a man almost entirely deserted by his people, a pariah at what should be his hour of triumph. In Arnoun, a family friend told me, "Fouad is a black sheep because of his staunch support for the Israelis." Although he frequently travels to Tel Aviv and the Persian Gulf, he almost never goes to Lebanon. In becoming an American, he has become, as he himself has confessed, "a stranger in the Arab world."

Ajami's is an immigrant's tale. It begins in Arnoun, a rocky hamlet in the south of Lebanon where Fouad al-Ajami was born on September 19, 1945. A prosperous tobacco-growing Shia family, the Ajamis had come to Arnoun from Iran in the 1850s. (Their name, Arabic for "Persian," gave away their origins.)

When Ajami was four, he moved with his family to Beirut, settling in the largely Armenian northeastern quarter, a neighborhood thick with orange orchards, pine trees and strawberry fields. As members of the rural Shia minority, the country's "hewers of wood and drawers of water," the Ajamis stood apart from the city's dominant groups, the Sunni Muslims and the Maronite Christians. "We were strangers to Beirut," he has written. "We wanted to pass undetected in the modern world of Beirut, to partake of its ways." For the young "Shia *assimilé*," as he has described himself, "anything Persian, anything Shia, was anathema . . . speaking Persianized Arabic was a threat to something unresolved in my identity." He tried desperately, but with little success, to pass among his Sunni peers. In the predominantly Sunni schools he attended, "Fouad was taunted for being a Shia, and for being short," one friend told me. "That left him with a lasting sense of bitterness toward the Sunnis."

In the 1950s, Arab nationalism appeared to hold out the promise of transcending the schisms between Sunni and Shia, and the confessional divisions separating Muslims and Christians. Like his classmates, Ajami fell under the spell of pan-Arabism's charismatic spokesman, the Egyptian leader Gamal Abdel Nasser. At the same time, he was falling under the spell of American culture, which offered relief from the "ancestral prohibitions and phobias" of his "cramped land." Watching John Wayne films, he "picked up American slang and a romance for the distant power casting its shadow across us." On July 15, 1958, the day after the bloody overthrow of the Iraqi monarchy by nationalist army officers, Ajami's two loves had their first of many clashes, when President Eisenhower sent the US Marines to Beirut to contain the spread of radical Arab nationalism. In their initial confrontation, Ajami chose Egypt's leader, defying his parents and hopping on a Damascus-bound bus for one of Nasser's mass rallies.

Ajami arrived in the United States in the fall of 1963, just before he turned eighteen. He did his graduate work at the

University of Washington, where he wrote his dissertation on international relations and world government. At the University of Washington, Ajami gravitated toward progressive Arab circles. Like his Arab peers, he was shaken by the humiliating defeat of the Arab countries in the 1967 war with Israel, and heartened by the emergence of the PLO. While steering clear of radicalism, he often expressed horror at Israel's brutal reprisal attacks against southern Lebanese villages in response to PLO raids.

In 1973, Ajami joined Princeton's political science department, commuting to work from his apartment in New York. He made a name for himself there as a vocal supporter of Palestinian self-determination. One friend remembers him as "a fairly typical advocate of Third World positions." Yet he was also acutely aware of the failings of Third World states, which he unsparingly diagnosed in "The Fate of Nonalignment," a brilliant essay in *Foreign Affairs*. In 1980, when Johns Hopkins offered him a position as director of Middle East Studies at SAIS, a Washington-based graduate program, he took it.

A year after arriving at SAIS, Ajami published his first and still best book, *The Arab Predicament*. An anatomy of the intellectual and political crisis that swept the Arab world following its defeat by Israel in the 1967 war, it is one of the most probing and subtle books ever written in English on the region. Ranging gracefully across political theory, literature and poetry, Ajami draws an elegant, often moving portrait of Arab intellectuals in their anguished efforts to put together a world that had come apart at the seams. The book did not offer a bold or original argument; like Isaiah Berlin's *Russian Thinkers*, it provided an interpretive survey—respectful even when critical—of other people's ideas. It was the book of a man who had grown disillusioned with Nasser, whose millenarian dream of restoring the "Arab nation" had run up against the hard fact that the "divisions of the Arab world were real, not contrived points on a map or a colonial trick." But pan-Arabism was not the only temptation to which the intellectuals had succumbed. There was radical socialism, and the Guevarist fantasies of the Palestinian revolution. There was Islamic fundamentalism, with its romance of authenticity and its embittered rejection of the West. And then there was the search for Western patronage, the way of Nasser's successor, Anwar Sadat, who forgot his own world and ended up being devoured by it.

Ajami's ambivalent chapter on Sadat makes for especially fascinating reading today. He praised Sadat for breaking with Nasserism and making peace with Israel, and perhaps saw something of himself in the "self-defined peasant from the dusty small village" who had "traveled far beyond the bounds of his world." But he also saw in Sadat's story the tragic parable of a man who had become more comfortable with Western admirers than with his own people. When Sadat spoke nostalgically of his village— as Ajami now speaks of Arnoun—he was pandering to the West. Arabs, a people of the cities, would not be "taken in by the myth of the village." Sadat's "American connection," Ajami suggested, gave him "a sense of psychological mobility," lifting some of the burdens imposed by his cramped world. And as his dependence on his American patrons deepened, "he became indifferent to the sensibilities of his own world."

Sadat was one example of the trap of seeking the West's approval and losing touch with one's roots; V. S. Naipaul was another. Naipaul, Ajami suggested in an incisive 1981 *New York Times* review of *Among the Believers*, exemplified the "dilemma of a gifted author led by his obsessive feelings regarding the people he is writing about to a difficult intellectual and moral bind." Third World exiles like Naipaul, Ajami wrote, "have a tendency to . . . look at their own countries and similar ones with a critical eye," yet "these same men usually approach the civilization of the West with awe and leave it unexamined." Ajami preferred the humane, nonjudgmental work of Polish travel writer Ryszard Kapuściński: "His eye for human folly is as sharp as V. S. Naipaul. His sympathy and sorrow, however, are far deeper."

The Arab Predicament was infused with sympathy and sorrow, but these qualities were ignored by the book's Arab critics in the West, who—displaying the ideological rigidity that is an unfortunate hallmark of exile politics—accused him of papering over the injustices of imperialism and "blaming the victim." To an extent, this was a fair criticism. Ajami paid little attention to imperialism, and even less to Israel's provocative role in the region. What is more, his argument that "the wounds that mattered were self-inflicted" endeared him to those who wanted to distract attention from Palestine. Doors flew open. On the recommendation of Bernard Lewis, the distinguished British Orientalist at Princeton and a strong supporter of Israel, Ajami became the first Arab to win the MacArthur "genius" prize in 1982; a year later, he became a member of the Council on Foreign Relations. The *New Republic* began to publish lengthy essays by Ajami, models of the form, which offer a tantalizing glimpse of the career he might have had in a less polarized intellectual climate. Pro-Israel intellectual circles groomed him as a rival to Edward Said, holding up his book as a corrective to *Orientalism*, Said's classic study of how the West imagined the East in the age of empire.

In fact, Ajami shared some of Said's anger about the Middle East. The Israelis, he wrote in an eloquent *New York Times* op-ed after the 1982 invasion of Lebanon, "came with a great delusion: that if you could pound men and women hard enough, if you could bring them to their knees, you could make peace with them." He urged the United States to withdraw from Lebanon in 1984, and advised it to open talks with the Iranian government. Throughout the 1980s, Ajami maintained a critical attitude toward America's interventions in the Middle East, stressing the limits of America's ability to influence or shape a "tormented world" it scarcely understood. "Our arguments dovetailed," says Said. "There was an unspoken assumption that we shared the same kind of politics."

But just below the surface there were profound differences of opinion. Hisham Milhem, a Lebanese journalist who knows both men well, explained their differences to me by contrasting their views on Joseph Conrad: "Edward and Fouad are both crazy about Conrad, but they see in him very different things. Edward sees the critic of empire, especially in *Heart of Darkness*. Fouad, on the other hand, admires the Polish exile in Western Europe who made a conscious break with the old country."

Yet the old world had as much of a grip on Ajami as it did on Said. In southern Lebanon, Palestinian guerrillas had set up a state within a state. They often behaved thuggishly toward Shia villagers, alienating their natural allies and recklessly exposing them to Israel's merciless reprisals. By the time Israeli tanks rolled into Lebanon in 1982, relations between the two communities had so deteriorated that some Shia greeted the invaders with rice and flowers. Like many of his fellow Shia, Ajami was fed up with the Palestinians, whose revolution had brought ruin to Lebanon. Arnoun itself had not been unscathed: a nearby Crusader castle, the majestic Beaufort, was now the scene of intense fighting.

In late May 1985, Ajami—now explicitly identifying himself as a Shia from southern Lebanon—sparred with Said on the *MacNeil/Lehrer Report* over the war between the PLO and the Shiite Amal militia, then raging in Beirut's refugee camps. A few months later, they came to verbal blows again, when Ajami was invited to speak at a Harvard conference on Islam and Muslim politics organized by Israeli-American academic Nadav Safran. After the Harvard *Crimson* revealed that the conference had been partly funded by the CIA, Ajami, at the urging of Said and the late Pakistani writer Eqbal Ahmad, joined a wave of speakers who were withdrawing from the conference. But Ajami, who was a protégé and friend of Safran, immediately regretted his decision. He wrote a blistering letter to Said and Ahmad a few weeks later, accusing them of "bringing the conflicts of the Middle East to this country" while "I have tried to go beyond them . . . Therefore, my friends, this is the parting of ways. I hope never to encounter you again, and we must cease communication. Yours sincerely, Fouad Ajami."

By now, the "Shia *assimilé*" had fervently embraced his Shia identity. Like Sadat, he began to rhapsodize about his "dusty village" in wistful tones. *The Vanished Imam*, his 1986 encomium to Musa al-Sadr, the Iranian cleric who led the Amal militia before mysteriously disappearing on a 1978 visit to Libya, offers important clues into Ajami's thinking of the time. A work of lyrical nationalist mythology, *The Vanished Imam* also provides a thinly veiled political memoir, recounting Ajami's disillusionment with Palestinians, Arabs and the left, and his conversion to old-fashioned tribal politics.

The marginalized Shia had found a home in Amal, and a spiritual leader in Sadr, a "big man" who is explicitly compared to Joseph Conrad's Lord Jim and credited with a far larger role than he actually played in Shia politics. Writing of Sadr, Ajami might have been describing himself. Sadr is an *Ajam*—a Persian—with "an outsider's eagerness to please." He is "suspicious of grand schemes," blessed with "a strong sense of pragmatism, of things that can and cannot be," thanks to which virtue he "came to be seen as an enemy of everything 'progressive.'" "Tired of the polemics," he alone is courageous enough to stand up to the Palestinians, warning them not to "seek a 'substitute homeland,' *watan badil*, in Lebanon." Unlike the Palestinians, Ajami tells us repeatedly, the Shia are realists, not dreamers; reformers, not revolutionaries. Throughout the book, a stark dichotomy is also drawn between Shia and Arab nationalism, although, as one of his Shia critics pointed out in a caustic review in the *International Journal of Middle Eastern Studies*, "allegiance to Arab nationalist ideals . . . was paramount" in Sadr's circles. The Shia of Ajami's imagination seem fundamentally different from other Arabs: a community that shares America's aversion to the Palestinians, a "model minority" worthy of the West's sympathy.

The Shia critic of the Palestinians cut an especially attractive profile in the eyes of the American media. Most American viewers of CBS News, which made him a highly paid consultant in 1985, had no idea that he was almost completely out of step with the community for which he claimed to speak. By the time *The Vanished Imam* appeared, the Shia, under the leadership of a new group, Hezbollah, an Islamist guerrilla movement with close ties to Iran, had launched a battle to liberate Lebanon from Israeli control. Israeli soldiers were now greeted with grenades and explosives, rather than rice and flowers, and Arnoun became a hotbed of Hezbollah support. Yet Ajami displayed little enthusiasm for *this* Shia struggle. He was also oddly silent about the behavior of the Israelis, who, from the 1982 invasion onward,

had killed far more Shia than either Arafat ("the Flying Dutch-
man of the Palestinian movement") or Hafez al-Assad (Syria's
"cruel enforcer"). The Shia, he suggested, were "beneficiaries of
Israel's Lebanon war."

By the mid-1980s, the Middle Eastern country closest to Ajami's
heart was not Lebanon but Israel. He returned from his trips to
the Jewish state boasting of traveling to the Occupied Territories under the guard of the Israel Defense Forces and of being
received at the home of Teddy Kollek, then Jerusalem's mayor.
The Israelis earned his admiration because they had something
the Palestinians notably lacked: power. They were also tough-
minded realists, who understood "what can and cannot be had
in the world of nations." The Palestinians, by contrast, were
romantics who imagined themselves to be "exempt from the
historical laws of gravity."

In 1986, Ajami had praised Musa al-Sadr as a realist for telling
the Palestinians to fight Israel in the Occupied Territories, rather
than in Lebanon. But when the Palestinians did exactly that, in
the First Intifada of 1987–93, it no longer seemed realistic to
Ajami, who then advised them to swallow the bitter pill of defeat
and pay for their bad choices. While Israeli troops shot down
children armed only with stones, Ajami told the Palestinians they
should give up on the idea of a sovereign state ("a phantom"),
even in the West Bank and Gaza. When the PLO announced its
support for a two-state solution at a 1988 conference in Algiers,
Ajami called the declaration "hollow," its concessions to Israel
inadequate. On the eve of the Madrid talks in the fall of 1991
he wrote, "It is far too late to introduce a new nation between
Israel and Jordan." Nor should the American government embark
on the "fool's errand" of pressuring Israel to make peace. Under
Ajami's direction, the Middle East program of SAIS became a
bastion of pro-Israel opinion. An increasing number of Israeli
and pro-Israel academics, many of them *New Republic* contrib-
utors, were invited as guest lecturers. "Rabbi Ajami," as some
people around SAIS referred to him, was also receiving significant
support from a Jewish family foundation in Baltimore, which

picked up the tab for the trips his students took to the Middle East every summer. Back in Lebanon, Ajami's growing reputation as an apologist for Israel reportedly placed considerable strains on family members in Arnoun.

Ajami also developed close ties during the 1980s to Kuwait and Saudi Arabia, which made him—as he often and proudly pointed out—the only Arab who traveled both to the Persian Gulf countries and to Israel. In 1985, he became an external examiner in the political science department at Kuwait University; he said, "the place seemed vibrant and open to me." His major patrons, however, were Saudi. He has traveled to Riyadh many times to raise money for his program, sometimes taking along friends like Martin Peretz; he has also vacationed in Prince Bandar's home in Aspen. Saudi hospitality—and Saudi Arabia's lavish support for SAIS—bred gratitude. At one meeting of the Council on Foreign Relations, Ajami told a group that, as one participant recalls, "the Saudi system was a lot stronger than we thought, that it was a system worth defending, and that it had nothing to apologize for." Throughout the 1980s and '90s, he faithfully echoed the Saudi line. "Rage against the West does not come naturally to the Gulf Arabs," he wrote in 1990. "No great tales of betrayal are told by the Arabs of the desert. These are Palestinian, Lebanese and North African tales."

This may explain why Iraq's invasion of Kuwait in 1990 aroused greater outrage in Ajami than any act of aggression in the recent history of the Middle East. Neither Israel's invasion of Lebanon nor the 1982 Sabra and Shatila massacre had caused him comparable consternation. Nor, for that matter, had Saddam's slaughter of the Kurds in Halabja in 1988. This is understandable, of course; we all react more emotionally when the victims are friends. But we don't all become publicists for war, as Ajami did that fateful summer, consummating his conversion to Pax Americana. What was remarkable was not only his fervent advocacy; it was his cavalier disregard for truth, his lurid rhetoric and his religious embrace of American power. In *Foreign Affairs*, Ajami, who knew better, described Iraq, the cradle of Mesopotamian civilization, a major publisher of Arabic literature and a center of the plastic arts, as "a brittle land . . . with little claim to culture and books and grand ideas." It was, in other words, a wasteland, led by a man who "conjures up Adolf Hitler."

Months before the war began, the son of Arnoun, now writing as an American, in the royal "we," declared that US troops "will have to stay in the Gulf and on a much larger scale" since "we have tangible interests in that land. We stand sentry there in blazing clear daylight." After the Gulf war, Ajami's cachet soared. In the early 1990s Harvard offered him a chair ("he turned it down because we expected him to be around and to work very hard," a professor told me), and the Council on Foreign Relations added him to its prestigious board of advisers last year. "The Gulf War was the crucible of change," says Augustus Richard Norton. "This immigrant from Arnoun, this man nobody had heard of from a place no one had heard of, had reached the peak of power. This was a true immigrant success story, one of those moments that make an immigrant grateful for America. And I think it implanted a deep sense of patriotism that wasn't present before."

And, as Ajami once wrote of Sadat, "outside approval gave him the courage to defy" the Arabs, especially when it came to Israel. On June 3, 1992, hardly a year after Gulf War I, Ajami spoke at a pro-Israel fundraiser. Kissinger, the keynote speaker, described Arabs as congenital liars. Ajami chimed in, expressing his doubts that democracy would ever work in the Arab world, and recounting a visit to a Bedouin village where he "insisted on only one thing: that [he] be spared the ceremony of eating with a Bedouin."

Since the signing of the Oslo Accords in 1993, Ajami has been a consistent critic of the peace process—from the right. He sang the praises of each of Israel's leaders, from the Likud's Benjamin Netanyahu, with his "filial devotion [to] the land he had agreed to relinquish," to Labor leader Ehud Barak, "an exemplary soldier." The Palestinians, he wrote, should be grateful to such men for "rescuing" them from defeat, and to Zionism for generously offering them "the possibility of their own national political revival." (True to form, the Palestinians showed "no gratitude.") A year before the destruction of Jenin, he proclaimed that "Israel is existentially through with the siege that had defined its history." Ajami's Likudnik conversion was sealed by telling revisions of arguments he had made earlier in his career. Where he had once argued that the 1982 invasion of Lebanon aimed to "undermine those in the Arab world who want some form of compromise," he now called it a response to "the challenge of Palestinian terror."

Did Ajami really believe all this? In a stray but revealing comment on Sadat in the *New Republic*, he left room for doubt. Sadat, he said, was "a son of the soil, who had the fellah's ability to look into the soul of powerful outsiders, to divine how he could get around them even as he gave them what they desired." Writing on politics, the man from Arnoun gave them what they desired. Writing on literature and poetry, he gave expression to the aesthete, the soulful elegist, even, at times, to the Arab. In his 1998 book, *The Dream Palace of the Arabs*, one senses, for the first time in years, Ajami's sympathy for the world he left behind, although there is something furtive, something ghostly about his affection, as if he were writing about a lover he has taught himself to spurn. On rare occasions, Ajami revealed this side of himself to his students, whisking them into his office. Once the door was firmly shut, he would recite the poetry of Nizar Qabbani and Adonis in Arabic, caressing each and every line. As he read, Sayres Rudy told me, "I could swear his heart was breaking."

September 11 exposed a major intelligence failure on Ajami's part. With his obsessive focus on the menace of Saddam and the treachery of Arafat, he had missed the big story. Fifteen of the nineteen hijackers hailed from what he had repeatedly called the "benign political order" of Saudi Arabia; the "Saudi way" he had praised had come undone. Yet the few criticisms that Ajami directed at his patrons in the weeks and months after September 11 were curiously muted, particularly in contrast to the rage of most American commentators. Ajami's venues in the American media, however, were willing to forgive his softness toward the Saudis. America was going to war with Muslims, and a trusted native informant was needed.

Other forces were working in Ajami's favor. For George W. Bush and the hawks in his entourage, Afghanistan was merely a prelude to the war they really wanted to fight—the war against Saddam that Ajami had been spoiling for since the end of Gulf War I. As a publicist for Gulf War II, Ajami has abandoned his longstanding emphasis on the limits of American influence in that "tormented region." The war is being sold as the first step in an American plan to effect democratic regime change across the region, and Ajami has stayed on message. We now find him writing in *Foreign Affairs* that "the driving motivation of a new American endeavor in Iraq and in neighboring Arab lands should be modernizing the Arab world." The opinion of the Arab street, where Iraq is recruiting thousands of new jihadists, is of no concern to him. "We have to live with this anti-Americanism," he sighed recently on CBS. "It's the congenital condition of the Arab world, and we have to discount a good deal of it as we press on with the task of liberating the Iraqis."

In fairness, Ajami has not completely discarded his wariness about American intervention. For there remains one country where American pressure will come to naught, and that is Israel, where it would "be hubris" to ask anything more of the Israelis, victims of "Arafat's war." To those who suggest that the Iraq campaign is doomed without an Israeli-Palestinian peace settlement, he says, "We can't hold our war hostage to Arafat's campaign of terror."

Fortunately, George W. Bush understands this. Ajami has commended Bush for staking out the "high moral ground" and for "putting Iran on notice" in his Axis of Evil speech. Above all, the president should not allow himself to be deterred by multilateralists like Secretary of State Colin Powell, "an unhappy, reluctant soldier, at heart a pessimist about American power." Unilateralism, Ajami says, is nothing to be ashamed of. It may make us hated in the "hostile landscape" of the Arab world, but, as he recently explained on the *NewsHour*, "It's the fate of a great power to stand sentry in that kind of a world."

It is no accident that the "sentry's solitude" has become the *idée fixe* of Ajami's writing in recent years. For it is a theme that resonates powerfully in his own life. Like the empire he serves, Ajami is more influential, and more isolated, than he has ever been. In recent years he has felt a need to defend this choice in heroic terms. "All a man can betray is his conscience," he solemnly writes in *The Dream Palace of the Arabs*, citing a passage from Conrad. "The solitude Conrad chose is loathed by politicized men and women."

It is a breathtakingly disingenuous remark. Ajami may be "a stranger in the Arab world," but he can hardly claim to be a stranger to its politics. That is why he is quoted, and courted, by Dick Cheney and Paul Wolfowitz. What Ajami abhors in "politicized men and women" is conviction itself. A leftist in the 1970s, a Shiite nationalist in the 1980s, an apologist for the Saudis in the 1990s, a critic-turned-lover of Israel, a skeptic-turned-enthusiast of American empire, he has observed no consistent principle in his career other than deference to power. His vaunted intellectual independence is a clever fiction. The only thing that makes him worth reading is his prose style, and even that has suffered of late. As Ajami observed of Naipaul more than twenty years ago, "He has become more and more predictable, too, with serious cost to his great gift as a writer," blinded by the "assumption that only men who live in remote, dark places are 'denied a clear vision of the world.'" Like Naipaul, Ajami has forgotten that "darkness is not only there but here as well."

{2003}

2

Kamel Daoud: Stranger Still

I first heard about the writer Kamel Daoud a few years ago, when an Algerian friend of mine told me I should read him if I wanted to understand how her country had changed in recent years. "If Algeria can produce a Kamel Daoud," she said, "I still have hope for Algeria." Reading his columns in *Le Quotidien d'Oran*, a French-language newspaper, I saw what she meant. Daoud had an original, epigrammatic style: playful, lyrical, brash. I could also see why he'd been accused of racism, even "self-hatred." After September 11, for example, he wrote that the Arabs had been "crashing" for centuries and that they would continue crashing so long as they were better known for hijacking planes than for making them. But this struck me as the glib provocation of an otherwise intelligent writer carried away by his metaphors.

The more I read Daoud, the more I sensed he was driven not by self-hatred but by disappointed love. Here was a writer in his early forties, a man my age, who believed that people in Algeria and the wider Muslim world deserved a great deal better than military rule or Islamism, the two-entrée menu they had been offered since the end of colonialism, and who said so with force and brio. Nothing, however, prepared me for his first novel, *The Meursault Investigation*, a thrilling retelling of Albert Camus's 1942 classic, *The Stranger*, from the perspective of the brother of the Arab killed by Meursault, Camus's antihero. The novel, which was first published in Algeria in 2013, not only breathes new life into *The Stranger*; it also offers a bracing critique of postcolonial

Algeria—a new country that Camus, a poor Frenchman born in Algiers, did not live to see.

What impressed me about Daoud's writing, both his journalism and his novel, was the fearlessness with which he defended the cause of individual liberty—a fearlessness that, it seemed to me, bordered on recklessness in a country where collectivist passions of nation and faith run high. I wondered whether his experience might provide clues as to the state of intellectual freedom in Algeria, a peculiar hybrid of electoral democracy and police state. Late last year, I had an answer of sorts. Daoud was no longer merely a writer. He was now someone you had to take a side on, in Algeria and in France.

His ordeal began on December 13, 2014, during a book tour in France, where *Meursault* received rapturous reviews, sold more than 100,000 copies and came two votes shy of winning the Prix Goncourt, the nation's most prestigious literary prize. He was on a popular late-night talk show called *On n'est pas couché* (We're Not Asleep), and he felt, he would tell me later, "as if I had all of Algeria on my shoulders." He insisted to the French-Lebanese journalist Léa Salamé, one of the panelists on the program, that he considered himself an Algerian, not an Arab—a view that's not uncommon in Algeria but that is opposed by Arab nationalists. He said that he spoke a distinct language called "Algerian," not Arabic. He said that he preferred to meet with God on foot, by himself, rather than in an "organized trip" to a mosque, and that religious orthodoxy had become an obstacle to progress in the Muslim world. Daoud said nothing on the program that he hadn't said in his columns or his novel. But saying it in France, the country that ruled Algeria from 1830 to 1962, got him noticed by people back home who tend to ignore the French-language press.

One of them was an obscure imam named Abdelfattah Hamadache, who had reportedly been an informer for the security services. Three days after Daoud's appearance on French television, Hamadache wrote on his Facebook page that Daoud—an "apostate" and "Zionized criminal"—should be put on trial for insulting Islam and publicly executed. It was not quite a call for Daoud's assassination: Hamadache was appealing to the state, not to freelance jihadists. But Algeria is a country in which more than seventy journalists were murdered by Islamist rebels during the civil war of the 1990s, the so-called Black Decade. Those murders were often preceded by anonymous threats in letters, leaflets or graffiti scrawled on the walls of mosques. Hamadache's "Facebook fatwa," as it became known, was something new, and uniquely brazen, for being signed in his own name. It provoked an outcry, and not only among liberals. Ali Belhadj, leader of the banned Islamic Salvation Front (FIS), harshly criticized Hamadache, asserting that he had no authority to call Daoud an apostate and that only God had the right to decide who was or wasn't a Muslim: a message, some said, that the FIS saw Hamadache as a tool of the state. Indeed, although the minister of religious affairs, Mohamed Aïssa, a mild-mannered man of Sufi leanings, came to Daoud's defense, the government otherwise maintained a strange neutrality, declining to respond when Daoud filed a complaint against Hamadache for incitement.

That neutrality reflects something deeper than political expedience. The principal lesson that the Algerian state drew from the decade-long war with Islamist insurgents was that Islamism could not be defeated on the battlefield: it had to be co-opted rather than crushed. In effect, Algeria is running a decade ahead of other countries where secular elites are clashing with powerful Islamist movements over the shape of new governments after the Arab uprisings. Now it is prosperous and has a growing sense of confidence that the Algerian model of power-sharing can and should be exported to neighbors like Libya and Tunisia. The Daoud Affair, however, is putting the Algerian model to the test.

By the time I flew to Oran, on January 15, the war over blasphemy had spread to France, when the offices of *Charlie Hebdo* were attacked by French jihadists, brothers of Algerian ancestry. In Oran, Daoud's supporters had been saying, "We are all Kamel Daoud"; now millions of people in Paris were saying "Je suis *Charlie*." I wondered how the events in Paris would affect Daoud's predicament. On my layover at Orly, I opened *Le Monde* to find an interview about *Charlie* with Daoud, who said he feared more "micro-9/11s."

To be an Algerian writer is to be a student of political violence. Algeria won its independence from France in 1962 after one of the world's longest and bloodiest wars of decolonization. Its political system, which people simply call the *pouvoir*, or power, is still strongly influenced by the mujahedeen, the "holy warriors" of the National Liberation Front (FLN) who fought against France. Algeria's seventy-eight-year-old president, Abdelaziz Bouteflika—who is now in his fourth term, and who governs from a wheelchair equipped with a microphone because his voice is so faint—joined the National Liberation Army in 1956. Rumored to be living in a villa outside Algiers, Bouteflika is able to work only a few hours a day. When Bouteflika was hospitalized in France in November, Daoud wrote of his regime, "Even the question of what comes after has become secondary: There's no life before death, why worry about life after death?" Bouteflika is not the only senior figure in the *pouvoir* whose time is running out. The heads of the army and the intelligence services are both in their mid-seventies. Algeria is facing a potential triple succession crisis at a moment of falling oil prices. A precipitous drop in oil prices could push Algeria toward a "violent rupture," Daoud says.

Whether the *pouvoir* has a transition plan for the post-Bouteflika era is anyone's guess, because its machinations are so obscure. This is deliberate: When the former French president Nicolas Sarkozy asked an Algerian minister why the government was so opaque, the minister reportedly replied, "Because that is our strength." The code of impenetrable secrecy, like so much else in Algeria, is a product of the War of Independence. Secrecy was a necessity for an anticolonial insurgency fighting one of the most powerful armies in the world, but it has remained the *pouvoir*'s modus operandi ever since independence. Algeria is governed as if the war never ended. Every new crisis—bread riots, the civil war, Berber protests, the Arab Spring—has justified a permanent war footing. And every emergency has delayed the question of "what happens after liberation," as Daoud puts it: "Is the goal to have enough food, enough housing? Why haven't we made happiness one of our goals?" This is a young man's question, but Algeria hasn't been run by young men since the early 1960s.

Today, Algeria's *décideurs*—the men who actually make decisions, as opposed to the politicians who bicker in its pluralist but impotent National Assembly—have two claims to legitimacy. The first is that they liberated Algeria from French rule. The second is that they defeated a wave of Islamist terrorism in the 1990s. In Daoud's view, neither achievement is enough. Algeria will be truly free only when it has been "liberated from its liberators." It is not simply a matter of overthrowing the government, which he believes was the great illusion of the Arab Spring. Society, too, needs to change if Algeria is to release itself from the fetters of authoritarianism and Islamic piety.

Daoud's writing has attracted many well-placed readers. He regularly receives calls from members of the *pouvoir*. Manuel Valls, the prime minister of France, recently called to say how much he admired *Meursault*. "Men in power are fascinated by people like me," Daoud said. "I don't have a state or an army, I'm just a guy with an apartment and a car. But I'm free, and they want to know, Why are you free?"

On January 16, the day I arrived in Algeria, thousands of protesters, including Hamadache, marched toward the Place de la poste in downtown Algiers after Friday prayers, in defiance of a ban on demonstrations in the capital. The Rally in Defense of the Prophet Muhammad had been called in protest against the Muhammad cartoon that ran on the cover of *Charlie Hebdo* after the massacre in Paris. Aïssa, the minister of religious affairs, opposed the demonstrations, but the anger over the cartoons was raw and easily fanned by Salafist preachers. "Je suis Muhammad" was a common slogan: a curious phrase with which to denounce blasphemy, because it is considered by some Muslims to be blasphemous to declare yourself the Prophet. (The slogan was promoted by the Arabic tabloid *Echorouk*, a platform for tirades against Daoud; it was later amended to "Je suis avec

Muhammad"—I am with Muhammad.) Young men waved the black flag of the Islamic State of Iraq and Syria and declared the Paris killers to be martyrs. Like many demonstrations in Algeria, it devolved into a riot, with shop windows smashed in the name of the Prophet. Hamadache was arrested in Belcourt, where Camus was raised, and briefly detained for his role in the rally.

The protests in Oran, where anti-Islamist sentiment runs high, were much smaller than in Algiers but still boisterous enough to hold up traffic. I was heading to my hotel from the airport with Robert Parks, an American academic who is a close friend of Daoud's. Parks, who has run a research center in Oran since 2006, had been telling me that Algeria was slowly but surely recovering its confidence. Algerians, he said, were grateful to have avoided the tumult of the Arab revolts, thanks to which they had been able to make a more sober, judicious and favorable appraisal of their own conditions. But when a group of young demonstrators marched toward us, he swerved into a back road: he was worried that we would be mistaken for Frenchmen.

The boldness with which Islamists took to the streets was a reminder of the deal that Bouteflika had cut with them shortly after coming to power in 1999. His "reconciliation project" offered amnesty to those who fought in the civil war of 1992–2002, provided they laid down their arms. The *pouvoir* never negotiated with the political wing of the FIS, preferring to settle matters with armed rebels behind closed doors. Security forces who were responsible for extrajudicial killings and disappearances were never charged. Islamist fighters made out even better. They came down from the *maquis*, the resistance in the mountains, and returned to the mosque. Many were reportedly given jobs and property. The paradox of the recent civil war is that while the Islamists failed to overthrow the state, Bouteflika's reconciliation project allowed them to increase their presence within it. Islamists are now, in effect, a wing of the *pouvoir,* which has not merely tolerated them but has allowed them to participate in the National Assembly. And their presence has the added attraction, to Algeria's generals, the most influential *décideurs*, of warning other Algerians—and the country's allies in Washington and

Paris—about what might lie in store if the army and the intelligence services loosen their grip.

There's no doubt that Algeria has made strides since the Black Decade. Although Bouteflika has hardly appeared in public since his stroke in 2013, he remains relatively popular, if only for lack of an alternative, and is widely credited with rebuilding Algeria after the civil war. When I reported from Algeria in 2003, a year after the war officially ended, it was a jittery, traumatized place, and people were still afraid of car bombs and fake checkpoints set up by rebels. Although radical jihadists are still active in the east and the south, today the country is largely safe, not only in the cities but on the roads connecting them. The new East–West highway, built with Chinese labor, has cut in half the drive from Algiers to Oran, once a ten-hour journey. The economy remains heavily dependent on natural gas and oil (more than 90 percent of its exports), but it has nearly $200 billion in foreign-currency reserves. Algeria has earned the admiration of Western powers, above all the United States, for its role in regional counterterrorism, for the expertise and efficiency of the intelligence services and for its resourceful diplomatic efforts in Tunisia, Libya and Mali. In the words of its energetic foreign minister, Ramtane Lamamra, Algeria is "an exporter of security and stability."

The *pouvoir* has been shrewd in maintaining that stability. There were antigovernment protests in early 2011, after the self-immolation of Mohamed Bouazizi in Tunisia, but the *pouvoir* swiftly contained them in the usual ways: deploying thousands of police officers in the capital; cutting prices on sugar, flour and oil; and offering cash handouts to young people who want (or claim they want) to start their own businesses. "The Arab Spring is a mosquito against which we shut the door of our country," Prime Minister Abdelmalek Sellal gloated in a speech, and then added a reference to a brand of insecticide: "If it ever tries to get in, we'll fight it with Fly-Tox."

The *pouvoir* is neither secular nor Islamist: it has pursued a policy of deliberate indecision, tolerating radical Islamists like Hamadache while at the same time turning a blind eye to what Parks described to me as a "fragile experiment" in cultural liberalization. The best place to witness that experiment is Oran, the birthplace of raï, an Algerian pop that fuses Arabic and Spanish music, disco and hip-hop. On my first night in Oran, only hours after the anti-*Charlie* demonstrations, I went to a nightclub with Parks and the poet Amina Mekahli, also a close friend of Daoud's. A fan of Philip Roth, Mekahli quoted from memory passages from *The Human Stain*, Roth's novel about Coleman Silk, a black college professor who passes for white; she said it spoke directly to the Algerian anguish of living a double life. Cabarets in Oran are basically speakeasies, but we had managed to talk our way in. A waiter brought us a bottle of Johnnie Walker Red Label, along with a plate of fresh fruit. Most of the clients were Algerians in their twenties and thirties. I was surrounded on all sides by leopard-skin pants, miniskirts, Louis Vuitton knockoff bags and lipstick. Mekahli introduced me to a friend of hers, whom she called Gigi, the "famous homo-sexual." She explained that Gigi, a sweet, androgynous man in his forties, plays matchmaker outside the bathroom; if a young man fancies a young woman, he tells Gigi, and when the girl emerges from the bathroom, he tells her of the man's interest. "What's interesting about Gigi," Mekahli said, "is that he's from a working-class neighborhood and accepted, though the word 'gay' is never mentioned." I was less enthralled than Mekahli, but then I remembered Camus's remark that Oran is a city where "one learns the virtues, provisional to be sure, of a certain kind of boredom."

Oran has changed since Camus's day, of course. Under French rule, it was a European city. After independence, the Europeans left en masse, and their homes were occupied by migrants from neighboring villages. Others found housing, grim but free, in Eastern bloc–style complexes built by the state. The skyline has grown taller in recent years: the Sheraton and Méridien hotels look as if they were imported from Dubai. Yet Oran has pre-served its languorous, Mediterranean character. In little cafés, men sip cups of black coffee and mint tea; seaside restaurants offer grilled fish, paella and breathtaking views of the Mediterra-nean, while corner stands serve *calentita*, a baguette stuffed with mashed chickpeas, a sandwich that Spanish settlers introduced to Algeria. On the street, most women wear hijabs. But at late-night cabarets like the one we went to, young people dance, drink and, as Camus wrote in 1939, "meet, eye and size up one another, happy to be alive and to cut a figure."

At midnight, when we arrived, the crowd seemed tentative, but when Cheba Dalila, a raï singer with a voice as deep as Nina Simone's, came on at 2 a.m., the dance floor filled up. She strode with her microphone from table to table, collecting bills from people who paid to have their names mentioned in her songs. The bass was so loud I felt it in my belly. A woman in tight jeans wore a T-shirt that said "Detroit 1983"; pairs of men danced with women when their interest was plainly in each other. I took a photograph, but Mekahli's son, Hadi, told me not to: "This place is run by the mafia." The "mafia" makes its money on bootleg liquor and prostitutes. Some of the women at the nightclub were apparently for hire. "For me," Mekahli said, "clubs like this are a reappropriation of Algerian identity. France doesn't exist here. The people here are totally decolonized."

When I first visited Daoud at his apartment in a gated community on the outskirts of Oran, he was in his pajamas, watching television with his twelve-year-old son. He was multitasking as he rattled off his latest news, typing out emails, checking his Facebook account, taking calls. He hardly looked up from his screen, and I feared that we would never get to talk. It would be easier, he said, if I stayed with him.

Two days later, when I checked out of my hotel, I sparked a minor diplomatic incident. The concierge came outside to talk to Daoud, who was waiting in his car. If I left, he said nervously, there would be no way of checking the whereabouts of the *étranger*—the foreigner. He could not afford to have another Hervé Gourdel on his hands: Gourdel, a French hiker, was kidnapped and beheaded by radical Islamists in September in the mountains of Kabylia. Daoud said he might have to notify the police. Housing an American, he joked, would doubtless turn out to be one more black mark against him, further proof that he had sold out to the forces of imperialism. Daoud knows how his critics think, in part because he used to think the same way. He is an ex-Islamist, and he has a defector's zeal. Two years into their marriage, Daoud says, his ex-wife became increasingly religious and started wearing the hijab. They divorced in 2008, after the birth of their daughter.

The great theme of Daoud's writing is the Algerian condition. To be Algerian, he argues, is to be "schizophrenic," torn between religious piety and liberal individualism. The liquor stores in Oran are legal but concealed; a ring of traffic forms around them on Thursday evening, the night before prayers. There is a growing acceptance of sex outside marriage, but women are seen as little more than prostitutes if they walk into a café for men. Algerians are becoming more modern, but on the down low, as if they were loath to admit it to themselves. Hypocrisy might be a step on the arduous road to a more tolerant civil society, but it exasperates Daoud. "The Islamists have at least made their choice," he said.

Daoud's campaign against Islamism has won him adoration, particularly among liberal, French-speaking Algerians, who hail him for staking out positions they share but are often too shy to express in public. But he is also widely reviled, not only among Islamists but among nationalists and leftists who see him as hostile to his own society. Daoud sometimes gives the impression of taunting them, as if he were spoiling for a fight. During the recent war in Gaza, he published a column titled, "Why I Am Not 'in Solidarity' with Palestine." Daoud wasn't in solidarity with Israel either; he just didn't like the implication that he *had* to be in solidarity with Palestine because he was a Muslim. He opposed Israel's bombing for anticolonial and humanitarian reasons, not religious or ethnic ones. As such, his hidden subject was Algeria; what he resented, in the call to solidarity with Palestine, was not the cause itself but the pressure to unify, once again, under the banner of Arab and Islamic identity.

The coercive pressure to unify has always been a defining feature of Algerian nationalism. During the struggle for independence, the leaders of the FLN, many of whom were Berbers, suppressed Berber identity politics in the name of national unity against the French. Since independence, as Daoud points out, Algerians have been taught to see themselves as belonging exclusively to the Arab-Islamic world and to deny what they know from their history and experience: that most are of Berber, not Arabic, ancestry; that a large minority still speaks either Berber, a language that only recently was recognized as a national language, or French, which became a "foreign language" after independence; and that even the Arabic most Algerians speak at home is a creole larded with words on loan from other tongues. (Hence Daoud's insistence on calling it "Algerian.") Far from representing an alternative to the ideology of Arab-Islamic unity, Algeria's Islamists preach a more religious version of it. As a result, Algeria remains, in Daoud's view, "stranded between the sky and the land. The land belongs to 'the liberators,'" while "the sky has been colonized by religious people who have appropriated it in the name of Allah." Algerians "have been persuaded that they are impotent; they can't even build a wall without Chinese help."

This sense of impotence finds physical expression in Algeria's decrepit infrastructure. "The streets of Oran are doomed to dust, pebbles and heat," Camus wrote in an essay. "If it rains, there is a deluge and a sea of mud." Once you're off the main roads, it's no better today. On a rainy night I drove with Daoud to a dinner in a secluded bourgeois neighborhood of Oran. The streets were a brown porridge, and we nearly got stuck. "What a mess," he exploded. Daoud, who is obsessed with cleanliness, thinks that Algeria's tolerance for dirt is a political symptom, even a spiritual one. Under French rule, Algerians were violently dispossessed of their land. Because the domestic interior was all that they owned, they came to see public space as something that didn't belong to them; as France's property, it was someone else's problem. After independence, it became the state's problem. Religion only reinforced the notion that everyday problems were in the hands of a higher authority. "Our ecological problems are also metaphysical," he said. "People who are waiting for the end of the world can't be bothered with the present."

Islamism thrives, he thinks, on this deeper malaise. The same sense of futility and boredom leads others to flee, even to risk death at sea. Daoud's younger brother is one of thousands of young Algerians—the so-called *harraga*—who have escaped to Europe by boat. He was picked up by a British ship and now lives, without papers, in the United Kingdom.

Daoud is no longer a practicing Muslim, and he describes himself as philosophically close to Buddhism. I asked him if there was anything about Islam he still admired. "The primacy of justice, rather than faith, is something I find very attractive," he said. "I also like the absence of intermediaries between the individual and God. The imam's only role is to officiate at prayers. Insofar as Islam is about the direct relationship between God and the believer, it's a very liberal faith."

He might have been describing the Islam that he knew as a child in Mesra, a village in northwestern Algeria. The Daouds, he said, "were sure of their faith, so they didn't feel they had to defend it, unlike the Islamists today, who are incredibly fragile." The same was true of his family's attachment to the land: they were patriots who lived through the War of Independence but felt no need to deny "the complexities of life under colonialism." In school, he learned "a single story," a black-and-white tale of infallible mujahedeen battling evil French settlers. At home, though, his grandparents told him about the impoverished French they knew in Mesra; about the Catholic priest who fed the family in times of shortage; about French soldiers who deserted their posts, rather than torture and kill. Later he would learn that his father's first great love was not his mother but a Frenchwoman with whom he was involved during the war.

The eldest of six children, Daoud was born in 1970, when Algeria was widely seen as a postcolonial success. Its president, Colonel Houari Boumediene, enigmatic and taciturn, was an authoritarian strongman, but he transformed Algeria into a regional player, a leader of the nonaligned movement. Under Boumediene, who seized power in a military coup three years after independence, the army became the dominant institution in Algerian life. Daoud's father, Mohamed, was a gendarme. In spite of his poverty, he was able, as "a member of a rising generation," to marry a woman from a prosperous, landed family outside of Mesra, socially his superior.

Mohamed Daoud, who studied in French schools, was the only member of the family who could read. He taught his son the alphabet and shared his small library of books in French. At the library in Mostaganem, the port city where Kamel Daoud attended school, he read Jules Verne, *Dune* and works of Greek mythology. But the book that most captivated him was *The Revival of the Religious Sciences*, by Abu Hamid al-Ghazali, an itinerant eleventh-century Persian theologian who, after a crisis of faith, tried to purify his soul through mystical experience. Daoud said that after reading al-Ghazali at age thirteen "the Quran was no longer enough for me. It was merely the visible face of a hidden text." In order to decipher that concealed, more sacred text, he became increasingly ascetic. He kept a stone in his mouth to prevent himself from speaking, after reading that silence opens the heart to God. Daoud wanted to be a writer, but he also wanted to become an imam. "It was a contradiction, but I didn't experience this as a contradiction," he said. "When you pray, you construct meaning, just as you do when you write. God is your only reader, but in essence, it's the same thing."

At first, the Quran won out. Religion was a more promising career path than literature for an ambitious Algerian teenager in the early 1980s. President Chadli Bendjedid, who came to power in 1979, two months after Boumediene's death, rolled back his predecessor's project of socialist land reform and began to liberalize the economy. The shops were flooded with Western consumer products, but "de-Boumedienization" left an ideological void. Bendjedid filled it with Islam and Arab identity. He put down the "Berber Spring" of 1980, a nonviolent movement that called for the recognition of Berber culture and language, intensified the Arabization of education and presided over a mosque-building spree.

Emboldened by these changes, the Islamist movement, which had been tightly controlled under Boumediene, began to train a generation of young militants. Daoud, a young Islamic mystic in a djellaba and turban, was recruited by his geography teacher, a member of an Islamist cell. He introduced him to the writings of Abul Ala Mawdudi, Sayyid Qutb and Hassan al-Banna— the founders of modern Sunni Islamism—and persuaded him that the individual salvation he sought could be achieved only through collective salvation, in the form of an Islamic state. Daoud grew a beard, handed out leaflets and became the imam of his high school. At an Islamist-run summer camp, "we lived as if we were companions of the Prophet." It was in camps and athletic clubs that the young militants of Algeria's emerging Islamic movement were indoctrinated, and Daoud appeared to be on his way to becoming a leader. But when he turned eighteen, Daoud quit the movement. "I felt I had the right to live and to rebel," he told me. "And I was tired. At a certain point, I no longer felt anything. I don't know if this is what losing faith means. But what's dangerous for a religious person isn't temptation, it's fatigue."

On October 5, 1988, three months after he broke with Islamism, Algeria experienced the first in a series of violent antigovernment demonstrations. Daoud went to Mostaganem, armed with a chain, hoping to "break stuff." By the time he arrived, the military had started to fire on people. An old man tried to use him as a human shield. He was saved by a woman who took him by the arm and, pretending that she was his mother, led him to safety. "I was furious at that generation of men, men who would hide behind a young man," he said. "It seemed very symbolic to me." Several hundred Algerians died in Black October. The following year, a new constitution was adopted, legalizing political parties other than the National Liberation Front and thereby dismantling the one-party state. The Islamic Salvation Front emerged as the country's most powerful opposition party.

In January 1992, the army canceled the second round of national elections, in order to prevent the Islamic Salvation Front from coming to power. Deprived of victory at the polls, Islamists took up arms, and a brutal civil war erupted. Daoud, who was studying French at the University of Oran, opposed the cancellation of the elections, but "I really didn't care. I was an individualist. I hated everyone. I looked at the events from a distance, and I thought, They're going to eat each other up." He had chosen a much more personal form of rebellion, in literature, music and beer, though he would not take his first sip of wine, which is specifically proscribed in the Quran, until he was thirty. He read Baudelaire, Borges and the Syrian poet Adonis, and began to write poetry and fiction.

After college, Daoud took a job as a crime reporter for a monthly tabloid called *Detective*. ("What made *The Wire* so great," he told me, "is that it's a collaboration between a writer and a policeman, the dogs of the world.") It was through traveling to small, remote towns, where he wrote about murder trials and sex crimes, that Daoud discovered what he calls "the real Algeria." When *Detective* folded in 1996, he went to work for *Le Quotidien d'Oran*. While other journalists complained of the danger they faced from Islamist rebels, Daoud rented a donkey and went out to interview them. He reported on some of the worst massacres of the civil war, including the 1998 killings in the village of Had Chekala, where more than eight hundred people were slaughtered. His work as a reporter, Daoud told me, left him suspicious of "hardened positions and grand analyses," and that sensibility infused the column he began writing for *Le Quotidien*. Daoud upheld no ideology, spoke in no one's name but his own. To his new admirers, this was something to celebrate: the emergence of an authentically Algerian free spirit. To his adversaries, Daoud became the face of an Algerian Me Generation: selfish, hollow, un-Algerian.

The Meursault Investigation arose from one of his columns. The premise is ingenious: that *The Stranger*, about the murder of an unnamed Arab on an Algiers beach, was a true story. It might as well have been, from the perspective of many Algerians; nationalist critics have long spoken about *The Stranger* as if the murder it described had actually happened and Camus, whose opposition to independence was difficult for many Algerian writers to forgive, had committed it. Daoud's stroke of inspiration was to take the next step and make Meursault, the fictive murderer, the author of Camus's novel. Just as "the Arab" is never named in *The Stranger*, so the name of Camus is never mentioned in *The Meursault Investigation*.

Meursault is a confessional monologue, in the style of Camus's novel *The Fall*, addressed by an Algerian named Harun to an unnamed Frenchman at a bar in Oran. Harun's brother, Musa, was murdered in 1942 by a French settler named Meursault, who went on to achieve fame by describing the killing in a novel called *The Other*. Now an old man, Harun is determined to give his brother a name and a story and to correct Meursault's version of events. For the first half of the book, he does just that, settling an old account that Algerian nationalists—and postcolonial critics like Edward Said, who derided Camus's "incapacitated colonial sensibility"—have had with *The Stranger*.

But the second half of Daoud's novel shows how little bearing that critique has on Algeria's present, denying the reader the easy satisfaction of anticolonial justice. Algeria, not Camus, is on trial here. Harun, we realize, is himself a stranger in a country overrun by religious fervor. The local mosque strikes him as so imposing "it prevents you from seeing God"; the man reciting the Quran sounds as if he were playing all the roles, from "torturer to victim." Men wander around in crumpled pajamas and slippers "as though Friday exempts them from the demands of civility." Friday is "not a day when God rested, it's a day when he decided to run away and never come back."

Harun reveals that he, too, has murdered. His victim, randomly chosen a few days after independence, was a Frenchman named Joseph Larquais, a *roumi* or stranger. His accomplice and enabler was his own mother, who wanted revenge for her son's murder. The new authorities chastise him not for the deed but for its timing: because he killed *after* July 5, 1962, Independence Day, his murder is not an act of liberation but an embarrassment for the regime. Looking for his brother, Harun has instead found his double: he is Meursault's Algerian brother, a murderer in equally absurd circumstances, a stranger in a land caught between "Allah and ennui." When an imam urges him to accept God before it's too late, Harun violently rejects his appeal, in almost exactly the same words that Meursault uses in his conversation with the priest who begs him to accept Christ before his execution. "I had so little time left I didn't want to waste it on God," he says. "None of his certainties was worth one hair on the head of the woman I loved." It is just one of the many lines lifted from Camus. *Meursault* is less a critique of *The Stranger* than its postcolonial sequel.

"*The Stranger* is a philosophical novel, but we're incapable of reading it as anything other than a colonial novel," Daoud told me when I asked him what drew him to Camus's fiction. "The most profound question in Camus is religious: What do you do in relation to God if God doesn't exist? The most powerful scene in *The Stranger* is the confrontation between the priest and the condemned man. Meursault is indifferent with women, with the judge, but he becomes choleric in the face of the priest. And here, in my novel, is someone revolting against God. Harun, for me, is a hero in a conservative society."

Meursault was published by Éditions Barzakh (under the title *Meursault, contre-enquête*) in 2013 to strong sales and widely admiring reviews in Algeria. Only when it was published the following year in France, by Actes Sud, a prestigious house in Arles—and even more so after it was nominated for the Goncourt in September 2014—did the novel stir controversy back home. A half century after independence, Algeria's intellectual life exists under the shadow of its former occupier. For many Algerian intellectuals, it was inconceivable that Daoud could have succeeded in France without the help of the ubiquitous but invisible and invariably sinister *main étrangère*, or "foreign hand."

In a sense, the "foreign hand" is French itself, the language that many Algerian writers still prefer to Arabic, but which for younger Algerians is now a foreign language: one they learn to speak only if it is spoken at home or if they choose to study it in school, as Daoud did. One Friday morning, I set out to meet the novelist Maïssa Bey, one of Algeria's most distinguished French-language writers, at her home in Sidi Bel Abbès, a quaint, dilapidated colonial town. It was the day of prayer, so the streets were deserted. Eucalyptus trees cast delicate shadows on the walls of buildings painted in bright shades of blue, pink and yellow. Bey, who was born in 1950, is the daughter of a nationalist schoolteacher who was tortured and killed by the French army when she was six. Like Daoud, she has written eloquently about Algeria's identity traumas, about the pluralism repressed by the rhetoric of national unity. Like Daoud, she has paid tribute to Camus as a fellow Algerian. "A lot of Algerians can't imagine you're not writing for France if you write in French," she told me. "It's as if the war never ended for them." The persistence of this colonial complex, she says, explains why there's such an acute sense of taboo among writers in Algeria today. "There are subjects you simply cannot touch, Islam above all. It's sacred, and even if you criticize the way it's practiced, not the religion itself, as Kamel did, your words will be twisted, and no one will know, because these rumors acquire a force, and they're manipulated by the *pouvoir*. And if you question the official discourse on Israel or on France's relationship to Algeria, you are inviting trouble."

The most surprising attack on Daoud has come not from a jihadist but from a fellow breaker of taboos, the novelist Rachid Boudjedra, who fled Algeria under a similar threat from Islamists four decades ago. Boudjedra, who is also published by Éditions Barzakh, came to prominence in 1969 when he published, in French, *The Repudiation*, about a young man whose father leaves his mother to marry a much younger woman. He avenges his mother's humiliation by sleeping with his stepmother; his gay brother kills himself after an affair with a Jewish man. Soaked in bodily fluids—blood, feces and semen—and filled with graphic depictions of sex and masturbation, *The Repudiation* was an extreme act of literary rebellion. Shortly after the book was published, Boudjedra went into exile in Paris, then Morocco, for the next six years. He still keeps an apartment in Paris and, after a brief period of writing in Arabic, he has returned to writing in French. If anyone was in a position to understand Daoud's predicament, it was Boudjedra. Instead he ridiculed Daoud's novel as "mediocre" on Ennahar, the Arabic satellite channel that on that same day gave a platform to Hamadache. He later called Daoud one of "those writers who are trying to get a literary visa. They go to France and lick their boots."

Boudjedra is a famously difficult man. But his disdain is not unique, and it reflects a more widespread class prejudice. Boudjedra, who fought in the War of Independence as a young man, is from a prominent rural family, while Daoud is a self-made man from a dusty village. One friend in the Algerian publishing business compares him to Rastignac, the parvenu who scales the social ladder in Balzac's Human Comedy. For leftist intellectuals in Algiers, that alone makes Daoud a provincial hustler rather than a genuine intellectual.

The day after I met Bey in Sidi Bel Abbes, I took the 8 a.m. train from Oran to Algiers, to visit some old friends, including the historian Daho Djerbal, whom I had first met here in 2003. Algiers felt very changed. Walking along rue Didouche Mourad, the main commercial drag, I saw a city to which life, at least commercial life, had returned. I passed a Swatch shop, jewelry stores, travel agencies and fashion boutiques. The sidewalk cafés were full. At the Place de la poste, hundreds of people, mostly men, were watching the Africa Cup on a giant outdoor television screen. I browsed in a lovely new bookstore, on the premises of a bookstore that had belonged to Joaquim Grau, a pied noir gunned down in 1994 by radical Islamists. The outdoor market that winds through Bab el Oued, a working-class neighborhood that was once an Islamist stronghold, was no less vibrant; the merchants' stalls were awash in Chinese electronic goods and clothing, CDs and DVDs and fresh produce.

At the offices of the historical journal he edits, Djerbal tried to persuade me that this normalcy was an optical illusion, the ephemeral effect of a consumption boom fueled by high oil prices. It couldn't last, and the reckoning with reality, he said, would not be pleasant. Djerbal gave me a *tour d'horizon* of the ravages of Algeria's economic liberalization—the capture and sale of key state industries by regime cronies, the accumulation of vast private fortunes, the emergence of a parasitic middle class that creates no wealth of its own. These were the people I saw in the shops of Rue Didouche Mourad, which he portrayed as a Potemkin village that would not survive the fall of oil prices or the failure of the Algerian state to diversify the economy. Perhaps the crash was coming soon, but I remembered hearing a similar chronicle of a disaster foretold from Djerbal twelve years ago.

When I changed the subject to Kamel Daoud, Djerbal grew uncharacteristically impatient, as if I'd asked him about someone beneath his pay grade. Daoud, he told me, was a part of the problem he had just described, a pampered child of the state he attacked. Surely, though, he had to admit that Daoud was a very good writer. Djerbal smiled. "Not good enough for the Goncourt. Besides, France will never give the Goncourt to an Algerian." He seemed to be savoring Daoud's loss. Daoud, he continued, "represents a stratum without historical legitimacy."

In Algeria, the term "historical legitimacy" is very specific. When the War of Independence broke out in 1954, the FLN proclaimed its "historical legitimacy" as the sole representative of the Algerian nation. To have legitimacy means that you represent a collective social force and therefore have the right to be heard. Most Algerian intellectuals set great store by legitimacy and by the implicit claim that they speak on behalf of a larger cause: the nation, the people, the working class, the Berbers. The fact that Daoud speaks only for himself may be what his critics find most unsettling about him.

One evening in Algiers, I provoked a four-hour row merely by mentioning Daoud's name. I was at a dinner party given by Samir Toumi, a writer who lives in an airy, elegant apartment in a Haussmann-style building across from the National Theater. The pro-Daoud faction was led by Sofiane Hadjadj, who runs Éditions Barzakh with his wife, Selma Hellal. (Together, they edited Daoud's novel.) The anti-Daoud faction was led by Ghania Mouffok, a radical journalist who admires his fiction but despises his column. Mouffok, whom I first met in Algiers in 2003, had just returned from reporting on the protests against the extraction of shale gas in the south, a historically marginalized region that is also the source of Algeria's riches, its gas and oil. The movement had rekindled her faith in Algeria's spirit of resistance. "When you think about all that we've gone through—more than a century of colonization, decades of dictatorship, a brutal civil war—it's astonishing that we're even able to raise our heads," Mouffok said. "This is what Kamel Daoud doesn't see."

With a glass of wine in one hand and a cigarette in the other, she laid out the case for the prosecution. Daoud "writes as if imperialism and capitalism didn't exist." He was "self-hating." It was "hardly a surprise that Kamel's narrator feels closer to the man who killed the Arab. You only have to read his columns." The novel was excellent, yet there was something "suspicious" about the book's success in France. "I think it comforts white readers," she said.

"Which country do you think was the first to want to translate Kamel's novel?" Hadjadj interjected. "Vietnam."

"I don't give a damn about whether the novel is translated in Vietnam," Mouffok said. "I'm worried about what French readers see in it."

She took a drag from her cigarette and paused. "Look, I adore Kamel. He was luminous on *We're Not Asleep*. He was beautiful, well spoken and sexy. A few days later I saw him on Echorouk television, and the guy interviewing talked to him as if he were an insect. I said to Kamel: 'Don't go on those shows, and don't behave as if you're guilty. Fight back. Algeria is a country that's failing, where you're not allowed to succeed and, if you do, people want you to fail. It's a hard country and it can be a brutal one.'"

I asked Mouffok why she could criticize Algeria so severely, when she condemned Daoud for doing much the same. She said she reserved her criticisms for the powerful, while Daoud attacks the people. "This is childish," Daoud said when I told him about Mouffok's criticisms. "I don't criticize 'the people,' I criticize *people*. You see that guy running a red light?"—we were in traffic—"I think he's responsible. If someone throws trash on the street, he's responsible. People like Ghania think the same thing, but they won't write it. Instead, they accuse me of hating Algeria, which is absurd. Of course capitalism exists, and when you have an empire, you also have imperialism. But imperialism doesn't explain everything. And it doesn't absolve us from solving our own problems."

In Mouffok's view, Daoud's belief in individual responsibility simply "reproduces the *pouvoir*'s contempt for the people." Accusing someone of being in league or even in sympathy with the *pouvoir* is, in Algeria, the ultimate trump card.

If Daoud shares the *pouvoir*'s dim view of the people, the *pouvoir* doesn't seem to appreciate him. When I met Hamid Grine, the minister of communication, he dismissed Daoud's concerns about the fatwa. "Kamel isn't any more threatened than others like him," he said. Hamadache, who started out as a professional dancer, was a crank without a following, and thus best ignored. "The case has attracted attention because it sells newspapers, but in the Algerian heartland, people are talking about the price of potatoes, not about Kamel Daoud."

As it happened, Grine called Daoud the day before. He was upset over a column that Daoud had just published, "The Other 'Je Suis Mohamed,'" praising Mohamed Aïssa, the minister of religious affairs, for his campaign against Islamist incitement on Algerian-owned Arabic satellite channels. ("Hamid would have preferred a column titled 'Je Suis Hamid,'" Daoud says.) Grine claimed that he was the first to defend Daoud, but his remarks were less than stirring. He had spoken privately to executives at the satellite channels that featured Hamadache, but, unlike Aïssa, he refrained from publicly reproaching them, because "in Algeria, we have a tradition of discretion." (A month after our conversation, Grine made statements echoing Aïssa's criticisms.)

Grine, who is sixty, is also a novelist who, like Daoud, writes in French. I told him that I enjoyed his novel *Camus in the Hookah Lounge*, about a man who hears a rumor that Camus is his biological father. He complained that his novel hadn't benefited from the "huge promotion team" that catapulted Daoud's book to success in France and hinted that his perspective on Camus might not have been welcome in Paris. The hero of *Camus in the Hookah Lounge* realizes that Camus was not his father and that Algerians have to abandon the fantasy of reclaiming Camus, as writers like Daoud and Bey have proposed.

"Camus wasn't an Algerian writer, he was a French writer," Grine said. "He was a colonizer of good will, a pied noir. Yes, he made gestures toward Algerians, but he was opposed to independence."

Grine hadn't read *Meursault*. "I'm sure it's excellent. My son has read it, and he enjoyed it. I only read what you see here," he said, pointing to the stack of official documents on his desk.

{2015}

3

The Life and Death of Juliano Mer-Khamis

On the afternoon of Monday, April 4, 2011, Juliano Mer-Khamis walked out of the Freedom Theater in the Jenin refugee camp and got into his old red Citroën. It was four o'clock, the sun was hot and the street crowded. He put his baby son, Jay, on his lap, placing the boy's fingers on the steering wheel; the babysitter sat next to them. As he set off, a man in a balaclava came out of an alleyway and told him to stop. He had a gun. The babysitter told Juliano to keep driving, but he stopped. The gunman shot him five times, then walked back down the alley. He left his mask in the street. Jay survived; the babysitter escaped with minor injuries. Juliano was dead. Later his body was handed over to the Israeli authorities, along with his car, computer, wallet and other effects.

Juliano was the founder of the Freedom Theater. He was an Israeli citizen, the son of a Jewish mother and therefore a Jew in the eyes of the Jewish state. But his father was a Palestinian from Nazareth, and Juliano was a passionate believer in the Palestinian cause. He would often say he was "100 percent Palestinian and 100 percent Jewish," but in Israel he was seldom allowed to forget he was the son of an Arab, and in Jenin he was seen as an Israeli, a Jew, no matter how much he did for the camp. Among the artists and intellectuals of Ramallah, however, he was admired for having left Israel to work in one of the toughest parts of the West Bank, and was accepted as an ally. Since its founding in 2006, the Freedom Theater had been under constant fire: local conservatives saw it as a corrupting influence, even a Zionist conspiracy; the Palestinian Authority resented what Juliano said about its "cooperation" with Israel; and Israel saw him as a troublemaker, if not a traitor.

Shortly after the murder, Mahmoud Abbas declared Juliano a *shaheed*, a martyr. But though he may have given his life to the Palestinian cause, he was not killed by an Israeli bullet. The man who shot him was Palestinian, and probably from the camp: no one else would have known how to navigate those streets, or how to disappear so quickly. The killing appeared to be a message from forces inside the camp. Juliano had spoken bluntly about the stifling effects of patriarchy, gender oppression and religious dogma; freedom, he argued, began with individual liberation, and without it freedom from occupation would mean nothing. This did not endear him to defenders of "tradition." Nor did the theater's productions, in which teenage boys and girls appeared onstage together. But risk was part of what inspired Juliano. In a 2008 interview, he joked that he would be killed by a "fucked-up Palestinian" for "corrupting the youth of Islam." The interview was posted on YouTube shortly after his murder.

The silence from the camp seemed to confirm the hypothesis: few people beyond those involved with the theater mourned Juliano, and no one came forward to identify the killer. For Israel's radical left, the murder was a devastating blow. Handsome and charismatic, Juliano was a symbol of the binational dream, a walking advertisement for solidarity and coexistence. For Palestinian artists and intellectuals his murder was "a hammer in the head," as George Ibrahim, head of the Qasaba Theater in Ramallah, put it. But right-wing commentators in Israel were delighted that a pro-Palestinian celebrity had been killed by a Palestinian. "He lived among snakes, and one of them killed him with its bites," Yehuda Dror wrote. "He proves to us once more that there is no one to talk to."

When I visited Jenin two months after the murder, almost everyone agreed that Juliano had angered many people in the camp, in spite of his efforts to win them over to his program of "cultural resistance," as he called it. No one was going to the theater, and the six members of his graduating class had left Jenin for Ramallah. The actor Nabil al-Raee, the theater's artistic director, and his wife, Micaela Miranda, an actress from Portugal, were working out of the house they had shared with Juliano and his family. They weren't sure when they would return to the theater, or whether it would survive. Nawal Staiti, an old friend of Juliano's, wouldn't get out of the car when she drove me to the theater. "I blame the camp," she said, bursting into tears. "They know who killed Juliano, and they aren't saying."

Two years after his murder, the theater Juliano created still stands in a converted stone house rented from the UN. But until the murder is solved, al-Raee told me, "we remain under threat." The question is from whom? Al-Raee no longer believes that Juliano was killed for challenging the ways of the camp; he thinks the killer was a hired hand, acting on behalf of more powerful forces inside the PA and Israel. At the theater, Juliano was seen as a political leader, not just a director: therefore his killing must have been an assassination. But elsewhere, one hears other theories, mostly to do with money, corruption and factional struggles. These theories have taken on a life of their own. The idea that Juliano was killed for introducing transgressive Western ideas about personal liberty to a community that adheres to a conservative form of Islam is no longer popular, except among Israeli Jews for whom it confirms old prejudices. As people in Jenin will tell you, violence against solidarity activists, even if they are Israeli, is almost unheard of in Palestine. That's what made the killing so unsettling.

It's possible, of course, that Juliano's murder had little to do with his work and more to do with the man himself. The most important question may not be who killed him, but why his killer, or killers, believed they could eliminate him with impunity. Whoever killed him knew that no one in the camp would rush to his defense. Juliano loved the camp—no one doubts that. But he seemed to forget that he was a guest there, and that the more deeply he penetrated the life of the camp, the more cautiously he had to tread.

෧

Juliano was the son of one of Jenin's most famous guests, Arna Mer, and many people will always remember him as her son. Arna Mer's work with children in the camp had made her a legendary figure. Born in 1929, she came from the Zionist aristocracy: her father, Gideon Mer, briefly directed Israel's ministry of health in the mid-1950s. At eighteen she joined the Palmach, the Jewish fighting brigades, and drove a jeep during the 1948 Arab-Israeli war. It was thrilling, she told Juliano in the documentary he made about her, *Arna's Children*, to be a young woman "driving people from place to place, and nobody could stop you." She would remain a Palmachnik—tough-talking, sometimes arrogant, always brutally direct—and she passed the style on to Juliano. The *keffiyeh* she wore in Jenin, which Palestinians assumed to be an expression of solidarity, was a homage to her days in the Palmach, when Zionists adopted the look of the fellahin whose land they coveted.

Arna became disillusioned with Zionism after taking part in an operation to drive the bedouin out of southern Palestine. Shortly after the war, she joined the Communist Party. She met Saliba Khamis, an intellectual from a Greek Orthodox family, at a party conference. Khamis was an emerging leader in "Red Nazareth," where the party was attracting support for protesting against Israel's harsh military government. Arna and Saliba married in 1953. To be in a mixed marriage was to be a good Communist; it expressed opposition to Zionism, and honored the principles of internationalism. Outside the party, and particularly among Jews, a mixed marriage was a source of unspeakable shame. Arna's father saw it as an act of rebellion that even he, a socialist, could not countenance. She was welcomed into the Khamis family, and shunned by her own.

Juliano, born in 1958, was the second of their three sons, and grew up in Nazareth and Haifa. It was a political household: Saliba wrote pieces in the party newspaper, *Al-Ittihad*, about the rise of anticolonial liberation movements; Arna had been a teacher but was fired for marrying an Arab, and spearheaded a popular campaign against the military government. The marriage was difficult. Arna was at heart an anarchist; Saliba a party man who was growing embittered at being denied a seat in the politburo. They disagreed fiercely about how to raise their sons: Saliba wanted them to be clean-cut young Communists, and was furious when Arna allowed them to grow their hair long. "Juliano grew up with a paradox," Osnat Trabelsi, the producer of *Arna's Children*, told me. "Outside, the oppressor was the Jew, but at home, the oppressor was Arab." Juliano later said he first learned about politics "at the end of my father's belt." When Juliano was ten, Saliba moved out. Juliano attended Jewish schools in Haifa and saw himself as a Jew—he even stopped speaking Arabic for a time. At the age of eighteen, he joined the paratroopers. Saliba and Arna were horrified: Juliano was now a soldier in the occupation they had both devoted their lives to fighting. He was stationed in Jenin.

Jenin has had a reputation for defiance since the Ottoman era, when residents refused to pay taxes to the sultan. Seized from Jordan on the first day of the 1967 war, it soon became a center of resistance to the Israeli occupation: the camp, which was set up in the early 1950s as a temporary shelter for refugees from Haifa and the neighboring villages, was known to be especially militant. By the time Juliano was stationed there, it had evolved into a densely populated slum with more than 10,000 residents. If a soldier killed an old woman or a child by accident, a weapon would be planted on the corpse: Juliano's job was to carry the bag with the weapons.

It wasn't long before he cracked. At a checkpoint in Jenin, his commanding officer asked him to search an elderly Palestinian man. Later he would claim that the man was a cousin, though he had never seen him before. No one disputes what happened next: Juliano refused his orders, punched his commanding officer and spent several months in prison. He would have been there longer had Arna not called Isser Harel, her cousin and the first head of the Mossad, and implored him to get her son released. He recovered in a mental hospital. His life as an Israeli Jew was over. He now flirted with the idea of joining the PLO: he still wanted to be a soldier, whatever side he was on. But he was no good at following orders. Instead, he enrolled at the Beit-Zvi School for the Performing Arts in Tel Aviv. There he could be an Arab or a Jew, or neither.

In 1985, Juliano Mer—he dropped "Khamis" from his name—starred in Amos Guttman's film *Bar 51*, a tale of obsessive love between a brother and sister, set in Tel Aviv's hedonistic underground. He seemed poised to become a star of Israel's emerging independent cinema. "Juliano had the material of great actors," Amos Gitai, who cast him in seven films, told me. But he was looking for something more intense. In 1987 he went to the Philippines, where he spent a year, mostly high on mushrooms. He lived in a tent, talked to monkeys and declared himself the son of God. His parents had him rescued. But he felt that something important had happened to him under the influence of the mushrooms: "I lost all my identities." As an actor this was no bad thing: "I have a gift, you are not only consciously un-nationalized, you are inside yourself divided. Use it!" He took the idea to the streets. In downtown Tel Aviv he would remove his clothes, cover himself in fake blood or olive oil or paint, and denounce Israel's response to the First Intifada, which had just broken out. His performances in Palestinian refugee camps were physically more demure but scarcely less provocative. "They think that if you replace the Israeli occupation with the Arafat occupation, it's going to be better," he said, "and I say no, fight both of them!"

He was sleeping on the beach, eating nothing but olives, labneh and garlic. He was saved by two women. The first was Mishmish Or, who found him one night in a bar wearing only his underwear. She was an Israeli Jew in her mid-twenties, the daughter of a Turkish father and an Egyptian mother, a costume designer, and the mother of a two-year-old daughter, Keshet. She took him home that night; he moved in, and became a stepfather to Keshet. The second was his mother, who asked him to help out with her new project. When the Israeli army shut down Palestinian schools after the outbreak of the intifada, Arna went to Jenin. "I have not come here for philanthropic reasons," she said, or to "show that there are nice Jews who help Arabs. I came to struggle against the Israeli occupation." Working closely with Nawal Staiti and Samira Zubeidi, both of them married to Fatah militants who were in and out of prison, Arna established an alternative education system called Care and Learning. She brought toys to people's homes and distributed banned resistance pamphlets. Israeli, Jewish, a former member of the Palmach and an atheist: everything about Arna was wrong in Jenin. But the parents of Jenin's children loved her.

More than 1,500 students from the camp attended her "children's centers," most of which were run out of people's homes. Arna, an accomplished sculptor, believed art could provide the children with a means of expressing their feelings about the occupation. She invited Juliano to teach drama therapy. And when she received the so-called alternative Nobel, the Right Livelihood Prize in Sweden, she built a theater with the proceeds. In 1993, the Stone Theater, named after the stones children threw at Israeli tanks, was established on the top floor of Samira Zubeidi's house. Juliano was there constantly, directing rehearsals, and filming his mother and the children for what became *Arna's Children*. The Stone Theater reunited the family: Saliba and Juliano's brothers came to performances, and Juliano began to call himself Mer-Khamis again. At first his students looked at him warily; they worried he might be "a spy for the occupation," as one of them told him. But he formed lasting friendships—among them with Samira Zubeidi's son Zacharia, who would later become a leader of the Al-Aqsa Martyrs Brigades, a militia of young men affiliated with Fatah, and a co-founder of the Freedom Theater.

Arna died of cancer in 1995, a few months after Saliba Khamis. No cemetery would bury her: she was now a traitor for her activities in Jenin. Juliano held a press conference at her home in Haifa. He said he would bury her in her garden if nowhere else would have her. Finally Ramot Menashe, a left-Zionist kibbutz in the hills of the Carmel, offered to take her. Juliano didn't set foot in Jenin for another seven years. He returned to his old life and made a name for himself as a daringly physical performer in Tel Aviv's Habima Theater. He played the gay prisoner in *Kiss of the Spider Woman*; he performed in Arthur Miller's *A View from the Bridge* and Tony Kushner's *Angels in America*. As Othello, he nearly strangled the actress playing Desdemona: an ambulance had to be called to resuscitate her. He often got into brawls: with directors, actors, even members of the audience.

But he was also settling down. In 2000, Or gave birth to their daughter Milay; along with Keshet they moved into Arna's old house in Haifa. But soon after the Second Intifada erupted in October 2000, Juliano turned their house into a base for organizing. This intifada, unlike the first, was armed, and Jenin was leading the way. Over the next three years, militants inside the camp—the "capital of terror," according to Israeli tabloids—sent an estimated thirty suicide bombers to Israel. In October 2001, two of Juliano's former students, Yusuf Sweitat and Nidal al-Jabali, carried out an attack. Two weeks earlier, Sweitat had rescued a girl from her classroom where an Israeli shell had exploded; she died as he was carrying her to hospital. Vowing to avenge her death, he and al-Jabali offered their services to Islamic Jihad. They drove a stolen jeep to a bus station in Hadera and opened fire. Four women were killed before the police killed Sweitat and al-Jabali.

Sweitat had been one of Juliano's favorite students. When he heard what had happened, Juliano decided to return to Jenin with his camera and complete the film about his mother. His first trip back was in May 2002; a month earlier, on April 2, more than a thousand soldiers had surrounded the camp and declared it a closed military zone. As the soldiers approached, Zacharia Zubeidi, speaking in Hebrew through a loudspeaker, warned them not to enter. The fighting went on for two weeks. The army demolished parts of the camp with armored bulldozers, supported by tanks. In the end, the camp lay in ruins. When Juliano arrived with two generators there had been no electricity for more than a month. His host was his former student Ala'a Sabbagh. They had first met ten years earlier, when Sabbagh was twelve years old and sitting in the rubble of his home after the army demolished it. Now Sabbagh was the leader of the Al-Aqsa Martyrs Brigade in Jenin, and Zacharia Zubeidi was his deputy. Zubeidi's mother, Samira, had been killed a month before the battle began: she was sitting on her porch when an Israeli sniper, possibly mistaking her for her son Taha, shot her; Taha was killed a few hours later. The Stone Theater, on the top floor of Samira's home, was demolished.

By night Juliano accompanied Sabbagh and Zubeidi on patrols, ate with them and slept in their hideouts. He spent seven months with men who were on Israel's hit list. Sabbagh was killed by a helicopter gunship in November 2002. Zubeidi, who replaced him at the head of the Al-Aqsa Brigades, soon became known in Israel as the Black Rat for his skill in dodging the army's attempts to kill him. In spite of his easy rapport with people in the camp, Juliano remained suspect, as an Israeli citizen, even among the fighters who were his friends. "They trusted him and didn't trust him," Or told me. "It was exciting for him."

Arna's Children was released internationally in 2004. It is a raw and upsetting film—above all, a son's elegy for his mother. We first see Arna at a checkpoint protesting against the closure of Jenin. She expresses her anger at the occupation and her belief that music and theater can show her students a way out of the occupation. In fact, she is raising the next intifada's martyrs. Ashraf, Yusuf, Nidal, Ala'a and Zacharia will all become fighters; only Zacharia will survive. Their decision to fight, as shown in the film, is as inevitable as it is tragic: they are patriots defending their homes, not Islamic zealots; their cause, it suggests, is no different from Arna's. The film is not an inspirational tale but a portrait of failure: you see the weakness of nonviolent resistance in the face of a violent occupation.

The film turned Juliano into a celebrity on the radical left. But he was having a hard time getting work on the Hebrew stage, partly because of his politics, but also because of his reputation for destructive behavior. One night he walked off the stage of the Habima Theater and punched a man who called him a traitor. He had never been more famous or less employable. He needed a break. He took his four-year-old daughter to India on a motorcycle trip; Milay sat in a basket he'd made for her. Four months into the trip, Or joined them for another two months. But when they returned, Or moved back to Tel Aviv with Milay, and Juliano stayed in Haifa. Again he began to spin his wheels. Lihi

Hanoch, his cousin, encouraged him to leave Israel, maybe move to New York, where he'd won the prize for best documentary at the Tribeca Film Festival. Instead, he went back to Jenin.

Arna's Children had been a success in the Jenin camp, where people had never seen themselves on film, much less depicted as freedom fighters. Juliano showed the film in a football stadium before an audience of more than three thousand. Every time one of the *shaheeds*—the martyrs—appeared on screen, the audience roared, and members of the Al-Aqsa Brigades fired their guns into the air. "You're shooting for nothing!" Amira Hass, the legendary *Haaretz* correspondent based in Ramallah complained to Zubeidi. "How much does each of those bullets cost?" The camp's resistance to the army during the invasion had been heroic, Hass told me, "But at the same time, men like Zacharia were living out a fantasy of armed struggle, where the very use of explosives, whether bullets fired in the air or human bombs exploded in buses, was glorified without thought for their long-term effects." *Arna's Children*, she worried, "might bolster the cult that Zubeidi and his friends were building around themselves." But it had its practical uses. It raised morale, and enabled young fighters to win positions in the Palestinian Authority—among them Zubeidi, who would soon collect a salary from the Ministry of Prisoner Affairs. It also helped to make them stars inside the camp, Zubeidi most of all.

Zubeidi first came to prominence in Israel a year before the release of *Arna's Children*, when he gave an interview to *Haaretz*. It was the beginning of a strange romance between the Israeli press and "Israel's number one wanted man in the area," alleged to be responsible for the deaths of at least six Israeli civilians. Zubeidi relished the spotlight and made himself available to reporters. He was a loose cannon who admitted he was no good at following orders. He spoke warmly of Arafat but otherwise expressed contempt for the PA, Mahmoud Abbas in particular: "Abu Mazen doesn't even control his pants," he said. (Still, he had no compunction about drawing a PA salary: like many of his fellow militants, he had become dependent on an organization whose existence he saw as humiliating to national aspirations.) He was comfortable among Israelis, and said his struggle was with the occupation, not with Jews. He spoke choppy but fluent Hebrew, which he'd learned in prison. He had an easy smile, a boyish charm.

Born in 1976, Zubeidi came from a family of militants. His father had been an English teacher but was banned from teaching because of his membership in Fatah; he worked in an iron foundry while Samira worked with Arna Mer. Zubeidi went to the children's centers and acted in Stone Theater productions, but school never held much interest for him. He spent his adolescence in street battles with Israeli soldiers, and in prison, where he joined Fatah. When the Oslo Agreements were signed in 1993, he joined the PA police but quit after a year. Under the name Jul Darawashe, he made a living in Israel as a contractor. When his cover was blown and he was deported, he turned to stealing cars in Israel and selling them in Jenin, until he discovered a new talent: making explosives. (Once, a bomb blew up while he was making it, leaving his face dark and pockmarked.) Sleeping in temporary hideouts, never far from his pistol, Zubeidi was always a step ahead of the Israelis. At least fourteen Palestinians were killed in Israeli operations against him. His ability to outwit his pursuers made him a local hero. By the time Juliano came to the camp to show *Arna's Children*, he was the most powerful man there.

Not long after the premiere, Juliano and Zubeidi started talking about relaunching Arna's project. It was their acquaintance Jonatan Stanczyk, the son of a Polish-Jewish father and an Israeli mother brought up in Stockholm, who drew up the plans for the Freedom Theater. The three of them opened it in February 2006. They knew that the camp was a quixotic location; most people there had never even seen a play performed. But that made it all the more exciting. Juliano would be the artistic director, Stanczyk the operations manager, while Zubeidi would protect the theater from anyone who threatened it. Zubeidi's support was indispensable: Juliano and Stanczyk—both outsiders, both Jews—could never have worked in the camp without his blessing and the legitimacy he conferred. But Zubeidi was a wanted man and in no position to defend the theater from Israel's threats: that was Juliano's job. He disarmed soldiers by addressing them in Hebrew; some recognized him from the movies.

Stanczyk supplied the start-up capital with money he had earned playing the Stockholm real estate market; the rest came from screenings of *Arna's Children*. Most of the original employees were volunteers; Stanczyk refused a salary. Juliano and his partners rented a building, and put up photographs of Che, Darwish, the novelist Ghassan Kanafani and Arna Mer in her keffiyeh. For the first few months, they slept on mattresses in the same room; Juliano hardly left the camp.

Juliano was startled by the changes in the camp since his mother's day. The physical damage had been repaired, but most children showed signs of post-traumatic stress disorder. Thanks to Israel's closures, Jenin was more isolated than ever; thanks to the rise in Islamic piety, it was more internally repressive. The inhabitants now suffered from two occupations: Israel's, and what Juliano called a "cultural-religious occupation" imposed from within. Juliano wanted to fight both of them. But in order to fight the second, he needed to win people's trust. And the camp was inevitably suspicious of outsiders, especially those who made an issue of their good intentions. It was also swarming with informers. Even Zubeidi's sponsorship could turn out to be a mixed blessing: it marked the theater as a Fatah project at a moment of intensifying Fatah-Hamas rivalry.

Juliano worked hard to woo the camp, and to remain somehow above the fray. Using his privileges as an Israeli citizen, he turned himself into a one-man relief organization. He brought food and medicine to people's homes. He drove pregnant women through checkpoints to hospitals in Israel, and children who had never seen the sea to the beaches of Haifa. If someone tried to shake him down for cash, he would give them a small job. In deference to the camp's ways, he never drank outside his house, and he threw away his empty whisky bottles in Haifa. When women from outside the camp came to work in the theater, he insisted they wear long sleeves. He lived very simply and refused to install an air conditioner in his house. He went to great lengths to prove that he was not beholden to Fatah, in spite of his alliance with Zubeidi.

The idea that, even under occupation, Palestinians could improve their situation, was central to Juliano's pitch. "Israel is destroying the neurological system of the society," he said, "which is culture, identity, communication," but "if you're going to keep blaming the occupation for all the problems of the Palestinians, you're going to end up in the same situation we're in today." He was careful not to denounce the armed resistance; that would have been heresy in the camp. But the next intifada, he declared, "will be cultural." Perhaps art could succeed where violence had failed. "We have to stand up again on our feet," he said. "We are now living on our knees."

The "we" was new. More and more Juliano spoke of himself as a Palestinian. The story of how he came to Palestine became an inspiring conversion narrative. "He never hid his history, the things that might make people uncomfortable," Khulood Badawi, a friend in Haifa, told me: he spoke of being "a killer" in the paratroopers, of his mother's work at the Stone Theater, of the political awakening that led him back to Jenin. "When I left Haifa," he said, "I left Israel. I left my work, I left my society, I left my friends. I live here." But Juliano never really left Israel or his friends there: on weekends, he was often in Haifa or in Tel Aviv. The story he told about his break with Israel was "mainly an instrumental declaration," Ruchama Marton, the founder of Physicians for Human Rights, told me. "He had to say this to work in Jenin. In the same week I would see Juliano one day in Tel Aviv and another in Jenin. Was he a different person? Sure, he spoke Arabic there and Hebrew here. It's not that he was lying. It was true and not true at the same time." The performance went over well enough. Juliano was the son of a local saint, and he pledged to continue her work, but he had larger ambitions than his mother: he wanted to transform the camp, not just to serve it. His ultimate aim was to train a group of professional actors, to stage productions that would be both artistically serious and politically provocative, and to create an independent media center for Palestinians in the West Bank and in Israel. Jenin was a base of operations, not a final destination.

He found his students by wandering through the camp, introducing himself to people and describing his vision. Some of the actors he attracted had been fighters, others were thieves: hard cases, just as he had been. Of his first six students, five were from Jenin, two were girls, and all faced ferocious opposition from people in their communities, for some of whom the theater might as well have been a brothel. It was a shameful place where boys and girls mixed; a place, as one visitor remarked to me, that "smelled of sex." Outsiders called the student actresses whores. One father threatened to disown his daughter. For the boys, it wasn't much easier. Juliano was a tough teacher, but he was also careful to build up his students' confidence. He told them they would be stars. And he paid them the ultimate compliment in Jenin: "You're not actors," he said, "you are freedom fighters."

But these "freedom fighters" couldn't perform without the cover of Zubeidi and his friends in the Al-Aqsa Brigades. Juliano was proud of his closeness to Zubeidi and the resistance; he could hardly object if its luster rubbed off on the theater. It was a major attraction for volunteers from Europe and America, who descended on the theater as if it were a revolutionary base. But Juliano was trading on his relationship to the resistance while promoting a nonviolent alternative. "Juliano understood that the methods of the Second Intifada had been a complete failure for the Palestinian cause," Jenny Nyman, the Finnish woman he married in 2007, says. "Even though he never spoke against the armed struggle, at the same time he said: 'Look what's happened to you. Isn't it time to take a break and build up the society again?' He wanted Zacharia to be a part of this. Zacharia was a big reason Juliano went back to Jenin, and he saw the theater as a way of saving him."

The young people who came to study in the theater were looking for a form of resistance that would allow them to live, rather than die as martyrs. This went against the grain in Jenin. "To be wanted by the army, to be a hero, was everyone's dream," a student called Faisal Abu Alheja told me. "But when I went to the theater, I said, this is a dangerous idea: it means we want to die. How can we have freedom if we die?" In the theater, he could "think without Fatah, without Hamas, without Islamic Jihad." Juliano forged strong relationships with young men whose fathers had been killed or spent long periods in prison. Mustapha Staiti, the son of Nawal Staiti, who worked with Arna Mer, was one of them. His father, Mohamad, a Fatah activist, had been in prison for much of his son's childhood. Under torture and other forms of physical duress, he'd lost much of his sight. He found God, and defected from Fatah to Hamas. After his release in 1995, he beat his children, and tried to get his daughters to cover themselves. Mustapha drifted away from his family and dabbled in radical Islam. He thought of becoming a fighter like his father, he told me; he was looking for "a way to get killed and just finish the story." It was then that Juliano re-entered his life, and promised his mother that he would look after her son. He took Mustapha to the theater, gave him a video camera, and introduced him to filmmaking. "Juliano took me under his wing, and I put down everything. My life became Juliano. He knew how we felt, he knew how to communicate with us, and he found an energy in the camp that he didn't find elsewhere."

It was at night, he said, drinking whisky with Juliano, that he learned the most. Juliano and Zubeidi shared a house, first in the camp, later in the city, where a number of staff members also rented rooms. There, members of the acting troupe and other friends of the theater were introduced to the pleasures of alcohol and hash, and met radical Israelis and foreigners. They were getting their first glimpse of a world beyond Jenin. It was a world Israel prevented them from entering, and the local enforcers of the cultural occupation didn't want them to see it either. Though the parties took place behind closed doors, rumors began to ripple through the camp. Girls and boys dancing onstage, fighters putting down their weapons to become actors, and now parties with drugs and sex: to some, it looked as though Juliano had come to foment a youth revolt. It was all part of an Israeli plan to weaken the resistance. One former Fatah activist told me he first understood this when he heard that children at the theater were being taught about the Holocaust: "First the Israelis destroyed the camp, then they gave us the theater."

The charge that the theater was a foreign project was hard to rebut. Although the administrative staff was largely from Jenin, most of the people running it were foreigners, and both Juliano and Stanczyk were Israeli citizens. The theater's stance was unusually radical for an NGO in Palestine. It refused to criticize the armed struggle or to parrot the PA's rhetoric about the peace process, positions that cost it some potential funding. It attacked the PA's collaboration with Israel and described itself as part of a struggle against occupation rather than another "capacity-building" organization. Yet the Freedom Theater depended as much as other NGOs on foreign money, and on the goodwill of its many guests from abroad. It had radical cachet because it was located in the camp, but its real roots lay elsewhere. Juliano conceived of the theater as a kind of revolutionary training base for soldiers in the "cultural intifada," but it looked more like a bohemian oasis in the midst of the camp's miseries.

Juliano was convinced that once people saw the results of his work, they would embrace it. His charisma worked wonders when he went abroad to raise money. His most ardent supporters were a group of aging New York radicals led by Constancia Romilly, the daughter of Jessica Mitford and the ex-wife of the civil rights leader James Forman, and Dorothy Zellner, a veteran of the Student Nonviolent Coordinating Committee. Friends from the civil rights era, and both red diaper babies, Romilly and Zellner met Juliano in 2006 at a screening of *Arna's Children* at NYU. The two women set up the Friends of the Freedom Theater, modeled on the support groups for SNCC. They held a fundraiser at the West Village flat of Romilly's friend Kathleen Chalfant, a well-known New York actress. Juliano talked about his mother's theater, and about his own efforts to rebuild a shattered community through art. His "most effective fundraising tool," Chalfant said, was to offer a nonviolent way of opposing the occupation. James Nicola and Linda Chapman, the heads of the New York Theater Workshop, were excited by Juliano, and became sponsors of the Freedom Theater. Nicola was impressed that

"Juliano's definition of freedom was much bigger than freedom from occupation," embracing women's liberation, freedom from religious oppression, personal and sexual freedom. Everyone who met Juliano in New York was beguiled: Danny Glover, Tony Kushner, the philanthropist and writer Jean Stein. Julian Schnabel cast him as a sheikh in *Miral*, Juliano's last performance on film. Eve Ensler invited him to stage *The Vagina Monologues* in Jenin. In a city of hyphenated identities his mixed identity made him all the more attractive, and more trustworthy. The theater became a popular cause for celebrities on the left: Vanessa Redgrave, Maya Angelou, the film producer James Schamus, Judith Butler, Slavoj Žižek, Noam Chomsky and the Lebanese novelist Elias Khoury.

Juliano urged supporters from the West to come to Jenin. Romilly often stayed with him in his home in the camp. One night Israeli tanks rolled up at three in the morning and ordered everyone out of their houses. "Juliano came downstairs in his boxer shorts, and said: 'We're not going out. They know that I'm here, and they know that I have foreign visitors.' He was very reassuring. We always felt safe." Juliano introduced her to Zubeidi. At the time, he was a wanted man and still lived underground. In the early days of the theater, he kept a low profile: the presence of a "terrorist" might discourage potential donors, Nyman told me. But he provided evidence of the theater's connection to the resistance, and some guests became enamored of him. The LA philanthropist Charles Annenberg, charmed by Zubeidi, wrote the Freedom Theater a $200,000 check, and made a rapturous documentary about his new friend, *Nobody Is Born a Terrorist*. "It was an absolutely terrible film," Nyman says, "but he gave us money and became a friend." (He was one of several wealthy American Jews supporting the theater; for Arabs, Nyman says, Juliano was "too Jewish.")

In July 2007, Zubeidi came out of the shadows: as part of an agreement between the PA and Israel, he promised not to engage in armed resistance in return for having his name removed from Israel's wanted list. Juliano saluted his decision. Zubeidi, he said, "left the armed resistance after being inspired by the theater, deciding that the only way forward was to join the cultural struggle against the Israeli occupation." In fact Zubeidi had little choice. He was one of 178 Fatah militiamen who accepted the amnesty; he could hardly defy the Fatah leadership. It was part of a series of political developments that transformed Jenin's political landscape. The PA, which had lost control of Jenin after the 2002 invasion, stepped up its efforts to impose itself on the camp—and to take over "security" responsibilities from Israel. In 2008, hundreds of PA security officers, funded by the US and trained in Jordan, entered Jenin, rounding up militants. The Jenin Development Plan was sweetened with economic and agrarian assistance and eased security restrictions for local merchants. Before long, the "reformed" security services in Jenin were fighting each other over territory and patronage.

Zubeidi was now free to sleep at home for the first time in five years, though he wasn't allowed to leave Jenin. But signing the amnesty did little to enhance his reputation inside the camp. Now that the Israelis were no longer giving him chase, his talent for survival counted against him. ("In Jenin you're not innocent until you're dead," one man told me.) Perhaps, some whispered, Zubeidi had survived because the Israelis wanted him alive; perhaps he'd been an informer all along. There had always been questions about his courage during the Battle of Jenin. Some of his critics cited a scene in *Arna's Children* as evidence: his predecessor as leader of the Al-Aqsa Brigades, Ala'a Sabbagh, who surrendered a week into the 2002 invasion, accuses Zubeidi of hiding with his group rather than continuing the fight. "At least I didn't surrender," Zubeidi replies, declaring that he would rather die than surrender. "If you wanted to die, why didn't you shoot the soldiers?" Sabbagh fires back. "You pretended to be dead." Ferocious recriminations about his acceptance of the amnesty came from Tali Fahima, an Israeli radical who had converted to Islam and spent nearly three years in prison for visiting Zubeidi in Jenin, and the attacks from Hamas, which had not ended its armed resistance and saw the amnesty as a betrayal, were more damaging still.

Even Gamal Abdel Nasser, Zubeidi said, "admitted his defeat, so why not me?" And he continued to attack the PA: "They are whores. Our leadership is garbage." But there was no denying that the amnesty had damaged his heroic image. His biggest defender was Juliano, and he drew closer to him, even as his friends in the Al-Aqsa Brigades warned him not to be "Juliano's man." ("Don't ask me to hold a guitar against an M16," a former Fatah activist in Jenin told me when I asked him what he thought of the theater.) The theater was connected to influential people far outside Jenin, and Zubeidi had always fancied being on a wider stage. "Zacharia is like Juliano," Abed Qusini, a journalist in Nablus, told me. "He used Juliano as much as Juliano used him. Juliano gave him a big name, and he wanted to be a leader in front of the world." Not that he had much to do with the theater's programming. "Let's face it," Nyman said, "he's not a culture person."

Not long after he was amnestied, Zubeidi built a stone and marble mansion in Jenin City with a view of the camp. It was in a neighborhood called the Mountain of Thieves; many of the residents are PA officials. No one could explain how Zubeidi was able to build his mansion on his wages from the Ministry of Prisoner Affairs. The PA suspected that, like many former militants, Zubeidi was selling guns. During the Second Intifada, Jenin had become an arms warehouse, and no one had better access to it than Zubeidi. He is believed to have invested his profits in real estate in Jenin and Nablus. He divided his house into flats, and became a landlord for a number of employees of the theater, including Juliano and al-Raee. It was safer for them in the hills.

In the spring of 2009, the theater staged *Animal Farm*, and Juliano realized he had enemies, not just critics, in the camp. The production was designed to shock. Actors appeared on stage dressed as pigs, violating Islamic taboo. In the last scene, army officers speaking Hebrew came to trade with the pigs: a dagger aimed at the Palestinian Authority. One night, someone tried to set the theater on fire; later the same evening, another Western-supported cultural organization in the camp, the Al-Kamandjâti Music Center, was burned to the ground. Soon there were anonymous leaflets denouncing the theater as a plot by

Jews and foreigners to "denigrate the memory of our martyrs." Juliano responded by taking his case to the community. He organized public meetings; he spoke to the local imams. "We faced our critics," al-Raee said. "We invited them to the theater and explained what we were doing."

The attention the theater was generating abroad made its work that much more difficult. The PA felt snubbed when in 2009 David Miliband came to the theater without consulting them. A perception arose that the theater was rich, though its operating annual budget never exceeded $450,000, modest for an organization of its size. Juliano had never handed out money, but he had gone out of his way to help people in the camp. According to Jamal Zubeidi, Zacharia's uncle, Juliano's reputation as a rainmaker created problems when he turned down people's requests: "So long as people thought he was supporting them, they saw him as a Palestinian. If they stopped thinking it, he became a Jew." The problem wasn't corruption, Nyman says, but its absence: "After Oslo, the whole NGO business became extremely corrupt, and basically meant lining your pockets and lining the pockets of your friends. The Freedom Theater wasn't like that. We were approached directly by Fatah officials who wanted a slice of the cake, but Juliano refused bribes." The theater's staff believed the arson attempt was carried out by a disgruntled Fatah member, not an Islamist.

Juliano's friends in Jenin told him the theater would be safer if he moved it from the camp to the city. The German-sponsored Cinema Jenin was there, and though it had had its problems, they hardly compared with the theater's. With Zubeidi acting as his front man—as an Israeli, Juliano couldn't purchase land—Juliano bought an empty lot in the city and began to build what he hoped would be a national theater, one as innovative and influential as the Habima Theater in Tel Aviv. He talked about his plans as if they were a fait accompli, though he had yet to secure a permit from the city. The theater in the camp, Juliano wrote in a letter to a group of supporters in July 2010, would be transformed into "an interactive TV studio" which would "serve all Palestinian artists, from Gaza, the West Bank, East Jerusalem,

Israel and the Palestinian diaspora, without the supervision of political parties, and certainly not of Israel."

The theater's work with children—the sort of unglamorous work that had won Arna so much love—began to suffer. Juliano complained that he was tired of "social work": he wanted to create real art, not plays for children. His behavior set off "a huge upheaval in the theater," Romilly told me. Stanczyk quit and returned to Stockholm. The friends of the theater in France withdrew their support, and the board in Jenin resigned. Frustrated by the resistance to his plans, Juliano spent more time in Haifa, where he directed a production of Ariel Dorfman's *Death and the Maiden*. He took his friends in the cast to see the theater in Jenin; he spoke of setting up a Freedom Theater branch in Haifa and leaving the theater in Jenin in the hands of local Palestinians. In Haifa he could escape from the scrutiny of the camp. For now, though, he told Amer Hlehel, one of the actors in *Death and the Maiden*, he had to go back to Jenin. "All my projects would be a lie" otherwise.

His next production with the Freedom Theater premiered in February 2011. It was an adaptation of *Alice in Wonderland* and told the story of a girl who refuses to marry the man her family has chosen for her. Juliano advertised the show by putting the actress Maryam Abu Khaled, dressed as the Red Queen, on the roof of his car with a megaphone and driving her around the camp. Some men told her never to show her face in their neighborhood again; she was afraid she might be stoned. But more than 10,000 people came to see the play, many of them from the camp. "There were kids in the camp who'd already seen the play who were staging demonstrations to see it again—Jenin-style demonstrations," Nyman told me. "It looked like we were becoming a big force in the community."

Not everyone in the camp was pleased by Juliano's success, and a stark reminder of his outsider status came when Jenin City refused to give him a permit to build the new theater. But Juliano didn't relent. In early March 2011, a German acting teacher at the theater, Stephan Wolf-Schönburg, proposed a production of Frank Wedekind's *Spring Awakening*, and Juliano agreed.

The 1906 play, a celebration of youthful sexual revolt, has been banned time and again for its treatment of homosexuality, incest, child abuse and suicide in fin-de-siècle Germany. Nyman thought the idea was "just crazy," but Juliano reminded her that Wolf-Schönburg had connections to the Goethe Institute and other potential sources of funding. He didn't want to discourage him.

Wolf-Schönburg, who is gay, told me he expected the actors at the theater to be "as interested as we were when we were young. Puberty, growing up, being in opposition toward parents and society." But it turned out to be harder than he'd thought when rehearsals began on March 14. Some actors pulled out and talked about the play in the camp; there was also opposition from members of the local board. Hlehel warned Juliano that he would be "committing suicide" if he went ahead with it, but Juliano replied that "putting on this play in Jenin would be a revolution." He had second thoughts, however, when an anonymous leaflet appeared denouncing him as a "Communist, an atheist and a Jew." If the theater didn't stop the production, it said, "we will be forced to speak in bullets." On March 28, Juliano, who was in Ramallah directing a production of Ionesco's *The Chairs*, canceled *Spring Awakening*. A week later, he returned to Jenin, where his killer was waiting for him.

Inside the theater, Juliano was mourned by his colleagues and students, but in the camp people were silent. The streets weren't flooded with people holding up his picture or waving Palestinian flags, as they usually are when a martyr dies. When a group from the theater went to the city to light candles in his memory, people asked why they were crying for a Jew. The camp seemed to be in a hurry to forget him. In Haifa, he was given a martyr's funeral. The service was mostly in Arabic, the only flags on display were Palestinian, and speaker after speaker—including Zubeidi, who addressed the crowd via mobile phone—praised him as a Palestinian hero.

The investigation of Juliano's murder has been fruitless. It wasn't clear who was responsible for investigating the murder of an Israeli citizen from a mixed Arab-Jewish background, living as a Palestinian in Jenin. Although they had collected all the evidence at the crime scene, the Israelis told Abeer Baker, Nyman's lawyer, that pursuing the case would be difficult because the murder took place under Palestinian sovereignty: Jenin is in Area A, formally under the jurisdiction of the PA. ("Suddenly the Palestinians have a state!" she said.) In May 2013 she received a letter from the authorities: "Unfortunately there is no development in this case that can help us bring people to justice."

The lack of progress has raised suspicions of a cover-up by Israel, but Baker is skeptical. The problem, she said, is indifference: "Juliano isn't a settler with political power. Deep inside they don't think he was killed because he was a Jew." The PA has been no more eager to find the killer. Shortly after the murder, it arrested a man with ties to Hamas, but he was soon released. Palestinian security conducted a preliminary investigation, and apparently concluded that the murder involved issues of money and power in the theater, but it made no further arrests. Baker speculated that the PA has shied away from the case because of "Fatah issues, or problems in Jenin over weapons." The PA's impotence has left Baker, a Palestinian citizen of Israel and a human rights lawyer, in the awkward position of "begging the Israelis to indict a Palestinian." "We don't care if the suspect is tried in Israel or the Occupied Territories," she said. "He's a murderer, and who said trials are any fairer under the Palestinian Authority? But we do want the suspect to be interrogated fairly, not placed in a Shabak cell and tortured. It's what Juliano would want. What am I supposed to do? Ask the Israelis to invade Jenin?"

The Israelis have been much more active in Jenin since the murder. The Freedom Theater has been a frequent target of military raids in the past two years. Most of the Palestinian members of the theater staff, and many of the actors, have been taken in for questioning, some for a few hours, others for weeks. Rami Hwayel, a shy young actor, was arrested at a checkpoint outside Ramallah; he spent thirty-one days in prison. In June 2012, al-Raee was woken up at 3:30 a.m. by Israeli soldiers at the house he shared with Zubeidi and taken to a nearby detention center.

He was interrogated for forty-eight hours, tied to a chair, and spent forty days in prison. His interrogators accused him of plotting Juliano's murder with Zubeidi. When he emerged from prison, people in Jenin were friendlier; the ordeal had gained al-Raee, who grew up in a camp outside Hebron and was always viewed with suspicion in Jenin, a bit of street credibility.

Zubeidi was never taken in for questioning by the Shabak. It was a strange omission. Zubeidi was Juliano's guardian angel, and no one had grieved his death more openly. A year after the murder, at the tenth anniversary of the invasion of the Jenin camp, he tried to put up a poster of Juliano beside the posters of the fighters who died fighting the Israeli army; when other former fighters took down the poster, he flew into a rage. Today, some people think this was a carefully staged performance. Everyone said that Zubeidi was the eyes and ears of the camp, so Juliano's friends expected him to live up to his promise and find the killer. But he very soon lost interest in the case, or so it seemed; when asked about it, he said it was in the hands of the authorities. In Ramallah, ex-comrades of Zubeidi told Tali Fahima that he was behind the murder. Juliano, they claimed, had discovered that Zubeidi had been diverting money for the theater in the city to his own real estate investments. The Shabak wasn't lifting a finger because Zubeidi had always been a useful source of information about the camp. Many of Juliano's friends in Israel, both Jews and Arabs, have come to believe that Zubeidi knows more than he's letting on. Some, Or included, believe he conspired in his best friend's assassination. (She also claims Juliano was carrying a suitcase filled with cash that he'd taken out of his safe in Haifa two weeks earlier, but no suitcase has been discovered.) Others suggest that the killing may have been a message to Zubeidi that he "no longer controlled the camp," which would explain why he expressed such guilt after the murder. But Zubeidi has kept his silence and discouraged others from probing. When he heard that Or was making inquiries about him in Ramallah, he warned her not to speak about him behind his back.

Zubeidi has spent most of the past year as a prisoner of the Palestinian Authority. His troubles began on December 28, 2011, when Israel revoked his pardon for unstated reasons and the PA recommended that he turn himself in, in order to avoid arrest or worse. He declined the advice, but in May 2012, when Qaddura Musa, the Jenin district governor, died of a heart attack after gunmen opened fire on his home, the PA put him in jail. One of the guns allegedly used in the raid was found in Zubeidi's home, though he maintains his innocence. He went on a hunger strike, supported by a petition drafted by the theater and its friends in the West. He was released in October 2012 and early this year returned to PA custody, saying he would otherwise risk assassination by Israel. Few I spoke to in Palestine took this claim seriously. "If Israel truly wanted him, it would have no difficulty reaching him where he is," I was told. He's in a facility outside Ramallah, too comfortable to be called a prison, with access to email, Facebook and his mobile phone. He receives visitors, and is in regular contact with his colleagues at the theater. No one there believes that Zubeidi could have been involved in Juliano's murder. Under PA custody, with his amnesty revoked, he is still an asset to them.

When I spoke to him by phone, he claimed the Shabak had hired a local hit man to kill Juliano because of the growing success of "cultural resistance." It's a view you often hear inside the theater, but almost never outside it, certainly not in the camp. The rumor in the camp is that Zubeidi supports the theater because it has supported him with a salary and other unnamed "benefits." When I mentioned this to him, he said I must have been talking to people in the PA. (I hadn't.) He praised Juliano for giving "an image of the Palestinian fighter as a human being, not a terrorist," and said: "The seeds that Juliano planted here are growing."

The theater is indeed flourishing. "The miracle of the Freedom Theater is that it continues to exist," Kathleen Chalfant told me. But one could also argue that the theater has benefited from Juliano's absence. Under Juliano it was wild, volatile and inspired; it has become calm, measured and diligent under Stanczyk, who returned from Stockholm the day after Juliano was killed, and resumed his role as general manager. The theater has raised its international profile, sending productions on tour in Europe and the US; it has also expanded its activities throughout the West Bank. Although Israel has continued to harass it, the anonymous threats have subsided, a modus vivendi has been established with the camp, and an eerie sort of normality has set in. For Juliano's old students, this shift in direction feels like a betrayal of their hero. One day a group of them was grumbling about the theater in the courtyard. It was less provocative, less radical, less ambitious, they said. There were hardly any girls onstage. But the theater couldn't be blamed if parents had taken their daughters out after Juliano was killed. And under Stanczyk's leadership, the entire enterprise has acquired something Juliano lacked, something he fought against all his life: a sense of limits. Most of the photographs of Juliano in the theater's offices have now been taken down. But Nabil al-Raee told me he can't go to work without thinking of him. The theater remains "a haunted place," his wife said. Some of Juliano's friends in Haifa haven't visited the theater since the murder; they don't feel welcome in the camp. Until the killer is found, Mishmish Or said, the theater will be "nothing but a crime scene." Jenny Nyman used to feel this way too. She was angry at the theater for continuing its work in a "tamer way." "Jul liked to say it's better to die on your feet than live on your knees. I thought the theater was just going down on its knees, like it's OK to shoot me if you think I say the wrong thing." But a few months ago, she went back to the theater. What struck her most was how quiet it seemed without Juliano.

{2013}

4

Edward Said: Palestinianism

When Edward Said joined the Columbia University English department in 1963, a rumor spread that he was a Jew from Alexandria. He might as well have been. Born in Jerusalem in 1935 to well-off Palestinian Christian parents, he had grown up in the twilight years of multicultural Cairo, where many of his classmates were Egyptian Jews. His piano teacher was Ignace Tiegerman, a Polish Jew who had moved to Cairo in 1931 and founded a French-speaking conservatoire. Said's closest friends at Princeton and Harvard, Arthur Gold, a brilliant Luftmensch prone to tormented idleness, and the future art critic Michael Fried, were Jews. His dissertation and first book were about Joseph Conrad's explorations of ambiguity and double identities. As Timothy Brennan writes in *Places of Mind*, the first comprehensive biography of Said, he was "a photo negative of his Jewish counterparts."

Said spent his first years at Columbia as a kind of an Arab Marrano, or crypto Palestinian, among Jewish and Wasp colleagues who were either indifferent or hostile to the Arab struggle with Israel. He published essays in the little magazines of the New York intellectuals, went to cocktail parties with Lionel Trilling and Mary McCarthy, and kept quiet about his identity and his politics. His parents, who were themselves estranged from Palestine (his father said Jerusalem reminded him of death), were relieved that their moody and contentious son was showing such prudence. Thanks to his father's service in the American

Expeditionary Forces during the First World War, Said was an American citizen, and if he was reinventing himself, well, that's what immigrants did in the New World. The Egyptian literary theorist Ihab Hassan had shed his Arab identity when he moved to the US and had never looked back.

But something in Said rebelled against the concealment and silence that the loss of Palestine had imposed, and that his father, William Said, had accepted, leaving behind not only the family's past in Jerusalem but also his Arab name, Wadie. After 1967, Said embraced the Palestinian struggle—an act of "affiliation," as he put it, a commitment based on belief, rather than "filiation." If Wadie chose to Americanize himself, adopting phrases like "hunky dory" and supporting the war in Vietnam, Edward chose to "Palestinize" himself.

In Cairo, Wadie Said had run a company that supplied office equipment to the British occupying army. Edward and his four sisters had a pampered childhood: servants, music lessons, family trips to New York, a holiday home in the Lebanese village of Dhour el Shweir ("mind-deadening rigours of relentlessly regulated summers," Said complained). As Palestinian members of the Anglican Church, they were a minority within a minority in Egypt. They gave their children English names and socialized mostly with other Arab Christians from Palestine, Lebanon and Syria. Wadie, who was proud of the whiteness of his skin and sometimes pretended he was from Cleveland, identified with America more than with Palestine. (The Saids celebrated Thanksgiving.) Edward also spent part of his childhood in the family's homeland, in the West Jerusalem neighborhood of Talbiyah, but after 1948, as he wrote in his memoir, "Palestine acquired a languid, almost dreamlike, aspect for me." It was only thanks to his aunt Nabiha, who did charitable work among Palestinian refugees in Cairo, that he became aware of the Nakba, which Wadie passed over in silence.

In his memoir, *Out of Place*, Said describes his parents as "amphibious Levantine creatures whose essential lostness was momentarily stayed by a kind of forgetfulness, a kind of daydream, that included elaborately catered dinner parties, outings to fashionable restaurants, the opera, ballet and concerts." He benefited from the daydream, as their world was shaken by the loss of Palestine, and, in 1952, the collapse of the Egyptian monarchy, which would eventually force the family to flee to Beirut. He read Balzac and Dostoevsky with his mother and saw Furtwängler conduct ("an emanation"). Yet he portrayed himself in his memoir as an unhappy, "delinquent" child, at the mercy of his father's strict discipline (and cane), vulnerable to his mother's caprice and emotional blackmail. The book's depiction of Wadie as a domestic tyrant infuriated his sisters, and Brennan has unearthed affectionate letters from father to son. Said described his memoir as a "documentary fiction," but Brennan largely confirms its accuracy.

He described Hilda, his mother, as "my closest and most intimate companion for the first twenty-five years of my life." (The intensity of the attachment was due in part to Hilda's loss of a baby boy the year before Edward was born.) Their relationship, Said wrote, had "shattering results for my later life as a man trying to establish a relationship . . . with other women." According to Brennan, Wadie sent his fifteen-year-old son to the Mount Hermon boarding school in rural Massachusetts not because of his rebellious behaviour at the British-run Victoria College, as Said later claimed, but because he feared that the "obsessive intimacies" with Hilda would hinder Edward's emotional development.

Said's letters home were "positively jaunty," full of enthusiasm for his adopted culture. But he chafed at the casual prejudice against Arabs (his classmates privately referred to him as a "wog"). He became a passionate anti-imperialist, expressing his support for the Palestinian cause and cheering on Nasser's revolution in Egypt, even though his father's business had been burned to the ground in nationalist protests. (Said's enthusiasm for Nasser, which his mother shared and which sat uneasily with his anti-authoritarian politics, was apparently undiminished by the murder of his childhood hero, Farid Haddad, a communist activist who was beaten to death in prison in 1959.) At Princeton, he met Ibrahim Abu-Lughod, a graduate student from Jaffa, who told him about the revolution in Algeria and schooled him in the Palestinian struggle. His ethnicity didn't go unnoticed on campus: a placement bureau form described him as "very dark, big" and "of Arab descent."

Said came into his own as an undergraduate, writing his senior thesis on André Gide and Graham Greene under the supervision of R. P. Blackmur, while continuing his piano studies with Erich Itor Kahn, a European Jewish émigré. His parents expected him to join the family business after graduation, but he had no intention of becoming his father's subordinate. At first he flirted with a career in medicine, a respectable compromise that his parents accepted. But his friend Arthur Gold persuaded him not to give up his real passions. Gold also introduced him to a book that would exert an enormous influence on his thinking, Vico's *New Science*. Vico's emphasis on historical beginnings as acts of human freedom gave Said the framework he needed as he contemplated a career as a professor of literature in the US.

The summer after graduation, while driving through the Swiss mountains, Said collided with, and killed, a motorcyclist; when he woke up, a priest was giving him the last rites. Only a few months later, he was in graduate school at Harvard. His mentor there was Harry Levin, the author of a study of realism that Said considered on a par with Erich Auerbach's *Mimesis*. As Brennan points out, Levin's belief in "universal interrelatedness" inspired Said's own practice of making unexpected connections between literary and cultural traditions, between fiction and contemporary philosophy. While seeing a psychoanalyst, attending Glenn Gould recitals in Boston and working on his Conrad dissertation, Said began to discover the ideas that would shape his imagination as a critic: Merleau-Ponty's phenomenology (the subject of his 1967 essay "The Labyrinth of Incarnations"), Lukács's analysis of "reification" and Sartre's theory of commitment.

At Harvard, Said also acquired a reputation for being irresistible to women. One of those women was Maire Jaanus, the daughter of Estonian refugees, whom he married at his family's summer home in Dour El Shweir in 1962. Jaanus, who worked on literature from the eighteenth century onward, referred to her new husband as "Saidus," and described him as a "vexing trinity": he "could have been a philosopher, a poet or a critic." She had left out his fourth aspect: membership in a large and overbearing family in which, Brennan writes, "uncles and aunts were almost as close as parents and no one kept secrets from anyone." Hilda found Jaanus chilly and distant. "Edward, it was only normal for us to be wary of a foreign girl marrying our son," she wrote to him. "But honest to God we tried hard to love her, do you remember *all* that happened before your wedding—your reaction? Edward we didn't know Maire then, we still don't know her, or know her even less. All we know and are sure of now is that she has no use for *any of us six*, in any way."

Hilda had already succeeded in sabotaging his love affair with a Lebanese Christian woman, seven years his senior, whom she considered unsuitable. Said was furious and refused to serve as his father's go-between with a business partner in New York, declaring that "my whole attitude to my past is in ruin." (Hilda responded by asking where he would be without his father's business.) He also wrote seventy pages of an unfinished novel, "Elegy," about a shady Lebanese Christian owner of a "failing printing company and a grubby stationery shop" and his sickly wife, "stuff[ed] away in a shabby apartment." Said didn't spare himself, including a mocking self-portrait of a clueless employee called Mufid who idles away his time on things that are "utterly lost on everyone else." Brennan presents the lost manuscript (and a story Said submitted around the same time to the *New Yorker*) as evidence of the novelist he might have become, but it seems more like a thwarted attempt to settle scores with his family and break free of the past. He put aside his literary ambitions, and grew estranged from Jaanus, whom he later divorced. In 1970 he married Mariam Cortas, a Lebanese Quaker whose family knew the Saids; they had two children, Wadie (a restoration of William's Arab name) and Najla. Hilda was overjoyed: she had regained her wayward son. In his private life, at least, filiation prevailed over affiliation. Said would seek out the company of other women, many of them high-profile academics, while quietly griping about the "bourgeois myth, which I now live, with increasing discomfort and unhappiness." But he never seriously contemplated giving up his life as a husband and father.

In his first few years in New York, Said "settled into Columbia life as an upstart member of the New York intellectuals." His relations with Trilling were cordial, but he found him "an impenetrable egoist" and drew closer to the radical literary critic Fred Dupee, a founding editor of *Partisan Review*. In his early literary journalism, Said marked his distance from the Cold War moralism of the New York intellectuals as well as from the conservative formalism of the New Critics by looking to Paris, where writers were taking what Brennan calls "insurgent positions on the politics of culture." His old mentor Harry Levin tried to check his enthusiasm for French theory, which, as he put it, "does not truly aim at the understanding of literature, but at deriving metaphysical paradigms from authors by superimposing certain abstractions supported by quotations taken out of context." Said would later tell Levin he'd been right all along. But theory served him well in establishing his intellectual independence, and aided his efforts to deprovincialize the study of literature—to make it more "worldly" (one of his favorite adjectives). He wrote variously on existentialism, phenomenology and structuralism, borrowing whatever he found useful.

Said's relationship to ideas was supple and pragmatic, and, as Brennan writes, he was often "drawn to writers he should have disliked." Conrad's bleakness and Swift's monarchism were anathema to him; so was Foucault's totalizing vision of power in which any and all resistance was destined to be swallowed up and neutralized. But Said found them all compelling as writers, and he sharpened his ideas by wrestling with theirs, in what he described as a form of counterpoint. Writers of the political right, he once said, can be "untimely, anxious witnesses to the dominant currents of their time." Brennan calls these interests "perverse allegiances," but they were also an expression of his commitment to intellectual freedom—and to the university as a sanctuary. While he styled himself an anti-imperialist, Said was mostly an old-fashioned liberal when it came to campus politics.

He supported the 1968 student strike against the war in Vietnam called by Students for a Democratic Society but recoiled from their attack on the university, and from what he saw as puerile anti-authoritarianism. When a group of striking students disrupted one of his lectures, he insisted that they leave and called security when they refused.

For Said, the excitement of 1968 lay not in the student uprising, which he saw as revolutionary theater, but in the Battle of Karameh in Jordan, where the Palestinian *fedayeen* fought bravely against the Israeli army. On his visits to Amman in 1969 and 1970, where he had his first, brief meeting with Yasser Arafat, Said had the experience of being "a visitor but also an exhilarated participant in the national revival that I saw taking place." In 1972, a year's Guggenheim fellowship took him to Beirut, where the PLO had set up headquarters after being forced out of Jordan. There he renewed his connection with a friend from Harvard, Hanna Mikhaïl, who had given up an academic career in the US to become a PLO cadre, taking the name Abu Omar. (He was killed in mysterious circumstances in 1976.) Mikhaïl in turn introduced him to Jean Genet, "a very strange bird given to long scary silences."

While in Beirut, Said immersed himself in the work of Ibn Khaldun, whose 1377 study of history, the *Muqaddimah*, became nearly as important to him as Vico's *New Science*, and received his political education from intellectuals in the orbit of the PLO who were struggling to make sense of the 1967 defeat. He met the Palestinian poet Mahmoud Darwish; the Lebanese novelist Elias Khoury; the Syrian Marxist Sadiq al-Azm (who had published a blistering anatomy of the Arab military failure); the Arab nationalist Constantine Zurayk (the author of a book on the 1948 war that popularized the term *Nakba*); and the PLO leader Kamal Nasser, who was killed by the Israelis only hours after he and Said had been at dinner together. In *Mawaqif*, a journal edited by the poet Adonis, Said made his own contribution to the literature of Arab self-criticism after the defeat, fretting—in the kind of essentializing language he would later condemn as "Orientalist"—that the "characteristic movement of the Arab is circular . . . repetition is therefore mistaken for novelty, especially since there is no sense of recognition."

The birth of the Palestinian guerrilla movement promised an end to the grim repetition of Arab political and intellectual life. The revolution's center was Beirut, and Said dreamed of staying on there with his family, but Mariam was against the idea. Having been made to feel unwelcome at the American University, he came to share her view: anyone of talent and initiative, he concluded, was "shelved, castrated or thrown out." But his year in Beirut led to a creative breakthrough. In his 1975 book, *Beginnings*, an ambitious study of modern theories of language, Said made a case for writing as "an act of taking hold of language (*prendre la parole*) in order to do something, not merely in order to repeat an idea verbatim." One critic saw in it "powerful intellectual tools . . . put in the service of Arab nationalist interests." In fact, it was a challenge to the rigidities of structuralism, not Zionism, but its political implications were clear: Said was arguing that intentional acts of language, especially speech, could short-circuit systems of power and become a form of resistance.

In November 1974, Said's argument was given a live demonstration before the world, when Arafat addressed the United Nations for the first time. Said helped draft the speech and added the closing line: "Don't let the olive branch fall from my hand." Although not opposed to armed resistance, he took a dim view of the PLO's cult of the gun and believed that nonviolent protest and diplomacy—the "olive branch"—were more effective weapons, given the enormous disparities in military power. The war for Palestine was, he understood, a war of clashing narratives and images: "In no modern conflict has rhetoric played so significant a part in legitimating one preposterous quote after another." He soon became the PLO's unofficial liaison with the US government. Although he felt closer to the secular leftism of the Democratic Front for the Liberation of Palestine than to the traditionalist nationalism of Fatah, he remained loyal to Arafat ("a genius at mediation") and in 1977 was elected to the Palestine National Council, the PLO's parliament in exile, as an independent.

Said's closest comrades on the American left were decidedly unimpressed by the PLO as a national liberation organization. Noam Chomsky—one of the few people Said allowed to call him "Ed," a nickname he hated—said it lacked any sense of strategic direction. Eqbal Ahmad, who had worked with the FLN during the Algerian struggle for independence, was even more scathing. Given the number of lavish dinners the PLO put on, he remarked that "banqueting" had become "the latest form of struggle." But Said, who had lost his father to cancer in 1971, found in Arafat a substitute father figure, a refugee who not only hadn't forgotten Palestine but had made it an international cause. For nearly two decades, Arafat called on him whenever the PLO wanted to send a message to the Americans. The US government recognized his value too: in 1978, the secretary of state, Cyrus Vance, told Said that the Carter administration would recognize the PLO and launch negotiations for a two-state settlement if Arafat accepted UN Resolution 242: a termination of the conflict, Israeli withdrawal from the Occupied Territories. Arafat wasn't interested. To Said's frustration, Arafat would always see him as a useful but somewhat suspect American professor, not a fellow fighter.

"The intellectual," Said wrote, "always stands between loneliness and alignment." His decision to align himself with a national liberation movement despised by many of his colleagues as a "terrorist" organization intensified his sense of loneliness and heightened his already acute sense of vulnerability and woundedness. In his introduction to *Orientalism*, which appeared in 1978, he wrote:

> The life of an Arab Palestinian in the West, particularly in America, is disheartening. There exists here an almost unanimous consensus that politically he does not exist, and when it is allowed that he does, it is either as a nuisance or as an oriental. The web of racism, cultural stereotypes, political imperialism, dehumanizing ideology holding the Arab or the Muslim is very strong indeed, and it is this web which every Palestinian has come to feel as his uniquely punishing destiny.

Orientalism not only made Said's reputation, it incited a debate that hasn't ended, and inaugurated a school of anti-Orientalist scholarship. Drawing on history, fiction, philology and philosophy, Said argued that the Arabs and Asians who had lived under British and French dominion had been captives not only of Western power, but of the image that Western writers had of them as mysterious, effeminate, timeless, immutable, irrational and, above all, incapable of self-government (he didn't discuss German or Russian versions of Orientalism). Orientalism, he claimed, had not merely reflected but influenced and shaped the practice of imperial domination. Still strongly influenced by Foucault's analysis of "discursive formations" and "power-knowledge," he depicted Orientalism as a discourse so pervasive as to be almost inescapable. In Said's account, even writers who appeared to praise non-Western cultures in relation to their own had participated in the representation of the Eastern "other" as essentially different. This was anything but a history of a distant past: Said made plain that he saw many of the best-known scholars of the Middle East, notably Bernard Lewis, as heirs of nineteenth-century Orientalism—and as apologists for, if not servants of, a new imperialism.

The value of Said's book was immediately evident to intellectuals who felt their treatment by Western scholarship had been no less punishing. "You are on the frontier—a Gramscian frontier," Cornel West wrote to him shortly after the book's publication. But Said was no man of the people; he wasn't even a defender of Middle Eastern cultural and political traditions. He made no secret of his love of Western "high" culture, even if he had assumed the task of exposing how deeply it had absorbed Orientalist mythologies. Unlike Eric Hobsbawm, whom he faulted for having a Eurocentric, top-down perspective of the short twentieth century, he took no interest in jazz or popular music. (His daughter, Najla, would score a small victory by turning him on to Sinéad O'Connor.) He was a critical, secular humanist widely mistaken for a radical opponent of the Western canon. In fact, the canon was his subject and remained so: he never once gave a course related to the Middle East at Columbia, and only late in his career did he begin teaching novels by writers from the Global South. While he insisted that literary representations had helped shape the Western "gaze," he didn't argue that writers such as Flaubert or Montesquieu were irreparably stained: their (mostly unconscious) complicity was another reason to study them. His was an ethics of complex resistance, not an escape from complexity.

Still, Said's bracing and accusatory tone, which gave *Orientalism* its rhetorical punch, helped fuel misperceptions. While he praised the work of Orientalist scholars, including Louis Massignon, Jacques Berque and Maxime Rodinson, he also sometimes implied that the entire tradition of Orientalist scholarship was a corrupted form of power-knowledge. But then what distinguished an eminent figure like Berque from Lewis or from a vulgar propagandist such as Daniel Pipes? And was all Western criticism—even Marxist criticism—of the failings of societies in the Arab and Islamic world to be dismissed as Orientalist? Said didn't answer these questions, which led some readers to assume that he thought all Western writing about the East was Orientalist and therefore unsalvageable. This wasn't his view at all, but he could be prickly. And his followers in post-colonial studies tended to be pricklier, as well as far less devoted to Western literature and culture than he was.

Some of the fiercest criticisms came from left-wing Arab intellectuals who hadn't left the region for academic posts in the West. In their view, Said's approach was indiscriminate and ended up reproducing the binary opposition of "East" and "West" he ostensibly opposed. They also felt that, by placing the emphasis on the Western gaze rather than on the imperialism that had formed it, Said had got things back to front. Orientalism, in this view, was a justificatory ideology that would fade away with the end of imperial domination. In the meantime, Sadiq al-Azm wrote in a long and forceful critique, the book risked giving comfort to Islamists in their denunciations of Marxism as a Western ideology and their campaign to ban the teaching of science. These criticisms reflected a fundamental misunderstanding of *Orientalism*: a study of literary representation exploring the culture of imperialism, not imperialism itself. Yet they also reflected a different set of priorities among intellectuals in the region, for whom the book was less urgently needed than it was for their counterparts in the West. Said did not take well to such critiques, denouncing al-Azm as a "Khomeini of the left."

But al-Azm had put his finger on one of *Orientalism*'s unintended effects: in spite of Said's own opposition to dogmatic anti-Westernism, to religious politics and any form of nativism, the book lent itself to a ritualized condemnation of Western scholarship and literature as "imperialist." Academic postcolonialism, which became a career path for a growing number of upper-middle-class graduate students from the Middle East and South Asia, would develop an increasingly orthodox critique of secularism and the Enlightenment, exasperating Said. Later in his career, he would find himself alternately embracing and lamenting the anti-Orientalist wave of scholarship he had spawned: a tribute to his influence, but, he felt, a misreading of his intentions. As if anticipating this wave, he wrote in *The World, the Text and the Critic* (1983) that "a breakthrough can become a trap, if it is used uncritically, repetitively, limitlessly." The history of ideas—and of politics—"is extravagantly illustrative of how the dictum 'solidarity before criticism' means the end of criticism . . . even in the very midst of a battle in which one is unmistakably on one side against another."

The World, the Text and the Critic was also Said's farewell to French theory. It wasn't surprising, he suggested, that Derrida's concept of undecidability and Foucault's Nietzschean skepticism about truth had flourished in Reagan's America: both provided sophisticated excuses for political quietism. This was an essentially Lukácsian critique of postmodernism as an expression of decadence. But his disenchantment also reflected a sense of personal betrayal: Foucault had abandoned the Palestinian cause; Derrida had wounded him by referring to him only as "un *ami*"—not by name—in his book on Genet. When Said's friend Jean Stein, the editor of *Grand Street*, asked him to review a book by Jean Baudrillard, he declined, saying that Baudrillard's ideas are "all sort of like little burps." He now preferred the company of Chomsky and John Berger, who believed that "there is always something beyond the reach of dominating systems." His own style became less cluttered and precious—more "transparent" and "worldly." He used it to demystify the ideology of Zionism in *The Question of Palestine* (1979), and to dissect the American media's tendentious portrayals of Muslims in *Covering Islam* (1981). But he also established himself as a belletrist, writing on Arabic fiction, bullfighting, tennis and belly dancing. He interviewed Gillo Pontecorvo, published essays on exile and Glenn Gould, and became the *Nation*'s classical music critic.

Said was more prominent than ever, and more exposed. Letters arrived at his home covered in swastikas or filled with used condoms. "You are now under surveillance and two of your associates know it," an anonymous correspondent wrote to him. "Don't think you're too small for this. Look for cameras—you won't find them." Informants at Princeton, Columbia and the Harvard alumni office assisted the FBI in an investigation that examined his banking and credit records, among other things. In 1985, Meir Kahane's Jewish Defense League called him a Nazi, and his office was firebombed and vandalized.

Beirut, where his mother lived, was still more dangerous for Said during the Lebanese Civil War. This wasn't simply due to the Israeli invasion in 1982, which led to the massacres of Sabra and Shatila by Israeli-backed Christian Phalangist militias and drove Arafat and the PLO out of Lebanon: Said also faced threats of assassination from Palestinians for expressing reservations about the efficacy of armed struggle. During his year in Beirut, he had written that his experience there made him aware of "the poverty of labels like left-wing and right-wing" when applied to Lebanese politics. Brennan seems unconvinced by this, but Said knew what he was talking about: while the Phalange had fascist sympathies, Lebanon's civil war was not so much an Arab version of the Spanish Civil War as a gruesome power struggle among competing sectarian groups, made even more murderous by the Syrian and Israeli interventions. The ultimate winners were the country's underdogs, the Shia, led by Hezbollah, which replaced the PLO as Lebanon's leading armed movement with the backing of Iran—"a regime of exceptionally retrograde cruelty," in Said's words. In the mid-1980s, armed clashes erupted between Palestinians and Shia in the refugee camps. Said deplored this development but had little to say about the rise of the Shia—or the growing appeal of political Islam, which clearly disturbed him. Still, there is little doubt that his distrust of identity politics reflected the chastening lessons of Lebanon, where politicized sectarianism had laid waste to his mother's adopted country. The war, he said, "began as a conflict over large areas of territory and in the end was fought over individual streets and sidewalks. And where did it lead? Nowhere."

The disaster in Lebanon also marked the end of the revolutionary phase of the Palestinian movement, when the PLO styled itself as a liberation movement in the tradition of the FLN and the ANC. Arafat and his men were now in Tunis, and the movement was adrift. Said's break with Arafat wouldn't take place for another decade, but the rift had begun. On his visits to Tunis, he later wrote, he saw former revolutionaries who "drank only Black Label Scotch whisky, traveled first class, drove fancy European cars, and were always surrounded by aides, bodyguards and hangers-on." In cautious, sometimes cryptic language, he began to express doubts about the movement's direction. "Our insistence on 'armed struggle,'" he wrote in *After the Last Sky* (1986), had "quickly turned into a worship of fetishized military postures, guns and slogans borrowed from theories of the people's war in Algeria and Vietnam." This emphasis "caused us to neglect the incredibly complex and far more important political and cultural aspects of our struggle, and it played right into the hands of Israel." For all Arafat's success in "connecting disparate segments of Palestinian life," no leader had appeared "so catastrophically to be implicated in setbacks."

But then, a year later, the First Intifada broke out. The Palestinians in the Occupied Territories were delivering a message to Israel, and to the "Tunisians" of the PLO, that could not have been more direct. Suddenly the movement's center of gravity shifted from the "exterior" to the "interior." Caught off guard, the leadership scrambled to impose itself on a revolt it had

neither launched nor foreseen. Said was elated, hailing the uprising (with no little hyperbole) as "surely the most impressive
and disciplined anticolonial insurrection in this century." In
November 1988, at a meeting of the Palestine National Council
in Algiers, Said and Mahmoud Darwish co-wrote the PLO's
statement in support of a two-state settlement. But within a
year Said was complaining openly to the Arab press about
the PLO's authoritarianism and corruption. He was furious
at Arafat's decision to support Saddam Hussein in the Gulf
war, which nearly bankrupted the organization and forced it
to the negotiating table prematurely. During the backchannel
negotiations between Israel and the Palestinians, Said looked
on aghast as the PLO prostrated itself before the US, the "big
white father," agreeing to arrangements that condemned Palestinians to continued occupation, even if they had a flag of their
own. Not surprisingly, betrayal was the theme of the unfinished
novel he worked on occasionally from 1987 to 1992; one of its
characters was a middle-aged Arab American professor, "cut off
from Arabs in the West, aware of Jews . . . powerless to change,
too honest to affiliate."

The betrayal became official in September 1993, with the
signing of the Oslo Accords— "an instrument of Palestinian
surrender, a Palestinian Versailles," as he wrote in the *London
Review of Books*. Not only had Arafat accepted a less generous
plan than the Carter-Vance offer he'd dismissed in 1978; more
humiliatingly, he had agreed to become Israel's gendarme in the
territories, policing Palestinian resistance rather than Palestinian
borders. Said never spoke to Arafat again. He would visit Israel-
Palestine and film a documentary for the BBC, but he didn't
feel at home in the West Bank, where political Islam was on
the rise, eclipsing the secular nationalism he had always advocated, and where the Palestinian Authority banned his books
because of his criticisms of Arafat. Exile, he decided, was a
"more liberated state" than a "final coming home"—and, in any
case, neither Israel nor the West Bank *was* home. When one of
Arafat's deputies was asked by a journalist about Said's critique
of Oslo, he replied that Said was an English professor whose

views about Palestinian politics were as pertinent as Chairman Arafat's opinion of a Shakespeare production.

Said felt wounded by his falling out with the PLO, but it left him a free man, capable of imagining a last, creative phase in the face of fatal illness. In 1991, he had been diagnosed with chronic lymphocytic leukaemia. Chemotherapy would leave his handsome face shrunken, an affront to his vanity as well as his health. While shuttling back and forth from hospital, he began to write his memoirs. *Out of Place* is revealing (and at times excruciatingly Freudian) in its depiction of the Said family romance, and of Said's teenage sexual frustrations. Brennan compares it to Mohamed Choukri's account of his life as a petty criminal and prostitute in Tangiers, *For Bread Alone*, but it's a poor analogy. If *Out of Place* recalls any other work, it is *Beer in the Snooker Club*, Waguih Ghali's novel about a group of doomed cosmopolitan Cairenes in the early Nasser years. As Nadine Gordimer put it, Said had finally written his novel.

But he wasn't ready to elegize the Palestinian cause, even if he had cut his ties to the leadership. Palestine was a symbol of justice denied and freedom to come, rather than a piece of bitterly contested real estate: Said wrote constantly and with furious eloquence about Israel's land grabs and Arafat's strategic failures. He also became a champion of a binational state for both peoples, an idea that had once been promoted by "cultural Zionists" such as Judah Magnes and Martin Buber, and long since been buried by the Zionist mainstream. Aware of this irony, Said once mischievously described himself as the "last Jewish intellectual." The "empty nationalism" that divided the land's inhabitants into "camps of Jews and non-Jews" supplied a vocabulary equipped "less for understanding than for reducing the world." The notion that Arabs and Jews in Palestine were condemned to hate one another contradicted everything his own life had taught him. Precisely because Jews had never been the "other" to him, he wasn't afraid that by acknowledging the Holocaust he would be supplying ammunition to Palestine's enemies. On the contrary, the Palestinian case was strengthened, not weakened, by recognition of the Jewish catastrophe during the war.

Said made this argument repeatedly, without fear of what other Arabs would say, but also without any suggestion of strategic genuflection to Jewish or Israeli sensitivities. "If we expect Israeli Jews not to use the Holocaust to justify appalling human rights abuses of the Palestinian people," he wrote, "we too have to go beyond such idiocies as saying that the Holocaust never took place, and that Israelis are all, man, woman and child, doomed to our eternal enmity and hostility." This statement appeared in a column for *Al-Hayat* in 2001, in which he compared the Arab taboo against contact with the "Zionist entity" to the taboo against performing Wagner in Israel. Both represented a refusal of complexity—not just a political failure but an imaginative one. In his writings in Arab newspapers, Said continued to excoriate the crimes of Israel and the US, but he paired these attacks with a forthright and pointed denunciation of Arab despotism.

In his later writings on culture and education, too, Said tried to persuade others to think "contrapuntally," acknowledging the injuries inflicted by imperialism, racism and other forms of domination while simultaneously promoting an ethos of inter-connectedness, pluralism and academic freedom. But he found himself increasingly embattled among the new generation of scholars of race and empire. When he appeared at Rutgers in 1993 to talk about his new book, *Culture and Imperialism*, "a black woman of some eminence"—a historian—asked him why, in the first part of his presentation, he had cited only European men. That he had mentioned C. L. R. James didn't count, she said, because James was dead. Said was confounded, not only because he'd been found "guilty of not mentioning living non-European non-males," but because "the general validity of the point made in *Orientalism* . . . was now being directed at me."

According to Brennan, "he was still grumbling" to friends about the Rutgers encounter months afterward. He largely kept his distance from the anti-PC brigade, but he struck up a corre-spondence with Camille Paglia and, in speeches, issued warnings about the rise of identity politics in universities. "Victimhood, alas, does not guarantee or necessarily enable an enhanced sense of humanity," he said. "To testify to a history of oppression is necessary, but it is not sufficient unless that history is redirected into intellectual process and universalized to include all sufferers." He went on:

> It does not finally matter *who* wrote what, but rather *how* a work is written and *how* it is read. The idea that because Plato and Aristotle are male and the products of a slave society they should be disqualified from receiving contemporary attention is as limited an idea as suggesting that *only* their work, because it was addressed to and about elites, should be read today. Marginality and homelessness are not, in my opinion, to be gloried in; they are to be brought to an end, so that more, and not fewer, people can enjoy the benefits of what has for centuries been denied the victims of race, class or gender.

The idea that education is "best advanced by focusing principally on *our own* separateness, our own ethnic identity, culture and traditions" struck him as a kind of apartheid pedagogy, implying that "subaltern, inferior or lesser races" were "unable to share in the general riches of human culture." Identity was "as boring a subject as one can imagine"; what excited him was the interaction of different identities and the promise—the "risk"—of universality. This vision lay at the heart of the youth musical ensemble he helped establish, the West-Eastern Divan Orchestra. The name alluded to Goethe's *West-östlicher Divan*, a collection of poems inspired by the Persian poet Hafez. The orchestra's co-founder was the conductor and pianist Daniel Barenboim, an Argentine-Israeli Said had met by chance in London in 1993, just as his relationship with Arafat was falling apart. Said described the meeting as "love at first sight."

Said, Barenboim and the cellist Yo-Yo Ma selected the original group of seventy-eight Arab and Israeli musicians for a workshop in Weimar; with Barenboim conducting, it evolved into a professional orchestra. The idea of bringing Arab and Israeli-Jewish musicians together was—and is—controversial. Some Palestinians, including Said's sister Grace, accused the orchestra of promoting "normalization" with Israel, even treason to the cause. Among his more radical acolytes there were complaints about his closeness to Barenboim (they spoke every day). Since Said's death, the orchestra has been boycotted by parts of the BDS movement.

Brennan wonders whether Said might have ended up approving a boycott against the orchestra he built, but has little sense of what the West-Eastern Divan meant to him. Said's increasing absorption in music wasn't a retreat from politics so much as a detour through aesthetics. While the Palestinian Authority tried to pass off an archipelago of bantustans as the prelude to freedom and independence, Said was trying to show what a binational future might look (and sound) like. In *Parallels and Paradoxes*, a book of conversations with Barenboim published in 2002, he identified with Goethe's belief that art "was all about a voyage to the 'other,'" and not concentrating on oneself, which is very much a minority view today." Said didn't imagine that the "voyage" would turn all the orchestra's members into binationalists like himself, or even lead them to a shared understanding of the region's history. But he had "become more interested in what can't be resolved and what is irreconcilable." The musicians no doubt reminded him of himself when he was studying the piano in Cairo, and he enjoyed listening to their "different but intertwined histories . . . without necessarily resolving them into each other." At times, he would correct their "culturally limiting perceptions." When an Arab musician told an Albanian Jew from Israel that he had no right to play Arabic music, Said responded: "What gives you the right to play Beethoven? You're not German."

Although as militant as ever in his defense of Palestinian rights, he never accepted the idea that Arabs should avoid contact with Israeli Jews. As he put it in an article for *Al-Hayat*: "How many Palestinian homes have been protected from demolition by antinormalization measures?" If Arab intellectuals wanted to do something for Palestine, they should go there to "give a lecture or help at a clinic" rather than "sit at home preventing others from doing so." Zionism, he said, "has tried to exclude non-Jews and we, by our unselective boycott of even the name

'Israel,' have actually *helped* rather than hindered this plan." That Said conceived the West-Eastern Divan as a challenge to Israel's exclusion of Palestinians—and as a response to the cultural isolation suffered by Palestinian musicians under occupation—was lost on his less imaginative Arab critics, who could only see it as making peace with the enemy.

Serving as Arafat's man in New York for nearly two decades had been an improbable role for a worldly, cosmopolitan man who dressed in Burberry suits, not keffiyehs. Said himself admitted that his relationship to the land of Palestine was "basically metaphorical." His Zionist critics cited this distance in order to belittle or even deny his Palestinian origins. They also used his relationship with the PLO to impugn his scholarship, insinuating that his books, and even his essays on critical theory and classical music, were merely subterfuges from the "professor of terror": Palestinian propaganda disguised as scholarship.

For all its crudeness, this charge has a grain of truth. All Said's writings were touched by his "affiliation." The burden of being a political spokesman, and his loyalty to Arafat, imposed certain limits on what he could say about the movement and the repressive governments of the Arab world: as Said often pointed out, affiliation could degenerate into filiation, into a familial structure of obedience and conformity. Only in his final decade did he express himself freely on the movement's failures and the region's dictatorships. But, as Brennan shows, the Palestinian struggle enriched Said far more than it constrained him. The themes that echo through his writing—the preference for exilic over rooted writing, the idea of "contrapuntal" criticism, the insistence on secular humanism, worldliness and universality—can all, indirectly, be traced to Palestine. Not to the land itself, or to the people, but to the metaphor, the region of the mind, that he fashioned out of them.

This was no small achievement. As Said wrote in a 1984 essay in the *London Review of Books*, Israel and its supporters had worked hard to deny Palestinians the "permission to narrate" their experience. He helped to restore that right, not only by describing their dispossession and oppression but also by

developing a powerful counter-myth to Zionism, which he sometimes called "Palestinianism." In his 1986 collaboration with the
Swiss photographer Jean Mohr, *After the Last Sky*, Said described
a nation of vivid fragments, rather than trying to assemble them
into a seamless whole. He had no interest in the folk nationalism of the refugee camps, with its romance of repatriation and
reclamation: the keys to old homes, women's embroidery, the
olive tree, the posters of Al-Aqsa mosque. Instead, he wrote of
Palestinians as witnesses to a century defined by ethnic cleansing,
wars of national liberation, and migration, in restless, nomadic
pursuit of freedom: "a counterpoint (if not a cacophony) of
multiple, almost desperate dramas."

Said's Palestinianism exemplified the qualities he admired:
open-ended and exploratory, resistant to the doctrinal and racial
fixity—the dark historical fatalism and exclusionary fear of the
other—that Zionism embodied. If Zionism was the song of a
single people, Palestinianism held out the hope of a nonsectar-
ian future for both peoples. Palestinian freedom, whether in the
form of a sovereign state neighboring Israel or—the position he
defended after Oslo—a binational state, represented "a beginning," a dynamic intervention in history, rather than a return
to origin. And yet his vision also looked to the past, betraying a
wistful attachment to his childhood memories of colonial Cairo,
where Arabs and Jews, Muslims and Christians had lived beside
one another.

Brennan's title alludes to Said's memoir, *Out of Place*, as
well as to his family's dispossession and his own experiences of
being attacked by Israel's apologists in the US, and later by the
Palestinian Authority. Yet the emphasis on place is misleading.
What captured Said's imagination wasn't place or territory so
much as time: the drama of beginnings, the defiance of late
style. Nor did he lack for a home: New York fitted him as well
as his bespoke suits. He once asked Ignace Tiegerman why he
hadn't left Cairo for Israel. "Why should I go there?" Tiegerman
replied. "Here I am unique." In New York, Said was unique, and
whatever loneliness he experienced was offset by his love of a
place where "you can be anywhere in it and still not be of it." In

New York he had a stage: a professorship at Columbia, where he was the highest-paid member of the humanities faculty; access to nightly talk shows and news stations, where he became the face of Palestine; and, not least, the world of literary parties and salons, where "Eduardo" (as friends teasingly called him) cut an alluring profile.

For all his admiration of men of the left who threw themselves into insurgent struggles—and although his own activism attracted the surveillance of the FBI—Said led the life of a celebrity intellectual. Brennan places him in the tradition of revolutionary intellectuals, but Said doesn't resemble Gramsci or Fanon so much as Susan Sontag, born two years before him, and, like him, a dissident heir of the New York intellectuals. Both were literary critics who first made a name for themselves as interpreters of French theory for Anglo-American audiences but later broke free of its textual games and jargon in favor of a more readerly style. Despite a shared loathing of American consumerism and provincialism, each was possessed of a peculiarly American energy and drive. They were each American in their rejection of cultural pessimism, and they shared a reverence for traditional Western culture: they may have expressed "radical styles of will," but they also invoked the authority of canonical critics. In their writings on photography, both drew inspiration from John Berger, moved, if not quite persuaded, by his insistence on the medium's insurrectionary potential. Their best-known books, *Orientalism* and *Illness as Metaphor*, both published in 1978, were quarrels with oppressive systems of representation by which they had felt personally victimized. They often wrote in praise of Marxist intellectuals but were never Marxists themselves. Neither took part in civil rights or labour struggles at home, devoting their political energies to foreign causes.

But unlike Sontag, who had a thick skin, Said remembered every slight he'd suffered, every award he'd been denied, every note he missed when he played the piano. According to Brennan, he lived "in agony" most of the time. The life of a closeted Palestinian would have been much easier. Sontag rose to prominence at a time when Jewish American intellectuals had won full entry to the American establishment; she was also white. For much of his career, Said was not just the lone Arab but the Palestinian, liable to be portrayed as an enemy of the Jews, as a dangerous radical who, as he put it, did "unspeakable, unmentionable things" when he wasn't giving lectures on Conrad and Jane Austen. Eventually even those lectures would come to be seen by his critics as a threat to Western culture, if not an extension of his work for the PLO. Said's insecurity, as much as his colonial origins, may explain why, unlike Sontag, he attached himself to institutions: Columbia, the Palestine National Council, the Century Club, the West-Eastern Divan Orchestra. Institutional affiliation wasn't simply a comfort; it offered an escape from feelings of awkwardness, of being "not quite right"—the original title of his memoir.

Brennan, a former student of Said's, writes with a restrained affection that only occasionally slips into defensiveness or hagiography. He understands that, in private, Said could be a prima donna, "a personality marked by impatience and vulnerability, by turns angry and romantic," playful and witty, capable of acts of generosity but also vain, in perpetual need of affirmation, and occasionally quite petty and vindictive. He shows us Said at home, preparing breakfast for Mariam, practicing Bach partitas, but we also catch glimpses of his less appealing side: the vulgar gusto he displayed in intellectual combat (before going onstage to debate Bernard Lewis he told his friends, in Arabic, that he was "going to fuck his mother"); his irrepressible competitiveness (when Mariam was struggling to learn Hebrew he grabbed her textbook and said: "I would finish this whole book in two weeks"). He was perpetually dissatisfied, insomniac, hypochondriac. "If Said had a cough he feared the onset of bronchitis," Salman Rushdie wrote after his death, "and if he felt a twinge he was certain his appendix was about to collapse."

Many illustrious friends and acquaintances—Philip Roth, Nadine Gordimer, Jacqueline Kennedy Onassis—make cameos in Brennan's biography, but there is little sense of the texture of these relationships. Of Said's personal life, we learn even less. After his second marriage, in 1970, other women recede from view, with one exception: his longtime mistress Dominique Eddé, a Lebanese novelist who published a perceptive study of Said's life and work, *Le Roman de sa pensée*, in 2017. While echoing several of Eddé's judgments about Said's work, Brennan characterizes their on-and-off relationship of more than two decades as a "brief affair" and ridicules her discreet book as the "largely autobiographical tell-all" of a scorned woman who hardly knew the man she professed to love. This ad hominem attack injects a bellicose note into a book that otherwise studiously ignores Said's private life. Brennan accuses Eddé of putting Said's name on a petition he had never seen. The petition, though Brennan doesn't mention the fact, was protesting a Holocaust denial conference in Beirut. Said added his own signature but withdrew it when he learned that Eddé was the author. After the conference was banned, Said claimed that he had removed his name on free speech grounds. According to Eddé, he apologized to her shortly before he died.

Brennan has, however, tracked down many of Said's early friends, including people whose names barely turn up in his writing, such as André Sharon, an Egyptian Jew who was at school with him in Cairo. He is also a confident guide to Said's work as a literary critic, though he is on less sure ground when writing about Middle Eastern politics or music (he includes Janáček in a list of "experimental composers").

Music supplied Said with more than metaphors in his writing: it provided him with the great theme of his final years, "late style," an idea he discovered in Adorno's writings on Beethoven. Adorno's belief that it was "part of . . . morality not to be at home in one's home" spoke powerfully to Said. And he was captivated by Adorno's argument that Beethoven's late piano sonatas exhibited an aesthetics not of harmony but of "intransigence, difficulty and unresolved contradiction." Far from being serene expressions of wisdom in old age, they were "catastrophes."

Said's vision of lateness differed from Adorno's, as Brennan says, in its emphasis on the creator's inner struggle. Lateness spoke directly to his own experience of exile, not just from the Palestine he had known but from the leadership, and explained his decision to uphold the ideals that had led him into the movement. The defiance and intransigence it expressed were spiritual cousins of what Palestinians call *sumud*, or steadfastness: better to accept the contradictions of exile and dissidence than the false harmony offered by the Oslo Accords, the "peace" of permanent occupation. Although he was in a constant state of rage and sorrow over Palestine, his fidelity to what he called "Palestinianism" grounded him.

In August 2003, I edited Said's last piece for the *Nation*: a review of Maynard Solomon's book on late Beethoven. We had become friendly over the previous few years, and he would occasionally call me, out of the blue, to give me a scoop or to chat about the politics of the Middle East. He seemed extremely anxious for the review to appear and called my boss to pressure me to run it sooner than planned (successfully, I might add). As it turned out, he had only a month to live. In the essay he celebrated Beethoven's late works for their "violence, experimental energy, and, most important, refusal to accept any ideal of a healing, inclusive restfulness that comes at the end of a fruitful career." The title, "Untimely Meditations," strikes me today as an accurate description of his late writings on binationalism, secular criticism, cross-cultural exchange and intellectual freedom, which have been obscured in recent years by his now canonical work on Orientalism and cultural imperialism. In his own late style, he found a new beginning.

{2021}

II

Equal in Paris

5

Richard Wright's Double Vision

When Richard Wright sailed to France in 1946, he was thirty-eight years old and already a legend, the author of two books hailed as classics as soon as they were published: the 1940 novel *Native Son*, and the 1945 memoir *Black Boy*. He was not only America's most famous (and commercially successful) black writer; he was an international literary celebrity—"the first black writer," in Paul Gilroy's words, "to be put forward as a major figure in world literature." In "choosing exile," as he put it, he hoped to free himself from American racism, and put an ocean between himself and the American Communist Party, in which he'd first come to prominence as a writer of proletarian fiction, only to find himself accused of subversive, "Trotskyist" tendencies. Almost as soon as he settled in Paris, a scene gathered around Wright—a handsome, brown-skinned man whose affable manner gave little hint of the ordeals he'd undergone—at the Café Monaco, a short walk from his Left Bank flat. French writers and black American expatriates alike flocked there to be in his presence. "Dick greeted everyone with boisterous condescension," Chester Himes remembered. "It was obvious he was the king thereabouts."

His place on the throne was shakier than he imagined. The novels he wrote in Paris failed to deliver on the promise of *Native Son*, his incendiary tale of a poor black chauffeur in Chicago, Bigger Thomas, who achieves a grisly sense of selfhood after killing two women: Mary Dalton, the daughter of his wealthy white employer; and Bess, his black girlfriend. The reputation of *Native Son*, too, went into decline, thanks in large part to another black American in Paris. In his 1949 essay "Everybody's Protest Novel," James Baldwin compared Wright's novel to a modern-day *Uncle Tom's Cabin* and, in a cruel aside, pictured "the contemporary Negro novelist and the dead New England woman locked together in a deadly, timeless battle; the one uttering merciless exhortations, the other shouting curses." In Baldwin's eyes, Wright was no less guilty than Beecher Stowe of insisting that it is a person's "categorization alone which is real and which cannot be transcended."

Wright never forgave Baldwin, whom, only a few years earlier, he had welcomed at his Brooklyn home with (in Baldwin's words) a "mockingly conspiratorial" smile that made the younger man feel "as though we were two black boys, in league against the world." Thanks to Wright, Baldwin had won the lucrative Eugene Saxton fellowship and secured a $900 renewal of his contract to write a novel. When the two men met at a café on the day that Baldwin's essay was published in the expatriate magazine *Zero*, Wright accused him of betrayal. "Richard thought that I was trying to destroy his novel and his reputation," Baldwin recalled in his 1961 account of their troubled friendship, "Alas, Poor Richard," published a year after Wright's death of a heart attack, "but it had not entered my mind that either of these *could* be destroyed, and certainly not by me."

In that essay, Baldwin admitted that Wright had sized up his intentions better than he had. "His work was the road-block in my road, the sphinx, really, whose riddles I had to answer before I could become myself . . . Richard was hurt because I had not given him credit for any human feelings or failings. And indeed I had not, he had never really been a human being for me, he had been an idol. And idols are created in order to be destroyed." Rereading Wright's work, he realized that his true subject was not racial oppression so much as "human loss and helplessness," his "unrelentingly bleak landscape . . . not merely that of the Deep South, or of Chicago, but that of the world, of the human heart." Perhaps, he suggested, "Richard Wright was never, really, the social and polemical writer he took himself to be"—or, rather, that Baldwin took him to be.

Wright's reputation has never quite recovered from Baldwin's blows. Nor was Baldwin the only black protégé to feel (as he put it) a "certain unadmitted relief" when Wright exited the scene. In his memoirs, Himes wrote that "Dick's death put an accelerator on my own life, which began to spin like a buzz saw." When, in 1963, Irving Howe published an essay in *Dissent* praising Wright's fiction over the work of Baldwin and Ralph Ellison, Ellison responded with an epic-length essay directed against Wright as much as against Howe. In Bigger Thomas, he argued, Wright had not created a black character recognizable to other black people, but rather "a near subhuman indictment of white oppression," crudely "designed to shock whites out of their apathy." Then came the zinger: "Wright could imagine Bigger, but Bigger could not possibly imagine Richard Wright."

The same could not be said of Ellison's hypercerebral protagonist in *Invisible Man*, whose ability to describe, and see beyond, his condition was a pointed rejoinder to Bigger Thomas's inarticulate and explosive rage. During their days together as intellectuals in the Communist Party, Ellison had taken a rather different view of Bigger's "revolutionary significance," as he put it in a letter to Wright, in which he argued that readers horrified by Bigger's violence "fail to see that what's *bad* in Bigger from the point of view of bourgeois society is *good* from our point of view . . . Would that all Negroes were as psychologically free as Bigger and as capable of positive action!" As for black critics who attacked the novel, "these bastards here are hollering their heads off because Bigger became a man rather than a political puppet! To hell with them."

Nearly three decades later, Ellison's initial response to *Native Son* was echoed by a writer he loathed: the Black Panther leader Eldridge Cleaver, who, in *Soul on Ice*, celebrated Bigger Thomas as "the black rebel of the ghetto," with "no trace . . . of the Martin Luther King–type self-effacing love for his oppressors." For Cleaver, who had practiced raping black women before graduating to white women, Bigger embodied an authentic, revolutionary black masculinity naturally despised by Baldwin, a gay man, who had tried to "drive the blade of Brutus into the corpse of Richard Wright."

The Black Power movement's patriarchal (and homophobic) embrace of Wright did little to salvage his literary reputation, especially with the rise of black feminism in the 1970s. In *Black Macho and the Myth of the Super Woman*, Michele Wallace traced the movement's "love affair with Black Macho" back to Wright's *Native Son*. His standing among black women writers had already been poisoned by his attack on Zora Neale Hurston, whom he accused, in his 1937 review of *Their Eyes Were Watching God*, of writing "in the safe and narrow orbit in which America likes to see the Negro live: between laughter and tears"— and of trafficking in "that facile sensuality that has dogged Negro expression since the days of Phyllis [*sic*] Wheatley."

In fairness, Wright had gone on to develop an increasingly passionate concern for women's rights during his travels in Spain, where he had been shocked by the oppression of women. And at the 1956 Conference of Black Writers and Artists in Paris, he denounced the absence of female speakers, insisting that black men could be free only if black women were also free. But— again, thanks to *Native Son*—he continued to be associated with the idea that, in Darryl Pinckney's words, "the black man can only come to life as the white man's nightmare, the defiler of white women." Black feminists weren't the only ones to take offense. The novelist David Bradley confessed in a 1986 essay for the *New York Times* that the first time he read *Native Son*: "I shed no tears for Bigger. I wanted him dead; by legal means, if possible, by lynching if necessary . . . I did not see Bigger Thomas as a symbol of any kind of black man. To me he was a sociopath, pure and simple, beyond sympathy or understanding . . . If the price of becoming a black writer was following the model of *Native Son*, I would just have to write like a honky."

Novelists seldom shake off some association with the murderers they invent. Dostoevsky is still remembered for Raskolnikov, Camus for Meursault. The difference in Wright's case is that Bigger Thomas has been nearly *all* that he is remembered for;

and he is not just blamed for Bigger but almost mistaken for him. Wright himself helped sow the confusion, playing the part of Bigger in a misbegotten film adaptation of *Native Son*, shot in Argentina in 1951. His own biography bore, on the surface, little resemblance to Bigger's: he was a child of the rural south, rather than the northern ghetto, not to mention a self-made intellectual and writer. But he had held a series of degrading menial jobs in hospitals and the postal service as a young man in Chicago, where he'd arrived in 1927 at nineteen, during the Great Black Migration, and he could identify all too well with Bigger's anger at the cruelties of a white world that was at best indifferent to black life. He had also known Bigger's fear of whites and their power—in his view, the "fundamental emotion guiding black personality and behavior," even if it sometimes appeared in "the disguise that is called Negro laughter."

With *Native Son*, Wright wanted to provoke not only whites but members of the black bourgeoisie, who considered the likes of Bigger Thomas an existential threat to their precarious status at the margins of white America. He was in search of a new voice, more staccato than lyrical, a brutal, plainspoken style that would throttle his readers. He was still frustrated over the sentimental praise he'd received for *Uncle Tom's Children*, his 1938 collection of stories about black life under segregation: "I found that I had written a book which even bankers' daughters could read and weep over and feel good about. I swore to myself that if I ever wrote another book, no one would weep over it; that it would be so hard and deep that they would have to face it without the consolation of tears."

Wright began writing *Native Son* after reading about a black man's murder of a white woman in the tabloids. The novel was a work of shocking and daring intransigence, both in its ridicule of liberal whites and, above all, in its violence. (Howe scarcely exaggerated when he wrote: "The day *Native Son* appeared, American culture changed forever.") After suffocating Mary Dalton with a pillow—he's terrified that she might alert her blind mother to his presence in her bedroom, and that he could be accused of rape —Bigger slices up her body and throws it into a fireplace. His violence is recounted as if it were the concentrated payback for hundreds of years of antiblack violence and humiliation—and with graphic relish. Whites are not the only ones to drown in this flood of revenge: Bigger also kills his girlfriend Bess lest she reveal his crime. Unlike the accidental manslaughter of Dalton, Bess's death is a premeditated murder. What makes Bigger's violence so horrifying is that Wright describes its logic from his perspective, bringing us into queasy complicity with his crimes. Wright conveys the exhilarating rush of adrenaline that Bigger feels after he kills: his proud sense of having accomplished "something that was all his own," an act of which no one would have imagined him capable or daring enough to execute. His ever-taut muscles relax, and "elation filled him." No longer subdued by fear, no longer "a black timid Negro boy," he discovers an enthralling sense of power over his oppressors, a "sense of wholeness," "like a man who had been somehow cheated, but had now evened the score." In his 1952 study *Black Skin, White Masks*, Frantz Fanon drew on *Native Son* to explain the violent impulses that racism creates in its victims. "Bigger Thomas is afraid, but of what is he afraid?" he writes. "Of himself. We don't yet know who he is, but he knows that fear will haunt the world once the world finds out." Wright, for Fanon, had shown that violence is a way to "put an end to the tension," to "feelings of not existing" in a white-dominated society: "The black man is a toy in the hands of the white man. So in order to break the vicious circle, he explodes." For Bigger, murder provides an irresistible glimpse of freedom; it is "disintoxicating," as Fanon would later write of anticolonial violence in *The Wretched of the Earth*. "I didn't want to kill," Bigger tells his lawyer, "but what I killed for, I *am*."

That middle-class black readers had little wish to be associated with Bigger is hardly surprising. But for Wright, Bigger Thomas was not—or rather not merely—a symbol of persecuted black masculinity so much as a symbol of the psychic injuries of oppression, rootlessness and dispossession under capitalism. In his essay "How Bigger Was Born," Wright explained that he had first met defiant men like Bigger while growing up in segregated Mississippi: men who "violated the Jim Crow laws of the South and got away with it, at least for a sweet brief spell," before they were "shot, hanged, maimed, lynched." But in Chicago and New York, he had "made the discovery that Bigger Thomas was not black all the time, and there were literally millions of him, everywhere. The extension of my sense of the personality of Bigger was the pivot of my life; it altered the complexion of my existence." As he became aware of "a vast, muddied pool of human life in America," he began to realize that segregation "was but an appendage of a far vaster and in many respects more ruthless and impersonal commodity-profit machine."

Wright did not portray Bigger Thomas as a heroic rebel; rather, he saw him as the humiliated, alienated and dangerous "product of a dislocated society," seething with fear and envy, susceptible to fantasies of power, domination and revenge: "he liked to hear of how Japan was conquering China; of how Hitler was running the Jews to the ground; of how Mussolini was invading Spain." (At one point, Bigger dreams of going to aviation school, only to muse, "maybe they right in not wanting us to fly . . . 'Cause if I took a plane up I'd take a couple of bombs along and drop 'em as sure as hell.") Wright believed that Bigger "carried within himself the potentialities of either Communism or Fascism." He also alluded obliquely to Marcus Garvey's back-to-Africa movement, whose fusion of black nationalism and militarist discipline fascinated him: "Someday," Bigger muses, "there would be a black man who would whip the black people into a tight band and together they would act and end fear and shame." In linking social atomization and fear, racism and authoritarianism, *Native Son* anticipated Arendt's *Origins of Totalitarianism*.

In his essay "Many Thousands Gone," an even harsher follow-up to "Everybody's Protest Novel," Baldwin criticized Wright for overlooking the traditions, rituals and family relationships that protect and fortify black communities in even the most appalling conditions. But Wright was not interested in the support structures or mutual aid that enabled black people to survive as a collective; he was drawn instead to individual outcasts and desperados who fell through the cracks and found themselves adrift, naked, in mass society. He was himself a loner, never at ease in his own family, and hostile to the church. He developed his loathing of religion as a child, thanks to his clashes with his grandmother, a stern Seventh Day Adventist who frowned on any reading other than the Bible. He might have been speaking about his own family when he wrote that Bigger "held toward them an attitude of iron reserve; he lived with them, but behind a wall, a curtain." His fiercest quarrels inside the Communist Party were with black militants who shared his working-class roots but distrusted him as an intellectual. Most of his romantic partners were white, including his wife, Ellen, the daughter of Polish Jewish immigrants, whom he met in the Party. Wright had a broad, black-Southern sense of humor, but he was an intensely private, almost impenetrable man of a certain coldness, all but impervious to the warmth of other suns. Although Baldwin left the church, the church never left him: his sentences are born aloft by its redemptive cadences, summoning "another country" where black Americans would at last be free. Wright doubted that such a country would ever exist in his homeland, and left, for good.

It has never been easy to read Wright. But that difficulty is not just a matter of his extreme bleakness, or of Baldwin's demolition of his work, or even of the scandal of his most unforgettable and terrifying creation, Bigger Thomas. Another major obstacle to Wright's reception has been the publishing industry. His 1938 novel about a day in the life of a black postal worker, *Lawd Today!*, written under the influence of Joyce, was never published in his lifetime, obscuring Wright's passion for modernism, and leaving the impression that he was simply a naturalist in the tradition of Dreiser. Under pressure from the Book-of-the-Month Club, the editors of his second novel, *Native Son*, suppressed crucial passages in which Wright described Bigger Thomas and Mary Dalton in bed: "the sharp bones of her hips move in a hard and veritable grind. Her mouth was open and her breath came slow and deep . . . He tightened his fingers on her breasts, kissing her again, feeling her move toward him." This is not a rape; this is consensual intimacy between a black man and a white woman, the taboo that the myth of the black rapist was intended to conceal. By deleting such passages, Wright's editors not only restored the image of the pure, virginal white woman, they deprived Bigger of a motive for his panic, magnifying the brutality of his crime and turning him into a monster. The original version of the novel wasn't published until 1992, when the Library of American brought out a restored edition of five of Wright's books. When Baldwin and Ellison took aim at *Native Son*, they were writing about the Book-of-the-Month Club's Bigger.

Black Boy also raised objections from the Book-of-the-Month club. The novelist Dorothy Canfield Fisher, a member of the selection committee, chastised him for overlooking white Americans who "have done what they could to lighten the dark stain of racial discrimination in our nation." (One black critic—W. E. B. Du Bois—shared this view, complaining that there was not "a single broad-minded, open-hearted white person in the book," and that Wright lacked the capacity for empathy, "even with his own parents.") The second half of the book, about Wright's often harrowing experiences in the North (later published under the title *American Hunger*), was also cut, so that the memoir might be read as a hopeful tale of exodus from Southern terror, rather than a caustic commentary on the pervasiveness of racism on both sides of the Mason-Dixon line.

Wright's publisher, Harper and Brothers, rejected the novel he considered to be his most important to date, written in between *Native Son* and *Black Boy*. An abridged version of *The Man Who Lived Underground* appeared in his posthumous collection *Eight Men* and attracted some influential admirers, including Howe, who declared its "sense of narrative rhythm" to be "superior to anything in his full-length novels." But it was not until 2021 that the novel appeared in print, followed by Wright's essay on the book, "Memories of My Grandmother." It is a short, riveting, intellectually exploratory work, with strong echoes of Dostoevsky, one of Wright's two greatest influences (the other being Dreiser). Wright began work on the novel in June 1941, after the Nazi invasion of the Soviet Union. Two weeks before the invasion, at the opening session of the fourth American Writers Congress, he had given a passionate speech against the war. When the Communist Party reversed its position, even suspending its campaign against racism in the war industries, Wright was furious: while Roosevelt had abolished discrimination in war production, the military remained segregated, and he refused to support a white man's army. (He was later drafted but declared psychologically unfit, apparently on grounds of his views about racism.) Although not yet ready to leave the party, he withdrew from all its activities, and poured all his energy into *The Man Who Lived Underground*.

Like *Native Son*, it was inspired by the tabloids: Wright had read a story in a detective magazine about a white man in California who'd lived for several months in a hideout. But Wright's protagonist, Fred Daniels, is black, and, unlike Bigger Thomas, he is innocent. The novel begins one Saturday evening when Daniels, a working-class, churchgoing man with a pregnant wife, is stopped by the police and accused of killing a white man in order to rape the white man's wife. They beat him with a black-jack and promise that if he signs a confession, he can go home. Although he's not guilty, he feels "condemned, inescapably guilty of some nameless deed," and agrees to confess, if only to end the agony and see his wife. Once they arrive at his flat, she goes into labor. They rush her to the hospital, where he manages to escape. He opens a sewer and climbs inside, sensing in "the whispering rush of the water" the "illusion of another world with other values and other laws."

As a number of critics have remarked, *The Man Who Lived Underground* feels startlingly contemporary in its treatment of police violence against an innocent black man.* Not surprisingly, it has been held up as a prescient indictment of the racist carceral state. But the book is no more of a "protest novel" than *Native Son*, and even less of a naturalist work. Its setting and atmosphere—chases through sewers, frenzied manhunts—recall those of noirish films like Fritz Lang's *M* and Carol Reed's *The Third Man*. Wright's writing combines the rhythms of hard-boiled

---

* The story of the interrogation is strikingly reminiscent of the 1989 Central Park Five case, in which a group of black and Latino minors were manipulated into confessing to the rape of a white jogger.

detective fiction with kinetic, almost phantasmagorical strokes, intensities of emotion and color. As Howe observed of *Native Son*, "naturalism pushed to an extreme turns here into something other than itself, a kind of expressionistic outburst, no longer a replica of the familiar social world but a self-contained emblem of grotesque emblems." For all that the novel reveals of police brutality and racism, Wright described *The Man Who Lived Underground* to his agent as a novel of ideas, rather than a novel about racial injustice: "The first time I've really tried to step beyond the straight black-white stuff."

Although Daniels is a victim of police violence, Wright's narrative hinges less on his victimization than on the mutations of his consciousness as he builds a new home for himself underground, illuminated by a single lightbulb. (Ellison, who was well aware of Wright's novella, equipped *his* underground man with 1,369 lightbulbs.) He steals money from a real estate and insurance company that has "collected hundreds of thousands of dollars in rent from poor colored folks," "not to spend, but just to keep around and look at." In a scene that evokes Marx's famous essay on "the mysterious character of the commodity form," Daniels "rubbed the money with his fingers, as though expecting it to reveal secret qualities. It's just like any other kind of paper, he observed with a musing smile." He turns the money into wallpaper, a "mocking symbol" of his exile from "the world that had rejected him." But when another man ends up being accused of the theft he commits, and kills himself, he concludes: "everybody's guilty." The contingency and artifice of the world outside, the "dead world of sunshine and rain he had left," leads him to the realization that "he was *all* people. In some utterable fashion he was *all* people and they were *he*." Racist persecution leads him to an awareness of what he shares with others, rather than sharpening his sense of identity.

One of the first readers of the manuscript was the German-Jewish psychiatrist Frederic Wertham. He sent Wright a poem in response:

The Freudians talk about the id
And bury it below
But Richard Wright took off the lid
And let us see the woe.

A professor at Johns Hopkins who moved in left-wing circles, Wertham shared Wright's conviction that there was "no other act . . . that so gathers together the threads of personal, social, political life of the nation as crime." Wright had contacted him after reading Wertham's *Dark Legend*, a study of an Italian immigrant youth who killed his sexually adventurous mother to defend the honor of his dead father. Wertham, in turn, published a remarkable study of *Native Son*, linking Bigger's bedroom panic to a repressed episode from Wright's childhood. They later joined forces to create the Lafargue Clinic, which provided cheap psychiatric counseling for people in Harlem. Wright's friendship with Wertham reflected his desire to fuse the insights of Marx and Freud—two of his favorite "poets," he called them—and apply them to the inner lives of oppressed people, especially victims of racism. "I'm convinced that the next great arena of discovery in the Negro will be the dark landscape of his own mind, what living in America has done to him," he wrote in his diary.

In his essay "Memories of My Grandmother," Wright explored his own "dark landscape," describing two experiences that lay behind the creation of the novel. The first—an encounter with the "strangely familiar," an idea that recurs throughout the book—took place in Chicago, shortly before his grandmother's death in 1934. Wright thought that he had "swept my life clean . . . of the religious influences of my grandmother," until he read a book that "miraculously linked my grandmother's life to my own in a most startling manner": Gertrude Stein's *Three Lives*. Reading Stein's story "Melanctha" in black vernacular speech at his grandmother's flat, "I suddenly began to hear the *English* language for the first time in my life! . . . But more than that; suddenly I began to hear my grandmother speak for the first time." Later, he read the story aloud in a basement on the South Side to a "group of illiterate, class-conscious Negro workers . . . and there were such howls of delight, such expressions of recognition, that I could barely finish."

In an artful series of moves, he connects the "quality of my grandmother's living" to a form of music she loathed as a sinner's genre, the blues, with their manner of "freely juxtaposing totally unrelated images and symbols and then tying them into some overall concept, mood, feeling," "a trait of Negro thinking and feeling." By imposing order, a strange order, on the fragments of a chaotic, ungovernable, intolerable reality, the blues marks "the advent of surrealism on the American scene." Wright was familiar with surrealism from his experience of psychoanalysis, but the blues represented a surrealism born of necessity, not from theory—not unlike the surrealism of the Martinican poet Aimé Césaire, whose epic *Notebook of Return to the Native Land* was published a few years earlier, years before he met André Breton, who discovered the work in a haberdashery shop in Fort-de-France.* Suddenly, Wright could see parallels with his grandmother's "ardent and volatile religious disposition," which he had previously found "illogical if not degrading." When he read about a white man who'd lived underground, he immediately thought of his grandmother, who, in her religious life, had retreated from the world: "Yes, I thought, here is where I can put a man outside of life and yet let him live within life, just as my grandmother had done." The "guilt theme" provided him with a "steady beat upon which I proceeded to improvise," as in jazz, with its "improvised, tone-colored melodies carried on in terms of rhythm." (Almost as an afterthought, he adds that this was linked, "in a rather muted way," to "the problem of the Negro," since "if you accuse a man of something he did not do . . . it has the power of upsetting his entire way of life.")

Wright was always a deeply self-reflexive writer, keen to analyze and explain his intentions. In his 1937 "Blueprint for Negro Writing," he had championed a program of radical, politically

---

* The idea that black life was surreal—or absurd—was common among black writers of Wright's generation. Inspired by the clinic that Wright helped found with Frederic Wertham, Ellison described black life in Harlem as fundamentally surreal in his 1948 essay "Harlem Is Nowhere."

engaged modernism, mocking his predecessors as "prim and decorous ambassadors who went a-begging to white America . . . dressed in the knee pants of servility." Still, "Memories of My Grandmother" stands out for its account of the writing he espoused, a homegrown modernism inspired by tabloids and pulp cinema, the blues and black working-class life, and a robust sense of the absurd. ("Absurdity," Himes remarked, "was the realest thing about Richard Wright.") None of the novels he went on to publish matched *The Man Who Lived Underground*, much less *Native Son*, but his next book, the wrenching memoir *Black Boy*, was infused with the same memories, the same "strangely familiar" juxtapositions of the "unrelated" that he believed defined black experience in America. According to Himes, Baldwin told Wright that it had left him and other black writers with little else to write.

In an essay published shortly after its publication, Ellison described *Black Boy* as a literary analogue of the blues: "an autobiographical chronicle of personal catastrophe expressed lyrically." That he'd lived to tell the tale was itself a near miracle: his early life was nearly as saturated with death and misery as his fiction. Born in rural Mississippi in 1908, he grew up in the epicenter of American apartheid. His grandfather had escaped slavery and joined the Union army, only to be deprived of his war pension; he hated white people "too much to talk of them." When Wright was three, his family moved to Memphis, Tennessee; a year later, his father abandoned them. His mother worked as a cook for a white family but soon became an invalid. He was largely raised by his austere grandmother, who looked so white she could have been a "pretty Victorian woman." It took him a while before he learned to "sense white people as 'white' people," because "many of my relatives were 'white'-looking people." He didn't have to go to school to realize race was a "construct"—and, in any case, no school in America would have taught him that.

To be a black male in the South was to be at constant risk of catching "the white death"—especially after the First World War ended, and black soldiers returned home to face a wave of antiblack violence. Wright's uncle was murdered by white men envious of his success in business; the brother of a classmate was lynched and castrated for sleeping with a white prostitute. Baldwin, in "Alas, Poor Richard," lamented that in Wright's fiction "there is a great space where sex ought to be; and what usually fills this space is violence," but antiblack violence, from property destruction to lynching, was the overwhelming reality of his childhood, and it was often ignited by rumors of sex between black men and white women. During his childhood, Wright's "feelings were governed by fear and I spoke to no one about them"—fear of white people, but also fear of his grand-mother's violence, and of abandonment by his mother, who was absent for long spells at a time. By the time he turned twelve, before he'd had a single year of formal education, "I had a con-ception of life that no experience would ever erase, a predilection for what was real that no argument could ever gainsay, a sense of the world that was mine and mine alone, a notion as to what life meant that no education could ever alter, a conviction that the meaning of living came only when one was struggling to wring a meaning out of meaningless suffering . . . The spirit I had caught gave me insight into the suffering of others, made me gravitate toward those whose feelings were like my own, made me sit for hours while others told me of their lives, made me strangely tender and cruel, violent and peaceful." This under-standing separated him from others, but it also drew him to what he called the "drama of human feeling which is hidden by the external drama of life."

Black Boy is unsparing in its account of the racism Wright faced both in the South and in the North, a corrosive battle against physical and mental annihilation that, he wrote, left a black man like himself "at war with himself . . . continuously at war with reality. He became inefficient, less able to see and judge the objective world." The memoir is also, at times, brutal—self-loathing, it could be argued—in its depiction of the "essential bleakness," the "cultural barrenness," of black life. Yet Wright's tone is searching and defiant, never succumbing to despair or resignation—a model, in Ellison's view, of how the "American

Negro impulse toward self-annihilation and going-underground" could be transformed into "a will to confront the world."

Even so, Wright's confrontations with America would soon leave him exhausted—and desperate to flee. Although he'd quit the Communist Party, he remained under FBI surveillance, because J. Edgar Hoover saw him as even more subversive than his former allies. *Black Boy* attracted denunciations from Southern segregationists like Mississippi senator Theodore Bilbo, who called it "the filthiest, lousiest, most obscene piece of writing that I have ever seen in print," intended to "plant the seeds of hate in every Negro in America against the white man of the South or against the white race anywhere." Even in New York, Wright and his wife, Ellen, had to set up a fake corporation so that they could buy a house, since no bank would give a black man a mortgage, especially a black man married to a white woman. They did not dare walk arm in arm on the street. His white leftist friends didn't provide much comfort either; even they couldn't understand why Harlem exploded in riots in 1943 after the killing of a black soldier by a white policeman. He felt "strangled by petty humiliations and daily insults . . . I need to live free if I am to expand."

In 1946, Wright accepted a formal invitation to visit France from Claude Lévi-Strauss. When he and Ellen arrived in Paris with their young daughter, Julia, after a four-day voyage at sea, a reporter asked him if the "black problem" was close to being resolved in America. "There is not a black problem in the United States, but a white problem," he replied. The existentialists embraced him as one of their own, and he declared that he had more freedom on a single block in Paris than in all of the United States. While Camus arranged for *Black Boy* to be published by Gallimard, Sartre and Beauvoir championed Wright as an exemplary *engagé* writer. As an outsider who wrote about (in Beauvoir's words) "the struggle of a man against the resistance of the world," and as a victim of racism who exposed the lie of the American dream, Wright was so appealing to Sartre and Beauvoir that, even amid their own spells of fellow-traveling, they were willing to overlook his hatred of Soviet Communism.

As if determined to play the role in which his French admirers had cast him, Wright sometimes spoke as though he'd made a sudden metamorphosis from black man to existential man: "I have no race except that which is forced upon me. I have no country except that to which I'm obliged to belong. I have no traditions. I have only the future." After all, he hadn't come all the way to France to write sequels to *Native Son* and *Black Boy*. He wanted to expand as a writer, both imaginatively and geographically. His fiction became more explicitly philosophical, featuring long—sometimes tortured—disquisitions on guilt, freedom and responsibility. He also began to travel, writing essayistic, introspective reportage about Spain, African independence struggles and the Bandung Conference—work that prefigured the New Journalism.

Wright's American friends were wary of his romance with the Parisian existentialists. Gertrude Stein confided in Carl Van Vechten: "You see I kept saying his books were not Negro, that is what I liked in them so much, but now when he isn't, do I like it so much?" Wright resented the notion that it was his obligation to represent what Stein called the "spirit of his race." He considered himself a novelist, not a "Negro novelist," the straitjacket imposed on him in the States. But the novels he published in France tended to vindicate those who believed that exile had cut him off from the sources of his deepest inspiration. *The Outsider* (1953), his most ambitious attempt at an existentialist fiction, was a long, unwieldy novel of ideas, by turns pulpy and ponderous, with a plot so improbable it might have caused a B film director to blush. Damon Cross, the protagonist, is a postal worker in Chicago who, after being presumed dead in a subway crash, walks away from his former life. A nihilist with "a propensity towards a certain coldness," Cross murders a black acquaintance who recognizes him and moves to Harlem under a new identity. There he immediately gets caught up in the factional struggles of the Communist Party, and murders several of its rank and file, either because they're about to discover his identity, or because they're somehow in his way. Killing is an expression of his freedom but also his rootlessness: where Fred Daniels feels guilty despite his innocence, Cross feels innocent despite his guilt. While evading a manhunt, he finds fleeting salvation in the arms of the wife of one of his victims, a young white painter; but she can see him only as an oppressed black man, a heroic figure of bruised nobility, rather than an existential outsider and criminal.

Cross's doppelganger is a brilliant district attorney in New York, Ely Houston, a white hunchback whose mind is as nihilistic as his, but who has chosen the law as a defense against his own criminal impulses. When Houston—whom he just happens to have met on the train from Chicago—discovers that he is behind the killings, he explains that "the first real clue" is the "list of the titles of the books you'd left in your room . . . Your Nietzsche, your Hegel, your Jaspers, your Heidegger, your Husserl, your Kierkegaard, and your Dostoevsky were the clues . . . I said to myself that we are dealing with a man who has wallowed in guilty thought." As a hunchback, Houston also intuitively senses Cross's suppressed fury as a man of color in a racist society. "This damned hump has given me more knowledge than all the books I read at the university."

"Dick's *Outsider*? He can tell a story, but what a meaningless, crazy, stupid story that is—don't you think so?" Beauvoir wrote to Nelson Algren, who replied, "He's trying his best to write like a Frenchman." Baldwin, a more astute if hardly more sympathetic critic, told a friend that Damon Cross reminded him of Bigger Thomas, albeit one who'd read "a few books which, far from changing him, simply affords him some kind of half-assed intellectual justification for his unhappy brutality." Indeed, for all its monologues about the meaning of freedom, *The Outsider* was a continuation of his earlier work: the gruesome murders and manhunt of *Native Son*; the black man's battles inside the Communist Party of *Black Boy*. But what felt grounded in those books now felt surreal and obsessional, an exile's fever dream. Wright's existentialism was less contrived, and more persuasive, before his alliance with the existentialists. He had forgotten what he told C. L. R. James while pointing to books by Kierkegaard in his library: "You see those books there? Everything that he writes in those books I knew before I had them."

Yet *The Outsider* is also a gutsy attempt to explore the Cold War mood of paranoia and fear, and to break out of the racial protest genre, to which, like so many black writers, Wright had been confined. It also provides a fascinating window onto Wright's imagination, evoking the grim isolation and the psychological claustrophobia of a black writer who had severed his connections to the world that had anchored him: family, country and comrades. In a powerful scene, Cross listens to a group of black men cracking jokes about whites, "feeling that the powerful white world had been lowered to their own humble plane by the magic of comic words." He laughs with them, only to wish that "he could lose himself in that kind of living! Were there not somewhere in this world rebels with whom he could feel at home, men who were outsiders because they had been born black and poor, but because they had thought their way through the many veils of illusion? But where were they? How could one find them?"

"All writing is a secret form of autobiography," Wright said, and so it is with *The Outsider*. It was, after all, Wright's sense of himself as an outsider—an intellectual, as well as a black pariah— that had led him into Communist Party, and out of it. The Cold War only intensified his feeling of isolation, caught between the far enemy of the Soviet Union and the near enemy that oppressed his people. Like Wright, Cross recoils at the Party's attempt "to destroy human subjectivity," while also deploring the hypocrisy of the West: "Even if Stalin had personally eaten 15 million human beings, it did not cancel the destruction of entire civilizations and the barbarous slaughter of countless millions by the arms of the Western world during the past 400 years." By the end of the novel Cross is alone and free. But the anarchic, antinomian liberty he has won by virtue of what he calls his "non-identity" turns out to be empty, and violently destructive. "Alone a man is nothing," he cries, just before he himself is murdered.

Wright drew the same lesson in France, as he met men and women who were forging a new, collective future for themselves, in anticolonial struggles for national independence. In "Alas, Poor Richard," Baldwin took him to task for ignoring the plight of Africans and Algerians in Paris and living as if he were an honorary white man. But Wright co-founded *Présence Africaine* with Aimé Césaire, Léopold Senghor and Alioune Diop, and helped organize its 1956 conference of Black Writers and Artists at the Sorbonne. Like most black writers in Paris, including Baldwin, he shied from declaring his support for the Algerian national liberation struggle, but he pointedly refused to sign a statement denouncing the Soviet invasion on Hungary unless it also condemned the war in Suez. He also wrote extensively about African and Asian independence movements—indeed, far more than Baldwin himself.

Wright's first travel book, *Black Power*, was based on a trip he made to the Gold Coast in 1953, at the urging of the pan-African intellectual George Padmore. For much of his time in what, four years later, would become Ghana, he felt out of sorts: the sun left him parched and sluggish, the food made him sick, and "my blackness did not help me" among Africans who did not see him as a brother. Kwame Nkrumah had invited him to give a speech but otherwise ignored him, arousing Wright's suspicion that Nkrumah saw him as an anti-communist spy. In his diary he described himself as "enervated, listless . . . I find myself longing to take a ship and go home." What troubled him most about the Gold Coast was the persistence of religious belief, which almost certainly reminded him of his puritanical grandmother. He felt as if Africans still "lived in a waking dream" and proposed that "AFRICAN LIFE MUST BE MILITARIZED," with a "temporary discipline" imposed to "unite the nation, sweep out tribal cobwebs, and place the feet of the masses upon a basis of reality. I'm not speaking of guns or secret police; I'm speaking of a method of taking people from one order of life and making them face what men, all men everywhere, must face." Without the recognition of necessity, there could be no freedom: for all of his anti-Communism, Wright remained wedded to the developmentalist, Western vision—and the *dirigiste* statism—of Soviet Marxism.

Yet his commitment to African independence was unwavering. "Europeans do not and cannot look upon Africa objectively. Back of their fear of African freedom lies an ocean of *guilt*." Africans, he insisted, must take their destiny into their own hands. He did not expect this to be easy. Not only had imperialism "shattered traditional tribal cultures that had once given meaning to people's lives"; it had also created a stratum of Western-educated people who had become estranged from their kin. The "young black French colonial" who returns home, he writes, "is dismayed to find that he's almost alone. The only people who are solidly against the imperialists are precisely those whose words and manner of living had evoked in him that sense of shame that made him want to disown native customs. They want national freedom, but unlike him, they do not want to prove anything." The "young man who spurned the fetish religion of his people returns and finds that the religion is the only thing that he has to work with . . . So, not believing in the customs of his people, he rolls up his sleeves and begins to organize that which he loathes."

Two years later, Wright went to Indonesia to cover the Bandung Conference of nonaligned countries, the subject of his 1956 book *The Color Curtain*. On his flight he met an Arab journalist, also on his way to Bandung, who showed him photographs of Palestinian refugees expelled from their villages. "I peered up into the face of the journalist; his eyes were unblinking, hot, fanatic. This man was religious . . . And the Jews had been spurred by religious dreams to build a state in Palestine . . . Irrationalism meeting irrationalism." When he arrived at the conference, he saw a white journalist being treated coolly by an Indonesian official, while he received his press card at once. At last, he laughed to himself, he was "a member of the master race," but he was "not proud of it." He was merely the beneficiary of "a racism that they have been taught too bitterly and too well." Western imperialism's great legacy among its former subjects, he argued, was an intense racial consciousness. The "naïve and childlike white Westerner would say, 'I'll support any legislation to eradicate racism,'" but "life is not that simple. Contrite words cannot now stop profound processes which white men set in motion on this earth some 400 years ago." Though alarmed by the fusion of "race and religion . . . swollen, sensitive, turbulent" into a strategy for mobilizing the masses, he was also moved by the display of Afro-Asian unity at Bandung, "a decisive moment in the consciousness of 65 percent of the human race" that seemed to promise a "de-Occidentalization of mankind" and therefore a time when "there will be no East or West."

White Man, Listen!, published in 1959, was Wright's most confessional account of the inner drama of decolonization. He dedicated it to Eric Williams, the prime minister of Trinidad and Tobago and author of *Capitalism and Slavery*, and to the "westernized and tragic elite of Africa, Asia and the West Indies, the lonely outsiders who exist precariously on the cliff-like margins of many cultures." The "'whiteness' of the white world," the spread of white supremacy in countries dominated by imperialism, had left native elites orphaned: they could never be fully Western, but neither could they find a haven in their own traditions. Wright borrowed Nietzsche's idea of the "frog perspective" to describe the relationship of colonized elites to the white world that had for so long restrictively defined their horizons: "A certain degree of hate combined with love (ambivalence) is always involved in this looking from below upward . . . He loves the object because he would like to resemble it. He hates the object because his chances of resembling it are remote."

Wright saw aspects of himself in the colonized elites of Africa and Asia, especially in their tendency to "hide their deepest reactions from those they fear would penalize them if they suspected what they really felt." Like Wright as a young man, many had been attracted to the nonracial, secular politics of the Communist Party, which had enabled the racially oppressed to "meet revolutionary fragments of the hostile race on a plane of equality." But with the rise of independence movements, and the birth of the nonaligned movement, Africans and Asians could now collectively express their "racial feelings . . . in all their turgid passion." Wright welcomed the fact that they could be "among themselves and could confess without shame," but the anti-Western articulations of Third World nationalism disturbed him. "My position is a split one. I'm black. I'm a man of the West . . . I see and understand the West; but I also see and understand the non- or anti-Western point of view. How is this possible? The double vision of mine stems from my being a product of Western civilization and from my racial identity." Wright did not see his "double vision" as a source of torment, as Du Bois had described "double consciousness" in *The Souls of Black Folk*. He considered it an intellectual asset, allowing him to "see both worlds from another and third point of view," and to see the colonized as both "victims of their own religious projections and victims of Western imperialism."

An anonymous reviewer in *El Moudjahid*, the French-language newspaper of the Algerian National Liberation Front—almost certainly Fanon—took strong exception to this claim. Wright's analysis of the psychic violence of whiteness in the lived experience and self-image of black and colonized elites echoed Fanon's in *Black Skin, White Masks*. And only six years earlier, Fanon had sent a fan letter to Wright, announcing his intention to write a book-length study of his work. But by the time *White Man, Listen!* appeared, Fanon had joined the Algerian national liberation struggle, and lost his interest in, and patience with, the private sorrows of colonized elites. "It is true," he wrote in his review, "that the drama of consciousness of a westernized Black, torn between his white culture and his negritude, can be very painful; but this drama, which, after all, kills no one, is too particular to be representative: the misfortune of the colonized African masses, exploited, subjugated, is first of all of a vital, material order; the spiritual rifts of the 'elite' are a luxury that they are unable to afford." He added that "it is hard to see why the black writer Richard Wright felt urged to solicit the 'understanding' of the 'white man' . . . Has history thus taught Richard Wright nothing?"

Indeed, it had. While Wright's sympathies lay with the colonized, he understood—in part thanks to his own struggles as a black Southern refugee made his way north in the Great Migration—that the road to freedom was mined with obstacles that were as much psychological as economic. (Fanon himself would later address this challenge in his chapter on the "pitfalls of national consciousness" in *The Wretched of the Earth*.) The violence and exploitation of imperialism, but also the Western education and secular styles of thought and ideology it had exported to the colonies, had created forms of dislocation—patterns of dependence, hierarchy, cultural schizophrenia—that political independence could not overcome overnight. Unsparing in its indictment of the West, but also alert to the destructive allure of nativism and other sectarian passions, Wright's assessment of the postcolonial condition was full of suggestive ambiguities. As Doris Lessing recognized, this ambivalence was an expression of lucidity—and courage. But Wright's candor came across to his contemporaries, especially his black contemporaries, as a churlish expression of skepticism, even disdain, toward the African motherland at the dawn of her emancipation. He seemed to have little to offer the colonized other than patronizing "tough love."

As a novelist, meanwhile, Wright looked more and more like Sonny Liston, knocked out by not one but two Muhammad Alis: Ellison, whose rhetorical pyrotechnics threw into embarrassing relief the leaden philosophizing of *The Outsider*; and Baldwin, whose winding, hypnotic sentences evoked the cadences of the church from which Wright had escaped. His personal life, too, was in crisis. His marriage to Ellen Wright fell apart; the young novelist William Gardner Smith seduced and ran away with his mistress. And he became convinced—with good reason—that the black expatriate journalist Richard Gibson was spying on him for the CIA. In his last year Wright slept with a revolver beside his bed. When friends made light of his paranoia, he said that "any black man who is not paranoid is in serious shape." Increasingly embittered, he rang up friends in the middle of the night—Sartre, the black cartoonist Ollie Harrington, the French anarchist Daniel Guérin—to vent his frustrations. He found solace at his country home, where he spent his time gardening and writing haikus that evoked the lost world of his youth: the sun and rain in the fields of Mississippi, black children in the alleys of Chicago tenements, the melancholy expression of his late mother. (A volume of Wright's haikus, collected by his daughter Julia, was published in 2019.) His late fiction, too, especially his short stories, expressed a longing for the speech, the humor and the blues sensibility of his people, working-class black Americans whose "traditions" he merely seemed to have left behind when he crossed the Atlantic. When Baldwin read the posthumous stories in *Eight Men*, he could "not avoid feeling that Wright, as he died, was acquiring a new tone, and a less uncertain esthetic distance, and a new depth."

Those traditions not only enriched his fiction; they also helped him to grasp the significance of decolonization, and to articulate a distinctively black internationalism, an original synthesis of Marxism, psychoanalysis and racial consciousness. For all his proud solitude, Wright never imagined that he was fighting merely for himself alone. Although he rejected the mysticism of "race," he believed fiercely in black liberation. In his last public speech, "The Situation of the Negro Artist and Intellectual in American Society," delivered at the American Church on the Quai d'Orsay on November 8, 1960, Wright described the world of black writers as a "nightmarish jungle," set up by a white publishing industry that was only too happy to see them tear one another apart in furies of almost Darwinian competition. He also thundered against black churches and concert halls for ostracizing Paul Robeson, who had been blacklisted and stripped of his passport. As much as he despised Robeson's Communism, he hated Robeson's racist enemies far more: the blacklisting of black intellectuals, he said, had led him to change "my position towards those who are fighting Communism." It emboldened him to know there were American agents in the audience. Shortly after his address, Wright fell ill in his intestinal tract; less than three weeks later, he was dead. (Julia Wright still believes that he was poisoned by the CIA; others blame the KGB.) Thomas Diop, an editor at *Présence Africaine*, gave the eulogy in a closed ceremony at Père Lachaise on December 3. "Dick's body was cremated," Himes writes, "the coffin consumed by flames as Dick's enemies showered praise on his body." "Listen to Dick," Ollie Harrington whispered to him. "He hears what they're saying about him."

{2021}

6

Chester Himes:
Writing Absurdity

On April 21, 1930, a fire broke out in the state penitentiary in Columbus, Ohio, a wretched, segregated prison where more than 4,000 men were packed into a facility built to hold 1,500. By the time it was extinguished, 322 prisoners lay dead, and the National Guard was called in to suppress rioting. Among the survivors was Chester Himes, a twenty-year-old black man serving a twenty-year sentence for armed robbery. Himes had already seen his share of troubles, but, as Lawrence Jackson writes in his impressive biography, they "did not inspire him" the way that "stumbling through the gore of two cell block tiers' worth of burned-alive men" did.[*] After the fire, Himes began to write fiction on a typewriter he had bought with his gambling winnings, and four years later he published a story about the fire in *Esquire*. As the prison was engulfed in flames, Himes had seen its clandestine eroticism come into the open, in a carnival of the damned. A convict called Broadway Rose put on a sex show, and the prison's "boy-girls" offered their services in cells covered by red curtains. In Himes's "To What Red Hell," it's the fire that enables this liberation of desire, before extinguishing it: "Oh, Lawd, ma man's dead," a black prisoner called Beautiful Slim says, mourning his lover. Yet death also has a leveling effect: Blackie, the white protagonist, observes that all the dead, white and black, have the same "smoke-blackened flesh."

---

[*]   *Chester B. Himes*, by Lawrence Jackson (Norton, 2017).

In his novels, Himes depicted the whole of American life as a prison inferno, a blaze of race, sex and power, where freedom could be achieved only in death, or murder. One of the most prolific American writers of his generation, as well as one of its most versatile, Himes published proletarian and prison fiction, bildungsromans, sex romps, blistering tales of interracial manners and flamboyant detective stories set in Harlem. The odd man out in a group of ambitious black male writers who came of age in the 1930s and 1940s and included Richard Wright (born 1908), Ralph Ellison (1914) and James Baldwin (1924), Himes has never quite entered the pantheon. His peers were condescending: Wright never took him seriously as an artist; Ellison, who saw him as little more than an ex-con with a pen, joked that Himes must have been the model for Bigger Thomas, the murderous antihero of Wright's 1940 novel, *Native Son*; Baldwin wrote that "Mr. Himes seems capable of some of the worst writing this side of the Atlantic." Jackson, whose previous book, *The Indignant Generation*, was a formidable history of black American writers from the Depression years to the civil rights era, writes brilliantly about Himes's fraught relations with his black peers as they competed for what little attention the white literary world was willing to grant them, a game Himes described as a "mean and undermining competition with your black brothers for the favors of white folks."

It was a game he could never win. Wright, Ellison and Baldwin were all determined to write the Great American Novel, and took Dostoevsky, Malraux and James as their models. Himes was a reader of European modernism, and of Hemingway and Faulkner ("my secret mentor"), but he mostly wrote genre fiction: existential potboilers, family dramas, ribald comedies, urban noirs. His prose was lean and gritty, and his plots often so dense with incident that they were difficult to follow. The intellectual seriousness of Ellison, the prophetic eloquence of Baldwin, the allegorical fire of Wright: these high notes eluded Himes. He remained just outside the gates of the literary establishment, grumbling at his exclusion. It was only in France, where Himes settled in 1953 and spent more than a decade, that he found himself celebrated as a major writer, the *poète maudit* of black America. Like his mentor Faulkner (and later Cormac McCarthy), Himes appealed to a Parisian readership convinced of the essential savagery of American life.

"What the great body of Americans most disliked" about his work, Himes believed, "was the fact that I came too close to the truth." He wasn't wrong in thinking that something beyond pure aesthetic judgment had prevented him from reaching a wider audience. Long before Himes left America for good, he had committed what, for black writers of the era, was a kind of treason: he depicted racism as a sin without the promise of redemption. Even at their bleakest, Himes's contemporaries hinted at a better world on the horizon. Wright, a socialist, held out the hope of collective action against racism and inequality. Ellison, a Cold War liberal, wrote scathingly about white benefactors in *Invisible Man* but believed in the promise of a racially inclusive American democracy. Baldwin, the gay stepson of a preacher, dreamed that romantic love between a white man and a black man might give birth to "another country." Himes was black American literature's one authentic nihilist. In his novels, solutions to what was then called the "Negro problem"—Communism, Cold War liberalism, integration, "race mixing"—are all subjected to withering ridicule. That he should even be asked to address the "Negro problem" he considered foolish and insulting, "as if this American dilemma of what to do with twenty million descendants of American slaves . . . was some riddle these poor folk had cooked up for the mortification of white intellect and could themselves solve at a moment's notice if they so desired." Merciless toward white liberals, he was equally severe with the black bourgeoisie he was born into. Being light-complexioned himself only intensified his rage at blacks who held themselves aloof from those with darker skin. In his 1945 novel, *If He Hollers Let Him Go*, Bob Jones, a black "leaderman" in an LA shipyard, is at a dinner party with a group of earnest middle-class blacks who ask his opinion on how to "integrate the people of this ghetto into the life of the community." "Well, now," he replies, "I think we ought to kill the colored residents and eat them. In that way we'll not only solve the race problem but alleviate the meat shortage as well."

With his scorn for liberal pieties, Himes won admirers among the black writers who emerged during the Black Power era, such as LeRoi Jones, John A. Williams and Ishmael Reed. And his legacy now? As Jackson writes, "history has borne out some of his vinegary judgments." Today, Himes's belief in the implacable force of white supremacism—what is now called Afro-pessimism—enjoys a growing vogue among black intellectuals. One can detect echoes of his jaundiced vision in Jordan Peele's recent horror film, *Get Out*, and in Paul Beatty's novel *The Sellout*. But, as if it were his destiny to remain just beyond the pale of literary approval, Himes, unlike Baldwin, flunks the contemporary "woke" test. As much as he deplored the prejudices of the black bourgeoisie and aligned himself with poorer, dark-skinned blacks, he was not above comparing one of his characters to an ape. His unsparing depiction of black poverty, his insistence on the sheer ugliness of social misery, seem rather dated in an age when black American writers, artists and filmmakers have been creating more redemptive visions of the inner city.

Then there is the matter of Himes's attitude toward women. Not only was he sometimes brutal toward the women in his life; he explicitly defended his brutality. "The only way to make a white woman listen is to pop her in the eye, or any woman for that matter," he wrote in his memoirs. "But it is presumed only right and justifiable for a black man to beat his own black woman when they need it. But how much more does a black man's white woman need it; maybe she needed it when she became his woman." Jackson refrains from citing this passage, which accurately identifies white hypocrisy only to rationalize spousal abuse, but he makes no secret of Himes's violence, or what drove it: "Chester took up his fists for really only one cause: the prerogative of patriarchy."

The youngest son of educated, middle-class parents, Himes started out on a path that looked relatively auspicious but strayed from it after a series of accidents, never to return. Those accidents came to acquire the appearance of fate—as if, as Jackson puts it, they were "comeuppance for overambition"—and a sense of fate would hang over Himes's novels of proud, articulate men, destroyed by forces beyond their control. He was born in 1909 in Jefferson City, the state capital of Missouri, across the street from the Lincoln Institute, where his father, Joseph, taught blacksmithing and wheelwrighting. Chester's parents were both children of former slaves, members of the "second generation" of African Americans in the postbellum era, but otherwise had little in common. Joseph Himes, a short, dark-skinned man with blue eyes, bowed legs and an aquiline nose, was a "contented and modest artisan" who educated his sons in black history but avoided confrontation with whites. Estelle, Chester's mother, was a pale-skinned beauty from a highly cultivated family of former slaves who were "light-bright-and-damn-near-white"; he described her in his memoir *The Quality of Hurt* (1971) as resembling "a white woman who had suffered a long siege of illness." Chester respected his father, but adored his mother: in his 1954 novel, *The Third Generation*, a wrenching portrait of the family's disintegration, he would depict the mother-son bond in explicitly Oedipal terms. A proud, restless woman who wrote sonnets and played Chopin études for pleasure, Estelle dreamed of what Jackson describes as an elusive "world of refinement and equal rights." Embarrassed by the folkways of poor Southern blacks—their ecstatic worship in church, their sexual mores, their accents—she preferred to mix with those who, like her, were partly descended from Southern aristocracy. She told her sons they must never think of themselves as "colored" or forget their "fine white blood" and kept them from playing with the children of poorer blacks. She was distraught when Chester's fine hair turned kinky, a reminder not only of her husband's "black blood," but her own. Chester's first exposure to the American race war took place inside his own black family.

In 1923, the family suffered a catastrophe that Chester would remember as its foundational trauma. They were living in Pine Bluff, Arkansas, where Joseph had taken a job at Branch Normal, a school for blacks at which Chester was introduced to Shakespeare and Chaucer. One day, in front of an audience of parents and students, Joseph Jr., the middle son, gave a chemistry presentation: a gunpowder demonstration in which he mixed ground saltpeter, ground charcoal and ground glass. Chester was supposed to lend his brother a hand, but Estelle forbade it as punishment for bad behavior. Joseph Jr. miscalculated the ingredients, and the contents of the mortar exploded in his face. Refused treatment at the local hospital because he was black, he was blinded. Chester blamed himself. "That one moment in my life hurt me as much as all the others put together."

To be closer to better medical care, the family moved to St Louis, Missouri. But Joseph couldn't find work as a teacher there, and joined the ranks of black manual workers. In 1924, the family moved again, to Cleveland, where they lived with Joseph's relatives close to Scovil Avenue, otherwise known as the "Bucket of Blood," home to poor, unemployed blacks, and to Eastern European immigrants working in the steel factories, which refused to employ their black neighbors. Estelle—increasingly distant from her husband, who had suffered a devastating loss in prestige, and resentful about having to share a home with his relatives, whom she considered beneath her—moved out with their disabled son. She returned a year later, when Joseph bought a large house on an all-white block, but the marriage continued to crumble. Chester rebelled by wrecking the family car and spending his money on prostitutes working in the "Bucket of Blood," where he lost his virginity to (in his words) "an old fat ugly whore sitting on a stool outside her hovel."

After high school, Chester took a summer job at a luxury hotel, where he had an accident nearly as serious as his brother's. While flirting with two white girls employed by the hotel, he stepped backward through the doors of an elevator. The car had already ascended to the floor above, and Himes fell between thirty and forty feet, shattering his chin, his jaw and all his teeth, as well as his pelvis and three vertebrae. Himes compared the experience to "spattering open like a ripe watermelon." Like his brother, he was turned away from the local hospital, allegedly because of space constraints, before being put into a full body cast at another. "The reality of his wounds and pains," Jackson suggests, "led him to a place of brittle irony with others, and self-pity with himself." The incident further chipped away at the fragile foundations of his parents' marriage. Estelle, the "rebellious dissenter," wanted to sue the hotel, but Joseph persuaded Chester to sign away his claim, since doing so entitled him to a secure pension.

Barely recovered from his injuries but determined to put on a brave face, Himes enrolled at the Ohio State University in Columbus, where he boarded with a black family—the dormitories and fraternity houses were barred to black students. Dressed in a coonskin coat and knickerbocker suit, he drove around town in a used Model T, drank "white mule" (a highly potent form of alcohol developed during Prohibition) and frequented the local bordellos. He avoided whites ("I simply didn't need them, didn't want to know them, and always felt that they couldn't reject me any more than I could reject them") but he was equally put off by the "'light-bright-and-damn-near-white' social clique"—his mother's people. Neglecting his studies, he befriended a thief called Benny Barnett, who taught him to steal cars and introduced him to Jean Lucinda Johnson, a precocious sixteen-year-old whose "skin was the warm reddish brown of a perfectly roasted turkey breast the moment it comes from the oven." She would become his first wife. Himes quit college at seventeen, and began to pack a .44-caliber Colt. "It was much later in life that I came to understand I simply hadn't accepted my status as a 'nigger,'" he wrote in his memoir, elevating his slide into crime as an intuitive revolt against racism. But he was also—in Hilton Als's words—"a child of the bourgeoisie in love with the stars in the gutter," and the gutter nearly swallowed him up. In 1928, he robbed a couple in Cleveland of four rings worth $5,000, and was arrested the next day in a pawn shop. The police forced a confession out of him by hanging him upside down and beating his testicles.

In his memoir, Himes claimed that "nothing happened in prison that I had not already encountered in outside life." Perhaps. But like Jean Genet, who was born a year after him, Himes found in prison a laboratory in which he could observe human behavior under duress. Initially terrified of being raped, he carried a knife to protect himself, but after the fire, Jackson writes, he came to consider "uncoerced situational homosexuality in prison a compensatory and human reflex to the despair of life behind bars." He fell hard for a prisoner known as Prince Rico, who wore a ukulele attached by shoestrings round his neck. In his otherwise frank memoirs—a second volume, *My Life of Absurdity*, appeared in 1976—Himes never mentions Rico, but his 1952 prison novel, *Cast the First Stone* (posthumously published unabridged as *Yesterday Will Make You Cry*), offers a tender account of their romance, though both Rico and Jimmy Monroe, the character based on Himes, appear in whiteface. "Out of all the things that touched him that spring," Himes wrote, "Rico touched him more than anything, Rico, with his morbid, brilliant, insane, unsteady mind and his frenzied beautiful mouth and kaleidoscopic moods and Mona Lisa smile and eyes of pure stardust . . . Poor little kid, he thought, what a terrible mistake that he was not a woman." In a 1952 letter to his friend Carl Van Vechten, Himes admitted, "I was in love with him more, perhaps, than I have ever been in love with anyone before or since."

Some of the black convicts, he wrote, sounding like his mother, struck him as "dull-witted, stupid, uneducated, practically illiterate, slightly above animals," but in the fire of 1930 he also witnessed their capacity for heroism and sacrifice. Before long, his dispatches from prison began to appear regularly in the black literary journal *Abbott's Monthly*, alongside the work of Richard Wright and Langston Hughes. Prison turned out to be an ideal writer's retreat. Thanks to the injuries he sustained in the elevator accident, he was assigned to the "cripple" ward, which meant that he couldn't be forced to do hard labor. He had a roof over his head, regular meals and all the time in the world. That he put his time to such good use showed how deeply influenced he was by his mother's drive and ambition, the values of the black middle class he claimed to despise.

Released from prison in 1936 for good behavior, Himes moved back to Cleveland and married Jean. The success of "To What Red Hell" had raised his expectations of a literary career: Meyer Levin, his editor, told him it had "received the greatest 'curtain

call' of any short story published in *Esquire*." But it would be
another two decades before he could live off his writing. By the
time he was freed, his brother Joseph Jr. had become the director of research for the Urban League, from which position he
would advance smoothly into the professional black middle class.
Already racked by guilt about his brother's blindness, Himes
now envied his success. He managed to pick up odd jobs with
the Federal Writers' Project, but as a black ex-convict who had
never finished college, he was mostly confined to manual labor.
He worked as a ditch-digger, a waiter, and as a groundskeeper
and butler on the estate of Louis Bromfield, a writer of popular
fiction whom he would later send up as the fascist industrialist
Louis Foster in *Lonely Crusade*. His short fiction was being
published, but his prison manuscript was rejected by Doubleday
as too "grim" for its readers.

In 1941, the Himeses moved to Los Angeles. This turned out
to be an even more bruising experience than prison. Chester
hoped to find work as a screenwriter but ended up working in the
shipyards for war production. Jean, meanwhile, became the co-
director of a charity working with the War and Navy Department
to provide leisure activities for soldiers—her success was, he felt,
an insult to his manhood. For all the racial discrimination he had
already endured, Himes insisted in his memoirs that until he came
to Los Angeles, with its brutal, racist police force, he had seen
"nothing racial about my hurt, unbelievable as this may seem."
Like most black writers of his generation, Himes fell into the
orbit of the Communist Party because of its commitment to racial
equality. He hung out with Dalton Trumbo and black veterans
of the Abraham Lincoln Brigade, wrote articles for the *People's
Daily World* and championed a "double V": a victory against
fascism abroad and racism at home. In an article called "Negro
Martyrs Are Needed," which included footnotes citing Marx and
Engels's correspondence, he excoriated the black middle class for
its cowardice, and advocated violent rebellion against "our native
American fascists." A month later, the FBI opened a file on him.

Himes's alliance with the party was intense but short-lived.
He recoiled at its paternalism and came to suspect that his white

comrades were driven by what he described, in an early short story, as a "queer sympathy for the underdog, sensual in its development." They imagined that they had liberated themselves from the prison of race when in fact they still couldn't see beyond its walls. After Pearl Harbor, he wrote, wartime Los Angeles seethed with a "tight, crazy feeling of race as thick in the street as gas fumes," and no one was above the fray. Himes captured the atmosphere better than anyone in his LA novels, *If He Hollers Let Him Go* and *Lonely Crusade*. But of all the injuries inflicted by racism, the one that he resented the most was its destruction of patriarchal masculinity. He had seen his father, an accomplished teacher, reduced to a "shrunken man" after his brother's accident. Now he appeared to be repeating his father's experience, since he was unable to support his wife. Worse, she was supporting him, having taken advantage of opportunities that were appearing for black women but not for black men. He felt like her "pimp," and the fact that "she didn't mind . . . hurt all the more." When he couldn't find work in the shipyards he turned to drink, and in the autumn of 1944 he jumped ship for New York, where he spent the next ten months. When Jean came to visit him, she "found me deeply involved in so many affairs that she tried to take her own life."

In New York, he hung out with his Harlem neighbors Langston Hughes and Ralph Ellison, who had also drifted from the party. In a short story about his New York experiences, published in 1945, he wrote: "I spent half my time thinking about murdering white men. The other half of the time taking my spite out in having white women. And in between, protesting, bellyaching, crying." Still, it was more pleasant than LA: as Himes wrote, New York hurt him "by accepting me." He sold *If He Hollers Let Him Go* to Bucklin Moon at Doubleday, who promised him that he would win the inaugural George Washington Carver Book Award, a prize for the best book about "American Negroes." The story unfolds over a few days in the life of Bob Jones, a man with two years of college who's working in a California shipyard. He is courting the light-skinned daughter of a local physician, but by the end of the novel has been arrested for the attempted rape of a white woman, a menacing "peroxide blonde" called Madge who has accused him mainly because he refuses to sleep with her.

Himes evokes his "trapped, cornered, physical fear," a state of being he shares with Bigger Thomas in Wright's *Native Son*, but the voice Jones speaks in—hardboiled, defiantly black—was unlike anything that had been heard before in American literature: "Race was a handicap, sure, I reasoned. But hell, I didn't have to marry it." As it turns out, he doesn't have a choice: for a black man, race is a forced marriage. Jones is a reasonable man and, precisely because he is a reasonable man, he is an angry man: "The only solution to the Negro problem is a revolution. We've got to make white people respect us and the only thing white people have ever respected is force." That voice won Himes acclaim—from Wright (for once), from the sociologist Horace Cayton, from Frantz Fanon, who admired its emphasis on the inherent violence of racial conflict—but it left his publisher deeply uncomfortable. Doubleday reneged on its promise, giving the Carver Award to Fannie Cook's *Mrs. Palmer's Honey*, a sentimental novel about an illiterate maid who becomes a cheerleader for the New Deal. Himes was even more disappointed by Doubleday's advertisement for that book, which implicitly smeared his own: Cook had written "an honest, intelligent novel, devoid of lynchings, mixed love affairs and profanity."

He poured his hurt into his next, supremely ambitious novel, *Lonely Crusade*, published in 1947, in which he explores the fractures on the home front: class struggle in the shipyards, battles among union organizers, conflicts in the Communist Party, Jewish paternalism and black anti-Semitism, and, not least, the impact of racism on sexual intimacy, both between black men and black women, and between black men and white women. The plot revolves around the pursuit of a mole in the Communist Party and culminates in a grisly revenge killing, but it draws its emotional force from a portrait of a marriage that resembled Himes's own. Lee Gordon, the protagonist, is a black union organizer at the Comstock Aircraft Corporation, married to a black striver called Ruth. He should be the "happiest man in the world," but instead he is consumed by fear of whites, and

sunk in a depression that leaves him feeling "castrated." There's
no way of escaping "white eyes—measuring him, calculating,
conspiring," nor can he take comfort in the company of other
black workers, who strike him as "either too loud or too sullen."
He allows himself to feel "a secret admiration for Japan," while
admitting this is "only the wishful yearning of the disinherited."
Ruth, for her part, has grown tired of being "a sponge for his
brutality," having realized that his fear "had beaten his life into
a weird infirmity, it was a disappointment, as it would have been
to any Negro girl with dreams." Feeling "emasculated" by his
more successful wife, he leaves her for a white communist, Jackie
Forks, who "could give him the illusion of manhood even while
denying that he possessed it, for to her he was the recipient of her
grace." When Ruth learns of the affair, she covers her face with
white powder, as if by magic it could bring him back.

Jean Himes broke down when she read the book and was
found weeping in the desert, a few miles from a ranch in the
Sierra Nevada that they were renting. She wasn't the only one
who couldn't stand it. As Himes remembered, "the left hated
it, the right hated it, Jews hated it, blacks hated it." His closest
literary friends weren't much more supportive. Wright offered
lukewarm praise of its "hard, biting, functional style," but
Ellison, who insisted that the blues sensibility enabled blacks to
"transcend" the "jagged grain" of racism, felt Himes was dangerously obsessed with the psychological damage racism caused.
Langston Hughes declined to blurb the novel, because the characters "behave so badly which makes it difficult to care very much
what happens to any of them." *Lonely Crusade* may have been
the most important novel by a black writer since *Native Son*, as
Jackson argues, but Himes couldn't afford another success of its
kind. He barely published a word for the next five years. In 1948,
he went to Yaddo to revise his prison novel but spent much of
his time getting drunk and trying to seduce Patricia Highsmith, a
twenty-six-year-old Barnard graduate from a Texas slaveholding
family who "consistently tried to tackle Chester on his own turf:
evil and sexuality." Himes was writing about his affair with Rico
while Highsmith, who was coming to terms with her own sexual

preference, was writing *Strangers on a Train*. She followed him into his room one night but rebuffed him when he tried to kiss her. The most significant piece of writing he did that year was a speech in Chicago on the "dilemma of the Negro artist." "If this plumbing for truth reveals within the Negro personality homicidal mania, lust for white women, a pathetic sense of inferiority, paradoxical anti-Semitism, arrogance, Uncle Tomism, hate and fear and self-hate," he said, "this then is the effect of oppression on the human personality." The writer who exposed this "truth," he added rather self-flatteringly, would be "reviled by the Negroes and the whites alike." No one applauded.

For the next few years, Himes lived in a room on Convent Avenue in Harlem, while plotting his escape to France, where Wright had urged him to move. He did occasional menial work, avoided his more successful friends and licked his wounds. He separated from Jean but was too ashamed to tell anyone, above all Ellison, who was soon to be lauded for *Invisible Man*. But in his hibernation Himes managed to finish two still underrated books, both quiet and intimate, with flashes of Faulknerian stream of consciousness: the prison novel, *Cast the First Stone*, and a thinly disguised portrait of his family, *The Third Generation*. The protagonist of *Cast the First Stone*, Jimmy Monroe, is a young white convict struggling to accept his love for another man. *The Third Generation* (originally titled *The Cord*) explores the ruinous consequences of black self-hatred but avoids political commentary, instead immersing the reader in the consciousness, the pleasures and agonies, of its characters. Himes sold both books in 1952, and began to show his face in public again.

"The first thing I desired now that I had money was to sleep with a white woman, and the only woman in the city I knew at the time who was likely to sleep with me was Vandi Haygood," Himes reported in his memoirs, as if she were merely an easy lay. In fact, as Jackson points out, Himes cared deeply for Haygood, who ran the Rosenwald Fund's fellowship program. He moved into her flat on Gramercy Park, but when he discovered she had another lover he beat her up so badly she couldn't leave the house for two weeks. He later threatened her at a party with a butcher's cleaver, and had to be subdued by his frenemy Ellison, which added humiliation to his embarrassment. Himes described his 1955 novel about their boozy, violent affair, *The End of a Primitive*, in which a black writer frees himself from his status as a "primitive" in the eyes of his white mistress by murdering her in their hotel room, as "rather exact except that I didn't kill her." Two days before he sailed to France in April 1953, he broke his big toe when he kicked her with his bare foot. He spent his last night in the States alone in a hotel room, "nursing my broken toe, and hating Vandi."

On the deck of the *Ile de France*, Himes met the woman with whom he would spend the next two years: Willa Thompson, the American ex-wife of a dentist and Nazi sympathizer from Luxembourg who had abused her for sheltering a downed Allied airman. Willa ("Alva" in Himes's memoir) was blonde, slender and emotionally brittle, a daughter of the New England upper class whose sophistication and reserve reminded him of his mother. Recognizing how "very hurt by life" she was, Himes writes, he had hesitated to kiss her, "as though kissing her would have been wrong. I wanted only to comfort her. How strange we blacks are. I did not want to make the slightest gesture that might disturb her, as though she were my patient and I were her nurse." When they finally made love in a cramped Paris hotel room, he took her "small, trembling body in my arms . . . What mattered to her was she had lost herself in the darkness of my race. She had hid from all her hurts and humiliations. In a strange and curious way, by becoming my mistress, the mistress of a man who'd never been entirely free, she had freed herself." But he soon separated from Thompson too, and threw himself into an affair with a highly unstable young German woman, Regine Fischer ("Marlene" in his memoir), and, as he put it, "tried to bury ambition, resentment, pity and all the rest, all the past hurts and future fears into her too-young, exaggeratedly tufted dark blonde German vagina." They moved into a room on the rue Buci, and had at one point so little money they had to eat "dog meat cooked with leeks to kill the odor." When she seemed to express renewed interest in her old boyfriend, the black expatriate communist Ollie Harrington, he beat her in what Jackson calls a "blind insensate fury." He said he couldn't help himself because he was a "dirty nigger-beast." She wasn't persuaded.

Himes didn't adjust easily to life abroad. Visiting Paris in the mid-1950s, Ellison found him "as tortured as ever," still "in love with a vision of absolute hell." Himes had no illusions that white Europeans would be different from American whites, but this knowledge was no help when he wanted to get a hotel room with a white woman. He gave up on learning French when his translator, hearing his French, replied: "You must forgive an uncultured Frenchman such as myself, but I do not understand English so well." He never felt entirely comfortable among his "soul brothers," the black American writers and artists in Paris who gathered around their "king" Richard Wright at the Café Monaco and the Café Tournon. "At times my soul brothers embarrassed me, bragging about their scars, their poor upbringing, and their unhappy childhood, to get some sympathy and some white pussy, and money, too, if they could. It was a new variety of Uncle Toming, a modern version." Himes reserved his hurts for the bedroom and the page, the only places he felt truly himself.

Escaping America was harder than it looked, and as ever he needed a trauma to inspire his imagination. A ten-month visit to New York in 1955 provided it in abundance. He arrived there a defeated man: his editor had rejected *The End of a Primitive* ("It's unthinkable for us, and I really wouldn't know who to suggest as a prospect for it in this country. Even with expurgation"). His relationship with Thompson, already frayed, was about to fall apart. That summer, Emmett Till, a fourteen-year-old African American in Mississippi, was lynched for allegedly whistling at a white woman. In New York, Himes was so down on his luck that he was forced to pawn his typewriter; each morning, he stood in line with other men hoping to get a day's work washing dishes. Meanwhile, he noticed *If He Hollers Let Him Go* being sold as a mass-market paperback at nearly every newsstand. With the help of a lawyer, he got a royalty cheque that enabled him to buy a ticket back to France. If he had stayed, he told a friend, he would have killed someone.

Only after he returned to Paris did Himes realize that, grim as his time in New York had been, it was a gold mine for his writing. In Harlem, he had studied "the way of life of the sporting classes, its underworld and vice and spoken language, its absurdities." And when he looked at himself—a "famous but destitute" novelist who could barely afford a typewriter—he had an epiphany: "My life itself was so absurd I saw everything as absurd." He began to take a more forgiving view of the soul brothers at the Café Tournon, for they too were absurd: "unique individuals, funny but not clowns, solemn but not serious, hurt but not suffering, sexualists but not whores." (He wrote a novel about the Tournon scene, *A Case of Rape*.) He understood now that he had always been "writing absurdity" even when he thought he'd been "writing realism," because "realism and absurdity are so similar in the lives of American blacks one cannot tell the difference."

Himes's first work of absurdism was a sexual farce called *Pinktoes*, black male slang for fetching white women. He based the heroine, Mamie Mason, "the uptown hostess with the mostess," on his cousin Mollie Moon (a friend but no relation of his editor at Doubleday), whose decadent interracial parties had helped promote the cause of "civil rights in the bedroom." As the jacket cover read, Mason "solved the integration problem with one bright idea: SEX." With *Pinktoes*, Himes declared riotous war on American puritanism, that secret sharer of white supremacy. He had often wondered why Americans censored the word "fuck," the profanity that "expressed the most pleasurable, the most meaningful, the most necessary function of human life. Was it a black word? Like nigger? But nigger got by. Nigger had always passed the censors. Must be passing for white." Himes had difficulty publishing the book: one editor told him he had "put too much burden on comic situation and done too little with plot and structure." But as Jackson writes, Himes was "more interested in brilliant virtuoso soloing than swinging a melody involving multiple complex parts." When *Pinktoes* was finally published in 1961, it became Himes's first bestseller, and prefigured the novels of black absurdists like Ishmael Reed and Paul Beatty.

Himes's real breakthrough, however, came with his series of comic noirs, set in Harlem, about the tough, seen-it-all detectives Coffin Ed Johnson and Grave Digger Jones, in which he put his 1955 "research" to inspired use. It was his French translator, Marcel Duhamel, the director of La Série Noire at Gallimard, who suggested that he try his hand at detective fiction. "We don't give a damn who's thinking what—only what they're doing," Duhamel advised him. He took this to heart. He depicted what he called "the big turbulent sea of black humanity which is Harlem," high and low, illuminating its garish surfaces while skirting the psychological interiority—and the hurt—that had been his speciality. He wrote the first novel in the series, *The Real Cool Killers*, while drinking two bottles of wine a day, washed down with Jamaican rum, and reading Faulkner's *Sanctuary*, his "bible of absurdity." He felt as if he was writing directly from "the American black's secret mind." The Coffin Ed Johnson and Grave Digger Jones novels were less "serious" than his earlier work, but in their irreverent vision of Harlem's human comedy, they expanded the terrain of American literary expression, and they were so stripped down and cartoonish that they suggested a kind of black Pop Art. One of those novels, *Cotton Comes to Harlem*, was made into a film by Ossie Davis in 1970, but Himes felt ripped off by the cinematic genre of Blaxploitation that his noirs had helped inspire. As Jackson puts it, he "considered himself the primary person exploited."

The Harlem novels were praised in Paris by Jean Cocteau and Jean Giono, who said he would "give you all of Hemingway, Dos Passos and Steinbeck for this Chester Himes." In a 1966 review in the *TLS*, Patricia Highsmith, his old Yaddo mate, called his detective fiction the work of a novelist who had "mellowed," thereby achieving genuine literary distinction. Himes celebrated his success by buying a Jaguar and boasting that it was his "main purpose" for writing crime fiction. In fact, he "only felt at home in my detective stories," which he came to consider his most important achievement. But it's possible that Himes also worried that he had retreated from the uncompromising fury of his novels of hurt. As Jackson notes, the Harlem novels were "blues tales," without "arguments about civil rights or the psychological dynamics of racial oppression." Although he wouldn't have admitted it, Himes was using the blues to transcend the absurd ordeals of black life, not unlike his old antagonist Ellison.

Off the page, Himes remained an angry loner. He distanced himself from Wright, feeling disrespected. When Wright died in 1960, he was the most prestigious black American writer left in Paris, but he declined to assume Wright's throne and suspected younger black writers of patronizing him. In his 1963 novel, *The Stone Face*, William Gardner Smith, one of the Tournon soul brothers, pictured a writer like Himes emerging "from his apartment now and then to drink heavily and launch an ironic tirade against the United States and the white world in general." The only black intellectual Himes praised without reservation was Malcolm X, whom he befriended on a brief visit to New York in 1962. As fellow ex-convicts from bourgeois homes with light-skinned mothers and dark-skinned fathers, they "understood each other perfectly," although Himes chastised him for allying himself with Arabs, whom he dismissed as "slave traders." (He modeled the Sheik in *The Real Cool Killers* on Malcolm.) Himes had left America, but it never left him, and he followed the urban revolts back home with close attention. During the hot summer of 1967, when his friend LeRoi Jones was arrested in Newark and charged with carrying a concealed revolver, he wrote that most black Americans "were never seen until they lie bloody and dead from a policeman's bullet on the hot dirty pavement of a ghetto street."

In 1967, Himes moved to southern Spain with Lesley Packard, a British journalist. They remained there until his death in 1984. Their bond was initially tested by Himes's numerous infidelities, but it evolved into a stable partnership, and they were married in 1978, as soon as Himes was able to get a divorce from Jean, his first wife. In perhaps his most famous commentary on interracial intimacy, Himes wrote: "Emotions between black men and white women are erratic, like a brush fire in a high wind." In his relationship with Packard, he found an exception to what had been, in his experience, a destructive pattern. Like absurdity, love required another country to bloom. They spent their best years in the coastal town of Moraira, ten of them under fascist rule: such were the paradoxes of exile. And exile it was: as Jackson makes clear, Himes had good reason to think that he couldn't survive as a black writer in America; to call him an "expatriate" is to see the pull factor but not the push. It was in Moraira that Himes wrote his memoirs, *The Quality of Hurt* and *My Life of Absurdity*. Widely dismissed when they were published, together they comprise one of the great autobiographies of literary exile, brave in its self-scrutiny, meticulous in its anatomy of the physical and emotional toll of racism, gripping in its portrait of a sensitive, volatile, sometimes monstrous man. Jackson's biography adds much to the record, but the memoirs, which deserve to be reprinted, remain indispensable for what Himes called their "hurting knowledge," which he had acquired at great cost. All his life, Himes confessed, he had been looking for "somewhere black people weren't considered the shit of the earth. It took me forty years to discover that such a place does not exist." By then, however, he could look back and laugh.

{2018}

7

"How does it feel to be a white man?": William Gardner Smith's Exile in Paris

In 1951, in an essay titled "I Choose Exile," the novelist Richard Wright explained his decision to resettle in Paris after the war. "It is because I love freedom," he declared, "and I tell you frankly that there is more freedom in one square block of Paris than there is in the entire United States of America!" Few of the black Americans who made Paris their home from the 1920s to the civil rights era would have quarreled with Wright's claim. For novelists such as Wright, Chester Himes and James Baldwin, for artists and musicians such as Josephine Baker, Sidney Bechet and Beauford Delaney, Paris offered a sanctuary from segregation and discrimination, as well as an escape from American puritanism—an experience as far as possible from the "damaged life" that Theodor Adorno considered to be characteristic of exile. You could stroll down the street with a white lover or spouse without being jeered at, much less physically assaulted; you could check into a hotel or rent an apartment wherever you wished so long as you could pay for it; you could enjoy, in short, something like normalcy, arguably the most seductive of Paris's gifts to black American exiles.

Baldwin, who moved to Paris in 1948, a year after Wright, embraced the gift at first but came to distrust it, suspecting that it was an illusion, and a costly one at that. While blacks "armed with American passports" were rarely the target of racism, Africans and Algerians from France's overseas colonies, he realized, were not so lucky. In his 1961 essay "Alas, Poor Richard," published just after Wright's death, he accused his mentor of celebrating Paris as a "city of refuge" while remaining silent about France's oppressive treatment of its colonial subjects: "It did not seem worthwhile to me to have fled the native fantasy only to embrace a foreign one."* Baldwin recalled that when an African joked to him that Wright mistook himself for a white man, he had risen to Wright's defense. But the remark led him to "wonder about the uses and hazards of expatriation":

> I did not think I was white, either, or I did not *think* I thought so. But the Africans might think I did, and who could blame them? . . . When the African said to me, *I believe he thinks he's white*, he meant that Richard cared more about his safety and comfort than he cared about the black condition . . . Richard was able, at last, to live in Paris exactly as he would have lived, had he been a white man, here, in America. This may seem desirable, but I wonder if it is. Richard paid the price such an illusion of safety demands. The price is a turning away from, ignorance of, all of the powers of darkness.

"Alas, Poor Richard," like Baldwin's famous critique of Wright's *Native Son*, was an exercise in self-portraiture, if not self-congratulation. By then Baldwin had come home to America and joined the civil rights struggle that Wright, nursing his wounds in his exile, preferred to observe from afar. But in his autobiographical story "This Morning, This Evening, So Soon," published in 1960, Baldwin implied that he too might

---

* One wonders if Baldwin read Wright's 1954 book on African independence struggles, *Black Power*, which contains a number of scathing criticisms of French colonialism: "It's a desperate young black French colonial who resolves to return to his homeland and face the wrath of white Frenchmen who'll kill him for his longing for the freedom of his own nation, but who'll give him the *Légion d' honneur* for being French."

have ended up the butt of an African's joke if he had stayed. The narrator, a black expatriate reflecting upon his estrangement from the Algerian "boys I used to know during my first years in Paris," remarks that "I once thought of the North Africans as my brothers and that is why I went to their cafés." But while he "could not fail to recognize" their "rage" at the French, which reminds him of his own rage at white Americans, "I could not hate the French, because they left me alone. And I love Paris, I will always love it."

Perhaps because he was grateful to the city that had "saved my life by allowing me to find out who I am," Baldwin never gave us a novel about the "uses and hazards of expatriation." This achievement belongs, instead, to a long-forgotten writer three years his junior, William Gardner Smith, a Philadelphian who moved to Paris in 1951 and died there in 1974, at the age of forty-seven, of leukemia. A journalist by trade, Smith published four novels and one work of nonfiction. The most striking of his books—and his deepest inquiry into the ambiguities of exile—is *The Stone Face*, a novel set in Paris against the backdrop of the Algerian War. Long out of print—the hardcover edition goes for $629.99 on Amazon, roughly $3 a page—it was published in 1963, the same year as *The Fire Next Time*. If it lacks Baldwin's prophetic eloquence, it radiates a similar sense of moral urgency. But where *The Fire Next Time* reflects Baldwin's return to his native land, his reckoning with its defining injustice, *The Stone Face* explores a black exile's discovery of the suffering of others: an injustice perpetrated by his host country, a place he initially mistakes for paradise.

Simeon Brown, the protagonist, is a young black American journalist and painter who begins to question France's self-image as a color-blind society as he witnesses the racism experienced by Algerians in Paris and becomes aware of their struggle for independence back home. At once a bildungsroman and a novel of commitment, *The Stone Face* resonates with contemporary concerns about privilege and identity, but its treatment of these questions is defiantly heterodox. Among the beneficiaries of privilege in the novel are Simeon's black expatriate peers, who refuse to support the Algerian struggle, partly because they're afraid of being expelled from France but also because they'd rather not be associated with a despised minority. They are not perpetrators of anti-Algerian racism, but they are passive bystanders, clinging to the inclusion they've been denied at home. *The Stone Face* is an antiracist novel about identity, but also a subtle and humane critique of a politics that is based narrowly on identity.

The Martinican poet Aimé Césaire memorably imagined a gathering of the oppressed at the "rendezvous of victory," but in *The Stone Face* the West's victims—black, Arab and Jew—are often bitterly at odds in their struggle for a place at the table. One of the Algerian characters explodes into an anti-Semitic tirade, accusing Algeria's Jews of being traitors to the national cause, worse than the colonialists themselves. Stung by this outburst, Simeon's Polish Jewish girlfriend, Maria, a concentration camp survivor, begs him to forget about race and the Algerian question and live a "normal" life, but, unlike her, Simeon does not have the option (or the desire) to fully disappear into whiteness. No one in *The Stone Face* is impervious to intolerance or moral blindness. (In a somewhat clumsy metaphor, both Simeon and Maria are visually impaired: one of his eyes was gouged out in a racist attack; she is undergoing surgery to avoid going blind.) The title alludes to the hateful face of racism, and Smith suggests it lies within all of us.

Fighting the stone face, Simeon learns, is not simply a matter of defending one's own people, and sometimes requires actively breaking with them. By the end of the novel, he has repudiated "racial" loyalty to his black American brethren in favor of a more dangerous solidarity with Algerian rebels. In its embrace of internationalism, the novel argues powerfully that exile needn't be a delusional fantasy or a solipsistic flight from one's ethical obligations. What matters, what is ultimately "black," for Smith, is not a question of one's identity or location but of conscience, and the action it inspires.

Born in 1927, Smith grew up in South Philadelphia, in a black working-class neighborhood of one of the North's most racist cities. By the time he was fourteen he had already been stripped naked and beaten with a rubber hose by police officers who felt that "I lacked proper respect." At nineteen he was assaulted at a nightclub by a mob of white sailors who thought that his light-skinned date was a white woman.

A precocious student of literature, Smith read the same novelists as most aspiring writers in mid-century America: Hemingway and Faulkner, Proust and Dostoyevsky. Keen to begin publishing, he turned down scholarships at Lincoln and Howard to take a job at a black-owned newspaper, the *Pittsburgh Courier*. But what really set him on his course as a novelist was being drafted into the army. In the summer of 1946 Smith went to occupied Berlin as a clerk-typist with the 661st TC Truck Company. He spent eight months in Germany, and by August 1947 he had completed a draft of a novel, *Dark Tide over Deutschland*. Farrar, Straus & Company paid him $500 for the manuscript and published it in 1948 under the title *Last of the Conquerors*. A reviewer in the *New York Times* described the novel—the story of a love affair between a black soldier in Berlin and a German woman, with strong echoes of *A Farewell to Arms*—as "a revealing example of the tendency of minority groups . . . to project themselves into a fantasy world in which they enjoy rights that are inherently, if not actually, theirs."

Yet the love between Hayes Dawkins and Ilse Mueller is no fantasy, even if it is endangered by the racism of the American army, which polices "fraternizing" between black soldiers and German women. To read *Last of the Conquerors* today is to grasp that it is out of such "fantasy worlds" that freedom is ultimately born. "I had lain on the beach many times," Hayes muses, "but never before with a white girl. A white girl. Here, away from the thought of differences for a while, it was odd how quickly I forgot it . . . Odd, it seemed to me, that here, in the land of hate, I should find this one all-important phase of democracy. And suddenly I felt bitter." More than any novel of its time, *Last of the Conquerors* captured the paradoxes of the black American soldier's experience in Europe. Hayes has come to the Old World as a "liberator," but he serves in a segregated army that, for all its talk of spreading democracy, has imported the racist practices of Jim Crow.* And like many of his fellow black soldiers, he has his first taste of freedom in the arms of a white German woman—and in a country that has slaughtered millions of people on racial grounds.

Hayes is keenly aware of his good fortune in Germany—and also of how strange and precarious it is: "*Wonder how many Negroes were lynched in the South this year . . . Wonder how many Congressmen are shouting white supremacy . . . Nice being here in Berlin. Nice being here in Germany where the Nazis were once rulers. Nice being so far away that I can wonder—but not be affected.*" Once his affair with Ilse is discovered, however, his superiors in the army do everything they can to keep the lovers apart, working closely with former Nazis in the local *polizei* no less eager to separate "the races." Nor is this the only prejudice they share. "Men, I forgot," Hayes's white captain says one evening, during an after-hours drinking session, "there was one good feature about Hitler and the Nazis":

> We waited for the one feature. "They got rid of the Jews." A bolt of tenseness landed in the room. You could not see or hear it, but you could feel it land. The German girls were especially struck . . . "Only thing. Only good thing they did . . . We ought to do that in the States . . . Jews take all the money . . . Take all the stores and banks. Greedy. Want everything. Don't leave anything for the people. Did it in Germany and Hitler was smart. Got rid of them. Doin' it now in the States. Take the country over and Americans ain't got nothing to say about it."

After returning to Philadelphia, Smith attended Temple University on the GI Bill, helped organize demonstrations against police brutality and studied Marx. (His ties to communists and Trotskyists raised the suspicion of the FBI, which would keep a file on him for the next two decades.) He married a black woman from the South Side, Mary Sewell; received a fellowship from Yaddo; and published a novel, *Anger at Innocence* (1950), a

---

* As James Q. Whitman has shown in *Hitler's American Model*, these practices were closely studied by Nazi jurists.

story about a love affair between a middle-aged white man and a white female pickpocket half his age. But for all his success, Smith felt suffocated by racism and McCarthyism, and feared, as he later told an interviewer on French television, that if he stayed in America he would end up killing someone. The Trinidadian Marxist C. James suggested that he try living in France and gave him Wright's address on the rue Monsieur le Prince near the Panthéon.

In 1951, the Smiths sailed to France. They moved into a tiny hotel room for $1.60 a night, until they could find an apartment. He found a job at Agence France Presse (AFP), profiled Wright for *Ebony*, and became a drinking companion of Chester Himes and the great cartoonist Ollie Harrington at the Café Tournon, a haunt of black writers and artists near the Luxembourg Gardens. He published a new novel, *South Street* (1954), about a black American radical who has returned from exile in Africa. But the reviews were lukewarm, and he felt that he'd "come to a dead end" and no longer wanted to follow "the road of protest." He took a long hiatus from fiction, divorced, and met the woman who became his second wife, Solange Royez, a schoolteacher from the French Alps whose mother had fled Nazi Germany as a child. Marrying a Frenchwoman reinforced his self-perception as an exile. So did the scrutiny of the American government, which declined to renew his passport in 1956, shortly after a visit he had made to East Berlin. For the next few years he lived in Paris as a "stateless" person.

"Youth was the most outstanding characteristic of William Gardner Smith—youth and naïveté," Himes wrote. But courage was another. Most of the black American exiles in Paris adhered to the unspoken agreement with the French government that, in return for sanctuary, they would not intervene in "internal" affairs, above all the sensitive question of French rule in Algeria, which was officially considered a part of France and divided into three departments. As Richard Gibson, a member of the Tournon circle, recalled, "There was a lot of sympathy for the Algerian national struggle among the American writers, but the problem was, how could you speak out and still stay in France?"

Even before the war of independence broke out in November 1954, Smith wrote about the oppression of Algerians in France. In an article for the *Pittsburgh Courier*, he described sitting on the terrace of the Café de Flore and overhearing racist chatter about an Algerian rug-seller who'd passed by: "A bell rings somewhere in your head. Echo from another land. You finish your beer and go home, tired, to bed." As Edward Said has written, "Because the exile sees things both in terms of what has been left behind and what is actual here and now, there is a double perspective that never sees things in isolation. From that juxtaposition one gets a better, perhaps even more universal idea of how to think, say, about a human rights issue."

Yet exile alone does not guarantee this "double perspective." It requires time, reflection and, above all, vigilance, since—as Baldwin observed acidly, and perhaps unfairly, of Wright—the adoptive country's acceptance, and pleasures, can prevent it from forming. In *The Stone Face*, Smith chronicles the emergence of Simeon's double perspective in three briskly told parts whose titles suggest his shifting identities: "The Fugitive," "The White Man" and "The Brother." When Simeon arrives in Paris in the spring of 1960, he is a refugee from America's race war—the first physical detail Smith supplies is that he has only one eye. Haunted by the monstrous face of his attacker, a "stone face" disfigured by rage, with "fanatic, sadistic and cold" eyes, he is trying, at the novel's opening, to reproduce it on canvas, the "*unman*, the face of discord, the face of destruction." This is, literally, art therapy: "I left to prevent myself from killing a man," he confesses.

At first, Paris enables Simeon to heal, as he rejoices in the disappearance of the color line and falls into the soft embrace of the black American expatriate scene. In swift, deft strokes, Smith sketches the geography of what the historian Tyler Stovall calls "Paris noir": the soul-food restaurant run by Leroy Haynes in Montmartre, the Tournon and Monaco cafés, the bookshop near Wright's apartment on rue Monsieur le Prince, the jazz clubs. Himes makes a cameo as the grouchy novelist James Benson, a "strange cat, a sort of hermit" who "disappears into his apartment with whatever girl he happens to be living with," and occasionally emerges to curse the white world and the American government. It's at the Tournon that Simeon first sees Maria, an aspiring actress determined to forget her childhood in the camps, where she was protected by a Nazi guard who took a twisted interest in her: "This child-role was a mask; there were night-mares inside her head." Smith tenderly describes the beginning of their love affair as a meeting of survivors in the city of refuge.

What shatters Simeon's idyll is his growing awareness that while he has fled the stone face in America, it is no less present in France—in the country where he's at last able to breathe freely. At first he's too happy to pay much attention to the headlines in the papers: MOSLEMS RIOT IN ALGIERS, FIFTY DEAD. But when he sees a man "with swarthy skin and long crinkly hair" pushing a vegetable cart, he wonders if he might be Algerian, and remembers how a group of white people in Philadelphia "had stared at him—and how he had stared back, sullen, defiant, detesting their nice clothes and leisure and lazy, inquisitive eyes." Soon after, Simeon gets into a scuffle with an Algerian man, and both of them end up in the back of a police wagon. Simeon notices that the sergeant addresses Hossein with the familiar *tu* while using the polite *vous* with him. While Hossein is locked up for the night, Simeon is released. "You don't understand," the police officer tells him. "You don't know how they are, *les Arabes* . . . They're a plague; you're a foreigner, you wouldn't know."

The next day he runs into Hossein, who asks him: "Hey! How does it feel to be a white man? . . . We're the niggers here! Know what the French call us—*bicot, melon, raton, nor'af.*" One of Hossein's friends, Ahmed, an introspective young medical student from a Berber family in Kabylia, invites him to dinner the following evening. They hop onto a bus together:

The further north the bus moved, the more drab became the build-ings, the streets and the people . . . It was like Harlem, Simeon thought, except that there were fewer cops in Harlem . . . The men he saw through the window of the bus had whiter skins and less frizzly hair, but they were in other ways like the Negroes in the United States. They adopted the same poses: "stashing" on corners, ready for and scared of the ever-possible "trouble," eyes sullen and distrusting.

Noticing that Simeon's attention has wandered, Ahmed asks him, "Where are you?" "Home," he replies.

Yet the Algerians, to Simeon's disappointment, do not "break into smiles and rush to embrace him shouting: 'Brother!' They kept their distance, considering him with caution, as they would a Frenchman—or an American." The fact that he is "racially" black does not make him an ally in their eyes; he must prove himself first. In *The Stone Face*, whiteness is not a skin color or a "racial" trait; it is, rather, a synonym for situational privilege. Relinquishing it, Smith suggests, is a difficult process, especially for an oppressed man who's barely begun to enjoy it. In a pivotal scene, Simeon brings his Algerian friends to a private club that he could never have joined in America. People at other tables whisper as they enter; the host is chillier than usual: "To his own astonishment, Simeon felt uneasy. Why was that?" Perhaps "he was afraid of something. Of losing something. Acceptance, perhaps. The word made him wince. Of feeling humiliation again. For one horrible instant he found himself *withdrawing* from the Algerians—the pariahs, the untouchables! . . . Sitting here with the Algerians he was a nigger again to the eyes that stared. A nigger to the outside eyes—that was what his emotions had fled." An argument erupts between a white woman and one of Simeon's friends, but Simeon, shamed by his initial response, rallies to his friend's defense and feels, for the first time, "at one with the Algerians. He felt strangely *free*—the wheel had turned full circle."

Simeon's black friends at the Tournon frown upon his decision to disavow his privilege: they have no desire to place their security in France in jeopardy. "Forget it, man," one of them says. "Algerians are white people. They feel like white people when they're with Negroes, don't make no mistake about it. A black man's got enough trouble in the world without going about defending white people." Maria is even more alarmed by Simeon's deepening attachment to his Algerian friends, one of whom—to Simeon's horror—has expressed a violent suspicion of Jews in her presence. Why, she asks, can't he "simply accept happiness" instead of "seeking complications"? After all, he fled a life of racism in America; must he continue to fight it here? "Perhaps the Negro who might want to marry you might not be able to flee," he replies. "Not forever. Because of something inside . . ."

That "something inside" is Simeon's conscience, and Smith describes what causes it to stir with extraordinary precision, in a remarkably authentic description of the Algerian War's impact on the *métropole*. As Simeon is taken into the confidence of his Algerian friends, he learns of the existence of detention centers and camps inside France, and of a network of French supporters for the resistance, the so-called *porteurs de valises*, or baggage carriers. He meets two young women, Algerian survivors of French prisons, one of whom was tortured in front of her father and fiancé with electrodes applied to her genitals; the other raped with a broken champagne bottle. And in the last pages of the novel, Smith provides a wrenching account of the police massacre of Algerian protestors on October 17, 1961—the only one that exists in the fiction of the period. (The first French novel to broach the topic, Didier Daeninckx's *Meurtres pour mémoire*, was published in 1984.) Smith's French publisher told him it was "very courageous to have written the book, but we can't publish it in France." Unlike his other books, *The Stone Face*, his only novel set in Paris, has never been translated into French.[*]

The October 17 massacre took place in response to a peaceful demonstration called by the National Liberation Front (FLN) to protest a curfew imposed on all Algerians in Paris. Its architect was the head of the Paris police, Maurice Papon, who had successfully concealed his involvement in the deportation of more than 1,600 Jews in Bordeaux during the war, and gone on to serve as the police prefect in the Constantinois region of Algeria, where he presided over the torture of rebel prisoners. The FLN had killed eleven policemen in the Paris region since August,

---

[*] Thanks in part to the reissue from New York Review of Books Classics, Smith's novel was translated into French in 2021, under the title *Le Visage de Pierre*.

and, at one of their funerals on October 2, Papon boasted that "for one hit taken we shall give back ten." Under his orders, the demonstration was brutally suppressed; hundreds of protesters were killed, some in the street that evening, their bodies thrown into the Seine; others were beaten to death inside police stations over the next few days.* As Smith writes: "Theoretically, French police charges were aimed at splitting demonstrations into small pockets, and dispersing the demonstrators; but it was clear that tonight the police were out for blood . . . Along the Seine, police lifted unconscious Algerians from the ground and tossed them into the river." Simeon sees a woman with a baby being clubbed, punches the officer who's attacking her, and ends up, again, in the back of a police van. But this time one of the Algerians riding alongside him says, "*Salut, frère*"—"Hello, brother."

The original draft of *The Stone Face* ended with Simeon heading to Africa, as his Algerian friends have urged him. In the final version, Simeon decides that it's time to go home, where civil rights activists are "fighting a battle harder than that of any guerrillas in any burnt mountains. Fighting the stone face." Some admirers of the novel have interpreted its conclusion as a regrettable failure of nerve, a retreat from the cosmopolitan solidarity it otherwise promotes—in Paul Gilroy's words, a "capitulation to the demands of a narrow version of cultural kinship that Smith's universalizing argument appears to have transcended." But there is another way of understanding Simeon's decision. The Algerian struggle has not only given him the courage to confront the stone face he fled; it has transformed his understanding of American racism by inscribing it in a wider history of Western domination. When Simeon refers to black Americans, he now calls them "America's Algerians."

A longing for home, if not Eden itself, is, of course, a recurring theme in the modern novel; Georg Lukács argued that the form

---

* In 1998, the French government acknowledged that a massacre had taken place but placed the death toll at "several dozen"; in *La Bataille de Paris*, Jean-Luc Einaudi estimates that 325 were killed. The most comprehensive study of the "battle of Paris," Jim House and Neil MacMaster's *Paris 1961: Algerians, State Terror, and Memory*, concludes that "a conclusive or definitive figure . . . will never be arrived at."

itself is shaped by a sense of "transcendental homelessness" in a world abandoned by God. In *The Stone Face*, the world has been deserted not by a higher power but by justice, which humans alone can create: in its absence, "home is where the hatred is," in the words of Gil Scott-Heron. Yet the critics of *The Stone Face* have a point. Smith obviously agonized over his exile from America, which separated him not only from his family but from black America at a time of revolutionary upheaval. "I sometimes feel guilty living way over here," he wrote his younger sister, "especially when I hear about 'freedom marches' and the like." But he had little interest in moving back to a country he disliked "not only racially, but also politically and culturally." Instead he left his job at AFP and went to Ghana, where W. E. B. Du Bois's widow, Shirley Graham Du Bois, had invited him to help her launch the independent state's first television station. He flew to Accra in August 1964 with Solange and their one-year-old daughter, Michèle, and moved into a big house on the sea provided by Kwame Nkrumah's government.

"For the first time in a long time I feel very useful!" he wrote his mother shortly after his arrival. "This country is going places—Nkrumah is a real African patriot, and he wants his country to develop fast. The people walk proud and tall." He met other prominent African American writers living in Accra, including Maya Angelou and Julian Mayfield, and spent an evening talking to Malcolm X when Malcolm swept into town in November, three months before his assassination. In those early days, Smith allowed himself to dream that he'd come back home. Sounding not unlike Simeon among the Algerians of northern Paris, he wrote that on the boulevards of Accra he "felt, sometimes, as though I were walking down a street in South Philadelphia, Harlem, or Chicago. These black people in their multicolored robes, with their laughter, with their rhythmic gait, were my cousins." In July 1965 he affirmed his bond with the African motherland when Solange gave birth to their son, Claude.

Smith's African dream, however, disintegrated even more rapidly than his Paris reverie. While the "visible signs of black sovereignty" in Nkrumah's Ghana still moved him, he saw that "the Black Power of Ghana" had "grave limitations." He also realized that "the idea of black American nationalists, summed up in the phrase, 'We are black, therefore we are brothers,' is incomprehensible in tribal societies where the hereditary enemies have, precisely, been black. For the Ibo of Eastern Nigeria, the Hausa of the North is a much more fearful, deadly and *real* adversary than the white-skinned men across the sea he will never sail." Early in the morning of February 24, 1966, he and Solange were awakened by gunfire. The army and the police had staged a coup against Nkrumah. When Smith arrived at his office, he was detained by a group of armed men and taken to a rebel-controlled police station. He and his family flew to Geneva that evening with all their belongings, before returning to Paris.

Not long after their return, Smith separated from Solange. He had fallen in love with a young Indian Jewish woman working at the Indian embassy, Ira Reuben, the daughter of a judge on the high court of Patna; they married as soon as his divorce was finalized. (Their daughter, Rachel, now a singer and actress, was born in 1971.) Restless as ever, he continued to travel for AFP. In the summer of 1967, he spent three weeks in Algeria and a month in the United States, where he saw his mother for the first time in sixteen years. This reporting became the basis of his book *Return to Black America* (1970), a fascinating study of the transformations among "America's Algerians." He interviewed not only Stokely Carmichael and other Black Power leaders but gangsters such as Ellsworth "Bumpy" Johnson, the king of the Harlem underworld, who reminded him of Ali La Pointe, an Algerian rebel who started out as a criminal in the casbah. Youth gangs, Smith wrote, were "becoming the hard core of the black nationalist movement . . . The same thing . . . occurred with Algerian gangs . . . during the Algerian liberation struggle." He marveled at the confidence exhibited by young black people, their fearlessness in confronting white supremacy, even "the way they moved, the way they acted." But "the real change, the real revolution, was *inside*. These black youths with whom I talked from coast to coast were much more different from most people of my generation than we were from the generation of our fathers."

What had triggered this cultural revolution among young black Americans, he argued, was the Second World War, when black soldiers like himself were

> uprooted from their tenant farms and ghettos and hurled across the ocean to do battle with white and yellow men in the name of freedom, democracy, and equality. The war opened up new horizons. Many black Americans came alive for the first time in the ruins of Berlin, the coffeehouses of Tokyo, the homes of Frenchmen or Italians. Members of a victorious army, they found respect and consideration for the first time—but from the former enemy!

Black America's revolution, he suggested, had been fueled not only by oppression but by the enlarged perspective and imaginative freedom that displacement and exile had afforded. Nothing less than a *"radical transformation of the surrounding white society itself,"* he concluded, could answer the revolution's demands for equality "in every sphere—political, economic, social, and psychological." Like Baldwin, who drew a similar portrait of the Black Power era in his 1972 essay *No Name in the Street*, Smith predicted that white America would do everything in its power to resist such a transformation.

Before his death in 1974, Smith proposed a novel he called "Man without a Country," about (in the words of his widow, Ira Gardner-Smith) "a black American who lives in France, who also lived in Africa, and because of these three continents—which all become part of him—he ceases to belong anywhere." He could not find a publisher. But in *Last of the Conquerors, The Stone Face* and *Return to Black America*, Smith left us with an extraordinary trilogy about the liberation, and the costs, of a black writer's exile in Europe. "The black person could live in greater peace with his environment in Copenhagen or Paris than in New York, not to speak of Birmingham or Jackson," he wrote:

> But he found it at times harder to live at peace with himself. The black man who established his home in Europe paid a heavy price. He paid it in a painful tearing of himself from his past . . . He

paid for it in guilt . . . He paid for it, finally, in a sort of rootlessness: for, seriously, who were all these peculiar people speaking Dutch, Danish, Italian, German, Spanish, French? . . . What did they know about the black skin's long, bitter, and soon triumphant odyssey? The black man, no matter how long he lived in Europe, drifted through these societies as an eternal "foreigner" among eternal strangers.

Yet the stranger did not regret his journey. As he wrote in his unpublished memoir, "Through Dark Eyes," "this rootlessness has its inconveniences, but it has an advantage too: it gives a certain perspective." Smith's perspective—a radical humanism both passionate and wise, sensitive to difference but committed to universalism, antiracist but averse to tribalism, disenchanted yet rebelliously hopeful—feels in dangerously short supply these days. It's time for his books to be restored to print, and for William Gardner Smith to be repatriated to the one country where he found a lasting home: the republic of letters.

{2020}

III

Signs Taken for Wonders

8

Claude Lévi-Strauss:
The Ends of Man

Austere, prickly, solitary, Claude Lévi-Strauss is the least fashionable, and most influential, of the postwar French theorists.
Lévi-Straussians are a nearly extinct tribe in Anglo-American
universities, far outnumbered by Foucauldians, Derrideans and
Deleuzians. But, in a paradox he might have enjoyed, his imprint
has been deeper. Like the Amerindian myths he anatomized in
obsessive detail in the four-volume *Mythologiques*, his ideas
have seeped into our thinking. From the significance of the incest
taboo, to the reasons we roast or boil our food, to the distinctions
we draw between nature and culture, the way we think about
behavior and the mind has been indelibly shaped by the writings
that bear his signature.

I say "bear his signature" because Lévi-Strauss saw himself as
a spiritual medium more than an author. "I don't have the feeling
that I write my books," he said. "I have the feeling that my books
get written through me . . . I never had, and still do not have, the
perception of feeling my personal identity." In *Tristes Tropiques*,
his memoir of his fieldwork among the Indians of Brazil, he
called the self "hateful." Everything he wrote aimed to puncture
the notions of will and agency that cluster around the human
subject. The critique of the subject was central to structuralism,
the school of thought he helped to found. He existed, he wrote
in the memoir's closing paragraphs, not as an individual, but as
"the stake . . . in the struggle between another society, made up
of several thousand nerve cells lodged in the anthill of my skull,

and my body, which serves as its robot." His work, he said, was just as mortal as he was: it would be "childish" to think he could escape the "common fate."

His style of structural anthropology long ago fell out of favor among ethnographers; its mathematical diagrams of cultural rules now look like relics of some mid-twentieth-century technocratic fantasy. Yet Lévi-Strauss, who died in 2009 at the age of one hundred, is in no danger of being forgotten. He is as much an icon as the brand of jeans with which he was often confused when he was teaching in New York in the 1940s. (At the suggestion of his employers he eventually adopted the "mutilated" name Claude L. Strauss.) But Patrick Wilcken has set himself an unenviable task, because Lévi-Strauss was the embodiment of *pudeur*, an exaggerated, almost prudish sense of discretion.* He was good at keeping secrets and at dodging interviewers' questions. (The interview, he said, was a "detestable genre.") Wilcken, who met him in 2005, found his glacial reserve impossible to crack and detected "a kind of emptiness, an isolation": "In the end, the mask had barely moved." To his credit, he doesn't try to remove the mask or to compete with *Tristes Tropiques*. Instead, he has written an absorbing, scrupulous account of Lévi-Strauss's career, recapturing both the grandeur and the idiosyncrasy of his intellectual project.

It was the mind and what he considered to be its formal patterns—particularly as revealed in art and storytelling—that fascinated Lévi-Strauss. Reading this biography one sometimes wonders whether he might in the future be thought of as a theorist of cognition and aesthetics who only happened, because of disciplinary prejudice, to take tribal cultures as his material. Like Freud, he believed that the deeper truths of culture are hidden from consciousness, lodged in a subterranean stratum of the brain the interpreter can never fully excavate. He came to believe that anthropologists would have to team up with neuroscientists to explain the mysterious patterns of behavior: a view, Wilcken suggests, that "presaged the cognitive revolution in the social sciences."

* Wilcken's biography, *Claude Lévi-Strauss: The Poet in the Laboratory*, was published by Bloomsbury in 2011.

More comfortable in the library than in the field, he was indifferent to what he called the "vast empirical stew" of life in tribal societies. The truth is he saw little of it: he conducted only about eight months of fieldwork in Brazil, spent no more than a couple of weeks at a time with any of the tribes he encountered, and didn't go back there until 1985, when he accompanied President François Mitterrand on an official visit. Edmund Leach spoke for many Anglo-American anthropologists when he complained in 1970 that Lévi-Strauss's analyses were "very far removed from the dirt and squalor that are the field anthropologist's normal stamping ground."

But Lévi-Strauss believed he could see better from a distance. It was in Paris—at the Laboratoire d'anthropologie sociale, the research institute he established in 1960, or in his sumptuous flat in the sixteenth arrondissement—that he did his real work, slipping into an imaginary world, reading the works of other ethnographers, conducting a kind of séance with his collection of tribal art. As *aides à penser*, he would listen to the Ring Cycle or Debussy's *Pelléas et Mélisande*, which he believed borrowed unconsciously from the structures of ancient myth. His aim was to discern the unconscious logic of the mind: what he called, in its raw, "unspoiled" state, "la pensée sauvage." Lévi-Strauss, Susan Sontag claimed in 1963, had "invented the profession of the anthropologist as a total occupation." Whether it was anthropology at all is debatable; that it was a remarkable effort to ask the Big Questions is not. Leach grudgingly conceded that Lévi-Strauss shared "with Freud a most remarkable capacity for leading us all unaware into the innermost recesses of our secret emotions," even if that made him a "poet in the laboratory" rather than a social scientist.

Anthropology, Lévi-Strauss wrote, "does not abandon the hope of one day awakening among the natural sciences, at the hour of the Last Judgment." But Wilcken suggests he might have preferred to wake up a novelist or, better yet, a composer. Like his teacher Marcel Mauss, he was the product of a uniquely French "amalgam of arts and ideas." His work owed much of its aura to its juxtaposition of the aesthetic and scientific, the rational and the mystical. But it wouldn't have been nearly as seductive had it not been for his style, which bridged what he considered the great divide in Western consciousness between the "intelligible" and the "sensible"—what can be apprehended by the senses. The little time that he spent in the field yielded some memorable passages, not just on customs and ritual, but on landscape, food and smell, which he described with extraordinary vividness and sensuality, as in his account of eating grubs from rotten tree trunks: "From the body spurted a whitish, fatty substance, which I managed to taste after some hesitation; it had the consistency and delicacy of butter, and the flavour of coconut milk."

Whether or not Lévi-Strauss was an "artist manqué," as Wilcken sees him, the aesthetic impulse ran deep. He was born into a family of artists. His great-grandfather was a violinist who performed for Napoléon III; his father, Raymond, a portrait painter. Lévi-Strauss *père* barely made ends meet, but he saved up to take his only child to see the Ring Cycle and Stravinsky's *Les Noces*. Claude drew, painted, took photographs, even wrote a trio for two violins and piano.

His maternal grandfather had been the rabbi of Versailles, but Judaism, he said, was "no more than a memory" at home. Still, as a Jew born in 1908, he felt the impact of the Dreyfus Affair. In a series of interviews conducted with Didier Eribon in the late 1980s and collected in *De près et de loin*, he spoke of being bullied at school, and of his embattled sense of difference as a member of a national community that didn't fully accept him. It's tempting to imagine that this alienation was what led him to the Mato Grosso, and inspired his radical defense of the equality of cultures in *Race and History*, his 1952 paper commissioned by UNESCO. Yet he was also a fierce advocate of assimilation in France, and instinctively hostile to cultural *métissage*. By the mid-1950s, hardly a decade after being chased out of Vichy France, he warned that his country was becoming "Muslim" in its rigidity and bookishness: "I cannot easily forgive Islam," he wrote, "for showing me our own image, and for forcing me to realize to what extent France is beginning to resemble a Muslim country."

He studied law and philosophy, then took the *agrégation* at the same time as Beauvoir and Merleau-Ponty. But he went through university "like a zombie," he said, too engrossed by his extra-curricular activities as a socialist militant. That passion seems to have vanished quite suddenly, but he continued to regard Marx as one of his "three mistresses," along with Freud and geology. In the late 1920s, he switched to anthropology, mostly as a "way of escape" from the "Turkish bath atmosphere of philosophical reflection," but also, he suggested, "because of a structural affinity between the civilizations it studies and my particular way of thinking." His first chance to study those civilizations came in 1934, when his adviser, Célestin Bouglé, arranged for him to take up a chair in sociology at the University of São Paulo. Bouglé promised him he'd find indigenous Brazilians wandering around the suburbs, but that turned out not to be true. The Brazilian ambassador in Paris, himself of indigenous ancestry, told him that Brazil's indigenous peoples had all been exterminated. That, too, turned out to be untrue. His four years in Brazil were hard. He clashed with his employers at the university and held on to his job thanks only to the intervention of his colleague Fernand Braudel. His recent marriage, to Dina, an ethnologist, was in trouble. The couple's friend Mário de Andrade, a poet and musician, "had a soft spot" for Dina, and it seems to have been reciprocated. The Lévi-Strausses divorced soon after they returned to France in 1939, but not before their famous, and nearly disastrous, expedition to Brazil's northwestern interior.

The team Lévi-Strauss assembled was large: "more like a travelling country fair than a scientific expedition." The authorities, nervous that they might become targets—a number of telegraph workers and missionaries had been killed by Indians—assigned them a minder, a young anthropologist called Luiz de Castro Faria. Lévi-Strauss, Castro Faria recalled, was a "silent, introspective" man who barely spoke: "For a Brazilian it was a very unusual experience." According to the anthropologist Alfred Métraux, who met Lévi-Strauss in São Paulo, "he looked like a Jew who had stepped out of an Egyptian painting: the same nose and a beard trimmed à la Sémite. I found him cold, stilted, in the French academic style . . . Lévi-Strauss hated Brazil."

This "supporting cast" would all but disappear from *Tristes Tropiques*. There Lévi-Strauss casts himself as a Rousseau-like solitary walker among the natives, a melancholy traveler at the edge of civilization. Wilcken's account of the expedition is like an ethnographic version of *Fitzcarraldo*, as Lévi-Strauss succumbs to depression and scribbles away at a play, a companion piece to Corneille's *Cinna*, about a "drifter who is beginning to doubt the validity of his adventures," while Dina is forced to return to São Paulo, eyes dripping with pus from an infection spread by the lambe-olho fly. The Nambikwara did not speak Portuguese, and he found their language "impossible to understand." When another group of Indians began to leave their village, Lévi-Strauss, gifts in hand, begged them to stay put so that he would have a more "authentic" ethnographic experience. "He wasn't cut out for the job," Castro Faria said years later in an interview with *Libération*, describing the expedition as "the price Lévi-Strauss paid to be recognized as a real anthropologist . . . He was truly 'a philosopher among the Indians.'"

Lévi-Strauss had no trouble admitting that he was "a library man, not a fieldworker"; and he didn't make any secret of his difficulties in *Tristes Tropiques*. ("I hate traveling and explorers" is its famous opening line.) But the memoir concealed the thinness of his research by its magisterial composure, and the authority, precision and visual intensity of his prose. His field notes, according to Wilcken, were "uneven" and "haphazard," a scattered collection of jottings, scraps and "doodles, childlike drawings of jaguars, armadillos, birds and fish," leaving the "impression of an artist trawling for ideas, rather than an academic at work." Yet *Tristes Tropiques* produced that "effect of the real" which Roland Barthes saw as central to the power of the realist novel. The artist manqué had no lack of imagination.

Before it became a memoir, *Tristes Tropiques* was the title of a "vaguely Conradian" novel that Lévi-Strauss began writing when he returned to Paris in 1939, and abandoned after fifty pages. By then he had gone back to teaching at a lycée, but in October 1940, he was forced out of his job under the first Jewish statute, and stripped of his citizenship; he would have ended up underground, or in a camp, had it not been for an invitation from the Rockefeller Foundation to teach at the New School for Social Research in New York. In March 1941, he boarded the *Capitaine Paul-Lemerle* along with 350 other "undesirables," among them Victor Serge, who described the ship as "a kind of floating concentration camp." Lévi-Strauss found the ascetic Serge unapproachable, but while docked in Casablanca he struck up a lasting friendship with André Breton, with whom, Wilcken writes, he shared "a modernist infatuation with the primitive and the subconscious."

Getting into the US wasn't easy. Lévi-Strauss was traveling with a trunk full of field notes and documents, and his papers weren't in order. But once he arrived in New York, in May 1941, he was enraptured by the city's "horizontal and vertical disorder," describing its fabric as "riddled with holes": "All you had to do was pick one and slip through it if, like Alice, you wanted to get to the other side of the looking glass." He befriended the anthropologist Franz Boas (who would die in his arms at a lunch held in his honor in 1942) and in his spare time joined Breton and Max Ernst on expeditions to the antique shops on Third Avenue, where cheap tribal artifacts were easy to come by. He learned another valuable lesson from these shops, with their displays of "previously scorned items": "The idea of beauty can take curious shapes."

He drew a similar lesson from the striking Sxwaixwe masks of the Salish tribes, with their protruding eyes and gaping mouths, at the American Museum of Natural History. "This unceasing renewal," he noted in his journal,

> this inventive assuredness . . . this scorn for the beaten track, bring about ever new improvisations . . . to get any idea of them, our times had to await the exceptional destiny of a Picasso. With this difference, however: that the daring feats of a single man . . . were already known and practiced by a whole indigenous culture for 150 years or even longer.

These words were reprinted in one of his last books, *The Way of the Masks*, in which he described the "carnal bond" he felt with the art of the northwest American coast. The idea of a beauty that transgressed traditional aesthetics was commonplace among his artist friends in New York, like Yves Tanguy, and Wilcken chides him for minimizing his debt to surrealism. But what he was proposing to do was different from the surrealist project: not to elevate this "savage modernism" in order to shock the Western spectator, but to understand it on its own terms, decipher its clandestine codes and laws, and carve a space inside Western reason for the thinking of its supposedly primitive Other.

For Lévi-Strauss's purposes, the surrealists were less help than another friend he made in New York, the exiled Russian linguist Roman Jakobson. Listening to Jakobson lecture was like reading "a detective story." Jakobson introduced him to Saussure's *Course in General Linguistics* of 1916, and to the idea that language was composed, acoustically, of phonemes or units of sound. These, Saussure argued, had no meaning in themselves, but acquired meaning by virtue of their difference from other phonemes. If this was structuralism, Lévi-Strauss realized, then he'd been "a structuralist without knowing it." Jakobson's ideas about language seemed to apply to the subject of his thesis: the rules governing marriage and exchange among the Nambikwara. Kinship, after all, was also a "relational system," structured by oppositions between men and women, endogamy and exogamy, nature and culture. Those unconscious rules, like the rules of language, were observed "with almost mathematical efficiency." This unexpected application of structural linguistics to anthropology enabled him to circumvent the problem of meaning and to analyze instead a formal network of relationships. It was in New York, not the Brazilian *cerrado*, that structural anthropology was born.

After the war Lévi-Strauss was in no hurry to go back to France. He'd seen how rough life there was: his parents, who had hidden in the Drôme during the war, were penniless, and his Paris studio had been ransacked. He wasn't convinced by France's makeover as a nation of Resistance heroes. France had lost, he told an OSS agent, and "the sooner people realized this the better for all concerned." His advice was not to waste time with trials: "Better to kill 50,000 collaborators immediately." He remained in New York as France's cultural attaché for a few years: he hosted lunches, introduced Camus and other writers to Chinatown and jazz clubs, and married a second time (they separated a year later). But he spent most of his time writing *The Elementary Structures of Kinship*. Published to great acclaim in 1949, a year after his return to France, it was a work of prodigious scope, though little of it was based on observations in the field.

At the heart of his analysis lay the incest taboo, a law that fascinated him because of its apparent universality. Lévi-Strauss's precursors had either grounded it in biology—as a protection against inbreeding—or claimed that the familiarity of close relatives tended to make them less appealing as sexual partners, an argument that showed little appreciation of Freud's work. Lévi-Strauss viewed the taboo as the law that ensures the passage from nature to culture and from endogamy to exogamy. By dividing women into sets of prohibited and possible spouses, and by forcing men to marry women from other families, the taboo enabled communication between groups and facilitated social reproduction. His analysis was influenced by Marcel Mauss's study of matrimonial exchange in *The Gift*, which explored the "triple obligation" of giving, receiving and returning. Mauss had hoped to discover the meaning behind such relations of reciprocity, but Lévi-Strauss was interested purely in the symbolic rules that governed the exchange of women.

There followed a series of intellectual landmarks, including *Race and History* (1952), *Tristes Tropiques* (1955), *Structural Anthropology* (1958) and *La Pensée sauvage* (1962). Plagued by anxiety that he'd never find an academic position worthy of his talents, he had given up hope of ever being appointed at the Collège de France. His Jewish name was against him, and his first two nominations were struck down. But in 1959 the Collège finally accepted him.

The two books that made him famous outside anthropology departments were *Tristes Tropiques* and *La Pensée sauvage*. They spoke to a national sense of decline in France, and in much of the West, at the time of decolonization. In *Race and History* he laid waste to the West's myth of progress, arguing that its narrative of evolution from primitive to civilized society was simply a form of "ethnocentrism." By the time he published *Tristes Tropiques*, the French had been defeated at Dien Bien Phu, and the Algerian struggle for independence had begun. It tapped into a widespread feeling of cultural pessimism.

Lévi-Strauss was far from being a champion of liberation movements. He would later describe the postcolonial states, with their dreary mimicry of Western technology, as more of a threat to tribal peoples than the colonial powers had been. Fanon's vision of a "new man" rising from the ashes of colonialism would have struck him as a fantasy. Yet there was a touching humbleness in his self-portrait as a homesick Western explorer, roaming among people with whom he could scarcely communicate, trying to "remain indifferent to . . . pretty girls sprawling stark naked in the sand laughing mockingly as they wriggled at my feet," and to maintain his equilibrium in South Asian cities. In the image of Nambikwara couples embracing, he found "the most truthful and moving expression of human love." Prostrating himself before an altar in an Indian village on the Burmese border, he wondered "what else . . . have I learned from the masters who taught me, the philosophers I have read . . . apart from a few scraps of wisdom which, when laid end to end, coincide with the meditation of the Sage at the foot of the tree?" Dismayed though he was at the thought of a future of crowds and pollution, he saw no point in fighting back: "The world began without man and will end without him."

La Pensée sauvage advanced a more radical critique of Western thought. It was a mistake, he argued, to think there was a difference in the ways primitive and civilized peoples reasoned: "The savage mind is logical in the same sense and the same fashion as ours." To imagine that it is driven merely by the struggle for subsistence (as in the functionalism of Malinowski) or governed by irrational or mystical feelings (as in Lévy-Bruhl) is merely a reflection of Western ethnocentrism. Primitive groups are just as "disinterested" as we are, and no less intellectual in their efforts to understand their surroundings. They are "bricoleurs," analyzing natural data on the basis of their sensory properties, which they organize and classify with considerable sophistication, following what he called a "logic of the concrete." Our method is to break up surface realities in search of the abstract truths underneath: a gain at the level of the intelligible, but a loss at the level of the sensible. The logic of the concrete is "all surface and no depth," and falsely imagines it can achieve total power over the environment, but it is also "beautifully balanced and rigorously logical" in its own fashion. Unfortunately, he wrote, most Western thinkers continued to posit an absolute distinction between primitive and civilized modes of thought—not least Sartre, whose *Critique of Dialectical Reason* he demolished in "History and Dialectic," the book's last chapter.

In his preface Lévi-Strauss described "History and Dialectic" as "a homage of admiration and respect," but he never much liked Sartre, whom he considered a cad for his treatment of Beauvoir. He disdained existentialism ("shopgirl metaphysics," he called it in *Tristes Tropiques*), and viewed Sartre's habit of speaking out on issues on which he had no expertise as ill-suited to a world of increasing complexity. "Sartre's view of the world and man," he wrote, "has the narrowness which has been traditionally credited to closed societies." His insistence on a "distinction between the primitive and the civilized" reminded Lévi-Strauss of "the way it would have been formulated by a Melanesian savage." But he reserved his sharpest criticisms for Sartre's Hegelian vision of history, which he described as a fairy tale about human agency, "the last refuge of a transcendental humanism." The goal of human science, he argued, "is not to constitute, but to dissolve man." Sartre, exposed as a man of the nineteenth century, never replied. The existentialist era had ended; the structuralist era had begun.

But Lévi-Strauss had no desire to lead the revolution he'd launched. He took no pride in his followers and claimed to be mystified, if not annoyed, by them. "This alleged structuralism is only an alibi offered for mediocrity," he said. "The best way to explain the current infatuation with structuralism is that French intellectuals and the cultured French public need new toys every ten or fifteen years." When Jacques Lacan drew on his ideas to argue that the unconscious was "structured like a language," he recoiled. Lacan had been a friend—he had introduced Lévi-Strauss to his third wife, Monique, his partner for the rest of his life—but he claimed not to understand Lacan's use of structuralism, and the friendship withered.

Lévi-Strauss was no more welcoming of fellow travelers outside academia. He admitted there were superficial resemblances between structuralism and new developments in the arts, but he mounted a scathing critique of serial composition and abstract painting in the "Overture" to *The Raw and the Cooked*. Luciano Berio's setting of texts from that book in *Sinfonia*, he said, left him "perplexed." Artistic innovation was the "sign of a state of crisis." Visual art that abandoned the attempt to reproduce nature inevitably became merely decorative, while atonal music divorced itself from the mythical structures that stir emotion. After Wagner and Stravinsky, he argued, Western music had plunged into an abyss of intellectual hermeticism.

The same charge would be made against Lévi-Strauss's own next project, the *Mythologiques* tetralogy published between 1964 and 1971, and against the shorter studies that followed, the so-called "petits mythologiques." He was beginning to give the impression of an artist exploring his obsessions without caring whether anyone else shared them. *Mythologiques* attempted an anatomy of mythological thought, based on what he called "mythemes," the contrasting elements out of which myths were built. He culled these from thousands of Amerindian myths and reassembled them, regardless of origin; he had a hunch that they were all part of a single overarching myth, and compared this somewhat fanciful method to the paintings and collages of his friend Max Ernst. *The Raw and the Cooked*, he announced, was "itself a kind of myth":

> It is in the last resort immaterial whether in this book the thought processes of the South American Indians take shape through the

medium of my thought, or whether mine takes place through the medium of theirs. What matters is that the human mind, regardless of the identity of those who happen to be giving it expression, should display an increasingly intelligible structure.

Wilcken argues that the appeal of myth for Lévi-Strauss was that it represented "the mind in the act of spontaneous creation, unfettered by reality . . . In a certain sense myth was the mind." Myth was, that is, the mind's way of achieving an imaginary, provisional resolution of intractable contradictions—of reaching an accommodation with an unacceptable reality.

With their emphasis on the *longue durée* of human culture, on invariant patterns, and on the tragic nature of existence (Lévi-Strauss's contradictions are, pointedly, never resolved outside myth), these books soon fell out of step with the intellectual mood in France. What Wilcken calls the "spell of structuralist meditation" was shattered by the *événements* of May 1968. Student radicals turned for wisdom to Henri Lefebvre, Guy Debord and Sartre, and antistructuralist graffiti appeared on the walls of the Sorbonne. Disgusted by the protests, Lévi-Strauss withdrew from the Collège until they were over. "I walked inside the occupied Sorbonne," he said, "with an ethnographic gaze." But there was little sign of his characteristic detachment in his analysis of the revolt, and he displayed no interest in the way relations formed among the young tribes making the revolution. The barricades, he complained, were built out of wood, an act of violence against trees. Always drawn to nature, he had become an environmentalist, of an antihumanist sort: "The right of the environment, which everyone talks about, is the right of the environment in regard to man, and not the right of man in regard to the environment."

Wilcken emphasizes the political shock of 1968, but the challenges to Lévi-Strauss's project were also theoretical. In *Of Grammatology*, Derrida did to Lévi-Strauss what Lévi-Strauss had done to Sartre in *La Pensée sauvage*. Like Lévi-Strauss, Derrida began with an obligatory homage, before proceeding to expose him as a naive Rousseauian—and, indeed, as an inverted ethnocentrist—in a ruthlessly close reading of a single chapter of *Tristes Tropiques*. Lévi-Strauss had described handing out sheets of paper and pencils to the Nambikwara, and concluded that writing was less a tool for "acquiring knowledge, or remembering or understanding," than for "increasing the authority and prestige" of some people over others: a means of imposing class division, exploitation and slavery. Derrida read Lévi-Strauss's chapter as a fable, in which the Western anthropologist spoils the innocence of a pre-literate people and writing is portrayed as a fall from the paradise of speech and orality, where the Nambikwara live in a state of "original and natural goodness." In Derrida's mocking description, Lévi-Strauss's structuralism, with its noble savages and its "logocentric" praise of the spoken word over writing, looked like a secular theology.

The poststructuralist demolition crew had arrived, and it aimed to take the house down from the inside. Inverting Lévi-Strauss's favored terms, Derrida and his allies celebrated diachrony over synchrony, events over structure, the exception over the rule, the periphery over the center, the variable over the invariant. But the master appeared not to notice that his house was crumbling. Instead, Lévi-Strauss "retreated into his own world of myths, masks and indigenous art." His work grew more intricate, more obsessional in its search for the mythical patterns created by the mind. While working on the tetralogy, he woke at five each morning, entering into "communion with the indigenous groups he was working on." As he put it, "I try to be the place through which the myths pass." Mystical talk like this left him vulnerable to criticism, particularly from Anglo-American anthropologists such as Rodney Needham, who described his work as a "surrealist enterprise . . . liberated from confinements of exactitude, logic and scholarly responsibility." When ethnographers pointed out exceptions to the incest taboo, the pillar of his analysis of the nature-culture opposition, he simply brushed them off, insisting all the more stubbornly on this sacred principle. The way actual communities functioned was of far less interest to him than the way the mind converted the materials of nature into culture, whether in the form of logical oppositions, mythic stories or, increasingly, art. He wrote with feverish passion about music, particularly the operas of Wagner, the "undeniable originator of the structural analysis of myth." Music, like myth, was a "machine for the suppression of time," the bearer of an almost occult power.

He traveled a little, mainly to Japan, a country he loved. He made one trip to Israel but felt estranged: he "didn't have the feeling of family." (Though he loathed Islam, he felt obliged, as a defender of indigenous peoples, to side with Palestine's Arabs, as he explained to Raymond Aron in a letter written after the 1967 war.) The *Mythologiques* ranged across North and South America, in an avowedly quixotic effort to grasp the whole of Amerindian myth, but he hardly left his laboratory except for a brief trip to British Columbia. The world was a place he preferred to avoid; it was becoming too large. The "hugeness of the human mass within which we live," he said, had made "humanity unmanageable." The beauty of indigenous civilizations like the Nambikwara, he believed, was that they lived face to face, in a setting of utter transparency. As he wrote in *Tristes Tropiques*, "I cherish the reflection . . . of an era when the human species was in proportion to the world it occupied."

Everywhere he looked he saw disproportion and decline. His rare comments on contemporary politics and society were a sour cocktail of Malthusianism and antimodernism. Addressing a UNESCO conference against racism in 1971, he argued that racial groups were equal but ought to remain separate. Anyone expecting a critique of racism instead heard a critique of racial mixing in the name of cultural preservation. In a world engulfed by excessive communication, a certain amount of racial hostility, even superiority, was an understandable form of self-defense. Racism was awful, but even worse was an antiracism that might lead humanity "toward a global civilization—a civilization that is the destroyer of those old particularisms, which had the honor of creating the aesthetic and spiritual values that make life worthwhile." Mutual tolerance, he said, depended on relative equality and sufficient physical distance between racial groups, scarce in a crowded, multicultural world. Lévi-Strauss seemed to relish the offense he'd caused: "This text caused a scandal and that was its goal." Members of the UNESCO staff, he said, "were dismayed that I had challenged a catechism that was for them all the more an article of faith because their acceptance of it . . . had allowed them to move from modest jobs in developing countries to sanctified positions as executives at international institutions."

By the end of the 1960s, Lévi-Strauss had become a Gaullist, a defender of order and tradition. Change unnerved him, whether it was the nomination of the first woman to the Académie française (Marguerite Yourcenar), or the emergence of more radical forms of anthropology that examined the discipline's complicity with empire or questioned the anthropologist's authority. Faced with a future he found unappetizing, he turned further inward. Wilcken says he was startled by Lévi-Strauss's "acid, but ironic nihilism" in conversation, but what seems to have upset him more was his lack of curiosity. When Wilcken asked him about the future of indigenous people in Brazil, he replied: "At my age, you don't think about the future." Wilcken struggles to remain detached, but it's clear that he is disappointed by Lévi-Strauss: disappointed that he disavowed his links with surrealism and modernism; disappointed that he disappeared into his laboratory; disappointed that he "ended up as a one-man school, peddling a type of analysis that had become so utterly idiosyncratic that it was impossible to build on"; disappointed that he "appeared sublimely unconcerned" about his legacy.

But Lévi-Strauss's repudiation of intellectual companionship, his rarefied hermeticism, his cranky prejudices, even his apparent indifference as to whether or not his work survived, may have been ploys, conscious or not, to keep people away. He scorned the Western concept of the self, but he was deeply attached to the idea of solitude. At a conference in 1974 on the cognitive sciences attended by Piaget, Gregory Bateson, Jacques Monod and others, Noam Chomsky asked Lévi-Strauss about a class he had taught with Jakobson, but got nowhere. Lévi-Strauss barely opened his mouth. He passed the time drawing "cats and other real and fantastical animals." Doodling, which allowed him to retreat into a private realm of the imagination, had been one of the sources of the artistic form of anthropology he had created after his journey to the Mato Grosso. His warnings about the death of civilization and the inexorable coarsening of society were also a retreat. Like the myths, they provided a temporary resolution to an intractable dilemma: his role as a public figure, and his distaste for it. He guarded his solitude until the end of his life and took considerable pains to prevent the kind of spectacular funeral procession that Sartre had. Before his death was announced to the press, he had already been buried near his country château in Lignerolles, at a small funeral attended only by his wife, close family and friends, and the town's mayor. The casket, at his request, was lowered in total silence.

{2011}

9

Not in the Mood: Jacques Derrida's Secrets

"Anyone reading these notes without knowing me," Jacques Derrida wrote in his diary in 1976, "without having read and understood *everything* of what I've written elsewhere, would remain blind and deaf to them, while he would *finally* feel that he was understanding easily." If you think you can understand me by reading my diaries, he might have been warning future biographers, think again. Derrida worried that the diaries might one day be privileged over his philosophical writing or, worse, used as a way of "finally" steering through the obstacles he had consciously placed between himself and his readers. Comprehension—particularly if acquired "easily," a Derridean slur—was one of the illusions of "mastery" that he set out to puncture. Language, for Derrida, is always saying more than we want it to say; it has a tendency to undermine itself, even to turn against itself; there is no final liberation into some utopia of clarity, transparency and understanding. Derrida, who died in 2004, never wrote a memoir; he claimed he'd been "denied narrative," as if it were a cruel punishment. Yet he wrote constantly about himself, in what his biographer Benoît Peeters calls "memoirs that are not memoirs."* The first half of *The Post Card* (1980) is an epistolary novel composed of *envois* to an unnamed lover. His 1991 essay "Circumfession," written in stream-of-consciousness as his mother lay dying, moves between reflections

___
* Peeters's *Derrida: A Biography* was published by Polity in 2012.

on circumcision, death and St. Augustine, and an elegiac remembrance of his childhood. His real ambition, Peeters suggests, was to be a poet or novelist; toward the end of his life, he spoke less of his philosophical legacy than of his desire to leave "traces in the history of the French language." By scattering his writing with clues and apparent confessions, he played a coy game of disclosure and concealment, inviting curiosity while refusing to show himself clearly. Still, his writings are a rich guide to the concerns that drove him: our longing for a reassuring "center" that could anchor thought; the West's troubled relationship to its colonial "other"; the agonies of Jewish identity; trauma and mourning; the power of the secret.

Peeters, whose previous book was a biography of Hergé, the creator of Tintin, is not a Derridean, but his book has qualities Derrida might have appreciated, above all a supreme patience with intellectual difficulty and abstention from moral judgment. He has done a heroic amount of research, interviewing more than a hundred of Derrida's friends and associates. He also had the cooperation of Derrida's widow, Marguerite. But his principal source of information is Derrida's own writing: some eighty books, as well as the many letters and journals in archives in France and at the University of California, Irvine, where he taught for many years. Derrida saved everything he wrote: he regarded every scrap as a "trace," an almost sacred emblem of survival—and all writing, from poetry to post-its, had philosophical implications. Peeters puts Derrida's professional writing and these traces on an equal footing, using the one to illuminate the other. We see his many sides: a loyal friend and irrepressible seducer; a critic of dogma who couldn't bring himself to admit his own errors; a man who loathed tribalism but was so thin-skinned and so in need of adoration that he ended up leading his own academic tribe.

Derrida's ancestors were Sephardic Jews from Spain who fled to Algeria during the Inquisition; they spoke Ladino, Hebrew and Arabic. But the Jews of Algeria—unlike the Muslim population—were made French citizens in 1870, four decades after the conquest, and by the time Derrida was born in 1930, his family no longer spoke any of its "native" languages. Growing up in El Biar, just outside Algiers, Jackie Derrida—he didn't become Jacques until he moved to Paris—often had the feeling that French was not his language: "I speak only one language," as he put it, "and it is not my own." Integration into the Republic had liberated Jews from their inferior status as natives, but they still faced severe anti-Semitism from the *colons* and the resentment of Algeria's Arabs and Berbers, the oppressed *indigènes* who remained disenfranchised. To be an Algerian Jew was to be caught between the opposing sides of what would soon become a war of decolonization.

The Derrida family home was a sanctuary, but even there, he said, he felt like a "precious but so vulnerable intruder," since he was born after the death of an older son, Paul, at three months. His mother, Georgette, whom he adored, insisted on finishing a poker game when she went into labor with him (she was to remain sparing with her affection). But the event that established Derrida's sense of being an outsider—the first "earthquake," as he put it—took place when the Vichy government stripped Algerian Jews of citizenship and he was expelled from school. Being moved to a school for Jewish children only sharpened his feelings of "ill-being," and he was relieved to return to his old school after the Allies landed. In an interview with Elisabeth Roudinesco many years later, Derrida said that, though "deeply wounded by anti-Semitism"—a wound that "has never completely healed"—he was too beset by "malaise" to enjoy "any kind of membership in a group." Yet Peeters gives the impression that Derrida was a well-adjusted young man, a reader of Gide, Sartre and Camus who was also good at football and confident with women.

At nineteen, he left Algeria for the first time to attend the lycée Louis-le-Grand in Paris, and then the École normale supérieure. There he began a long, tortured relationship with the *grandes écoles*. His teachers often complained that they couldn't understand his papers: Foucault wasn't sure whether to give him an A or an F. Derrida's *caïman*—the supervisor of his *agrégation*—was the Marxist philosopher Louis Althusser, who immediately spotted his brilliance, though he too had trouble making sense of his writing. Derrida's thesis on Husserl revealed him to be, in the philosopher Jean-Luc Nancy's words, "fully armed and helmeted, like Athena." All he lacked was "a certain youth, with its playfulness." As a student he had frequent bouts of anxiety and depression. "I'm no good for anything except taking the world apart and putting it together again (and I manage the latter less and less frequently)," he wrote to a friend.

The world of his childhood was already coming apart when, after a spell at Harvard, where he married Marguerite Aucouturier, a psychoanalyst and the mother of his two older sons, Derrida returned home in 1957, at the height of the war of independence, to do his military service, teaching at a school southwest of Algiers. Derrida's postcolonialist admirers will be disappointed, and his conservative critics surprised, to learn that he opposed both the FLN and the partisans of Algérie française, holding out for a third way that might allow natives and settlers to share the country, perhaps in a federation with France. (In 1952, Derrida wrote a paper for a history class on "our African empire": the idea of Algeria as an independent, majority-ruled republic was at that time as inconceivable to him as it was to Camus.) When a close friend serving in Brazza wrote to him about the torture of an Arab teenager, Derrida was horrified but refused to take a position: "Any attempt to justify or condemn either group is not just obscene, just a way of quieting one's conscience, but also abstract, 'empty.'"

In 1959, Derrida and Marguerite returned to France. After a miserable stint teaching philosophy at a lycée in the provinces, which ended in a nervous collapse, he landed a job as a lecturer at the Sorbonne. But his psychological state was precarious, his thoughts never far from his family in Algeria. In 1961, a year before independence, the historian Pierre Nora, a lycée classmate, published a scathing little book, *Les Français d'Algérie*, pillorying the *colons* as genocidal in their hatred of Arabs. Derrida sent Nora a nineteen-page single-spaced letter. He agreed that independence was now inevitable but recoiled from Nora's "harshly aggressive" tone, his "desire to humiliate." One couldn't blame the *pieds noirs* while letting the true "masters," the French government, off the hook. He was particularly angered by Nora's scathing depiction of liberals like Derrida as de facto supporters of colonial rule.

Impressed by the letter, Nora suggested that they publish their debate, but Derrida preferred not to. "I realize that I love [Algeria] more and more, love it madly," he wrote to Nora after spending a final summer there in 1961, "which does not contradict the aversion I have long stated for it." After independence came in July 1962, Derrida's relatives—fifteen of them—camped out at the flat he and Marguerite shared outside Paris, before moving to Nice. Derrida, who would return to Algeria only twice, often spoke of his "nostalgeria"; he continued to insist that "a different type of settlement" might have led to less suffering. Peeters suggests that Derrida had Algeria in mind when he expressed the hope that Israelis and Palestinians might find a way to live in a single, binational state. His experience of the Algerian war accounts for the moral sensitivity—the attention to nuance, the refusal to choose sides, as well as the occasional utopianism—of his political thinking.

Derrida's early work was written in the shadow of decolonization. His first book, a translation of Husserl's forty-three–page *Origin of Geometry* preceded by a 170-page introduction, was published in 1962, but it wasn't until 1967 that he made his mark. That year he published three books of astonishing audacity that, taken together, amounted to a declaration of war on structuralism, then all the rage in France: *Speech and Phenomena*, another study of Husserl; *Writing and Difference*, a collection of essays originally published in journals like *Tel Quel* and *Critique*; and his masterwork, *Of Grammatology*. Few read the formidably dense *Of Grammatology* from cover to cover, but it acquired tremendous cachet; a year later, its cover made an appearance in Godard's *Le Gai Savoir*. What was *Of Grammatology* about? When Madeleine, the heroine of Jeffrey Eugenides's campus novel *The Marriage Plot*, asks a young theory-head this question, she is immediately set straight: "If it was 'about' anything, then it was about the need to stop thinking of books as being about things."

That's not so far off. In all three books, Derrida's argument was that Western thought from Plato to Rousseau to Lévi-Strauss had been hopelessly entangled in the illusion that language might provide us with access to a reality beyond language, beyond metaphor: an unmediated experience of truth and being which he called "presence." Even Heidegger, a radical critic of metaphysics, had failed to escape its snares. This illusion, according to Derrida, was the corollary of a long history of "logocentrism": a privileging of the spoken word as the repository of "presence," at the expense of writing, which had been denigrated as a "dangerous supplement," alienated from the voice, secondary, parasitic, even deceitful.

Derrida wanted not only to liberate writing from the "repression" of speech, but to demonstrate that speech itself was a form of writing, a way of referring to things that aren't there. If logocentrism was a "metaphysics of presence," what he proposed was a poetics of absence—a philosophical echo of Mallarmé's remark that what defines "rose" as a word is "*l'absence de toute rose*." Derrida, a passionate reader of Mallarmé, made a similar argument about language by drawing on—and radicalizing—Saussure's *Course in General Linguistics*. Saussure had argued that words acquire their meaning through their difference from other words—specifically from the differences between phonemes—rather than from their referents. Derrida went a step further, arguing that meaning itself is subject to what he deliberately misspelled as *différance*, a pun on the verb *différer*, which means both "to differ" and "to defer." (He spelled *différance* with an "a" rather than an "e" because it could only be read, not heard: a mark of the primacy of writing over speech.) The meaning of what we say, or write (a distinction without a difference, for Derrida), is always "undecidable"; it hardly takes shape before it dissolves again in an endless process of differing and deferring.

This set of moves—first, demonstrating that the terms of a binary opposition were in a "violent hierarchy" (speech over writing); second, that that the hierarchy could be inverted, so that the dominant term (speech) is shown to be dependent on, even to be a species of the subordinate term (writing); and third, proposing a new, provisional concept of writing (*différance*) in order to "disorganize" the "inherited order"—was a strategy typical of deconstruction, the label given to Derrida's character-istic mode of analysis. (Derrida would reject this description of deconstruction, just as he refused to call it a form of critique, or method, or indeed to give it any positive definition at all; to do so would be to give it an identity as susceptible to deconstruction as any other. Deconstruction was, rather, a process that could be revealed as being at work in a text.) Again and again in his writ-ings, Derrida took the fundamental oppositions (good/evil, dark/light, inside/outside, reason/madness) that, structuralists such as Claude Lévi-Strauss had argued, organize the way we think about the world, and showed how they undid themselves in the canonical texts of the Western tradition. And if you believe, as Derrida did, that our subjectivity is "constituted" in and through language, you have to bid farewell to the idea of a stable, unified self. That notion is another of those reassuring fictions—like God, Spinoza's "substance," Hegel's *Geist*, Heidegger's "being," Lévi-Strauss's structures—we have devised in order to escape *différance* and find some anchor, some "meaning of meanings." We would be better off, he suggested, if we abandoned this search for foundations, and these God-terms, in favor of a "Nietzschean affirmation, that is the joyous affirmation of the play of the world and the innocence of becoming . . . This affirmation then determines the non-center otherwise than as loss of the center. And it plays without security."

With these words in *Writing and Difference*, Derrida introduced the themes of what would become known as poststructuralism. I quoted one of the more accessible passages: Derrida's writing pushes the limits of intelligibility, as if that were a requirement of any philosophy devoted to the traps and snares of language. The sheer difficulty of his writing no doubt contributed to its aura, but the main source of its appeal lay in the creativity of Derri-da's reading—or misreading—of the philosophical canon. The Belgian-born literary critic Paul de Man, who founded a school of poststructuralist criticism at Yale and became one of Derrida's closest friends, recognized his reading of the Western tradition for what it was: "a good story." He showed that Derrida's Rousseau was a straw man, and that logocentrism had been deconstructed in Rousseau's writings as nimbly as in Derrida's. (Rather than engage de Man directly, Derrida simply lifted his notion that major works of literature deconstruct themselves.) Analytic philosophers were even less persuaded by Derrida's claims and accused him of everything from nihilism to "terrorist obscurantism." (A notable exception was Richard Rorty, who understood that persuasion wasn't Derrida's purpose and that he was an heir of system-destroyers such as Wittgenstein, who used "satires, parodies, aphorisms" to subvert the efforts of mainstream philosophy to "ground" its claims.) But Derrida's fable enchanted literary radicals: it allowed partisans of *différance* to imagine themselves as revolutionaries: one Marxist follower of Derrida argued that the speech/writing distinction was analogous to the bourgeois/proletariat dialectic; a group of young feminists, including Derrida's friend and fellow Algerian Jew Hélène Cixous, teased out the implications of *différance* for gender. Derrida—paying them homage and seeing an opportunity to expand his following—began to speak of "phallogocentrism."

He, however, refused to spell out his own politics. He was a philosopher, not a polemicist. He considered himself a man of the left, but the call to choose sides in the class struggle or the Cold War struck him as a betrayal of deconstructionist first principles, an abandonment of the doubt and skepticism he cultivated in his work. He also had reason to be careful. The Parisian academic scene was intensely polarized, a war zone of "camps, strategic alliances, maneuvers of encirclement and exclusion," in Derrida's words. Teaching at the École normale in the late 1960s, he refused to join any of the various *groupuscules*, at the risk of raising suspicions that he was secretly a Maoist, a Stalinist or, worse, an idealist reactionary. He remained loyal to Althusser, his old *caïman*, during his frequent breakdowns, and did everything in his power to ensure that Althusser received fair legal treatment and medical attention after he strangled his wife in 1980, but he loathed the "intellectual terrorism" of Althusser's Maoist acolytes, who goaded him to declare his support for the Cultural

Revolution. When Lacan heard that Derrida was acquiring a following among Lacanians for his writings on Freud, he told him: "You can't bear my already having said what you want to say." Lacan later made a feeble attempt to apologize, taking "Derrida's hand warmly in his oily palms," in Peeters's words, and sending him a copy of his *Ecrits*, only to betray him later in one of his lectures, when he pointedly revealed something that Derrida had told him in confidence. Derrida never forgave him.

Not that Derrida shied away from intellectual battle. "Parricide is philosophy's theatrical fiction," he wrote, and he showed himself to be a ruthless practitioner. The subject of his first major paper, delivered in 1963 and reprinted in *Writing and Difference*, was his former professor, Foucault, who'd become a star after the publication of *Madness and Civilization*. After introducing himself as "an admiring and grateful disciple," Derrida fastened on a passage in Descartes that he claimed Foucault had misread—a fatal error, he said, since "Foucault's entire project can be pinpointed in these few allusive and somewhat enigmatic pages." The "maddest aspect of his project," he went on, was Foucault's attempt to "let madness speak for itself," something it could not possibly do in the imperial language of reason. (In the lecture, Derrida drew a suggestive comparison with the "anticolonial revolution," which "can only liberate itself from factual Europe or the empirical West" by adopting the West's "values, language, sciences, techniques and weapons.") Foucault was so stunned by this piece of oneupmanship that he thanked Derrida: "Only the blind will find your critique severe." (He would have his revenge years later, belittling deconstruction as a "piece of petty pedagogy.") Foucault was not the only father to be slain: in a lengthy critique of *Tristes Tropiques*, Derrida portrayed Lévi-Strauss as a sentimental Rousseauian, keen to protect speech-based tribes from the corruptions of literate societies. "Aren't you playing a philosophical farce by scrutinizing my texts with a care that would be more justified if they had been written by Spinoza, Descartes or Kant?" Lévi-Strauss asked in a testy letter to *Cahiers pour l'analyse*, the Marxist-Lacanian journal where Derrida's essay first appeared.

The accusation that he was a prankster would trail Derrida for years, but he persisted: the distinctions between philosophy and "non-philosophy," between seriousness and frivolity, even between sense and nonsense, were precisely the kinds of binary opposition he wanted to collapse. His wildest book, *Glas* (1974), was a hypertext *avant la lettre* featuring two columns of text: on the left, an essay on Hegel's family; on the right, a breathless, relentlessly punning homage to his friend Jean Genet, dilating on his treatment of flowers, crime and hard-ons. The objective was to produce "a contamination of a great philosophical discourse by a literary text that is reputedly scandalous." (It was also to challenge *père* Sartre, author of the massive Genet portrait *Saint Genet*.) *Glas* seems to have left Genet, the contaminating agent, at a loss for words, as it did most readers.

Derrida's closest intellectual comrade in the late 1960s and early 1970s was the writer and editor Philippe Sollers, who published a number of Derrida's early essays in *Tel Quel*. But the friendship soured. Sollers wanted *Tel Quel* to become the cultural journal of the French Communist Party (PCF) and enforced strict obedience to the Moscow line. At a dinner with the Derridas, one *telquelian* launched into a passionate defense of the Soviet invasion of Prague, where Marguerite's relatives lived. It did not go down well. Sollers was also worried that Derrida's reputation might eclipse his own, suspecting that Derrida's essay in praise of his novel, *Numbers*, was a covert "attempt at appropriation." In 1967, Sollers had secretly married the Bulgarian literary theorist Julia Kristeva, whose career he was also keen to promote over Derrida's. Rebuffed in their efforts to capture the cultural apparatus of the PCF, in the early 1970s Sollers and Kristeva converted to Maoism. This led to a deepening estrangement from Derrida, whose friend Lucien Bianco, a distinguished Sinologist, had disabused him of any illusions about revolutionary China. When Derrida gave an interview to *La Nouvelle Critique*, a PCF literary journal, Sollers and Kristeva protested by "boycotting" a dinner in his honor. Derrida's *Tel Quel* years were over. Years later, in her novel *The Samurai*, Kristeva would mockingly depict Derrida as Saïda, founder of "condestruction theory," a man who was so attractive to American feminists that they "all became 'condestructivists.'"

It's no wonder that Derrida considered the Paris scene "asphyx-iating." Although widely seen as a leader of *la pensée '68*, he was out of step with his milieu; he was not so much a radical as a tortured left-liberal who still viewed politics through the prism of Algeria. He also had a strong distaste for the public *prises de position* by which French intellectuals transformed themselves into celebrities. While Deleuze, Foucault and Bourdieu made interventions in the press on everything from the state of prisons to the Iranian revolution, Derrida kept his distance from politics in the 1970s and much of the 1980s. When the Nouveaux Philosophes, led by Bernard-Henri Lévy and André Glucksmann, began to preen themselves on television, accusing philosophers of Derrida's generation of failing to join the great struggle against Soviet totalitarianism, Deleuze retaliated in a withering interview. Derrida thought that some "clearly demarcated silences" would be more effective, although he did get into a fistfight with Lévy.

Derrida's main cause in the 1970s and early 1980s was defending the teaching of philosophy in lycées against the reforms proposed by Giscard d'Estaing's minister of education, René Haby. He founded the Greph (Groupe de recherches sur l'enseignement philosophique) and, according to one colleague, "never drew back from the most humdrum tasks." Haby's reform was shelved, and when Mitterrand came to power, Derrida had friends in the administration, including the president's adviser Régis Debray, a former student at the École normale. These connections soon came in handy: in December 1981, Derrida undertook his most daring political mission, a trip to Prague to help Czech dissidents. As he was about to leave for Paris, he was arrested and drugs were planted in his luggage; he was interro-gated for six hours and thrown into a dark cell. ("So, prison, did you discover how it smells?" Genet asked him.) The Mitterrand administration intervened, and he was released to great fanfare, his photograph appearing in the press for the first time: a form of exposure Derrida found especially humiliating, since he had long refused to have his picture taken.

This terrifying night in Prague made him feel vulnerable, and reopened the wound of his expulsion from school. His failure to receive a major appointment in France—in spite of the efforts of Paul Ricoeur at the University of Paris Nanterre and Pierre Bourdieu at the Collège de France—increased his sense of rejection. Though he began teaching at the École des hautes études en sciences sociales, he was happiest lecturing in the US: first at Johns Hopkins, then at Yale with Paul de Man, and finally at Irvine and NYU. Thanks not least to Gayatri Chakravorty Spivak's 1976 translation of *Of Grammatology*, he had become a star in the American academy. His style of reading was widely, if not always convincingly, imitated: professors of comparative literature hunted down the aporias of nineteenth-century novels; students who hadn't read Husserl or Hegel armed themselves for war against the metaphysics of presence. Exiled from its roots in philosophy, deconstruction would turn into an all-purpose tool for anyone attacking racial and sexual "essentialisms": feminists, postcolonialists, queer theorists, transgender activists. The spread of deconstruction in the New World seemed limitless; "America *is* deconstruction," Derrida joked. It reached—or, as Derrida might have said, "contaminated"—everything from aesthetics to theology, from history to anthropology, and did much to open "non-philosophy" to philosophy. Only analytic philosophy—whose opposition Derrida preferred to call "resistance," as if it were a Freudian reaction-formation—remained impermeable.

The experience in Prague of being pressured to confess and made to feel guilty converged with his growing obsession with what he called the question of the secret. "If a right to a secret is not maintained," he said, "we are in a totalitarian space." His own biggest secret was his long relationship with the philosopher Sylviane Agacinski, which began in the early 1970s. Marguerite was aware of the relationship, as she was of Derrida's many affairs, but he didn't want anyone else to know, above all his sons. (Peeters speculates that the death of his brother led him to be an extremely protective father—a "Jewish mother," in the words of a family friend.) Agacinski's first book was published in a series Derrida edited for Flammarion, and she

was the program director of the International College of Philosophy, which Derrida headed. When Derrida wrote *The Post
Card* (1980), with its suggestive *envois* to an unnamed lover, his
seventeen-year-old son, Pierre, was so upset by the book's "disguised confidences" that he stopped reading his father's work,
moved in with an Israeli-American protégé of Derrida's, Avital
Ronell, and changed his last name. The name Derrida, he said,
"wasn't really mine"—an act of filial repudiation that Derrida
wrestled with in his short book *Passions*.

In 1984, Agacinsky got pregnant and insisted on having the
child against Derrida's wishes. The affair ended there. ("To the
devil with the child, the only thing we ever will have discussed,
the child, the child, the child," he had written in *The Post Card*.)
Derrida acknowledged that he was the father two years later, at
Marguerite's urging, but he had no contact with his son Daniel,
who was raised by Agacinski; she eventually married the Socialist
politician Lionel Jospin. The story was revealed in the press when
Jospin ran for president in 2002, an episode Derrida found so
unbearable that he told an interviewer he wasn't in the mood to
vote. When Jospin came third behind Chirac and Le Pen in the first
round of the election, Agacinski broke her long silence. "So it's a
question of *mood*, yet again!" she wrote. "I hadn't thought it could
play such a decisive role on election day. Let's hope at least that
the philosopher will be in a better mood for the second round."
Once Jospin became prime minister, she tore into Derrida's call
for "unconditional hospitality" for undocumented immigrants,
a swipe at her husband's policies: "There is nothing more *condi-
tional* than hospitality. The unconditional, in general, answers the
longing of beautiful souls for the absolute and the pure . . . But it
gives up the attempt to think through reality as it is."

Much more damaging to Derrida was the revelation by a
young Flemish scholar in 1987 that his friend Paul de Man, who
had died four years earlier, had written more than a hundred
articles during the war for the pro-Nazi Belgian newspaper *Le
Soir*. In one article, de Man had reassured his readers that, contrary to the warnings of vulgar anti-Semites, European literature
had not been contaminated by Jews (*enjuivée*); in another, he

contemplated with apparent equanimity the eventual disappearance of Jews from Europe. The revelations weren't just a personal blow to Derrida; they were a threat to his intellectual project. This wasn't the first time deconstruction had been accused of being soft on Nazism. Victor Farias's devastating study had shown that Heidegger's Nazi sympathies were far deeper than had been realized—and less easily disentangled from his work— and put deconstruction in an uncomfortable position. Derrida was not uncritical of Heidegger: his insistence that "you can think only in the language of the other," a notion he borrowed from Emmanuel Levinas, was an implicit critique of Heidegger's belief that "you can think only in your language, your own language." But deconstruction also owed a lot to Heidegger's critique of metaphysics, and Derrida was prickly when critics put it to him that Heidegger's thought might be tainted by his Nazism.

The de Man affair hit still closer to home. Out of a ferocious sense of loyalty—and a fear that guilt by association with Nazism might jeopardize deconstruction—Derrida gave no quarter to de Man's critics. His friend's "declared and underscored intention," he argued in a long essay as fanciful as it was troubled, was to criticize vulgar anti-Semitism, "but to scoff at vulgar anti-Semitism, is that also to scoff at or mock the vulgarity of anti-Semitism?" De Man, he implied, was a deconstructive partisan fighter, using the language of Nazism to subvert it. He defended de Man's silence after the war, imagining—in the absence of any textual "traces"—that he had been tortured by the memory of what he'd done. To have apologized would have been pious, at best: it was nobler for de Man to keep his secret and suffer quietly. Derrida's opponents pounced on the essay: one American critic claimed that deconstruction was "a vast amnesty project for the politics of collaboration during World War II." That was unfair. But Derrida's inability to come clean about de Man—and his refusal to brook dissent among his followers—carried deconstruction to an impasse. "The whole affair was a disaster," Avital Ronell told Peeters. "In certain ways, we never got over it."

Derrida was unable to condemn his friend's behavior because he was less concerned about de Man's war than his own. The

attack on de Man struck him as the latest in a series of mali-
cious attacks on deconstruction. He had reason to feel that he
was fighting on all fronts: against the Nouveaux Philosophes;
against Anglo-American analytic philosophers who considered
him a charlatan; against Jürgen Habermas and his followers in
Germany, who denounced deconstruction for what they saw as
its Heideggerian irrationalism. Derrida, who had refused to join
the communists and Maoists in Paris, was now leading a party of
his own, and, publicly at least, he was as inflexible as any leader.
He never expressed regret over his response to the de Man affair.
But in his last two decades, he began to evolve into a different
sort of thinker, a globally attuned ethicist, as if in response to the
charges made by his adversaries. He spoke less of Heidegger than
of Levinas and Walter Benjamin, whose radical Jewish messian-
ism struck a chord with him. Deconstruction, he now claimed,
had always been about justice, all the more so for having been
silent about it. He continued to pun—deconstruction, in French,
would be nothing without puns—but the Joycean mischief of
works like *Glas* and *The Post Card* subsided, as new, more
somber themes emerged: responsibility to the other (a theme
taken from Levinas), memory ("the trace"), Islam and the West,
democracy, globalization and its discontents, and sovereignty. He
began to write more explicitly about his Algerian-Jewish roots, as
if he wanted the world to know who he was after years of hiding
from view. In his autobiographical essay "Circumfession," composed in fifty-nine paragraphs, one for each year he had lived,
Derrida remembered his own ritual circumcision and speculated
that circumcision was "all I've ever talked about." The roots of
deconstruction lay in the "writing of the body," in the writing
that marked difference.

In *Specters of Marx* (1993), Derrida delivered on an old promise
to write about the founder of historical materialism. He took off
from the first line in *The Communist Manifesto*, "A specter is
haunting Europe," portraying Marx as obsessed with ghosts:
the inventor of what he called "hauntology." With the collapse
of Communism, Marx himself had become a ghost, as an entire
generation of French intellectuals, from Lévy and Glucksmann to

Sollers and Kristeva, denounced him as fervently as they had once embraced him. Once again, Derrida was luxuriating in philosophy's figurative language. Yet his denunciations of the new world order, and his insistence that the specter of Marx would continue to haunt capitalism, revealed an old-fashioned moral outrage he might have once found embarrassing, even suspect. As well as taking up the cause of illegal immigrants, he condemned Israel's occupation of Palestine (but also attacked the "anti-Semitic propaganda that often—too often—tends, in the Arab world, to give renewed credit to the monstrous Protocols"), and called for a peaceful resolution of the civil war in Algeria. Long accused of being a radical critic of the West, Derrida revealed himself to be the conscientious social democrat that he probably always was: an advocate of a new Europe, open to "the other," conscious of its "totalitarian, genocidal and colonialist crimes," and willing to stand up to American hegemony. After September 11, 2001, he was reconciled with Habermas: Bush's war on terror made them realize how much they had in common, whatever their disagreements about Heidegger. Like any leader, Derrida knew when to strike tactical alliances, and when to lower the volume: on a trip to China, where deconstruction was expanding its zone of influence, he agreed not to discuss the death penalty in his lectures.

Never one to turn down an invitation, he pursued an extraordinarily punishing travel schedule, delivering lectures across the world even after he was diagnosed with pancreatic cancer in spring 2003. There was something compulsive about this, and in his final interview with *Le Monde*, he admitted that he had "never learned to live." To learn to live, he explained, is to learn to die, and he could never resign himself to death. His greatest fear, he said, was that "a month after my death *there will be nothing left*. Nothing except what has been copyrighted and deposited in libraries." These were his beloved traces, which he hoped would outlive him. He died in October 2004, his last request, in defiance of Jewish tradition, that he not be buried too quickly. He wanted to give resurrection a chance.

{2012}

10

Roland Barthes's Autofictions

In 1978, Roland Barthes embarked on a series of lectures titled "Preparation of the Novel" at the Collège de France. The novel? Which novel? The one that Barthes had long planned to write, of course. But he didn't know quite how to begin, and he kept getting distracted. As Laurent Binet writes in his recent novel, *The Seventh Function of Language*, "All year, he has talked to his students about Japanese haikus, photography, the signifier and the signified, Pascalian diversions, café waiters, dressing gowns, and lecture-hall seating—about everything but the novel." The novel never got written. On February 25, 1980, Barthes was run over by a laundry van while crossing the street after a lunch with François Mitterrand. He died a month later.

There was always something incongruous about Barthes's ambition to write a novel. He made no secret of being bored by the great novels of the nineteenth century: "Has anyone ever read Proust, Balzac, *War and Peace*, word for word?" Although he had been a champion of the experimental "new novel" of Alain Robbe-Grillet and Michel Butor in the 1950s, his best writing was inspired by photography, theater, painting, music and, not least, consumer culture. Still, he remained haunted by the unwritten novel, as if it were proof of his illegitimacy as a mere critic. According to Tiphaine Samoyault in her superb biography, Barthes often felt like an impostor, which might explain the endearing notes of self-deprecation that punctuate his writing.* As the novelist Philippe Sollers writes in his enjoyably grouchy homage, *The Friendship of Roland Barthes*, "He didn't realize that what he had done was considerable."

Nor did he realize that, by failing to write the novel, he had instead invented a new, aphoristic genre, a bricolage of aesthetic reflection, memoir, philosophy and cultural criticism: a "New New New novel," as Robbe-Grillet called it. Barthes's influence left its mark on the novels of his friend Italo Calvino and his former student Georges Perec. Writers like Geoff Dyer, Ben Lerner, Teju Cole, Sheila Heti and Maggie Nelson are almost unimaginable without Barthes, not to mention the school of contemporary French writing known as "autofiction," associated with writers such as Annie Ernaux.

Barthes claimed that he was incapable of writing an old-fashioned novel because he could not invent "proper names." Yet he did create one unforgettable character: Roland Barthes, or "R.B.," as he called himself in his 1975 memoir *Roland Barthes by Roland Barthes*. Although he never entirely abandoned the rarefied language of theory, most of his work can be read as a self-portrait, a discreet yet impassioned record of his tastes, his moods, his loves and his vulnerabilities. As Susan Sontag put it, he was a "devout, ingenious student of himself."

In his memoir, Barthes portrays himself as a self-effacing aesthete captivated by modernist innovation but secretly, a bit guiltily, a classicist, "in the rear guard of the avant-garde"; a plump sensualist who dislikes the conventions of bourgeois society but not so much that he wants to sacrifice its pleasures on the altar of a puritanical revolution; a gay man who lives with his mother, devoted simultaneously to the fleeting thrills of cruising and the dependable comforts of domesticity. He is a flirt, easily bored, invariably dissatisfied. If he is committed to anything, it is to the infinitely paradoxical nature of the self, and to the refusal of any attempt to deny it in the name of a singular meaning. He wrote of himself, "He dreams of a world which would be *exempt from meaning* (as one is from military service)."

---

* Samoyault's *Barthes: A Biography* was published by Polity in 2018.

Barthes wasn't the most original of postwar French thinkers; he did not transform the way we think about kinship relations, prisons or linguistics, much less (as Samoyault unconvincingly claims) open "a path for thinking about a new order of the world and our knowledge of it." Nor did he aspire to lead an intellectual revolution: more than any of his peers, Barthes discarded the heroic model of the "universal intellectual" that Sartre had pioneered. But he was the only French theorist who can be said to inspire genuine love—a subject on which he wrote some of his most memorable pages. The joy of reading him is that you always feel you're in the presence of a friend who accepts your moods and imperfections, and sympathizes with your desire not to be pigeonholed.

Barthes was born in 1915 in Cherbourg. When he was eleven months old, his father, an officer in the merchant navy, was killed at sea by the Germans; the body was never recovered. The state stepped in to pay for Roland's living expenses and his education. His mother, Henriette, a bookbinder, had little money of her own but came from a highly cultured Protestant family. Her father had been a well-known scientist and colonial officer in West Africa; her mother ran a literary salon where Paul Valéry was a frequent guest. Henriette moved with her son to Bayonne, a small port town in the southwest where they were among the few Protestants, a status that, along with his early awareness of his homosexuality, left him with an acute sense of belonging to a minority.

He grew up in Bayonne and Paris, where his mother found an apartment in 1924. His geography scarcely changed as an adult: he divided his time between his apartment in Paris and his house in Urt, hardly ten miles from Bayonne, where he set up an office identical to his home office on the rue Servandoni, next to Saint-Sulpice. Barthes needed such routines or, as he put it, "structures," to write. The foundational structure was his bond with Henriette, with whom he lived until her death. Nothing would threaten it: not her tempestuous love affair with André Salzedo, a Jewish industrial ceramist and a married man, with whom she had a son, Barthes's half-brother Michel, in 1927; or his own nocturnal adventures (he always returned home after cruising). As he wrote in his memoir, "No father to kill, no family to hate, no milieu to reject: great Oedipal frustration!"

As a student in Paris at the Lycée Montaigne and later at Louis-le-Grand, Barthes immersed himself in all that was new: the music of Debussy, the poetry of Mallarmé, the writings of Nietzsche and Gide. He flirted with writing a novel, but complained to his friend Philippe Rebeyrol (later a distinguished diplomat) that the novel was "by definition an anti-artistic genre," too burdened by psychology: he wanted to write something in "the 'tonality' of Art." (In any case, his life was "just too pleasant" to write a novel.) Instead he practiced the piano, wrote sonatinas and took singing lessons with Charles Panzéra, whom he would later use to illustrate his concept of the "grain of the voice," the trace of "the body in the voice as it sings, the hand as it writes, the limb as it performs." Theater was his other passion: at the Sorbonne, he helped found the Groupe de théâtre antique and performed in its productions. His experiences onstage left him with what Sontag called a "profound love of appearances."

In the era of the Popular Front, Barthes was an instinctive anti-fascist, an admirer of the moderate Socialist leader Jean Jaurès: "Everything he says is wise, noble, human and above all kindly." In a 1939 letter he wrote eloquently of his "hatred against the stench of this country," but he steered clear of revolutionary rhetoric. ("I am liberal in order not to be a killer," he wrote in his memoir.) He was, in any case, fighting a more personal war with pulmonary tuberculosis. In 1942, Barthes was confined at the sanatorium of Saint-Hilaire-du-Touvet. He spent the last year of the war lying for eighteen hours a day in a reclined position, with his head lowered, in silence.

At Saint-Hilaire Barthes fell in love with a fellow patient, Robert David. His letters to David, which are reprinted in *Album* (a newly translated selection of his correspondence), prefigure the themes he would explore in his 1977 book *A Lover's Discourse*:

> Love illuminates for us our imperfection. It is nothing other than
> the uncanny movement of our consciousness comparing two

unequal terms—on the one hand, all the perfection and plenitude of the beloved; on the other hand, all the misery, thirst, and destitution of ourselves—and the fierce desire to unite these two such disparate terms.

Remarkably, Barthes seems never to have suffered the torments of the closet; he accepted his desires without guilt or ambivalence. "I'm already really quite *self-affirmed*," he wrote a heterosexual friend in 1942, though, discreet as ever, he added that "self-affirmation mustn't become ostentation."

By the time Barthes left the sanatorium in 1946, he was, in his own words, "a Sartrean and a Marxist." He had fallen under the influence of another patient, a Trotskyist survivor of Buchenwald who had impressed him as much for his personal qualities—"the moral freedom, the serenity, the elegant distance," as Samoyault puts it—as for his analysis of the class struggle. Barthes's Marxism was heterodox and deeply anti-Stalinist. "Communism cannot be a hope," he wrote to Robert David. "Marxism yes, perhaps, but neither Russia nor the French Communist Party are really Marxist."

That conviction was reinforced in Bucharest, where he taught at the French Institute in the late 1940s. Romanian culture was then being purged of "Western" influences, including homosexuality. Barthes, who shared an apartment with his mother above the French library, did his best to protect its collection from the local censors and was soon appointed France's cultural attaché before being expelled. In a brilliant paper on the semiotics of the new "Romanian science," he showed how "nationalism" and "cosmopolitanism," epithets for "Western" feelings, were transformed into the virtues of "patriotism" and "internationalism" when applied to Communism.

Barthes deepened his critique of Stalinist writing, in which the "sole content" of language is "the separation between Good and Evil," in his first book, *Writing Degree Zero* (1953). Although he still considered himself a Marxist, he had seen in Bucharest how easily Marxism could lend itself to "police-state writing"—and to aesthetic banality. French communist writers were "keeping alive a bourgeois writing which bourgeois writers have themselves condemned long ago." He also implicitly distanced himself from his hero Sartre, who had defined revolutionary prose as an expression of political commitment.

For Barthes, writing was revolutionary only insofar as it was revolutionary in form, and the qualities he admired in radical literature were opacity, complexity and elusiveness, a defiance of the communication that Sartre had seen as its goal: "Rooted in something beyond language, it develops like a seed, not like a line." He advocated a "neutral writing," cleansed of symbolism, psychology and self-conscious literariness, like the flat, inexpressive style of Meursault, Camus's narrator in *The Stranger*. "Literature is like phosphorous," he wrote. "It shines with its maximum brilliance at the moment when it attempts to die." As Samoyault astutely observes, rather than denounce Sartre, Barthes "incorporated"—and transcended—him.

The writer Barthes championed most passionately in the 1950s was Brecht, who had created a theater "purified of bourgeois structures" that at the same time avoided the pieties of left-wing didacticism. Brecht's Marxism, Samoyault writes, supplied Barthes with "a method of reading, a principle of demystification." Barthes used this method, along with the tools of structuralist linguistics, in his 1957 collection of newspaper columns, *Mythologies*. In sly, pithy essays on wrestling matches, *steak-frites*, cruises, striptease, Greta Garbo's face, Einstein's brain and the new Citroën, he unveiled the process of "mystification which transforms petit bourgeois culture into a universal nature." The book soon became nearly as mythical as its subjects, for its sharp critique of French consumer culture at the height of the Trente Glorieuses. But what distinguished Barthes from the dour analysts of the Frankfurt School was, as Samoyault writes, his playful ability to "connect desire with critique": the essays in *Mythologies* have "a certain theatricality . . . both magnificently comic and at the same time pedagogic."

Published against the backdrop of the war in Algeria, *Mythologies* was also Barthes's most radical book, an evisceration of the self-congratulatory myths that underpinned France's *mission civilisatrice* in the colonies. "Wine's mythology," for example, did not go unappreciated by "the big Algerian settlers who impose on the Muslims, on the very land of which they have been dispossessed, a crop from which they have no use, while they actually lack bread." In his concluding theoretical chapter, Barthes examined a *Paris Match* cover showing a black soldier saluting the tricolor—a "*good Negro who salutes us like one of our own boys*," he acidly observed—to show that "*myth hides nothing*: its function is to distort, not to make disappear."

Barthes was not, however, a man of the barricades. When the writer and philosopher Maurice Blanchot asked him to sign the 1960 "Manifesto of the 121," a declaration in support of insubordination against the Algerian war, Barthes declined, explaining that he felt "repugnance toward anything that could resemble a *gesture* in the life of a writer." The heroics of intellectual engagement, and the calcified "doxa" he felt they encouraged, were anathema to him. He recoiled from public debate, and harbored a profound bias against the spoken word. (Fascism, he said, is "any regime that not only prevents one from speaking but above all *obliges* one to speak.") He did not conceal his erotic leanings—he dedicated the first volume of his *Critical Essays*, published in 1964, to his lover François Braunschweig, an eighteen-year-old law student—but the "political liberation of sexuality" struck him as "a double transgression, of politics by the sexual, and conversely." His own morality, he wrote, was "the courage of discretion": "It is courageous not to be courageous."

When the student demonstrations of May 1968 broke out, Barthes was hurt by the graffiti that said "Structures do not take to the streets," but, with his horror of the spoken word, he had little sympathy for the movement's speechifying, and he was now a middle-aged member of the establishment, chairman of the sixth section of the École pratique des hautes études. Nor could he deny having been infatuated with structuralism's "dream of scientificity." From the mid-1950s until nearly the end of the 1960s, he had been a diligent student of Ferdinand de Saussure, Roman Jakobson and other linguistic theorists, applying their insights to everything from Michelet and Racine to the language of fashion and the Eiffel Tower. But Barthes eventually chafed against the rigidity of structuralism and abandoned it much as he had Marxism: "quietly and without fuss, on tiptoe as always," as Robbe-Grillet remarked.

By May 1968 he had already embraced the next trend, later known as "poststructuralism," which celebrated the endless play, the restless and fugitive nature of signs. Interpretative systems, he decided, were a kind of tyranny imposed on the reader, and structuralism was no less guilty of this than Marxism and Freudianism—a conclusion he reached around the same time as his friend the *"toujours fidèle"* Susan Sontag did in *Against Interpretation*. In his 1968 essay "The Death of the Author," he argued that reading itself had to be liberated from the repressive "function of the author." He showed what the liberation of the reader might look like in two books published in 1970: *S/Z*, a virtuosic, paragraph-by-paragraph reading of a little-known Balzac short story about a castrato singer disguised as a woman, and *Empire of Signs*, his exquisite travelogue about Japan.

Barthes had fallen in love with Japan after his first visit in 1966. But he was the first to acknowledge that the "country I am calling Japan" was an imaginary country, and he was happy for the actual place to remain elusive. (As he confessed in a letter written in 1942, "I have no curiosity about facts, I am only curious—but fanatically so—about humans.") Nothing pleased him more than the "rustle" of a language he did not understand: at last, language was freed from meaning, from the referential property that he called "stickiness," and converted into pure sound. Not surprisingly, Barthes's favorite contemporary artist was Cy Twombly, whose paintings resembled illegible scribbles—a style that Barthes, an amateur artist, emulated in his own drawings.

While Barthes learned a bit of Japanese, he had little interest in literatures other than French, and virtually none in French fiction written in former colonies such as Morocco, where he taught in the early 1970s and often spent his holidays, mostly in search of boys. (His loathing of colonialism did not extend to sexual tourism.) His taste in contemporary French literature ran to faddish practitioners of "neutral writing," since his aversion to meaning left him indifferent to novels with psychological, much less historical, themes. He never wrote about Georges Perec, the most innovative French novelist to emerge in the 1960s, who shared his fascination with language, writing and the mythologies of consumer society. Perec was crushed by the "silence" of his "master," insisting that his novels had "no other existence than those which your reading of them may provide." But Perec was a Jew who had lost his parents in the war, and the void that lies at the center of his work is their disappearance in the Holocaust, not the *satori*, the emptiness of the haikus that Barthes adored. Perec's novels were too "sticky," too heavy with meaning for Barthes, who, as Sontag observed, "had little feeling for the tragic."

Still, poststructuralism encouraged Barthes's most appealing quality, the grain of his voice, and his writing increasingly assumed its own *petite musique*, liberal in its use of quotation marks, italics and parentheses. At the time of Barthes's defection from the structuralist camp, Claude Lévi-Strauss wrote him, "There is an eclecticism that comes across in the excessive liking you show for subjectivity, for feelings." If Barthes was no longer capable of making distinctions between "symbolic forms" and "the insignificant contents that men and the centuries can pour into them," perhaps, Lévi-Strauss speculated, structuralism had always been "far from his true nature." Was the emperor of structuralist anthropology taking a jab at Barthes's homosexuality, implying that he was too soft and feminine for the rigors of science? Perhaps, but he was not alone in expressing disdain for Barthes, whose autobiographical writings provoked frequent accusations of frivolousness or pandering among academics.

Barthes won election to the Collège de France by only a slender margin in 1975. Even Foucault, who had supported his candidacy, raised his eyebrows when, two years later, Barthes published *A Lover's Discourse*. That book grew out of his obsessive love for a young Romanian man, an ordeal that led him to undertake an ill-fated analysis with Jacques Lacan ("an old fool with an old fogey," as Barthes described their sessions). A delicate, often rapturous sequence of fragments about the many states of ardor, longing and infatuation, it bathed unapologetically in the sort of rhetoric that Foucault had dismantled in the first volume of his *History of Sexuality*, published a year earlier.

But Barthes's originality lay precisely in his riffs on ordinary experiences, which were met with glacial indifference, or smug dissection, from his peers. He democratized semiology by showing that we are all amateur semiologists when we are in love, obsessively reading the behavior of the beloved for signs of affection returned or denied. In his 1973 manifesto *The Pleasure of the Text* he defended another value held in disdain by "the political policeman and the psychoanalytical policeman." He aligned himself with readers, with "the modest practices of a Sunday painter and an amateur pianist," as Samoyault puts it, not with pedagogues, and winked at them knowingly, admitting that he, too, had a tendency to "boldly skip (no one is watching)."

The writers in Paris who best understood the anti-elitist thrust of Barthes's late work were the novelist Philippe Sollers and his partner, the Bulgarian literary theorist Julia Kristeva, who edited the poststructuralist literary journal *Tel Quel*. They formed a strange triangle, as even Sollers—in his self-flattering words, "the only heterosexual man to have had the benefit of representing something for Barthes"—concedes. While Barthes was rhapsodizing about pleasure and desire, Sollers and Kristeva were cheerleading the Chinese Cultural Revolution, plastering the *Tel Quel* offices with the sayings of Chairman Mao. Barthes did not share their enthusiasm, but he was grateful for their friendship, and Kristeva's convoluted theories about abjection made him feel "so inferior . . . so reduced to nonexistence."

In 1974, he joined them on an expedition to China. Barthes passed his time reading *Bouvard and Pécuchet* while Sollers played ping-pong with professors of Marxist philosophy. The puritanism of Mao's China (a "Desert of Flirtation") repulsed Barthes. "What can you know about a people, if you don't know their sex?" he asked Sollers. He worried that he would have "to pay for the Revolution with everything I love: 'free' discourse exempt from all repetition, and immorality." His diary of the trip, however, contained little criticism of Maoist China (Simon Leys called it "a tiny trickle of lukewarm water"). Barthes insisted that he was not "choosing" China, but "what the intellectual public wants is a *choice*: one was to come out of China like a bull crashing out of the *toril* in the crowded arena: furious or triumphant." He had gone to China for the same reason that (in the face of considerable Parisian criticism) he had gone to lunch with President Valéry Giscard d'Estaing: "out of curiosity, a taste for hearing things, a bit like a myth-hunter on the prowl."

By the early 1970s, Barthes was writing on what he called a "trapeze without any safety net, ever since I've no longer had the nets of structuralism, semiology or Marxism." But being Barthes was more than enough, and for all his protests against meaning, he ended up producing some of French literature's most moving writing on desire, love, and loss. The loss that affected him more deeply than any was that of his mother, who died in 1977, at eighty-four.

Barthes often spoke in his "Preparation for the Novel" lectures about Dante's idea of the *vita nuova*, of starting out anew. But the thought of a new life without his mother was unfathomable to him. Although Barthes devoted much of his spare time to cruising, he was otherwise a strict monogamist: he lived his entire life, after all, with a single woman, who supplied him with an image of "the Sovereign Good." Henriette Barthes was the one person from whom he scrupulously concealed his homosexuality, and one suspects that his reason had less to do with a fear of reproach than with a fear that she might mistake his other desires for infidelity. Her death left him almost paralyzed. When asked what he planned to teach the following semester, he replied, "I'll show some photos of my mother, and remain silent." Over the next year he took notes about his loss on more than three hundred index cards.

A number of the ideas in those index cards—published posthumously as *Mourning Diary*—were reworked in his last and greatest work, *Camera Lucida*, in which Barthes most fully realized his dream of "the novelistic without the novel . . . a writing of life." *Camera Lucida* is a book about photography and mourning, and about how a single photograph allowed him to mourn Henriette's death. Photography has usually been understood in relation to painting, but Barthes likened it, strikingly, to "a kind of primitive theatre . . . a figuration of the motionless and made-up face beneath which we see the dead." In a famous distinction, he argued that each photograph attracted our interest by way of two basic elements: the *studium*, "a kind of general, enthusiastic commitment," and the *punctum*, a detail that "pricks me (but also bruises me, is poignant to me)."

On his desk as he wrote *Camera Lucida* was a photograph of five-year-old Henriette, in the winter garden of the house where she was born. It is the only photograph he discusses that is not reproduced in the book. "At most it would interest your *studium*: period, clothes, photogeny," he writes. "But in it, for you, no wound." The *punctum* in the winter garden photograph, for Barthes, is the "untenable paradox" of her character, "the assertion of a gentleness," and it leads him to remember having "nursed her" while she lay dying, when she "had become my little girl, uniting for me with that essential child she was in her first photograph." In one of the final images in Barthes's work, Henriette, whose kindness permeated her son's writing, is briefly raised from the dead, and Barthes, who was unable to go on after her death, achieves instead the miracle of birth: "I who had not procreated, I had, in her very illness, engendered my mother." That Barthes, the most irreligious of French writers, left us with a vision of the immaculate conception was a paradox he might have savored.

{2018}

11

Solitary Passions: Alain Robbe-Grillet's Secret Room

By the time he was elected to the Académie française in 2004, Alain Robbe-Grillet had suffered a cruel fate: he had all the renown he could have hoped for but few readers to show for it. The literary movement he'd launched half a century earlier—the nouveau roman—had ground to a halt. The new novel—antipsychological and anti-expressive, stripped of individualized characters, temporal continuity and meaning itself—was no longer new. Like the total serialism championed by his contemporary Pierre Boulez, it seemed all the more dated for heralding a future that had failed to arrive. In the US, where he'd once enjoyed a cultish notoriety alongside Beckett and Genet, Robbe-Grillet was now to be found in second-hand bookshops. Passionately anticlerical, a self-confessed sadist, Robbe-Grillet had always relished his unofficial title, the "pope of the nouveau roman," but now the joke was wearing thin: no one wants to lead a church without a congregation. His parting gesture was to preside over a black mass. He called it *Un roman sentimental*.

Published six months before his death in 2008, it is the story of a fourteen-year-old girl called Gigi, and her initiation into S&M under the tutelage of her father, lover and master, a man known as the Professor. That's a sanitized summary of the proceedings, described in meticulous prose in 239 numbered paragraphs over little more than a hundred pages. Fayard, his publisher, was worried enough to have the book wrapped in plastic with an advisory notice. It's not hard to see why. France had been rocked by a series of scandals over child pornography, and Robbe-Grillet's novel was a work of unrelenting and graphic sadism, in which women—or rather, barely pubescent girls—exist to be raped, tortured and murdered. Some are eaten alive by dogs ("so they conserve the memory of the delicious scent and flavor of the thing that it is their mission to hunt down"), while others are given a "commercially banned ointment" that causes them to come so violently they die. Robbe-Grillet's proclivities were well known—Fredric Jameson called his sensibility "sado-aestheticism"—but they had never before found such gruesome expression.

Back in the news for the first time in years, Robbe-Grillet had a lot of explaining to do. Always a forceful spokesman for his own work, he took up the task with his usual gusto, describing *Un roman sentimental*, with a wink, as a book of "Flaubertian precision." (He never missed a chance to tip his hat to the canon, even as he seemed to ask us not to take him at his word.) His aim was to purge himself of violent fantasies that he claimed were widely shared. Yes, he had "loved little girls" since he was twelve, but he had never acted on his fantasies. In fact he had "mastered" them. And he continued in this half-facetious, half-moralizing vein: "Someone who writes about his perversion is someone who has control over it." He warned of a new "literary correctness" ("when one writes something incorrect, it's as if one were committing it"), and seemed hurt by an interviewer's suggestion that he had written a "masturbatory" novel. On the contrary, *Un roman sentimental* was, "like all my novels," a Brechtian work, written in a glacial style so as to distance the reader from the book's infernal preoccupations.

Un roman sentimental was greeted with derision in France. Its author was a dirty old man, or a lunatic, or both. Robbe-Grillet seemed shaken by the reception. He now insisted that, although the novel's prose was "irreproachable," it wasn't really a part of his oeuvre: it grew out of erotic notebooks he'd been keeping since he was an adolescent. The notebooks were separate from his literary journals, he said, as if a fortress defended the one from the porno-guerrilla attacks of the other. He had a point. Although the prose is unmistakably Robbe-Grillet's, the questions raised by *Un roman sentimental* were rather different from those raised by the novels that made his reputation. His early masterpieces were narrative puzzles; each revolved, teasingly, around a blind spot or cavity. In *Le Voyeur*, the 1955 novel that brought him to prominence, we never learn if Mathias, a traveling watch salesman, has killed the precocious Jacqueline or merely fantasized about doing so: the crime scene, but not his anxious search for an alibi, has been erased from the narrative ("the abnormal, excessive, suspicious, inexplicable time amounted to forty minutes—if not fifty"). Not only are we denied a resolution, but our thwarted attempt to find one, to assign guilt and fill that maddening cavity, becomes the real story of *Le Voyeur*. The novel's "clarity reveals everything except itself," Maurice Blanchot wrote in his magisterial review. "It is as if we were seeing everything, without anything being visible. The result is strange." Robbe-Grillet's mother said it was "a fine book," though she would rather it had not been written by her son. "It's a good thing you wrote that novel," a psychoanalyst told him. "If you hadn't, you might have murdered a young woman." (Robbe-Grillet would often cite this diagnosis with approval; he enjoyed his role as the resident psychopath in the republic of letters.)

Olga Bernal, one of Robbe-Grillet's most perceptive early interpreters (he had an army of them when the nouveau roman was still new), called her 1964 study of his work *Le Roman de l'absence*. "At the center of Robbe-Grillet's world," she wrote, "there is not *something*; there is an *absence* of something. His novels become, as a result, the story of an absence, of a 'gap at the heart of reality.'" They are full of intricate, almost fanatically clinical descriptions of the surfaces of everyday reality, but the crucial things are left to the imagination, as if he were bent on revealing—no doubt, mocking—our desire to make sense of a senseless world. In *Un roman sentimental*, nothing is left to the imagination: it is a crime scene brazenly told from the standpoint of the perpetrators.

But the book is not an outlier in Robbe-Grillet's work or an old man's folly. The boundaries between his two journals were more porous than he suggested. *Un roman sentimental* was hardly the first time that he'd explored the topic of pedophilia or of sadism. Sexual criminality lay at the heart of Robbe-Grillet's nouveau roman: the original, unspeakable absence that drives his unresolved plots. *Un roman sentimental* existed as an idea, and an inspiration, long before it was written. Consider Robbe-Grillet's 1962 story "La Chambre secrète," dedicated to Gustave Moreau. It begins: "The first thing to be seen is a red stain, of a deep, dark, shiny red, with almost black shadows. It is in the form of an irregular rosette, sharply outlined, extending in several directions in wide outflows of unequal length, dividing and dwindling afterward into single sinuous streaks." The red stain is blood, flowing from the breast of a woman in chains, whose long black hair is "spread out in a complicated wavy disorder over a heavily folded cloth, of velvet perhaps." As her killer, a man in a cape, escapes, his face is "seen only in a vague profile, but one senses in it a violent exaltation." When we read in one of the final sentences that smoke from an incense burner is "rising vertically, toward the top of the canvas," we realize that what we've been reading is a description of a painting such as Moreau might have done. The "secret room" is, literally, the chamber where S&M is practiced, but it seems also to refer to the forbidden imagination that fueled Robbe-Grillet's writing, and that, by his own mischievous account, prevented him from committing murder. Until *Un roman sentimental*, he allowed us only glimpses of his *chambre secrète*, but it was there all along.

As he confessed at the beginning of his 1985 memoir, *Le Miroir qui revient* (translated in 1988 as *Ghosts in the Mirror*), "I have never spoken of anything but myself." The Breton coast, with its dunes, cliffs and seagulls, so powerfully described in *Le Voyeur*, was his childhood *lieu de mémoire*. *La Jalousie*, the story of a love triangle on a banana plantation, was one that he himself had lived. Yet at the time it would have seemed crude to look for biographical clues in his fictions. (No one seemed to notice that he pilfered unashamedly from *série noire* detective fiction and other pulp genres.) For the Marxist critic Lucien Goldmann, Robbe-Grillet's depiction of an inert object world reflected man's alienation under late capitalism. For Barthes, the fiction reflected nothing except the surfaces of modern life, which it described with depersonalized accuracy, having dismissed individual psychology as an anachronism. Barthes argued that Robbe-Grillet had created an "objective literature," one "turned toward the object" (rather than to consciousness), but his use of the term "objective" was widely misunderstood to imply that Robbe-Grillet was somehow impartial, or neutral. "One is entitled to wonder: what principle of selection guides Robbe-Grillet in choosing one object for description rather than another?" Irving Howe asked in a mocking review. "Why a tomato rather than a cucumber?" Another, related misconception, which Barthes was also responsible for spreading, was that Robbe-Grillet required "only one mode of perception: the sense of sight." Never mind that his novels were nearly as rich in sounds as in images: he was the novelist of "the gaze." His detractors, citing his training as an agronomist who specialized in the diseases of the banana, belittled him as a scientist implausibly moonlighting as a novelist. Robbe-Grillet particularly resented the insinuation that he wrote with a "scientific eye," or—the "supreme injury"—that his descriptions of place were "geometrical": geometry, he protested, was an "exact science of measurements," while he was interested in topology, the subjective properties of space, not topography, its quantitative ones.

Still, he didn't protest too much: the confusion prompted by his work added to its aura, and he had a hand in stoking it. He boasted that he had "nothing to express," and seemed to enjoy taunting readers who looked for meaning beneath the surface. "The reality in question is a strictly material one," he wrote in the mordant foreword to his 1959 novel, *Dans le labyrinthe*. "The reader is therefore requested to see in it only the objects, actions, words and events which are described, without attempting to give them either more or less meaning than in his own life, or his own death." Ever the unreliable narrator—and mostly an unreliable commentator on his books—Robbe-Grillet knew that he was asking the reader to do the impossible: as he admitted elsewhere, "no sooner does one describe an empty corridor than metaphysics comes rushing headlong into it."

Empty spaces, resembling nothing in actuality yet described as if by a camera, were a Robbe-Grillet specialty. These labyrinths reminded some critics of Kafka, but they were deliberately drained of meaning: Robbe-Grillet revered Kafka but loathed Max Brod's theological reading of his work. The opening line of his masterpiece, *La Jalousie* (1957), reads like an architectural diagram: "Now the shadow of the column—the column which supports the southwest corner of the roof—divides the corresponding corridor of the veranda into two equal parts." The prose seldom wavers from this sterile, descriptive rigor, yet its eerie rhythms and hypnotic repetitions—and its curious absence of affect—create a sense of mounting disquiet. A woman called A . . . has cocktails with her neighbor Franck, whose wife is never able to join them. This scene is repeated again and again, without any firm temporal indication, except that it is happening now; and with such slight variations that the reviewer from *Le Monde* thought he'd been sent a defective copy. Who is observing this scene? We're never told, we never see more than "he" sees, and we can never be sure whether he's seeing, remembering or imagining it. The absent narrator is usually taken to be the woman's jealous husband, spying on her and Franck through a slatted shutter (a *jalousie*), but he (or perhaps more precisely it) is never referred to in the first or third person. As Blanchot wrote, he is a "pure anonymous presence," his role in the triangle implied by an empty place setting at the table. But what this phantom notices is hardly disinterested: A . . . and Franck drinking cognac and soda on the veranda, chatting about a novel set in Africa in which a white woman is sleeping with the natives; the number of banana trees on the plantation, which he counts for pages and pages; a crushed centipede that leaves a dark stain on the wall; the image (or perhaps a fantasy) of A . . . and Franck in a car crash that sets off a brush fire, making the same "sound the centipede makes, motionless again on the wall." In *La Jalousie*, published the same year as the Battle of Algiers, the loss of control over a woman seeped into a more generalized fear of colonial disorder. Its dispassionate yet obsessional prose was expressive, almost in spite of itself. It suggested a latent violence, hidden by a great labor of repression.

In Robbe-Grillet, the gaze invariably belongs to a murderer or a madman. In his imagination, objectivity is a kind of derangement, a monstrous will to power. This skepticism had its roots in his childhood. He was born in 1922 in Brest, his mother's hometown, but brought up in Paris. His parents were, in his words, "right-wing anarchists": they read aloud from *L'Action française* at the dinner table, loathed Léon Blum and the Third Republic, and believed that France had to be protected from "Judeo-Bolshevism"; yet they had inherited from their own left-wing fathers a hatred of the "sacred union of the army and the church" and were eccentrically nonconformist. Still, they preferred the Germans to the British, and when France fell to the Nazis welcomed the occupiers as defenders of "order."

At the time of Vichy, Robbe-Grillet was in Paris at the National Institute of Agronomy (which Michel Houellebecq, who found his work "indigestible," would attend).* Unable to return to Brest, he ended up in Nuremberg as a forced laborer assembling Panzer tanks. He had never questioned his parents' support for Pétain and found the war a shattering experience. He stood at a lathe in a factory for seventy-two hours a week and lived on rotten potatoes; he saw a group of soldiers arrest a man in hospital, who bawled "like a beast being led to slaughter"; he experienced "the fundamental *strangeness* of my own relation with the world," a feeling of "exteriority, almost of extra-territoriality," as if "I was there by mistake." After this "Bavarian interlude," "a respect for order at all costs could now only make me profoundly suspicious . . . We'd just seen where that got us." When he finally returned to Brest, the town had been flattened and was being rebuilt as an American-style city. Yet "instead of crying over these ruins,"

---

* After Robbe-Grillet's death, Houellebecq wrote that Robbe-Grillet "reminded me of Agro, and he even reminded me of something much more precise, something that only former Agro students know: Alain Robbe-Grillet reminded me of soil-cutting."

he recalled in *Préface à une vie d'écrivain* (2005), "we felt on the contrary a great euphoria. The world was there for the making."

Like many of his peers, Robbe-Grillet hoped that socialism would rise from the ashes of fascism and war, but four days of "building socialism" with a brigade of volunteers in Bulgaria left him suspicious of the left—and, he said, of any truth claims. He decided now that truth had "always and only served oppression." The literature of commitment, whether socialist realist or existentialist, struck him as a moral luxury: "I had seen the face of death and didn't feel I was in the best position to give my fellow citizens public moral lessons." For a few years after the war, he found relief from his all-pervading uncertainty in science, as a researcher with the Institut des fruits et agrumes coloniaux, studying diseases of the banana tree in Guinea, Morocco, Guadeloupe and Martinique. But there were "ghosts I couldn't come to terms with," and this "world of concepts, cleanness, virtue" failed to exorcise them. Writing was "the most promising arena in which to act out this permanent imbalance: the fight to the death between order and freedom, the insoluble conflict between rational classification and subversion."

After being hospitalized in Martinique with a variety of tropical diseases, Robbe-Grillet left his job and returned to Paris. He spent his days in an artificial insemination lab taking vaginal smears from sterile rats injected with urine from mares in foal; at night, in a tiny garret above his parents' flat on rue Gassendi, he worked on his first novel, *Un régicide*. Gallimard turned it down, but in 1953 his second novel, *Les Gommes*, was accepted by Jérôme Lindon at Editions de Minuit, Beckett's publisher. *Les Gommes* was both a neo-noir and a modern rewriting of the Oedipus myth, about a police inspector investigating a murder that has not yet taken place: he ends up killing the suspect, who may be his father. The critic Jean Cayrol read *Les Gommes* as an allegory about the German occupation and the French Resistance: "Sadly," Robbe-Grillet later wrote, "I had been on the other side."

Les Gommes won the Prix Fénéon and the admiration of Barthes, who saw in its affectless prose a model of "writing degree zero," ignoring what Cayrol and others took to be its allegorical dimensions. *Le Voyeur* and *La Jalousie* followed over the next four years. As an adviser to Lindon, Robbe-Grillet began shepherding to publication the novels of Michel Butor, Nathalie Sarraute, Claude Simon, Robert Pinget and Marguerite Duras, who were soon known as the "école de Minuit." These writers drew on different models, but with their detached sensibility and rejection of nineteenth-century dramatic conventions, they had enough in common for Émile Henriot of *Le Monde* to declare the birth of the nouveau roman in 1957, the movement's annus mirabilis. "Henriot was kind," Robbe-Grillet recalled, "with a charming incomprehension, naive about what we were doing . . . He thought literature had ended with Balzac." Robbe-Grillet's own view was that Balzac ("an Ice Age in the history of litera-ture") had nearly destroyed the novel: "Who is that omniscient, omnipresent narrator appearing everywhere at once, simultane-ously seeing the outside and the inside of things . . . knowing the present, the past and the future of every enterprise?" he asked in his 1963 manifesto, *Pour un nouveau roman*. "It can only be God."

One novelist accused Robbe-Grillet of wanting to "saw off the branch we're sitting on." He replied that "the branch in question actually died of natural causes." The ancestor of the nouveau roman, he suggested, was Flaubert, who had injected a revolutionary element of uncertainty and doubt into narration. What struck him most powerfully about *Madame Bovary* was the narrator's opening reference to *nous*, "we": "That *nous* . . . signified that there was *somebody*"—not a God-like narrator —"who was speaking." Then came Proust, Kafka, Joyce and Faulkner. But the novel—the French novel, he meant—was now at risk of regression, thanks to the vogue for existentialism and committed literature, which emphasized political and ethical concerns over formal ones. Just as Boulez argued that composers had to "fight the past to survive," so Robbe-Grillet argued that "the novel's forms must evolve in order to remain alive."

The chief obstacle to innovation was Sartre, who had opened the way for the nouveau roman with his phenomenological novel

La Nausée but failed to explore its radical implications, caving in to the old myth of "depth": the idea that the "surface of things" is a "mask of their heart, a sentiment that led to every kind of metaphysical transcendence." Like Lévi-Strauss, Robbe-Grillet saw Sartre as a ninteenth-century holdover, clinging to the fables of reason, historical progress and, worst of all, humanism. Sartre still thought the world meant something and that it was the job of the writer to reveal its meaning; so did Camus, the philosopher of the absurd. "The world is neither significant nor absurd. It *is*, quite simply," Robbe-Grillet wrote in a passage with Heideggerian undertones. "That, in any case, is the most remarkable thing about it." The task was to liberate the novel from the "tyranny of significations," an idea that Susan Sontag soon lifted in *Against Interpretation*. Depth, character and humanism, as Robbe-Grillet saw it, were "obsolete notions" that stood in the way of what Barthes called the pleasure of the text, and Sontag the "erotics of art." Robbe-Grillet denounced them with a Nietzschean delight. Character: "How much we've heard about character! . . . Fifty years of disease, the death notice signed many times over by the most serious essayists, yet nothing has yet managed to knock it off the pedestal on which the nineteenth century had placed it." Humanism: "Is there not . . . a certain fraudulence in this word *human* which is always being thrown in our faces?" Fortunately, "the exclusive cult of the 'human' has given way to a larger consciousness, one that is less anthropocentric." This was as much a philosophical project as a literary one. The critique of Western humanism, the attack on "transcendence" and metaphysics, the assault on truth as a rhetoric of domination, the rebellion against the philosopher who was taken to embody these ideas, Sartre: Robbe-Grillet got there first, and Foucault among others would celebrate him as a radical thinker, a playful, nihilist *maître à penser*.

From the late 1950s to the mid-1960s, Robbe-Grillet enjoyed unmatched prestige as a champion and practitioner of the nouveau roman: an influence on Perec and Modiano, Calvino and Cortázar; the darling of the avant-garde literary journal *Tel Quel*. Grove's combined edition of *La Jalousie* and *Dans le labyrinthe* sold 40,000 copies in the US, where Robbe-Grillet was taken on a widely publicized tour of "forty universities and forty-three cocktail parties." He also rose to prominence in the world of cinema, both as the screenwriter of Alain Resnais's *Last Year at Marienbad*—in which a glamorously distressed couple talk endlessly about whether or not they met the year before in a deserted hotel—and as the director of his own kinky, enigmatic films. The unresolved mystery à la Robbe-Grillet acquired such avant-garde cachet—thanks above all to his friend Michelangelo Antonioni's *L'Avventura*—that Pauline Kael grumbled about a "creeping Marienbadism." When "The Talk of the Town" told him "we didn't feel we had completely understood" the plot of *Last Year at Marienbad*, Robbe-Grillet replied: "Moi non plus." He was well spoken, well traveled and, with his wavy black hair and moustache, rather dashing: the novelist as matinée idol, as likely to be seen at Cannes as at a literary festival.

The virile looks, however, were deceptive, as his wife, Catherine, discovered. She was the daughter of Armenians from Iran; they met in 1951 in the Gare de Lyon, as they were both boarding a train to Istanbul. He was instantly taken with her. Barely out of her teens, not quite five feet tall and only forty kilos, Catherine Rstakian "looked so young then that everyone thought she was still a child." She inspired in him (as he later wrote) "desperate feelings of paternal love—incestuous, needless to say." The relationship began immediately, but with one condition, imposed by Catherine: there could be no penetration, since she had undergone a painful clandestine abortion the year before and didn't want to risk another. Six years later, on a boat from Zadar to Dubrovnik, she changed her mind, only to learn that her fiancé was impotent. He had other things in mind for his "petite fille," as he called her. "His fantasies turned obsessively around sadistic domination of (very) young women, by default little girls," she wrote in her memoir of their life together, *Alain*. He gave her "drawings of little girls, bloodied." ("Reassure yourself, he never transgressed the limits of the law," she adds.) Shortly after they were married in 1957, they drew up a contract in five pages, outlining the "special rights of the husband over his young wife, during private séances," where she would submit to torture, whipping and other humiliations. If she performed her duties with "kindness and effort," she would be paid in cash, which she could use for "expensive holidays, private purchases, or lavish generosity on behalf of third parties."

Catherine Robbe-Grillet never signed the contract, which "clashed with my erotic imagination": "A Master imposed himself, he didn't negotiate." Writing under the male pseudonym Jean de Berg, she had explored her erotic imagination in an S&M novel, *L'Image*, published in 1956 by Minuit. He respected her wishes, and never asked for an explanation. When they moved into the Château du Mesnil-au-Grain, a seventeenth-century mansion in Normandy, it was Catherine, not Alain, who became the house dominatrix—France's most legendary practitioner—as if she were "substituting myself for Alain." He was remarkably solicitous of her needs, and she of his. He welcomed her lover, Vincent, so long as Vincent agreed to be his disciple (there could only be one Master in the house). She also shared her mistresses with him, and dressed up as Lolita when they had dinner with Nabokov. She was "content, even proud," when Alain fell for Catherine Jourdain, a stunning blonde who seduced him on the beach in Djerba, where he was directing her in his 1969 film *L'Éden et après*; she read every letter he wrote to Jourdain. The affair appears to have been the closest thing to a conventional heterosexual relationship he had, but he was overwhelmed by her "voraciousness" in bed, and she failed to be "the docile slave he dreamed of." When the affair ended, Robbe-Grillet lost interest in sex. He felt burdened when Catherine offered him a close friend of hers as a birthday gift in 1975; the next year he announced his retirement from "all erotic activity between two people or with several." From then on, she says, he "isolated himself in an ivory tower populated with prepubescent fantasies, in the pursuit, in his 'retirement,' of the waking dreams in his *Roman sentimental* —reveries of a solitary sadist."

Renouncing sex seems to have liberated Robbe-Grillet to write about it more explicitly. His novels of the 1970s and 1980s were full of S&M subplots; so were his films, in which beautiful young women invariably appeared without clothes, often tied up, while older, intellectual men devised unusual (and humiliating) forms of ravishment, such as cracking eggs on their naked bellies. In what soon became known as the "nouveau nouveau roman," he surrendered to fantasy and emphatically abandoned any attempt at realistic representation. Robbe-Grillet's frustration with nineteenth-century convention, in *Pour un nouveau roman*, was that it "reconciled" readers to their alienation from the world of objects; he wanted to depict this immutable rift between people and "things"—and between people—without the consolations of humanism, and thus to recover a sense of reality. "The discovery of reality," he argued, "will continue only if we abandon outworn forms." There was always a tension in the earlier work between the deadpan and the deadly earnest—between the prankster and the scientist—but the nouveau nouveau roman took a more overtly playful, textual turn: the new work was a gleeful flight from the real, a fantastical *jeu d'esprit* that unfolded within the narrow confines of narrative practice, drawing on what he called "generative themes": formal elements whose manipulation he compared to the techniques of modern music and painting. Narrators battle for control of the text; characters (who aren't, of course, characters) appear under different names, defying our attempts to identify them. Even the sex is textual: the bodies we see are usually images of images—models on billboards, or mutilated mannequins.

   The nouveau nouveau roman was launched by Robbe-Grillet's zany 1970 novel *Projet pour une révolution à New York*, inspired by a three-day visit to Manhattan. An army of revolutionary rapists is carrying out attacks in the subway; "crime," one character explains, "is indispensable to the revolution . . . Rape, murder, arson are the three metaphoric acts which will free the blacks, the impoverished proletariat and the intellectual workers from their slavery, and at the same time the bourgeoisie from its sexual complexes." The allusion to these "metaphoric acts" was a giveaway. Metaphor, for Robbe-Grillet, was the origin, and original sin, of fiction-making: a violation of the purely descriptive and thus a "rape" of reality. The "revolution" refers, above all, to the author's failed attempt to write a novel that coheres; it begins and ends in metaphor.

But the metaphor of rape was not a random choice: Robbe-Grillet seemed peculiarly drawn to it. A girl called Laura is held hostage in a high-rise; another female prisoner is burned alive, her body "twisting in a paroxysm of suffering." The pace is antic, yet circular, a sequence of looping repetitions of the novel's "generative themes": not only rape, but bondage, the nature of narrative, the relationship between art, crime and revolutionary violence. The story is a breathless sequence of false starts and "traps," no doubt intended to expose the deceptive lure of narrative, and inviting us—if we haven't given up—to compose our own novel. (The nouveau nouveau roman was a choose-your-own-adventure novel for theory-heads.) Robbe-Grillet studiously avoids describing New York in realistic terms: like Kafka's America, it's a phantom city—a figure of urban apocalypse. The noir elements that were so haunting in his earlier novels now incline to farce, amusing enough but in the end wearying. The writer who had parodied older forms—Greek tragedy, noir, the novel of matrimonial betrayal—now seemed to be parodying himself:

> The first scene goes very fast. Evidently it has already been rehearsed several times: everyone knows his part by heart. Words and gestures follow each other in a relaxed, continuous manner, the links as imperceptible as the necessary elements of some properly lubricated machinery.
>
> Then there is a gap, a blank space, a pause of indeterminate length during which nothing happens, not even the anticipation of what will come next.
>
> And suddenly the action resumes, without warning, and the same scene occurs again . . . But which scene?

By now, most readers in France had ceased to care; even his intellectual champions lost interest, although Barthes stood by him. "Transgression" had come to mean *l'écriture féminine* and gay erotica; Robbe-Grillet's hetero-sadist fixations looked decidedly démodé, quite possibly reactionary. (Fredric Jameson wondered whether his books had become "unreadable since feminism.") At the party for Barthes's 1977 inaugural lecture at the Collège de France, Foucault confronted Robbe-Grillet: "I have told you this already and I will say it again, Alain: when it comes to sex, you are, and always have been misguided!" Barthes rose to his defense, reminding Foucault that Robbe-Grillet was, at the very least, a pervert. Foucault replied: "Ça ne suffit pas!"

There was no denying Robbe-Grillet's growing isolation from the Parisian avant-garde. He spent more of his time tending his cacti at the chateau in Normandy, while Catherine whipped her guests in the *chambre secrète.** America, where "French theory" was all the rage on campus, proved more welcoming. He became a lecturer at New York University in the early 1970s and ended up teaching there for more than two decades. He found a new following among American practitioners of deconstruction and—a particular pleasure for him—artists and composers. (American writers had little interest in his work, and the indifference was mutual: Robbe-Grillet admired Burroughs and Nabokov but disdained the "pseudo-realism of Saul Bellow and Mailer.") He had always had a predilection for modern painting and music, and his ambition for the nouveau nouveau roman was to win the same liberties that had freed painters from the obligation to represent "reality" or to mine its surfaces for buried (psychological or political) meanings. Pop artists recognized a fellow Warholian in his deadpan descriptions of coffee pots, billboards and "things" in the world; conceptual artists admired his juxtaposition of readymade forms as narrative collage; minimalist composers heard a literary analogue of Reich and Glass in his use of churning repetitions with tiny, flickering variations. (In *Robbe-Grillet Cleansing Every Object in Sight*, a homage by his friend the painter Mark Tansey, a figure appears in a desert,

---

* I originally referred to those on the receiving end of Catherine Robbe-Grillet's whip as her "clients." After the essay was published, she wrote the *London Review of Books* to correct "an inaccuracy which, in view of the reputation of the *LRB*, is likely to be taken as gospel: I have *never* received 'clients', either in my 'chambre secrète' or anywhere else; neither before Alain's death, nor after. I have only ever been a dominatrix for my personal pleasure, never *ever* for money!"

scrubbing stones as if to remove any "signification.") There were intriguing collaborations with Rauschenberg, Johns and—most strikingly—Magritte, in a 1975 book called *La Belle Captive*.

After *La Belle Captive*, the best Robbe-Grillet novels appeared under the names of other writers: Italo Calvino (*If on a Winter's Night a Traveler*), Paul Auster (*The New York Trilogy*) and, later, Jean-Philippe Toussaint and Tom McCarthy. In 2001, he published a sort of spy-thriller, a nouveau nouveau roman set in a ravaged postwar Berlin, but its title, *La Reprise*—"resumption," "repetition," even "rerun"—captured all too well the experience of reading it. Most of the later novels seem tossed off, as fodder for dreary dissertations on "transgressive literature."

A new voice emerged toward the end of his career in a trilogy of lightly fictionalized memoirs that he called "romanesques." Having assailed the idea that anything might be beneath the surface of his prose, he now disclosed his autobiographical inspirations with self-deprecating wit and an affection for the world of which few imagined him capable. He wrote of how the music of the Breton waves had shaped his sentences, and, in a darker vein, of the perversions that lurked at the edges of his novels. The "beneficiaries of my first erotic practices" were a collection of china dolls, which he would dress and undress. He "cheerfully dreamed of the massacre of my classmates," reserving the pretty ones for "long, drawn-out torture sessions tied to the chestnut trees in the playground." In *Les Derniers Jours de Corinthe*, the second of these romanesques, he wrote that while working in Martinique he had become infatuated with a "pink and blonde" girl who had "the air of a bonbon"; Marianne, the twelve-year-old daughter of a local magistrate, would sit on his knee, "conscious without doubt" of the effect these "lascivious demonstrations" had on him.

Most striking of all, though, was his account in *Le Miroir qui revient* of growing up in a collaborationist family, a reckoning that was all the more powerful for being free of shame or apology. Robbe-Grillet made no secret of his parents' prejudices, or of their enthusiasm for the Germans, yet he portrayed them with disarming tenderness. His father, a sapper in World War I, had returned home with a collection of scars and a limp, but otherwise "as elegant as ever, ready to throw himself wholeheartedly into the most dubious causes." He founded a fascist groupuscule, the Renaissance Socialiste Nationale, in 1936, but when Pétain came to power he refused, out of pure obstinacy, to put up a poster of the Maréchal; he did put it up when the war ended, to spite the Americans. Robbe-Grillet's mother was a lover of animals (and, it seems, of women) who kept mollusks as pets and hid a bat under her blouse,

> to the great terror of uninitiated visitors, who thought they were hallucinating when at table they looked at their impassive hostess whose tea they were politely sipping, and saw the creature suddenly emerge from its hiding place through the narrow opening of a white collar with large lapels, to clamber awkwardly over her breast and neck spreading its huge, black, silky wings.

He shared with his mother a passion for "nooks," and for classifying things, like the "mouth parts of lobsters and sea urchins." The most memorable—perhaps the only—characters he ever created, his parents as they appeared here suggested what Robbe-Grillet might have done if he'd been a more conventional novelist.

This confessional turn caused a gratifying stir, although his scandalous success at an outwardly conventional genre soon left him uneasy. By the mid-1980s the French literary scene— partly as a result of the nouveau roman—had seen "a violent reaction against any attempt to escape the norms of traditional expression-representation." Worried that he might be "sliding into the slippery slope of the prevailing discourse" and jeopardizing his reputation as an avant-garde prankster, he insisted that his romanesques were as elusive and unreliable as his novels. He noted that one of the recurring characters, Henri de Corinthe, was a fictional creation, inspired by Goethe's "Fiancée of Corinth," itself based on a Greek legend. Still, the romanesques had all the personality and warmth that he had forsworn, and gave ample display of storytelling gifts that he'd done his best to hide. He was now an establishment figure: a member of the Académie (though he was never inducted in an official ceremony, since he refused to wear the required uniform), the subject of an extensive portrait on the radio station France Culture, and even an actor—Raúl Ruiz cast him as Edmond de Goncourt in his 1999 Proust adaptation, *Le Temps retrouvé*. Perhaps it was "time to resume the terrorist activities of the years 1955–60."

One way to read *Un roman sentimental* is as a return to literary terrorism: an old man's bid to be the bad boy again. The story is fairly typical Sadean fare. Gigi, a fourteen-year-old girl and a very eager student of sexual transgression, reads an obscene eighteenth-century novel with her father (and lover), the Professor. She's bored by the "scenes of couplings according to conjugal norms," but turned on by the tale of a "great feast . . . where a victorious sultan, for the sole pleasure of his court, tortured to death the 900 girls delivered the previous night as war trophies, almost all virgins." As a reward for her ardor, the Professor gives her a "toy," a thirteen-year-old girl "endowed with various precocious charms," whom she submits to a number of sexual tortures before consigning her to a dungeon, her body covered with "artfully painted lash marks." A harem of child sex slaves—virgin *belles captives*—are violently deflowered, in scenes described with Robbe-Grillet's obsessional precision: murderously large dildos, seats made of nails, sliced and grilled breasts.

It's hard not to be repelled by *Un roman sentimental*. When it came under fire in France, Robbe-Grillet, who once compared his novels to uncommitted crimes, claimed somewhat disingenuously not to understand what all the fuss was about. He had never laid a hand on an underage girl; what harm, he asked with a grin, could he have done by writing about his fantasies? This was a reasonable enough defense: *Un roman sentimental* is a work of fiction, not an incitement to crime, much less a criminal act. Or that was my view when I started the book; as the atrocities piled up, each more unspeakable than the last, I wondered what my reaction would have been if the novel had been set on a slave plantation or in a concentration camp. It is a severe test of any reader's civil libertarian convictions.

On closer inspection, however, *Un roman sentimental* is not simply an impotent man's fantasy of dominance over a group of helpless girls. Robbe-Grillet's novels were always laid with traps and, as Blanchot warned, the central illusion of his novels is their impression of total legibility. The secret of *Un roman sentimental* is hiding in plain sight. The title is not, or not merely, a prank: this is, in fact, a sentimental ode to his two great loves.

The first is writing. An "adult fairy tale," the novel opens in a void, perhaps the blank page of the novel we're reading. "At first sight, the place in which I find myself is neutral, white, so to speak: not dazzlingly white, rather of a nondescript hue, deceptive, ephemeral, altogether absent." Suddenly, the (never identified) narrator's eyes are drawn to a painting, a "forest landscape" where a naked young girl is bathing. This is the girl he calls Gigi. The world depicted in *Un roman sentimental* is not only unreal, but an artifice, inspired by a painting and peopled by ghosts in the mirror. We are not far from Robbe-Grillet's 1962 homage to Moreau, "La Chambre secrète," also an elaborate staging of an imaginary painting. The passion Robbe-Grillet describes in such outrageous detail is, perhaps, less important than what he called his "passion to describe": the solitary passion that defined the nouveau roman.

Robbe-Grillet's other great love was his wife Catherine, his *petite fille*. Their marriage, an unbroken pact of complicity over more than half a century, bears a close resemblance to the relationship of the couple in *Un roman sentimental*. It's no accident that Gigi is also called Djinn, a word that sounds like the English "Jean," which was Catherine's pseudonym as a writer of S&M. Gigi/Djinn resembles Jean de Berg in other ways: she's the brilliant pupil who absorbs the wisdom of her Master and surpasses him in the art of sexual cruelty. (She even seems to be the ideal Robbe-Grillet reader, impressed by an erotic novel's "precise description, objective, without superfluous words.") The ornate, almost comically rarefied prose here is less reminiscent of Sade than of the Robbe-Grillets' unsigned marital contract. The last line of this, the last novel Robbe-Grillet published, is unexpectedly declamatory, and unexpectedly moving: "Thus shall we for ever live in celestial fortresses." His own celestial fortress was literature itself, the secret room of the imagination. Literature had been his freedom from truth and certainty, and a playpen for his criminal passions and victimless crimes. In her memoir *Alain*, Catherine Robbe-Grillet, who still works out of a *chambre secrète* at the Château du Mesnil-au-Grain, described her husband's last novel as "his bouquet." She knew the flowers were for her.

{2014}

12

The Banality of Islamism: Michel Houellebecq's *Submission*

Michel Houellebecq's novel about a Muslim takeover of France is a melancholy tribute to the pleasure of surrender. It's 2022, a charismatic Islamist politician called Mohammed Ben Abbes has become president, and France has fallen under his spell. Houellebecq's timing could hardly have been better: *Soumission* was published on January 7, 2015, the day of the *Charlie Hebdo* massacre. The novel was hailed by the right as a prophetic warning, a fictional cousin of Éric Zemmour's anti-Muslim tirade, *Le Suicide français*, and attacked by the left, in the words of Alain Jakubowicz, as "the best Christmas gift he could have given to Marine Le Pen." Both Houellebecq's admirers and his detractors assumed that he still believed Islam was what he'd once called it: "the stupidest religion." But Houellebecq has had second thoughts, and although his novel is deeply reactionary, it is not Islamophobic.

Houellebecq is not the first to imagine an Islamic France. In 1959, three years before he presided over the end of Algérie française, Charles de Gaulle told his confidant Alain Peyrefitte that France would have to withdraw from Algeria, because the alternative—full French citizenship for the *indigènes*—would turn it into an Islamic state:

> Do you believe that the French nation can absorb 10 million Muslims, who tomorrow will be 20 million and the day after 40

million? If we adopt integration, if all the Arabs and Berbers of Algeria were considered as Frenchmen, what would prevent them from coming to settle in mainland France where the standard of living is so much higher? My village would no longer be called Colombey-les-Deux-Eglises, but Colombey-les-Deux-Mosquées!

Two decades later, when Peyrefitte revealed de Gaulle's remarks, the hero of the Resistance sounded a lot like Jean-Marie Le Pen. But fear of Islam, and of Muslims, has never been the exclusive property of the far right in France: it has always been rooted in the widespread demographic nightmare of being overrun by Muslims, of the coming "Eurabia."

Houellebecq's novel is sprinkled with winking allusions to anti-Muslim conspiracy theorists like Bat Ye'or, the doyenne of Eurabia literature. But in *Soumission*, France's Islamization isn't brought about by the Muslim birth rate, the rage of the banlieues or the excesses of multiculturalism—the unholy trinity of the far right—and it isn't something to be feared, much less resisted. Rather, it's born of a marriage (arranged, of course) between a rudderless political establishment and a peaceful Islamist party. The Muslim Fraternity party is led by Ben Abbes, a Muslim de Gaulle (Houellebecq's comparison) who towers above his rivals. Houellebecq says his novel should be read as "the book of a sad historian," but the way it observes the passing of French secularism is more bemused than sad. There is never any question in *Soumission* that France doesn't deserve its fate.

Houellebecq has long been denounced as a reactionary, not unfairly. But he writes novels, not manifestos, in spite of their topical surfaces. His singular theme has been the miserable solitude of middle-class white Frenchmen, men of "absolute normality." The typical Houellebecq hero is a bored, alienated, self-pitying man who is losing his place in society, at work and, worst of all, in the bedroom. In a ruthless, zero-sum sexual marketplace, he loses out to men who are more powerful or more virile. Houellebecq is notorious for his pornographic depictions of sex, but there's a point to the detail: his heroes inhabit a pornographic universe, the inevitable result, as he sees it, of the sexual liberation of the 1960s. He can be brutally funny about his self-pitying heroes, yet he also feels sorry for them, even a touch sentimental. In the 2010 novel *The Map and the Territory*, Houellebecq himself appears as a character, only to be murdered in a scene of carnivalesque cruelty. When he was thought to have gone missing during his tour to promote that novel, it was rumored that he'd been kidnapped by Al Qaeda. He hadn't, but the idea clearly had a masochistic appeal: Houellebecq played himself in a mock documentary, *The Kidnapping of Michel Houellebecq*, released last year, in which his feckless kidnappers befriend him, in a reverse Stockholm syndrome, allowing him to enjoy a rare reprieve.

The narrator of *Soumission*, François, is a solitary, alcoholic forty-four-year-old bachelor who teaches literature at the Sorbonne. He's a scholar of J. K. Huysmans, his one "faithful friend." Huysmans is best known as the author of *À Rebours*, a masterpiece of the late nineteenth-century Decadent movement, but Houellebecq is more interested in Huysmans's later spiritual writings, produced after he embraced Catholic mysticism and entered a monastery. The question that drives much of the narrative is whether, like Huysmans, François can overcome his atheism and find redemption in the church. When he's not thinking about Huysmans, François is thinking about his diminishing sexual opportunities. He has on average one girlfriend "per year," but they invariably tell him they've "met someone." His latest girlfriend is Myriam, a pretty Jewish student with a stereotypically warm, tight-knit family, a remarkable gift for oral sex and a tender patience for his eccentricities. But his "abnormal honesty" is wearing thin with her. When he lazily defends patriarchy one evening at his flat, she walks out on him before their sushi arrives. Soon she has another reason to abandon not just François but France: the irresistible rise of Mohammed Ben Abbes and the Muslim Fraternity.

Paris is burning when the novel opens, just before the first round of the 2022 presidential elections. The *identitaires*, fascist militants who call themselves "indigenous" Europeans and oppose "Muslim colonization," are fighting with jihadists for control of the streets. The violence hasn't spread to François's neighborhood in the thirteenth arrondissement, but one day he finds a group of young Muslim men blocking the campus entrance, waiting to escort their burqa-clad "sisters." François used to take comfort in the saying "après moi, le déluge." Now he's not sure he'll die in time to avoid it.

In the first round of elections, the Front National wins, with a third of the vote, followed by the Socialists and the Muslim Fraternity with a fifth each. Faced with the prospect of a Front National victory, François Hollande presents himself as "the last rampart of the republican order." But Hollande's speech elicits only "brief but perceptible chuckles," and it's Ben Abbes who begins to emerge as the most plausible consensus candidate for parties opposed to the Front National. His Muslim Fraternity is the only party capable of imposing order in the banlieues, and it has offered to relinquish control of most ministries as long as it can have the ministry of education. Ben Abbes's rhetoric is silken in its moderation, and he's careful to assuage the fears of Jewish religious authorities. Although a graduate of the École nationale d'administration, he affects the airs of "an old Tunisian spice salesman" and speaks in a "suave and purring" voice. "The nastiest, most aggressive journalists," François observes, become "hypnotized and soft in the presence of Mohammed Ben Abbes." He also notices that the women in burqas are strutting around campus "as if they were already masters of the land."

Unpersuaded by Ben Abbes's appeals to interfaith harmony, Jews begin to leave en masse for Israel, Myriam and her family among them. But the real tragedy belongs to François, who's stuck in France: "There is no Israel for me," he sighs. Fearing civil war, he retreats to the countryside. On his way to Rocamadour, he drives through a ravaged landscape—at a filling station he finds a cashier in a pool of blood and the corpses of two young North Africans—and learns that dozens of voting stations have been attacked, and the elections suspended. Conveniently, he stumbles on Alain Tanneur, a retired intelligence officer married to one of his colleagues. Tanneur has a holiday house in Martel, a town named after Charles Martel, who defeated the Arabs at Poitiers in 732, putting a stop to the Muslim advance to the north. Over dinner, Tanneur, who "gave the impression of almost abnormal intellectual agility," provides François with a report on the backroom negotiations in Paris and predicts that the center right Union for a Popular Movement will soon drop its opposition to Ben Abbes's candidacy. The UMP shares Ben Abbes's social conservatism, and, after all, "the true agenda of the UMP, like the Socialist Party, is the disappearance of France, its integration into a federated European Union." As Tanneur notes, Ben Abbes's project is fundamentally a European one, an attempt to revive the Holy Roman Empire: "In a sense he's only resuming de Gaulle's ambition, that of a great Arab politician in France, and I assure you he does not lack for allies." The former spy turns out to be right: with the support of the Socialists and the UMP, Ben Abbes becomes president.

After his discussion with Tanneur, François goes to see the Black Madonna at Rocamadour, hoping for the sort of revelation experienced by Huysmans. Instead he feels "deserted by the Spirit," and walks glumly back down the steps to the car park. On his return to Paris, his life gets worse. His parents die. As a non-Muslim, he's forced into early retirement (with a monthly pension of €3,000, thanks to the Saudis and Qataris, who are now funding the French education system). Myriam writes from Tel Aviv that she has "met someone." He has a glimmer of hope during an expensive series of encounters with two prostitutes, but that "miracle" isn't repeated, and he's soon bedeviled by eczema and hemorrhoids. Turning one last time to his faithful friend, he makes a pilgrimage to Ligugé, near Poitiers, where Huysmans became a monk.

France meanwhile is "recovering an optimism it hadn't known since the end of the Trente Glorieuses, a half-century ago . . . The reconstruction of the Roman Empire was underway." Crime falls by a factor of ten in "difficult" neighborhoods, while unemployment vanishes because women no longer work. Ben Abbes's "moderate" Islam is moderate insofar as it is nonviolent, but on issues of gender and the "dignity" of the family it could hardly be more regressive. Women are forced to cover themselves in public, and polygamy is introduced. Yet the general mood is one of "a tacit and languid acceptance." And not only in France: when social spending is radically cut, the Gulf monarchies supply the difference. Everyone, it seems, wants Ben Abbes's France to succeed.

On his way back from Ligugé, François discovers that Ben Abbes's France has plans for him, too. First he's asked to edit the Pléiade edition of Huysmans. Then, at a reception for the reopening of the Islamic Sorbonne—a very Parisian affair, but without any women—he's introduced to its new director, Robert Rediger, who invites him to dinner. Rediger is a man of his times: a convert to Islam and an ally of Ben Abbes. (The name is a twist on Robert Redeker, a right-wing journalist who in 2006 went into hiding after receiving death threats for his attacks on Islam; *rédiger* means "to redraft.") He lives on the rue des Arènes— one of the oldest streets in Paris, near the arena of Lutèce—in a house that belonged to the writer and publisher Jean Paulhan, who also edited the *Nouvelle Revue française*. As François waits for Rediger to make his entrance, he notices a fifteen-year-old girl with long black hair who runs away when he sees her. It's Aïcha, Rediger's new wife, his third. "She's going to be very upset because you shouldn't have seen her without her veil."

Rediger would like him to return to the university. There's just one condition: he must become a Muslim. Rediger, author of the bestselling *Ten Questions about Islam*, is a proselytizer: "I seem to have developed an entirely unexpected gift for vulgarization." He knows that the "three hours of religious proselytism" in his book aren't going to persuade François, but an appeal to reason and self-interest just might. As a young man, Rediger had flirted with the Catholic right, with its celebration of tradition, patri- archy and faith. Without Christianity, he believed, European countries like France had become "bodies without a soul— zombies." But now only the more muscular Islam could revive the zombies of Europe. This revelation came to him one Easter, when he passed the bar of the Hotel Métropole in Brussels, only to find it was closing down that evening:

I was stupefied . . . To think that until then one could order sandwiches and beers, Viennese chocolates and cakes with cream in this absolute masterpiece of decorative art, that one could live everyday life surrounded by beauty, and that all this could disappear in one stroke in a European capital! . . . Yes, that was the moment when I understood: Europe had already committed suicide . . . The next day, I went to see an imam in Zaventem. And the day after that—Easter Monday—in the presence of a dozen witnesses, I pronounced the ritual formula of conversion to Islam.

Rediger's "new Muslim friends," he tells François, have never reproached him for his youthful adventures on the Catholic right; they understood that in his "search for a way out of atheist humanism" he would "turn at first toward my tradition of origin." When François reads *Ten Questions about Islam*, he discovers that Rediger has remained faithful to the Nietzschean philosophy of his youth. His arguments in favor of Islam are an appeal to his former right-wing allies to put aside their "irrational hostility to Islam" since, in every other respect, "they were perfectly in agreement with Muslims." Like Don Fabrizio in *The Leopard*, Rediger understands that everything must change so that everything can remain the same. Submission doesn't have to mean self-renunciation.

Or does it? Describing his embrace of Islam, Rediger settles on a nearby literary analogy. As he reminds François, they are in the house where Anne Desclos, Jean Paulhan's lover, wrote *The Story of O*. For all its "ostentatious kitsch," Rediger says, *The Story of O* captured "the astonishing and simple idea . . . that the summit of human happiness resides in the most absolute submission." His fellow Muslims might "find it blasphemous, but for me there's a relationship between the absolute submission of woman to man, such as *The Story of O* describes it, and the submission of man to God, as Islam envisages it." And surely a literary man like François should be able to appreciate the literary splendor of the Quran, a "mystical praise poem" that can only be recited in Arabic because it "rests on the idea . . . at the heart of poetry, of the unity of sound and meaning." Rediger promises François that if he converts, he will not only get his job back, but he will be able to get "three wives without difficulty," chosen for him by an experienced matchmaker. For the first time in his adult life, François finds himself thinking about God, or rather, Allah. Over a bottle of rum, he comforts himself with the thought that "I was a relatively insignificant individual, that God certainly had better things to do, but the terrifying idea persisted that he was going to become aware of my existence."

Soumission derives its name from the original meaning of the Arabic "al-Islam"—voluntary submission, or surrender, to the will of God. In that sense, the novel is a faithful rendering of Islam's meaning. François is under no compulsion to convert, other than the usual inducements of professional ambition and sex, the typical motors of the French novel. Ben Abbes's arrival is greeted with relief, the war between the *identitaires* and the jihadists is brought to an end, and Islamization proceeds not so much by conquest as by persuasion. The national patrimony— the Sorbonne, the Paulhan *hôtel particulier*—now belongs to the Gulf sheikhdoms, and on campus the miniskirt has given way to the burqa, but otherwise France is unchanged. In fact it's even a bit better off. As Houellebecq says, the entire novel unfolds in an "ambience of resignation."

Is Houellebecq condemning the French for capitulating to Islam, or worse, accusing them of "collaboration"? His critics have pointed out that the structure of *Soumission* resembles narratives about Vichy: a confused period of civil unrest; an exodus to the countryside; and accommodation to the new regime. But really, far from damning the French for embracing Ben Abbes, Houellebecq is suggesting that they could do much worse: indeed, that they are already doing much worse. And, as Houellebecq reminds us, "moderate Muslims are not Nazis."

Perhaps this is all just a Swiftian stunt. Perhaps Houellebecq is saying that France has sunk so low that even Islam would be preferable to the state religion of *laïcité*. But I don't think so. *Soumission* is too ambiguous to be read as satire—or, for that matter, as nightmare. There are strong indications, both in the novel and in interviews, that Houellebecq sees Islam as a solution, if not *the* solution, to the crisis of French civilization. Yes, civilization, that word evocative of the *longue durée*, religion, tradition, shared values and, not least, clashes with civilizational rivals. But the word is unavoidable. What has always made his writing so perverse is the way it jumps between microsociology and the aerial view of history. (His novels almost always take place at some point in the future, allowing the present to be depicted as a just-vanished past.) Houellebecq has an unerring, Balzacian flair for detail, and his novels provide an acute, disenchanted anatomy of French middle-class life: TV dinners, petty intrigues at the workplace, tourism, sex. But since his characters are never more than sociological types, without much of an interior life, he needs to find another narrative for them: hence the role played by history. For Houellebecq, history is the story of the rise and fall of civilizations. The only lasting civilizations, as he sees it, rest on a solid foundation of shared religious values. Once those values disintegrate, a civilization slides into inexorable decline, and becomes susceptible to what, in *The Elementary Particles* (1998), he called a "metaphysical mutation," a sudden and decisive transformation of its values. These metaphysical mutations are the engine of history. Politics and economics—the stuff materialists get worked up about—are of secondary importance. (By any objective measure, France isn't doing so badly: people work less and make more, and have a higher life expectancy than the OECD average. The "crisis" of the French model is partly phantasmagorical.)

Houellebecq is not a believer himself. But he isn't happy about it. As Marc Weitzmann writes in the *Magazine littéraire*, he is a "disappointed mystic" who believes that "the technological revolution and its rationalism have condemned the West to death, to nihilism," and that "regeneration can come only from another religion." In *The Elementary Particles*, the new religion was Comtean positivism; in *Soumission* it's Islam. According to Houellebecq, *Soumission* was inspired by the crisis of faith he suffered after the deaths of his parents (and his dog). Atheism, he realized, couldn't console him, and it became clear to him that he couldn't turn to Christianity either. His original plan had been for François to follow in Huysmans's footsteps and embrace Catholicism while staring at the Black Madonna. But Houellebecq couldn't write the scene: it struck him as a "deception." For Houellebecq, France's dilemma resembles his own: France has attempted to replace God with the secular religion of republican citizenship and laïcité, but at the price of leaving deeper questions unanswered. And the abandonment of God has left France without a sense of direction or purpose: "The search for meaning has returned. People aren't content to live without God." This isn't a new argument, but Houellebecq turns it to a very different end by suggesting that Islam, a younger and more confident religion, might be a better vehicle for setting Europe back on track than Catholicism, which has "run its course."

It's quite a volte-face. In *The Elementary Particles*, Islam is described as "the most stupid, false and obscure of all religions . . . doomed just as surely as Christianity." In *Platform* (2001), Islam is the absolute Other: Michel Renault, the narrator, has "a vision of migratory flows crisscrossing Europe like blood vessels" while he talks to his father's Muslim housekeeper; "Muslims appeared as clots that were only slowly reabsorbed." Later, Renault finds a reason to "feel hatred for Muslims" when his girlfriend dies in a bombing carried out by Islamic terrorists in Thailand: "Every time I heard that a Palestinian terrorist, or a Palestinian child or a pregnant Palestinian woman, had been gunned down in the Gaza Strip, I felt a quiver of enthusiasm at the thought that it meant one less Muslim."

Houellebecq changed his mind about Islam after reading the Quran. It "turns out to be much better than I thought," he told the *Paris Review*. "The most obvious conclusion is that the jihadists are bad Muslims . . . an honest reading will conclude that a holy war of aggression is not generally sanctioned, prayer alone is valid." In *Soumission*, Houellebecq writes about Islam with curiosity, fascination, even a hint of envy. Islam is a more convincing "image of the future" than Catholicism precisely because it provides a more reliable vessel for a faith-based, patriarchal order where sex is insulated from the marketplace, men and women have clearly defined roles, and social harmony prevails over moral permissiveness, class conflict and crime, the ills of liberal capitalism. (Even its loopholes have the virtue of not being hypocritical: thanks to polygamy, men no longer need mistresses or sex clubs.) Ben Abbes—whom Houellebecq describes as a "very ambitious and gifted man" and compares to Napoleon—is depicted as the only politician in France who has a credible strategy for restoring order. He has something else that his non-Muslim colleagues conspicuously lack: a plan for reviving the continent, by enlarging it to include the countries of the southern Mediterranean basin. That other politicians rally to him is evidence less of their spinelessness than of their recognition that the republic is a sinking ship, and that they had better get onboard with a winner. Once he's in power, the results speak for themselves. At the beginning of the novel, François worries that his best years are behind him; on the last page, he is contemplating a conversion to Islam with serenity and "no regrets."

Because the drama of *Soumission* hinges on whether François will follow the rest of France and embrace the new order, some critics have argued that Islam is merely a device, a mirror held up to reveal the corruptions of French society: the complacency of its civil servants; the cynicism of its politicians; the longing for a strongman to rescue the country. But Houellebecq's own remarks about the novel suggest otherwise, and this is where the reactionary—indeed, delusional—cast of his politics becomes even more pronounced. He seems to believe that the Muslim Fraternity is a plausible, even a needed, political force. Muslims in France, he says, are in "an actually schizophrenic situation." They "have more in common with the extreme right than with the left" because of their views on gay rights, abortion and other social issues, but they can't vote for the Front National. Instead, they vote for parties of the left that hold socially progressive views they reject. "For those reasons . . . a Muslim party makes a lot of sense." This argument has a semblance of logic (some Muslims in France are indeed socially conservative), but it also depends on a self-defined, coherent Muslim community which, as Olivier Roy has argued, doesn't exist. Muslims in France are a population, not a community, and they don't vote as a bloc.

Most Muslims aren't particularly observant, and those who are practice in a variety of ways. There are also secular Muslims—the current minister of education, Najat Vallaud-Belkacem, the daughter of Moroccan parents, is one—who fervently support republican values and laïcité, partly as a protection against autocratic defenders of the faith. Houellebecq sees neither the divisions within Islam, nor its fragility.

To grasp the complexity of Islamic practices in France, Houellebecq would have to write about Muslims, rather than "Islam." But his discovery of the Quran hasn't made him any more curious about the lives of actual Muslims in France. Islam-obsessed though his earlier fiction was, its only Muslim characters were prostitutes, housekeepers, terrorists and native informants who echoed his reasons for loathing Islam. Despite being far more sympathetic to Islam, *Soumission* is similarly starved of actual Muslims: the only ones with speaking parts are converts; the only Muslim François seems to know personally is a call girl. Houellebecq's beloved Ben Abbes is as aloof as de Gaulle, although that distance is defensible in the case of a politician. It doesn't occur to Houellebecq that some French Muslims might take exception to the country's most powerful faith—not Catholicism, but laïcité—for reasons that have as much to do with the injuries of discrimination as with the claims of faith. The situation in the banlieues is duly mentioned, but only as a problem of social order: thanks to Ben Abbes, the "delinquent" zones are quiet. (Not the least of Ben Abbes's virtues is that he knows how to control "his" people.) Why so many Muslims inhabit these zones, Houellebecq never says: the "sad historian" points to the battle of Poitiers, as a reminder of the antiquity of this clash of civilizations, but doesn't mention the history of colonization that brought Muslims to France, or the racism and inequality that are still the lot of third-generation "immigrants."

I had the strange experience of reading *Soumission* in Algeria, where Islamic theocracy has never been a merely theoretical proposition, and the damage wrought by Islam in power is a commonplace in contemporary fiction. In Kamel Daoud's recent novel *The Mersault Investigation*, for example, the narrator complains that "in a few years, the only bar that will still be open will be in paradise, at the end of the world," and launches into a ten-page tirade against Friday prayer. While François seems resigned to losing Myriam, Daoud's narrator is tormented by the memory of a free-spirited, "insubordinate" woman who embraced "her body as a gift, not a sin or shame." But what really sets novels like Daoud's apart from *Soumission* is not their critique of faith-based politics so much as their spirit of defiance and rebellion: their *insoumission*. At the beginning of *Soumission*, Houellebecq says that while the style of a novel matters and "the musicality of phrases have their importance," "an author is above all a human being, present in his books." He is distressingly present in *Soumission*. Houellebecq, who once dreamed of a world "delivered from Islam," now dreams that Islam might deliver France from its impasse. The contrast, however, is only superficial: the fantasy of surrender to a superior force remains. Houellebecq has often been compared to his reactionary ancestor Céline, but Céline's writing had a wild, insurgent spirit; Houellebecq's luxuriates in *ressentiment*, helplessness and defeat. *Soumission* is the work of a nihilist not a hater—the *jeu d'esprit* of a man without convictions. Whether or not France deserves Mohammed Ben Abbes, it has found in Houellebecq a sly and witty chronicler—and a fittingly louche symbol—of its malaise.

{2015}

IV

Lessons of Darkness

13

Suffering as Identity:
Claude Lanzmann

The life of Claude Lanzmann, Claude Lanzmann declares at the beginning of his memoir, has been "a rich, multifaceted and unique story." Self-flattery is characteristically Lanzmannian, but its truth in this case can hardly be denied. He has lived on a grand scale. A teenage fighter in the Resistance, he became Sartre's protégé in the early 1950s as an editor at *Les Temps modernes*. He also became—with Sartre's blessing—Beauvoir's lover, "the only man with whom Simone de Beauvoir lived a quasi-marital existence." He marched with the left against the wars in Algeria and Vietnam; moonlighted in Beijing as an unofficial conduit between Mao and de Gaulle; and fell under the spell of Frantz Fanon in Tunis. Writing for the glossies at the height of the Nouvelle Vague, he interviewed Bardot, Moreau, Deneuve, Belmondo and Gainsbourg: "I met them all . . . and, I can say without vanity, I helped some of them make a qualitative leap in their careers." He had a brief, stormy marriage to the actress Judith Magne, and was Michel Piccoli's best man at his marriage to Juliette Gréco. He knew how to woo his subjects off and on the page. "You are the only one who talked about me as I would have wished," the novelist Albert Cohen told him.

It was a charmed life, particularly for a Jew who'd spent his youth on the run from the Gestapo and the collaborationist Milice. But the war never really ended for Lanzmann. Seventy-five thousand Jews were deported by Vichy, and, as Beauvoir writes in her memoir *La Force des choses*, "his rancor with respect to the goys never went away." Once he tired of covering the dolce vita, Lanzmann began a second, more celebrated career as a chronicler of the Holocaust. *Shoah*, released in 1985 after more than a decade of labor, is a powerful nine-and-a-half-hour investigation, composed almost entirely of oral testimony. Neither a conventional documentary nor a fictional recreation but, as Lanzmann called it, "a fiction of the real," *Shoah* revealed the way the Holocaust reverberated, as trauma, in the present. It was soon declared a masterpiece.

Lanzmann says that his fans have long pleaded with him to tell his story, but he wasn't sure he had the energy for "such a massive undertaking." As an intellectual dignitary, he was guaranteed a warm reception in France when his memoir, *The Patagonian Hare*, was published three years ago by Gallimard; Philippe Sollers called it a "metaphysical event." It's an unbridled piece of self-celebration, dictated to his assistant editor at *Les Temps modernes* in what Lanzmann calls his "naturally epic" style. There is a lot of name-checking but no real discussion of ideas: neither the existential Marxism that defined the *Temps modernes* circle, nor its battles over Communism, receive much attention. If he had any memorable discussions with his colleagues, he has chosen not to share them: as Beauvoir recognized, Lanzmann was a man of action. He was, he tells us, a courageous fighter in the *maquis*, as well as a fearless skier, a daring mountaineer, a natural-born pilot, an author of "visionary" journalism, an athlete in the sack (no compliment is too small to mention, even the praises of a prostitute he visited in his teens). He has triumphed as a writer and filmmaker by virtue of a talent for "entering into the reasons and the madness, the lies and the silences of those I wished to portray . . . I consider myself a seer." Even the films he merely planned to make are masterpieces. There is, for example, the unmade meditation on totalitarianism in Pyongyang, where, as part of a left-wing writers' delegation in the late 1950s, he had a near fling with a nurse that ended disastrously when they were caught in Lanzmann's hotel room by his minders. This "insolent, intriguing beauty," with bright red lipstick and a napalm scar underneath her breast, was put on trial for consorting with Lanzmann, who says he has "never in the intervening fifty years . . . stopped thinking about her." He even scouted for locations for a film about their brief encounter when he returned to Pyongyang four decades later. He didn't try to find her.

The guillotine and more generally capital punishment have been "the abiding obsession of my life," Lanzmann says in his first chapter and goes on to invoke Algerian independence fighters executed in French jails, the White Rose conspirators Sophie and Hans Scholl, Stalin's victims at the Moscow trials, the Chinese murdered in Nanjing, the anarchists put to death in Franco's Spain. These images are intercut with grisly scenes from Greuze and Goya, history and representation merging into a Popular Front–style fresco of twentieth-century martyrs. Lanzmann believes, he says, in "the universality of victims, as of executioners. All victims are alike, all executioners are alike." But when he turns to the twenty-first century, the wars the United States has launched in the Muslim world do not rate a mention; nor do Israel's invasions of Lebanon and Gaza. Instead, we are given a long, detailed description of a video showing a hostage being slaughtered by Islamic terrorists—one of twenty he says he has watched. He feels as if he were "that hostage with the vacant eyes, this man waiting for the blade to fall." He is distressed that such execution videos—"an unprecedented qualitative leap in the history of global barbarism"—have been censored "in the name of some dubious code of ethics." It's a strange comment to come from a filmmaker who has denounced visual representations of the Holocaust as sacrilegious, and who has said that if he were to discover footage of Jews being asphyxiated in the gas chamber, he would destroy it.

Lanzmann's memoir owes its title to a hare he nearly ran over while driving through a village in Patagonia. It reminded him of the hares that sneaked under the barbed wire at Birkenau: a symbol of freedom and the tenacious will to live. He almost called his book *The Youth of the World*, and you can see why: he has lived a long life while still seeing the world as a child does, divided between the forces of light and darkness. His view is understandable: the world he knew as a child was a battlefield. Claude remembers seeing his father with a butcher's knife raised over his mother's head "as though to strike her down," and her daring him to try. In 1934, when Claude was nine, Paulette Lanzmann moved out. Claude and his younger brother, Jacques, were packed off to a boarding house, their little sister, Evelyne, to a farm. A year later, Armand Lanzmann and his new wife reassembled the family in Brioude, in the Auvergne. Paulette moved to Paris, married a Serbian-Jewish surrealist poet called Monny de Boully, and barely saw her children for several years.

The Vichy government wasted little time in passing anti-Semitic laws after the fall of France in June 1940. Secular, assimilated Jews of Eastern European origin, the Lanzmanns lived in fear of a knock on the door from the Gestapo. As a boarder at the Lycée Blaise-Pascal in Clermont-Ferrand, Claude joined the Jeunesses Communistes. The Party supplied him and his comrades with weapons and Resistance pamphlets. At night, they practiced shooting in the school cellars. He collected guns at the local railway station under the Gestapo's nose and laid ambushes. Among the local leaders of the Unified Movement of the Resistance (MUR) was Lanzmann's father, but it was only in February 1944 that "each of us learned what the other had been doing." Armand proposed to integrate forty members of Claude's group into the MUR; Claude's Party handlers congratulated him; he felt as if he'd been awarded "the Order of Lenin." But the Party double-crossed his father. When the MUR weapons were delivered, the Party told Claude and his men to grab as many guns as they could and report to another group in the *maquis*. He refused to betray his father, and fell, he says, under a Party death sentence, which wasn't lifted until after the war.

Lanzmann's relationship with his mother was much more strained. Paulette had abandoned the family and "faded from my memory" until she returned to Brioude in 1942. He came to love her again because he adored her second husband, Monny, a charming, worldly man, a friend of Breton and Aragon. (Monny introduced Claude to his first love, "my nibbling Elise.") But he was embarrassed by his mother's "terrible stammer" and "big nose." That nose, "obviously, shockingly Jewish," got her and Monny arrested by the Gestapo. Paulette, pretending to be Arab, pointed to a photograph of Goering: "Look, your own field marshal looks more Jewish than I do!" They were released. Later, on what he remembers with shame as the Day of the Boot, he and his mother were in a shoe shop when he became terrified that her nose might tip off the Gestapo. He ran out, ready to leave his mother to her fate: "That afternoon I behaved like a dyed-in-the-wool anti-Semite."

After the war, at the salons Paulette hosted in her Paris flat, Lanzmann met every famous person from Cocteau to the poet Francis Ponge. His friends at the Lycée Louis-le-Grand, where he enrolled as a boarder, were no less impressive. Jean Cau, later Sartre's secretary, shared his anger at a student protest in support of the Fascist writer Robert Brasillach, on trial for collaboration. (That Brasillach had once been a student at Louis-le-Grand counted more with their classmates than his anti-Semitism.) Lanzmann and Cau formed a groupuscule with the future novelists Michel Tournier and Michel Butor, and the charismatic Gilles Deleuze.

Lanzmann was not the only one to fall for Deleuze, who began an affair with his sister, Evelyne, a sixteen-year-old with "the body of a pin-up, huge cobalt-blue eyes and a beautiful Semitic nose." It didn't end well. Deleuze asked Lanzmann to tell his sister he wanted to break up with her; Lanzmann refused but never forgave Deleuze. Evelyne, heartbroken, married the artist Serge Rezvani, became an actress, had a nose job, and changed her name to Evelyne Rey. But when she ran into Deleuze again she became his mistress, living in a gloomy flat he rented for her. When he broke things off for good, Evelyne fell back into depression. She went on to have a successful career on the stage, but after a string of tormented affairs with famous men of the left, including Sartre, she killed herself. She was thirty-six. Lanzmann's elegy for her is one of the few moments of sorrow, or regret, in *The Patagonian Hare*.

It was in 1952 that Lanzmann met Sartre and Beauvoir. Sartre was his hero, his savior: "By describing in perfect detail what I had felt on 'the day of the Boot' " in his *Réflexions sur la question juive*, Sartre "truly cured me." Impressed by a series of articles on East Germany Lanzmann had published in *Le Monde*, Sartre invited him to an editorial meeting of *Les Temps modernes*. Lanzmann was enthralled. Sartre took him under his wing, and he would later become the journal's editor in chief. Although he made his living writing celebrity profiles for *Elle* and *France Observateur*, he saved his best work for Sartre, notably the 1958 article "Le Curé d'Uruffe," a lengthy investigation of a murder committed by a priest, and an indictment of the Church. Writing it, Lanzmann learned "lessons that would repay me a hundred-fold during the making of *Shoah*, which in many respects can be considered a criminal investigation."

As for Beauvoir: "From the first, I loved the veil of her voice, her blue eyes, the purity of her face and more especially of her nostrils." According to Hazel Rowley's joint biography of Beauvoir and Sartre, Lanzmann's interest began as a bet with Jean Cau as to who could seduce her first. He invited her to a movie, and they ended up in her flat. There had been five men in her life, she said, and he was to be the sixth. They lived together for seven years, and remained close until Beauvoir's death in 1986, a year after her essay in praise of *Shoah* appeared on the front page of *Le Monde*.

Beauvoir was seventeen years older than Lanzmann and excited by his raw spontaneity, a "foreign" temperament that made her feel close to him. Lanzmann's wartime record also appealed to her; she, like Sartre, had done little to resist the Nazis. "Thanks to him a thousand things were restored to me," she writes in *La Force des choses*, "joys, astonishments, anxieties and the freshness of the world." They saw Josephine Baker, skied in the Alps, drove through the backroads of Yugoslavia, watched the bullfights in Pamplona and holidayed with Sartre in Saint-Tropez. They were bound by the causes of the left, above all the opposition to the war in Algeria. They signed the Manifeste des 121, a petition in support of soldiers who refused to serve. They went with Sartre to Rome to visit the dying Fanon; there are echoes of Fanon's belief in recovering identity and dignity through violence in *Shoah*'s depiction of the Warsaw Ghetto uprising, and in Lanzmann's rhetoric about the "reappropriation of violence" by the warriors of modern Israel. The relationship was not free of tensions. Beauvoir, Lanzmann recalls, was susceptible to sudden fits of sobbing, while Lanzmann, according to Beauvoir, was prone to tantrums, impulsive and highly impressionable. He sometimes woke up from dreams shouting: "You're all Kapos!"

Their relationship was, at all times, transparent to Sartre, the head of what they called the Family. He read Beauvoir's letters to Lanzmann before Lanzmann did. Meanwhile, Lanzmann had introduced his sister to Sartre—she had been acting in a production of *Huis Clos*—and she had become his secret mistress. (His *maîtresse en titre*, Michelle Vian, learned of the relationship only after Sartre's death.) Sartre, he says, was a courtly, almost fatherly lover; Evelyne's years with him were the happiest of her life. Lanzmann makes little of the incestuous ambience around the Family, but Beauvoir did, both in her memoir and in her letters to Nelson Algren. Lanzmann, she wrote to Algren, "asks for motherly tenderness, rather than something else." She indulged him at editorial meetings, where he was the only person allowed to criticize Sartre to his face. Privately, though, she worried that the *père* "had drifted too far from his own truth" under the influence of his intensely pro-Soviet *fils*, who "called each step Sartre made toward the Communists progress." Beauvoir recognized Lanzmann's boundless faith in the PCF as "the flipside of a profound pessimism," but it exasperated her: in a man of such obvious intelligence, "his Manichaeism astonished me."

Lanzmann's romance with the Soviet Union, which had been "like a sky above my head," had run its course by the end of the 1950s. Although he wept when Stalin died, he shared Sartre and Beauvoir's horror at the Soviet tanks in Budapest in 1956. Solidarity trips to North Korea and China—then in the midst of the "rectification campaign," described in all its garish fanaticism in *The Patagonian Hare*—put an end to any enthusiasm he still had for the communist project.

The Manichaeism of his outlook remained, however. In 1952, he went to Israel for the first time. He spent two months there, and might have stayed longer, he says, if Beauvoir hadn't begged him to return. The visit was the birth of an abiding passion. In *Réflexions sur la question juive*, Sartre had argued that the anti-Semite "creates" the Jew, but in Israel, Lanzmann reported to Sartre and Beauvoir, he had discovered a vibrant Jewish world; far from the anti-Semite's gaze, Israel's Jews went on being Jews. He noticed that the state wasn't above lying about living conditions in order to attract new immigrants, but even this impressed him as a way of getting things done. Before long, his uncomplicated belief in the pioneers of the Soviet Union, building socialism in the face of capitalist aggression, would be transferred to the sabras of Israel, creating a kibbutznik society in the face of Arab hostility.

Lanzmann's relationship to Israel became a source of friction with Sartre in the 1960s. Like most people on the French left, Sartre was sympathetic to Israel, but he had also supported the FLN in Algeria and viewed Nasser as a fellow progressive. A friend of both the Jews and the Arabs, he felt helplessly torn. Lanzmann had chosen sides after Ben Bella gave a speech promising to send troops to liberate Palestine. He felt betrayed, since a young Algerian rebel he'd met in Tunisia—the country's current president, Abdelaziz Bouteflika—had told him that Algeria had much to learn from Israel. "For me, it was over: I had thought it was possible to believe both in an independent Algeria and the state of Israel. I was wrong."

A few months before the 1967 war, *Les Temps modernes* published a special issue on the Arab-Israeli conflict, more than a thousand pages long, featuring contributions by both Arab and Israeli writers. At the invitation of Mohamed Heikal, the editor of *al-Ahram* and a confidant of Nasser, the Family traveled to Cairo. As Lanzmann recalls, Nasser, a "tall, timid man who impressed by his soft voice and dark, handsome eyes," looked him in the eye, "addressing himself to me alone," knowing of his special bond with Israel. Although Sartre accused his Egyptian hosts of leaving the refugees in Gaza "to rot, surviving on handouts," Lanzmann suspected that his mentor viewed him as a liability, "preventing him from truly enjoying the seductions of the Arab world." The quarrel intensified in Israel, the trip's next stop, when Sartre refused to meet anyone in uniform: "an obstinate refusal to even try to understand Israel" and its "primordial mission" of defense, Lanzmann felt. When de Gaulle announced an arms embargo against Israel in early June, Lanzmann pressured Sartre into signing a pro-Israel petition; Sartre immediately regretted it. Their relationship never recovered.

At a rally in Paris on June 2, Lanzmann declared that the destruction of Israel—a "second annihilation"—would be worse than the Holocaust: "Israel is my freedom. Without Israel, I feel naked and vulnerable." Lanzmann was hardly alone among French Jewish intellectuals. Most shared his sense that Israel faced imminent destruction, rejoiced in its lightning victory and felt betrayed by de Gaulle's press conference of November 27, 1967, in which, using language not heard in public since the war, he described the Jews as "an élite people, sure of themselves and domineering." Yet there was much that rang true in de Gaulle's warning that the occupation would not proceed "without oppression, repression, expulsions"; that "resistance" was bound to follow and that Israel would call it "terrorism." The messianic zeal with which Israel rushed to conquer and colonize the West Bank soon troubled Jewish liberals like Pierre Vidal-Naquet and Jean Daniel, the editor of the *Nouvel Observateur*, but Lanzmann's attachment to Israel grew only fiercer.

After the Six-Day War, Lanzmann returned to Israel. He spent time with troops on the border with Egypt during the War of Attrition, and met his second wife, the Berlin-born Angelika Schrobsdorff. He was in Paris for *le joli Mai*, but experienced it "from the outside, like a curious, disinterested spectator, never believing in the realization of the Second Coming in the history of mankind." The resurrection of the Jewish kingdom in Israel was another matter. Though a critic of his own society, he felt little kinship with left-wing Israelis like Uri Avnery, "whose sarcastic way of pulling his country to pieces until there was not one stone standing on another had always irritated me." Lanzmann's first film was an admiring portrait of the Jewish state. Released in 1973, *Pourquoi Israël* led to a summons from Alouph Hareven, director-general of the Ministry of Foreign Affairs. Hareven told him that Israel had a mission for him: "It's not a matter of making a film *about* the Shoah, but a film that *is* the Shoah. We believe you are the only person who can make this film."

Lanzmann accepted the assignment. The Foreign Ministry's support for him reflected a shift in priorities. Until the 1960s, Israel had shown little interest in the Holocaust. The survivors, their stories, the Yiddish many of them spoke—these were all seen as shameful reminders of Jewish weakness, of the life in exile that the Jewish state had at last brought to an end. But with the Eichmann trial, and particularly after the 1967 war, Israel discovered that the Holocaust could be a powerful weapon in its ideological arsenal. Lanzmann, however, had more serious artistic ambitions for his film than the Foreign Ministry, which, impatient with his slowness, withdrew funding after a few years, before a single reel was shot. Lanzmann turned to the new prime minister, Menachem Begin, who put him in touch with a former member of Mossad, a "secret man devoid of emotions." He promised that Israel would sponsor the film so long as it ran no longer than two hours and was completed in eighteen months. Lanzmann agreed to the conditions, knowing he could never meet them. He ended up shooting 350 hours of film in half a dozen countries; the editing alone took more than five years. Despite his loyalty to Israel, his loyalty to *Shoah* came first, and he was prepared to do almost anything to make it his way.

Shoah is an austere, antispectacular film, without archival footage, newsreels or a single corpse. Lanzmann "showed nothing at all," Godard complained. That was because there was nothing to show: the Nazis had gone to great lengths to conceal the extermination; for all their scrupulous record-keeping, they left behind no photographs of death in the gas chambers of Birkenau or the gas trucks in Chelmno. They hid the evidence of the extermination even as it was taking place, weaving pine tree branches into the barbed wire of the camps as camouflage, using geese to drown out cries, and burning the bodies of those who'd been asphyxiated. As Filip Müller—a member of the Sonderkommando at Auschwitz, the Special Unit of Jews who disposed of the bodies—explains in *Shoah*, Jews were forced to refer to corpses as *Figuren* ("puppets") or *Schmattes* ("rags"), and were beaten if they didn't. Other filmmakers had compensated for the absence of images by showing newsreels of Nazi rallies, or photographs of corpses piled up in liberated concentration camps. Lanzmann chose instead to base his film on the testimony of survivors, perpetrators and bystanders. Their words—often heard over slow, spectral tracking shots of trains and forests in the killing fields of Poland—provided a grueling account of the "life" of the death camps: the cold, the brutality of the guards, the panic that gripped people as they were herded into the gas chambers.

In *The Patagonian Hare*, Lanzmann describes the making of *Shoah* as a kind of hallucinatory voyage, and himself as a pioneer in the desolate ruins of the camps, "spellbound, in thrall to the truth being revealed to me . . . I was the first person to return to the scene of the crime, to those who had never spoken." In fact, many of Lanzmann's witnesses had already spoken. Müller had published a book on his time in Auschwitz; so had Rudolf Vrba, another member of the Sonderkommando. What Lanzmann did was to get his subjects to act out their experiences. In some cases they did so on location: Lanzmann flew Simon Srebnik from Israel to Poland, and filmed him rowing up the Narew River, singing the Prussian military song that had won him fame—and saved his life—when he was a child in Chelmno. He rented a steam train from Polish Railways and persuaded a man who had transported Jews from Warsaw and Bialystok to Treblinka to drive it again. He persuaded Franz Suchomel, an SS guard at Treblinka, now a portly retiree, to perform the eerily cheerful Treblinka anthem Jews were forced to sing on entering the camp.

The skills Lanzmann learned in the *maquis* came in handy. When former Nazis refused to be interviewed, suspecting he was Jewish, he took a nom de guerre, Claude-Marie Sorel, and set up a fake historical institute that happened to share a postal address with *Les Temps modernes*. He showed up unannounced at the houses of those he wanted to talk to, and tried to win them over with flattery, cash and the occasional feast. Lanzmann treated Suchomel and his wife to a sumptuous lunch while his cinematographer, Willy Lubtchansky, whose father was gassed at Auschwitz, looked on in horror. When Suchomel hesitated to appear on screen, Lanzmann filmed him from a small cylindrical camera hidden in the handbag of his translator. (On one occasion, their cover was blown, and the pair were assaulted by the son of an Einsatzgruppen officer.) He often promised his subjects anonymity, only to withhold it in the film.

Lanzmann argues that it was necessary to "deceive the deceivers," and it's hard not to root for him as he describes the tricks he used to fool the perpetrators. But his ruthless behavior was not reserved for Nazis; anyone who failed to do as he wished was an obstacle to be overcome. He was furious, for example, with the translator Barbara Janicka, a Polish Catholic, when she translated *Ziydki*, "little Yid," as "Jew," sanitizing the "incredible violence of the Polish responses": "It is a constant failing of female interpreters—even the best of them, especially the best— they give in to their fears, their emotions." The survivors were not insulated from Lanzmann's bullying: he was determined to get them to re-enact their stories ("our common task, our shared duty"). In one of the film's most famous scenes, Lanzmann interviews Abraham Bomba, the barber at Treblinka, who cut people's hair just before they entered the gas chambers. He rented a barbershop in Tel Aviv, and suggested that Bomba pretend to give a haircut: the "familiar motions," he claimed, might ease "the task of speech and actions he needed to perform before the camera." Bomba broke down, recalling the moment he was asked to cut the hair of the wife and sister of a friend.

> BOMBA: I can't. It's too horrible. Please.
> LANZMANN: We have to do it. You know it.
> BOMBA: I won't be able to do it.
> LANZMANN: You have to do it. I know it's very hard. I know and I apologize.
> BOMBA: Don't make me go on, please.
> LANZMANN: Please. We must go on.

"I was like the state of Israel with its immigrants," he writes, in defense of his methods. "In the end, as everyone knows, I betrayed no one: *Shoah* exists as it should exist." At the time of the film's release, most viewers agreed. Before long, it inspired an enormous body of academic literature, in film studies, psychoanalysis, comparative literature and Holocaust studies. For its admirers, *Shoah* became an object of worship. The stark, enigmatic title—the term "Shoah," Hebrew for "catastrophe," had been officially adopted in Israel in 1953 but was then scarcely known in the West—enhanced its aura. As Lanzmann recalls, "not speaking Hebrew, I did not understand its meaning, which was another way of not naming it . . . Shoah was a signifier with no signified, a brief, opaque utterance." No one contributed more to the sacralization of *Shoah* than its director. Lanzmann called his film "an incarnation, a resurrection," an "originary event," a Western, even a symphony; he compared it to the plays of Shakespeare. *Shoah*, in Lanzmann's rapt description, was a *Gesamtkunstwerk* of the Holocaust, as darkly transcendent as the event itself.

When Pauline Kael panned the film—"*Shoah* is a long moan. It's saying: 'We've always been oppressed, and we'll be oppressed again'"—the *New Yorker* received a flurry of outraged letters. But in the twenty-seven years since its release, the film's defects have come into sharper focus. There is no discussion of anti-Bolshevism and Social Darwinism, as integral to Nazi ideology as anti-Semitism; no account of the invasion of the Soviet Union, which accelerated the process of extermination; and hardly a mention of non-Jewish victims—Gypsies, or the mentally ill or homosexuals. The lack of context was deliberate. Citing a story told by Primo Levi in *If This Is a Man*, Lanzmann argued that attempting to understand the Holocaust was a form of "madness," "an absolute obscenity." Levi, desperately thirsty, grabbed an icicle, and an SS officer took it from him, shouting, "*Hier ist kein warum*": "Here, there is no why." But Levi continued to try to understand the horrors he witnessed; he didn't elevate the SS officer's command into a taboo. As Dominick LaCapra argued, Lanzmann appeared to be insisting not only on a *Bilderverbot*, a prohibition on images, but a *Warumverbot*, a prohibition on explanation itself. In the absence of explanation and historical context, and with non-Jewish victims removed from the picture, Lanzmann's Holocaust is the story of Jews facing an eternally hostile Gentile world where another genocide is always a latent possibility. "The worst crime" when making a film about the Holocaust, he said, "is to consider [it] as *past*."

Witnesses who might have quarreled with his interpretation were excluded from the film. This was particularly true in the treatment of Poland, where most of the exterminations took place. We don't hear from Marek Edelman, one of the leaders of the Warsaw Ghetto rising, probably because his disenchanted view clashed with Lanzmann's stirring account of it, at the end of *Shoah*, as a resurrection from the ashes. A member of the Bund, hostile to Zionism, Edelman remained in Poland instead of settling in Israel, which he called a "historic failure." Also missing from *Shoah* was Wladislaw Bartoszewski, a member of a clandestine network that rescued Polish Jews during the war. Lanzmann interviewed him in Warsaw, but found him "boring," "incapable of reliving the past"; his testimony ended up on the cutting-room floor.

Lanzmann insists that he left out "nothing essential" about Poland in *Shoah*, and that he captured "the real, true Poland," where the people living near the gas chambers and death convoys "ate and . . . made love in the unbearable stench of charred flesh." The Nazis interviewed in *Shoah* come off rather better than the Poles, a rogues' gallery of Jew haters. When *Shoah* was shown in Warsaw, a "tsunami" of anger greeted it. Polish reactions were, in part, a denial of reality. Lanzmann had not invented Polish anti-Semitism, as he points out; indeed, he found enough of it in Poland to confirm the worst stereotypes. But what this anti-Semitism explained about the Holocaust was less clear. The Polish villagers in *Shoah*—who were themselves regarded by the Germans as scarcely more human than the Jews—would not have been capable of organizing anything more than a drunken pogrom: industrialized killing was beyond not only their imagination but their competence. Lanzmann, however, alleges that the Nazis set up camps in Poland because they could count on Polish complicity, a claim no historian credits. "It would have been impossible to have death camps in France," he says. "The French peasants would not have stood for it." In fact, French peasants were known to dig into the lavatories of deported Jews in search of gold; the French government, on its own initiative, passed anti-Jewish laws more severe than the Nuremberg laws and oversaw the deportations of Jewish children.

Defending his depiction of Poland, Lanzmann says that his "most ardent supporter" was Jan Karski, a representative of the Polish government in exile who made two visits to the Warsaw Ghetto in 1942, and reported his findings both to Anthony Eden and to Roosevelt. Until Lanzmann approached him for an interview in 1977, he had not spoken in public of his wartime mission. His appearance in *Shoah* and in *The Karski Report*, an addendum released last year, is indeed shattering: Lanzmann deserves enormous credit for conducting the interview. Karski praised *Shoah* as "the greatest film that has ever been made about the tragedy of the Jews" but sharply criticized Lanzmann's failure to interview Bartoszewski. Karski did not say this to defend his people—in his report, he deplored the Poles' "inflexible, often pitiless" attitude toward their Jewish compatriots—but because he believed Bartoszewski's absence left the impression that "the Jews were abandoned by all of humanity," rather than by "those who held political and spiritual power." Karski's Holocaust was an unprecedented chapter in the history of political cruelty; Lanzmann's Shoah was an eschatological event in the history of the Jews: incomparable, inexplicable, surrounded by what he called a "sacred flame." "The destiny and the history of the Jewish people," he said in an interview with *Cahiers du cinéma*, "cannot be compared to that of any other people." Even the hatred aimed at them was exceptional, he said, insisting that anti-Semitism was of a different order from other forms of racism.

In an amusing scene in his memoir, Lanzmann meets a group of American Jewish moguls while he's trying to get funds to complete his film. They ask him what his message is. He replies that he has none and leaves the meeting empty-handed. But

Lanzmann's message becomes clear in the last few minutes of *Shoah*, when we see a group of Israeli soldiers at a memorial for the Warsaw Ghetto uprising. As Esther Benbassa, a French scholar of Judaism, writes in *Suffering as Identity*, *Shoah* helped raise the destruction of the Jews "to the level of an event possessing intense transcendental meaning, while conferring qualities of the same order, redemptive in this case, on the creation of the state of Israel." Lanzmann's next film was an adulatory portrait of the Israel Defense Forces. He began *Tsahal* in 1987, the year the First Intifada exploded, and completed it seven years later. Yitzhak Rabin (who had offered to finance a film on the 1948 war) put the army at his disposal, and Lanzmann conducted extensive interviews with senior military officials, including Ehud Barak and Ariel Sharon.

In *Tsahal*, Lanzmann's style of questioning soldiers is avuncular, chummy, even doting at times. He hugs them at pilot school, admires their equipment, compliments them on their looks. The lesson of the Holocaust—the need to remain vigilant in the face of anti-Semitism—is emphasized by his subjects at every turn. Lanzmann says he wanted to show that "the soldiers in this young army, sons and grandsons of Filip Müller and his companions in catastrophe, are, deep down, the same men their fathers were." The difference is that they have an army, and, as Lanzmann put it, "this army represents a victory of the Jewish people over themselves." In taking up arms, the Jews, like the colonized in Fanon, have been reborn as new men, all the while retaining an unusual sensitivity to life. Because of the Holocaust, the army "is not like other armies": Jewish soldiers "do not have violence in their blood." This has all the subtlety of a nationalist anthem, and Lanzmann admits in *The Patagonian Hare*, "I was shown much more than I chose to show": the army's drones, for example, "a magnificent Israeli invention." There is, however, no lack of military hardware on display in *Tsahal*, which offers a striking visual counterpoint to *Shoah*. In *Shoah*, the machinery of life (trains, trucks) is transformed into the machinery of death; in *Tsahal*, the machinery of death (fighter jets, tanks) is transformed into the machinery of life. Much of the film is an ode to the Merkava tank, seen in slow, languorous takes in the desert, an embodiment of the Jews' reappropriation of violence. "Do you like tanks?" Lanzmann asks a young soldier. "Yes, very much. I like to drive them. I like to shoot from them. A tank is a beautiful machine." *Tsahal* is about redemption through force. As one officer puts it, "in order to survive, we must chase them . . . Assault, assault, but with a plan."

Who "they" are, and why they might oppose Israel, is never explained. The "enemy" is not even named for much of the film. Two hours into *Tsahal*, Lanzmann conducts a token interview at a checkpoint with an unidentified Palestinian man returning from Dubai with his wife ("Do you work in oil?" "No, in buildings"); otherwise the Arabs are voiceless. When Lanzmann interviews Sharon on his farm, a gentle shepherd surrounded by a flock of sheep, he avoids the topic of Sabra and Shatila. The Lebanon disaster over which Sharon presided gave birth to a movement of refusenik soldiers, but Lanzmann, signer of the Manifeste des 121, does not speak to any of them. "As far as Israel is concerned," he writes in his memoir, "I have always been more susceptible to what unites Israelis than what divides them."

Tsahal is not a sentimental film or an explicitly boosterish one. It is solemn in tone; the hardened men of the IDF admit that Israel faces serious moral and political challenges. As a public figure, particularly in his demagogic speeches at pro-Israel rallies, Lanzmann has shown far less restraint. In 2011 at a rally in Paris where he was introduced as the "conscience of the Jewish people," Lanzmann, flanked by Bernard-Henri Lévy, gave a robust defense of the blockade of Gaza. Once again, Israel was being scapegoated, "charged with every crime, above all with the original sin of existing." He ridiculed the humanitarian concerns of "so-called peace activists":

Gaza is overflowing with goods. There are televisions, iPhones and iPads . . . No one in Gaza dies of malnutrition or suffers from thirst or hunger. Where are the emaciated people? Have we seen images of the emaciated? You can be sure if there were any, Hamas would be using them as propaganda . . . Mr. Goldstone,

Gaza is not the Warsaw Ghetto. [Cheers] Israel doesn't want to starve Gaza. Every day it sends hundreds of trucks to the northern border of Gaza . . . Do not imagine, decent people, that Gaza is a fraternal, classless society. There is a Gaza of the poor and a Gaza of the rich, the very rich . . . living in sumptuous homes who have never lifted a finger . . . for the so-called brothers from the refugee camps.

In fact, Gaza might be experiencing a serious food crisis were it not for international humanitarian assistance. During the last war, in which more than a thousand people were killed under Israeli bombardment, 80 percent of the strip's agricultural crops were destroyed. According to a recent report by Physicians for Human Rights–Israel, the majority of Gazans—900,000 people out of population of 1.5 million—"do not have the self-sufficient means to grow or purchase the bare minimum of food for themselves and their families." Lanzmann is right, in one sense: Gaza is not the Warsaw Ghetto, where six thousand people were dying each month in 1942; Israel's aim in Palestine is politicide, the destruction of Palestine as a viable political entity, not genocide. But his rhetorical moves will be disquietingly familiar to anyone who has seen his interview in *Shoah* with the Warsaw Ghetto administrator Franz Grassler: the insistence on the humanitarian intentions of the occupier, providing food and "maintaining" the ghetto; the belittling, the mockery of people's suffering.

"Everybody is somebody's Jew," Primo Levi told an Italian journalist after the massacres in Sabra and Shatila. The bitter ironies of Israel's treatment of the Palestinians—all too evident to Levi, who had seen men and women in Auschwitz reduced to ghosts "who march and labor in silence," known in the camps as "Muslims"—are invisible to Lanzmann. He is fond of quoting Emil Fackenheim's remark that the murdered Jews of Europe are "the presence of an absence," but refuses to see that the Jewish state was also created "in the presence of absence," as the Palestinian poet Mahmoud Darwish wrote. Only a few years after the war, Holocaust survivors found themselves living in the homes of another people who had been driven into exile, and on the ruins of destroyed villages. The Ben Shemen forest, where Lanzmann spoke with survivors of the Sonderkommando in *Shoah*, is only four kilometers east of Lod, where tens of thousands of Arabs were forcibly expelled in 1948. The Nakba—Arabic for "catastrophe," or Shoah—has yet to end.

The Nakba's traces in contemporary Israel have been the subject of a deeply Lanzmannian film, *Route 181*, a four-hour documentary co-directed by Eyal Sivan, a French-Israeli Jew, and Michel Khleifi, a Palestinian citizen of Israel. In 2003, Sivan and Khleifi spent two months traveling along the border outlined by the UN in Resolution 181, the 1947 partition plan, interviewing Arabs and Jews. Like *Shoah* and *Tsahal*, the film cuts between oral testimony and slow tracking shots of roads and infrastructure. Among those interviewed is an Arab barber in Lod who recalls the expulsions while cutting a man's hair: an obvious, provocative allusion to the barbershop scene in *Shoah*. Sivan and Khleifi insisted that their intention was not to compare the Nakba to the Holocaust, but to show the thread that links them. Outraged by this scene, Lanzmann denounced Sivan as an anti-Semite, and, with Alain Finkielkraut, successfully lobbied the Ministry of Culture to prevent the film being shown at a documentary festival at the Pompidou Center. Lanzmann, Sivan said, "is the only intellectual in the world whom you are not allowed to quote."

Since the outbreak of the Second Intifada, the French Jewish community has been swept by a wave of *communautarisme*, or identity politics. Anti-Semitism is one reason: clannishness is understandable in the face of incidents like last month's killings in Toulouse.* But anti-Semitism alone can't explain the Jewish community's turn inward, or its drift to the right. A few years ago, troubled by the increasingly bellicose tenor of Jewish politics in France, Jean Daniel published a striking little book called *The Jewish Prison*. This prison, unlike anti-Semitism, was self-imposed, and made up of three invisible walls: the idea of the

---

* In March 2012, the French jihadist Mohammed Merah murdered seven people in southwestern France, including three children and a teacher at a Jewish school, before being killed in a police siege.

Chosen People, Holocaust remembrance and support for the state of Israel. Having trapped themselves inside these walls, the prosperous, assimilated Jews of the West were less and less able to see themselves clearly or to appreciate the suffering of others—particularly the Palestinians living behind the "separation fence." Over the last four decades, Claude Lanzmann has played a formidable role not only in building this prison but in keeping watch over it. That a chronicler of the Holocaust could become a mystical champion of military force, an unswerving defender of Israel's war against the Palestinian people and a skilled denier of its crimes, is a remarkable story, but you won't find it in Lanzmann's memoir.

{2012}

14

Brothers in Arms:
Jean-Pierre Melville's War

In August 1943, Jean-Pierre Grumbach, a former soldier in the seventy-first artillery regiment in Fontainebleau, arrived in London. Grumbach, an Alsatian Jew from Paris, twenty-five years old, wanted to offer his services to the Forces Françaises Combattantes (FFC)—de Gaulle's Free French. His journey had begun seven months earlier in Marseille, where he had distributed pamphlets for the Resistance under cover of his work in the textile trade. After crossing into Spain through the Pyrenees, he had presented himself at the British consulate in Barcelona, where an official arranged for him to stay in a clandestine hotel until he could be transported to Gibraltar. But on the night of December 1, Grumbach sat with a group of ten other passengers in a fishing boat whose motor wouldn't start. At 3 a.m. the captain left to find a mechanic, but by the time he returned the air tank was empty. He went off again, ordering the passengers to stay put. Minutes later, the boat was seized by a Spanish patrol. Grumbach was detained for more than a month on suspicion of being a spy or a commando, then transferred to a naval prison, where he remained until late May, when he was cleared after an investigation. A month later he boarded a ship to London with a group of eighty other French citizens. "The volunteer Grumbach produced a very good impression," his interrogator in London wrote, and issued him a Number One visa. To the left of the photograph on his FFC visa, Grumbach wrote: "I wish to serve under the name of Melville, Jean-Pierre."

Herman Melville had been Grumbach's literary god, alongside Poe and Jack London, ever since he'd read *Pierre, or The Ambiguities* as a teenager. He "made the war" with his new name, and by the time it was over so many people knew him as Melville that there was no question of going back to Grumbach. Even Melville found himself getting confused: "I forget that when I say Melville, it's not me."

Yet Melville did not merely lift the name, he made it his own. In his thirteen films, Melville created an austere, somber aesthetic: even his color films appear to be in black and white. His protagonists, whether resistants, gangsters or priests, are solitary "men without women," in the words of Volker Schlöndorff, who worked as his assistant in the early 1960s. Driven by duty, they move inexorably toward their fate, which is often death. Paris is usually their home, and it's depicted as if it were always night, a city of slick cabarets, backroom poker games and garages where you can get a makeover for a newly stolen car—or a gun. In their fleeting appearances, even the city's monuments acquire a desolate air. In the words of the director Philippe Labro, Melville's films are suffused with "solitude, violence, mystery, a passion for risk and the aftertaste of the unpredictable and the inevitable."

Melville was a loner and a curmudgeon, with more than a touch of Bartleby. He built his own studio so that he wouldn't have to take orders from anyone and lived there with his wife and three cats. (The staircase from the studio to the flat upstairs features in nearly every Melville film.) He hated shooting because he had to wake up early and change out of his pajamas. He could be charming but on set was often a tyrant; he considered it a betrayal when his actors became romantically involved. He was a great talker, with a deep, velvety voice, but he hated cliques and industry schmoozing. One of the fathers of the Nouvelle Vague, he soon fell out with his "children." "I desire only one thing in life: to be left alone," he said. Individualism was something he revered, especially as portrayed in American gangster films and westerns. He described himself as an "anarchist of the right" but was in no way a political reactionary. "If I had been profoundly on the right, I couldn't make the films I make," he told the

Portuguese critic Rui Nogueira in *Le Cinéma selon Melville*, a book of interviews published two years before his death in 1973. What he was, he explained, was "backward-looking. I shun the world of the present, which I never manage to love."

Melville's refuge was his desk, where he wrote his scripts and edited in the middle of the night, with his sunglasses on and all the windows and shutters closed. He believed art was "possible only when the creator is alone, when he isolates himself from the rest of the world." (He preferred the term "creator" to "director" since he considered writing and editing to be the most important aspects of his work.) Several of his movies, including his three great films about the war, were adaptations of novels. In the first scene of *Le Silence de la mer* (1949), a man leaves a suitcase on the street; another man opens it to find, underneath some pressed shirts, the 1942 novel of the Resistance by Vercors on which the film is based. The pages of the novel reveal the credits: a device, as André Bazin noted, that Robert Bresson borrowed for his 1951 adaptation of Georges Bernanos's *Diary of a Country Priest*.

Melville's early films were bookish and rather talky. But in the early 1960s he began to cut back his dialogue. The first seven minutes of *Le Samouraï* (1967), in which Alain Delon plays the hitman Jef Costello, unfold silently; the heist in *Le Cercle rouge* (1970) goes on for half an hour without a sound, until Yves Montand's character disables the security system of a jewelry store with a single rifle shot. Men, almost always men, are quietly, diligently at work in Melville's films: they break safes and rob banks, organize escapes from prisons and moving trains, prepare themselves to commit murder. These wordless *longueurs* aren't entirely silent. Melville orchestrated ticking clocks, footsteps, barking dogs, rain and wind. He also used music sparely to brilliant effect, working with some of France's best film composers, including Martial Solal, Paul Misraki and Georges Delerue. But there was sometimes so little dialogue that his assistants wondered what the actors were supposed to do. "*On va dilater*," he would tell them—"We're going to stretch out"—like a jazz musician discussing how to improvise on the basis of a sketch. According to Bernard Stora, his assistant on *Le Cercle rouge*, the point of "stretching" a short passage of dialogue, or a scene, was to heighten its power, and slow down time. Melville's acts of "dilation" sometimes seem superfluous, even perverse, only to acquire meaning later on, like the languorous shot in *Le Cercle rouge* of a barmaid handing a red rose to Corey, the robber played by Delon, just before he falls into a trap laid by the police.

The minimalism of Melville's films—and their indifference to psychological motivation and melodramatic convention—provoked comment that he was imitating Bresson. Melville testily pointed out that he had used "Bressonian" techniques before Bresson himself: so it was Bresson who was "Melville-izing." The observation was accurate enough, but even Bazin, who acknowledged its truth, credited Bresson with carrying Melville's innovations to their "final conclusion," as if Bresson had made art out of a lesser filmmaker's tricks. Melville isn't even mentioned in Paul Schrader's canonical account of the "transcendental style" in cinema, though Scorsese's *Taxi Driver* (1976), based on a script by Schrader, owes much to Melville's vision of the underworld. The unflattering comparison with Bresson suggests genre prejudice—and perhaps other prejudices as well. Melville, an atheist Jew, made *polars*, *policiers* and political thrillers, while Bresson, a fervent Catholic, made arthouse films with spiritual ambitions. The grace which occasionally falls on Bresson's characters never finds the underground conspirators in Melville. They live in a fallen world from which the only sanctuary is brotherhood, and the only escape death.

What did Melville really know of the world he put on screen? He described the war as the "rare time when one encounters virtue," and as "the most beautiful years of my life." But he remained discreet, even secretive, about his experiences, and ruled out ever making a movie of them, though he flirted with the idea of writing a novel about the battles inside the Resistance. When Bertrand Tavernier, who worked as his assistant on *Léon Morin, prêtre* (1961), asked him what he did during the war, Melville said he'd "gone to England so he could see *The Life and Death of Colonel Blimp*." He was so cagey that some of his closest colleagues—including Schlöndorff, whom the childless

Melville regarded as a son—wondered if his Resistance past was a myth, all part of the same persona as his Stetson and Ray-Bans.

Thanks to two recent books—Bertrand Teissier's biography *Jean-Pierre Melville: Le Solitaire* and *Jean-Pierre Melville, une vie*, an unusually illuminating coffee-table book by the film critic Antoine de Baecque—we have a much fuller picture not only of Melville's war but of the ways it shaped his films.[*] As de Baecque writes: "Melville would remain a man the war had fashioned, faithful to a vanished time." While the sets of his films were expressionistic confections, not faithful recreations—Melville aimed for authenticity, not realism—their themes, especially brotherhood and betrayal, came directly from the war. As he told Nogueira, "what people tend to take for imagination" in his films is "in reality an effect of memory."

The same observation might be made of Patrick Modiano, whose noirish investigations of wartime Paris, spun from newspaper clippings and phone listings, often recall Melville's cinema. Their work converges, too, in a shared feeling for Nazi-occupied Paris, their fascination with the underworlds of crime and collaboration, and their obsession with the war's traces in the present. But the differences are more striking. Modiano, the son of a Jewish wartime profiteer who may have been part of collaborationist networks, was born in 1945, and has written to excavate the suppressed memories of the war, especially his father's. His novels turn on the trauma of not knowing his own past, of being the child of a war he never experienced directly. Melville, who was born in 1917, told Nogueira that to be a filmmaker, you have to be "constantly 'traumatizable,'" yet his films show little outward evidence of trauma: they have a defiant serenity, the cool logic of dreams. Melville had no interest in shattering the silence around the war. He was not a breaker of taboos, like Marcel Ophüls in his scathing documentary of French complicity, *The Sorrow and the Pity* (1969), or, in a different way, Louis Malle in his ambiguous portrait of a collaborator, *Lacombe, Lucien* (1974). If he was silent about what he had seen, he shared that

---

[*] *Jean-Pierre Melville, Le Solitaire* (Fayard), and *Jean-Pierre Melville, une vie* (Seuil) were both published in 2018.

silence with everyone who had lived through the war, whatever side they had been on. Melville himself made no secret of his friendships with former collaborators. "I have friends in the SS," he said, adding that he liked people who "get wet, who do something, and I believe that people who risk their life for a cause, bad or good, are interesting people. I don't like neutral people very much." For Melville, the silence of former combatants did not signify repression or shame but rather a kind of honor among those who had lived in the shadows.

Melville grew up in a middle-class home in the ninth arrondissement not far from Galeries Lafayette. His father, Jules Grumbach, who came from a family of Polish-Jewish butchers who'd settled in Alsace in the nineteenth century, sold *schmattes* (rags). Jules and his wife, Berthe, were fervent believers in the Republic, close to the Socialist Party. Their eldest son, Jacques, born in 1901, went on to become a writer for the party's weekly, *Le Populaire*, and the confidant of its editor, Léon Blum, the future prime minister. Jean-Pierre—the youngest of four—was a dreamer, with little interest in school or the fate of the Republic. He made his first movies at six, when his parents gave him a hand-cranked Pathé-Baby, graduated to a 16mm camera at twelve, and as a teenager became a connoisseur of Hollywood movies (French cinema bored him). His first mentor in what he called the "fantastic American science of showbusiness" was his uncle Arthur, an antiques dealer friendly with Maurice Chevalier and Josephine Baker. Arthur introduced him to the circus, then to nightclubs and music halls. As de Baecque points out, Melville's gangster films invariably include a "fetish" scene in a cabaret, a place set deep in "the heart of Jean-Pierre Grumbach's native land."

When Melville was fifteen, his father died of a heart attack. (He preferred to wear black, he once said, because he was permanently in mourning for his father.) Two years later, he dropped out of school to work as a courier for a diamond company, then as a wedding photographer, but he could never hold down a job since he was always sneaking off to go to the movies. A cad and *coureur* who boasted of sleeping with the family's maids, Melville grew more serious after being drafted in 1937. He joined the

Communist Party, perhaps as a way of distinguishing himself from his Socialist brother—an infatuation that ended abruptly in August 1939 over the Hitler-Stalin Pact, the only time that Melville said he'd contemplated suicide.

When France fell to the Germans, Jacques, whose name appeared on a Gestapo list, went underground, producing a clandestine edition of *Le Populaire*. Melville soon joined him and their sister, Janine, in the Resistance, working as a fur trader in the free zone outside Castres in the Languedoc. The Grumbachs belonged to a tiny minority of *résistants*, always at risk of a Gestapo raid or denunciation by collaborators. He did not see himself as particularly courageous. "The opportunity to distinguish myself by making a choice was never offered: I was Jewish. And for a Jew, being a member of the Resistance was infinitely less heroic than for someone who wasn't. Who, or what, could prove to me that if I hadn't been Jewish, I would have made the right choice?"

In November 1942 Melville followed Jacques, who had set out a few weeks before to cross the Pyrenees into Spain, carrying a large sum of cash for de Gaulle. He didn't learn until the end of the war that Jacques never made it past the frontier. His *passeur* Lazare Cabrero, a Spanish republican, shot him in the head, took his money and buried his body. A decade later, the corpse was discovered and Cabrero arrested. At the trial, he claimed that Jacques had broken his ankle, leaving him no choice: his orders were to kill the seriously wounded rather than abandon them in the mountains and so compromise the security of the convoy. In May 1953, Cabrero was acquitted; Melville did not appeal the judge's decision. Forty years later, Cabrero, dying of cancer, offered to send Jacques's son his father's watch and the money he'd stolen in return for absolution. He refused the request.

Melville served with the Free French for two years. A month after being dispatched to Algiers in October 1943, he joined the artillery. They were first shipped to Bizerte and Bône, then to Italy, where they fought alongside American troops near Naples. In May 1944, during the battle of Monte Cassino, Melville was part of the first wave of Allied soldiers crossing the Garigliano

River, whose waters were said to have run red with blood during the battle. Under an apple tree in Cassino, Melville placed a cigarette in the mouth of a young man who'd been shot. "He took two drags and then he died. Imagine, springtime in the Italian countryside . . . and here is this young man dying at twenty. Reality always surpasses cinema in war films."

Demobilized in 1945, Melville returned to Paris, moving into a small apartment in Montmartre. He had decided that *Le Silence de la mer* would be his first film when he read Cyril Connolly's translation, *Put Out the Light*, during the Blitz. The book tells the story of an elderly Frenchman and his teenage niece who are forced to put a German officer up in their home. Unusually sensitive, Werner von Ebrennac is keen to persuade his hosts of Germany's "civilizing" mission in France, whose culture he professes to love. The uncle and niece put up with his monologues but refuse to respond. Instead of overcoming their silence, he is overcome by theirs, and eventually shamed into a recognition of Hitler's barbarism.

Vercors was the pen name of Jean Bruller, an illustrator and engraver. Bruller's family had been forced to house a German officer during the Occupation. When Éditions de Minuit published the novel in February 1942, not even his wife knew that he was the author. He considered the novel to be the collective property of the Resistance; fearful that it would be vulgarized, he initially declined to give the rights to Melville, whose only film credit at that point was a short feature—later disavowed—about a circus clown. "You can prevent me from showing a film based on your work, but you can't prevent me from shooting it," Melville told him. "I will show it to you, and it will be so faithful you will not be able to refuse me."

Vercors was persuaded and invited Melville to shoot at his country home in Villiers-sur-Morin, where the German officer had stayed. Jean-Marie Robain, who played the uncle, and Nicole Stéphane, who played the niece, had also been in the Resistance. For the role of von Ebrennac, Melville chose the Swiss-American actor Howard Vernon, who was known for playing villainous Nazi officers. "You were so good at playing a Nazi bastard,"

Melville told him, "but you'll be just as good playing a sympathetic Nazi." The twenty-seven-day shoot was spread out over a year since Melville constantly had to interrupt filming to raise more money. He made the film in near secrecy, as if he were still in the Resistance, mostly to avoid detection by the film studio unions, dominated by the Communist-led Confédération générale du travail, which would have required him to work with a crew that he couldn't yet afford, and otherwise limit what he saw as his independence. (The CGT accused Melville of "making a film with the Rothschilds' money," because he'd cast Stéphane, the daughter of Baron James-Henri de Rothschild.) On the last day of the shoot, Vercors's wife returned home early and complained that the German officer had shown more respect for their house than the film crew had. "But Madame," Melville replied, "the German wasn't making a movie!"

In November 1948, Melville screened the finished film to two dozen Resistance veterans, including Vercors, Paul Éluard, Louis Aragon, Claude Bourdet, who wore (in the words of one witness) "the severe gaze of those who are right by decree." All but one of them approved the film. It's not hard to see why. *Le Silence de la mer* honors the novel that inspired it, as well as the ideal of Resistance. But it also captures what Vercors meant by his title: the "submerged life of hidden and conflicting feelings, desires and thoughts." The uncle and niece speak only when von Ebrennac expresses grave reservations about Hitler's war. But Melville suggests that their silence disguises emotions other than noble defiance: curiosity, tenderness, compassion, even love. This is particularly true of Stéphane's character, who seems to be falling for the officer, leaving the impression that her struggle is as much with herself as with him. What distinguishes her symbolic "resistance" from a more passive *attentisme* is an inner decision that is somehow visible in her face, filmed by Henri Decaë in contrasts of light and shadow.

Melville said that, in *Le Silence de la mer*, he wanted to make an "anticinematic" film, "composed exclusively of images and sounds, from which movement and action would be practically banned." The film was revolutionary in another way: it was shot by a small crew on location, using natural light and funded independently. After making an adaptation of Jean Cocteau's *Les Enfants terribles* in 1950, for which Cocteau would take most of the credit, Melville pursued his dream of creating his own studio. He built a flat over a warehouse he found on the rue Jenner, and moved in with his wife, Florence, whom he married in 1952. Florence would tolerate his many infidelities, and was, in Teissier's description, a "woman of the shadows"; no photograph of the couple exists. (When Melville was interviewed in *Lui* in 1965, the profile was illustrated with a photograph of a nude woman in his office: it wasn't Florence but his secretary and confidant Annie Méliant.)

The first film Melville made at Studio Jenner was his fourth, *Bob le flambeur* (1955). Bob Montagné, the aging ex-thief played by Roger Duchesne, is a gambler on a permanent losing streak who begins to plot a comeback after hearing, on the morning of the Grand Prix horse race, that the safe at the Deauville casino contains 800 million francs. The film ends in a wry joke: Bob breaks his losing streak at the tables on the night of the heist, wins big and forgets to follow through on the plan he'd hatched; the heist's violent failure ends in his arrest and in the death of his young protégé Paulo. "There's always a *Bridge on the River Kwai* that dozes at the bottom of my heart," Melville said. "I love the fact that effort is useless. Climbing toward failure is an altogether human thing."

Bob le flambeur was not a *policier*, but rather, as he stressed, a "comedy of *moeurs*," an affectionate, laid-back study of the criminal underworld of Montmartre and Pigalle: "heaven and hell," as Melville announces in a voiceover at the beginning of the film. Bob is an ex-con, but he's also a man of dignity, honor and chivalry, a member of a dying breed of noble thugs. He spends much of his time looking after Paulo, showing him the ropes, and setting him up with Anne, a young woman Bob had been too chivalrous, and perhaps too weary, to seduce himself. Even Commissaire Ledru describes him as a "friend," though he fears, rightly, that he'll have to arrest him again one day. "I don't believe in friendship," Melville told Nogueira. "It's one of those things that I don't believe in, that I don't know myself, but that I like to show in my films." (A friend, Melville said, is someone you can call in the middle of the night to "tell him, 'Be nice, find your revolver and come immediately,' and to hear him respond, 'OK, I'm coming.' Who does that for anyone?")

The casual style of *Bob le flambeur* looks forward to the Nouvelle Vague, rather than to the pared-down, meticulous thrillers Melville would go on to make. But it is the first time we see a masculine underground based on honor codes among "brothers," where women are an ever-present temptation and threat: the heist is compromised when Paulo, keen to impress Anne, leaks the Deauville plot. (Isabelle Corey, who played Anne, was a fifteen-year-old nonprofessional Melville spotted while driving around the place de la Madeleine.) His partner on the script was Auguste Le Breton, the author of *Rififi* and a former criminal, who showed him around Pigalle at night. Roger Duchesne, who played Bob, was a regular at L'Heure bleue, a cabaret on rue Pigalle where French stars had fraternized with German officers. Banned from working during the postwar *épuration* for collaboration, Duchesne robbed a bank of 800 million francs—the same sum Bob tries to steal in Deauville—then cooled his heels in prison writing adventure novels. When Melville tracked him down, he was selling scrap metal in Saint-Ouen. Duchesne wasn't much of an actor, but he had a sleepy charm. He'd also seen men get shot, and explained to Daniel Cauchy, who played Paulo, that he would jump back, not forward, when he heard gunfire. Melville had no objections to working with a collaborator. "Like the former fighters," Labro said, "he liked to face his enemies . . . He was attracted to drifters and marginals."

What you remember about *Bob le flambeur*, long after you've forgotten the plot, is its mood: a vibraphonist playing by himself in a club that's just closed; an American soldier on a motorcycle, picking up a young woman in a drowsy street at sunrise. Melville filmed these scenes as if he just happened to catch them, with the offhand elegance of Brassaï. The film's editing was often scrappy, but this, too, charmed the future filmmakers of the Nouvelle Vague. In *Cahiers du cinéma*, Claude Chabrol praised Melville for his "imperfect cinema," his "art of seizing the unusual or poetic detail." ("We could never have made the films we made if it hadn't been for Melville," he wrote later.) This sort of praise would soothe Melville's wounded ego after *Two Men in Manhattan* (1959), a caper about the murder of a French UN official, flopped. In Godard's *À bout de souffle* (1960), Michel Poiccard, the criminal played by Jean-Paul Belmondo, asks for Bob Montagné, and Melville appears in a cameo as Parvulesco, the novelist interviewed by Jean Seberg's character. Godard told Melville to "talk about women the way you usually do with me." Melville drew on Nabokov, "whom I'd seen in a television interview, being himself, pretentious, intoxicated by himself, a little cynical and naive." When Seberg asks what his greatest ambition is, he says: "To become immortal, then die."

Throughout the early 1960s, Melville met Godard every Saturday for dinner at the home of Georges de Beauregard, their producer. As Teissier writes, both hid behind outsized personas and outsized sunglasses, and for a while they were inseparable. Melville was a witness when Godard married Anna Karina; Godard paid tribute to Melville in *Vivre sa vie* (1962), where the character played by Karina is shot to death outside the Studio Jenner. After Karina miscarried, Godard smashed his television and ripped his own clothes. "Why did you destroy your own things rather than hers?" Melville asked. He was astonished when Godard asked him "seriously what was more important: Anna or the cinema?" (Obviously it was the cinema.) Godard broke off the friendship after Melville raised questions about the direction of his work; as Melville saw it, Godard had been "spoiled by Aragon's flattery."

Melville was, in any event, coming to the end of his New Wave period, having "preached in the desert from 1947–57." For him, the New Wave wasn't a style or sensibility, but merely "an artisanal system of production," and he didn't like being the "head of an enormous family of totally illegitimate children whom I didn't want to recognize. Hence the break." After the failure of *Two Men in Manhattan* (1959), "I no longer had the least intention of continuing to make films that didn't succeed. I'd had enough of being an *auteur maudit*, known only by a little chapel of the cinema-mad."

Free of the cinephile chapel, Melville set his next film in the Catholic Church, and hired two of France's biggest stars, Belmondo and Emmanuelle Riva, whom he'd seen in Resnais's *Hiroshima mon amour*. *Léon Morin, prêtre*, an adaptation of Béatrix Beck's Goncourt-winning novel, is an anomaly in Melville's cinema, both for its subject matter and its melodrama. But it is also one of his most visually ravishing films. Riva plays Barny, a communist and atheist, a friend of the *maquisards* and young widow of a Jewish man, living with her young daughter in an Alpine village under German occupation. One day, on a whim, she decides to walk into the confessional chamber of the local church and declare, "Religion is the opium of the people." The priest's reply surprises her: "Not exactly. The bourgeoisie made it so, distorting it to their advantage." A relationship of sorts begins, half conversational duel, half unrequited love affair.

The priest, Léon Morin, is a secondary figure in Beck's novel, but Melville made him a central character, and turned the story into a contest of wills between the sacred and the profane, faith and eros. (Beck was furious that Melville had focused on "what was sexual and scandalous.") Belmondo, who plays Morin, is a left-wing rebel, a Resistance theologian who hides Jews, but what fascinated Melville was that he "loves to excite women and yet doesn't sleep with them. He's Don Juan." Barny is stirred by Morin's radical interpretation of the scripture, and eventually converts to Catholicism; but it is his charisma, not his faith, that persuades her, and what she really desires isn't salvation but physical love. Melville appears to sympathize with her frustrated longing, but by the end of the film, which ends with Morin's rejection of her, she is punished for failing to transcend her desires and accept God's grace. Barny—the widow of one Jew and the employee of another—is as close to being a Jew as someone can be without actually being one. Her world, one is tempted to say, is Melville's (Jewish, earthly, sensuous), while Morin's is Bresson's (Catholic, spiritual, ascetic). *Léon Morin, prêtre* is an atheist's tormented—sexist, cruel—homage to the Catholic faith, a film in the transcendental style about the impossibility of transcendence. More than any of his films, it crystalized his distrust of carnal love, his belief that solitary commitment to a cause is preferable to emotional dependence on others.

In his great gangster films of the 1960s and 1970s, Melville transposed the aesthetic sensibility of *Léon Morin, prêtre*—its severity, its admiring portrait of a celibate male loner—onto the criminal milieu of *Bob le flambeur*. What he left out was no less crucial. The comedy of manners in *Bob le flambeur* gives way to an atmosphere of almost relentless solemnity: instead of modern jazz, we hear ominous percussion and symphonic chords. Gone, too, is the clash of philosophies and the attention to female experience in *Léon Morin, prêtre*. Melville's gangsters (and the cops who pursue them) are almost priestly in their renunciation of worldly pleasures. He said that he had created a "cinema without women because, if I may offer my excuses to women (whom I love greatly), man can achieve sublimation only outside his desires, his libido and his complexes." His focus now was on a different kind of chase, featuring cops and outlaws, hunters and hunted, pushing the genre almost to the point of abstraction.

Melville's first gangster film was *Le Doulos* (1962), with Belmondo and Serge Reggiani, based on a *polar* by Pierre Lesou. It's a tangled story of brotherhood and betrayal among criminals, revolving around the question of whether Silien, the cocky young thug played by Belmondo, is a savior or a *doulos*—an informer. But the most riveting thing about the film isn't its story but its look. "Doulos" also means "hat," and most of the characters wear fedoras, as if they've wandered in from a William Wyler or John Huston film. The sets, too, "bear witness to my passion for the American cinema," Melville said. The phone booth in the métro is an American one; the bar resembles a coffee shop in Manhattan; the police interrogation room, with its Venetian blinds, is an exact copy of the one in Rouben Mamoulian's *City Streets* (1931), itself a copy of a New York City police station. The point of this "fetishistic extraterritoriality" (de Baecque's phrase) wasn't to "disorient" the viewer, Melville explained, but rather to produce a "bewitchment . . . that he surrenders to without remarking on it."

Melville set four more films in this hardboiled wonderland: *Le Deuxième Souffle* (1966), *Le Samouraï* (1967), *Le Cercle rouge* (1970) and *Un flic* (1973). With the exception of *Un Flic*, they were hits, though critics complained that Melville had sold out to Hollywood and betrayed the New Wave. The influential critic Serge Daney dismissed Melville's thrillers as advertisements for trench coats. "You are in a cinema which copies or reproduces another cinema, without the slightest relationship with French society," Tavernier wrote five years after his former employer's death. But Melville had no interest in commenting on French society. And while he worshiped classical Hollywood cinema, his love affair with America as a country came to an end during the shooting of *L'Aîné des Ferchaux* in 1963, a picaresque road movie based on a Simenon novel. The story follows Dieudonné Ferchaux (Charles Vanel), a corrupt banker on the run from justice, and his secretary Michel Maudet, a former paratrooper and would-be boxer (Belmondo), as they drive from New York to Louisiana, chased by the FBI. A buddy film like *Bob le flambeur*, it's little more than a curiosity, notable largely for being Melville's first film in color. Before leaving for the States, where he shot most of the outdoor scenes, Melville was considering moving there; he had loved America "like crazy and without reservation," he told Nogueira, until he saw American racism up close. "Blacks are right to revolt . . . No one can reproach them for wanting to fight . . . The reason I didn't want to live in America is that I would have become a witness of a black sub-proletariat . . . and I couldn't bear that."

He would never set foot in the US again. But far from discouraging him, staying in France freed him to pursue his cinematic dream of "America" unburdened by reality. He continued to pay tribute to Hollywood films: the screenplay he wrote for *Le Samouraï* was a barely disguised reworking of *This Gun for Hire* (1942); *Le Cercle rouge* is a western, only moved to 1970s Paris and featuring cars rather than horses. Still, his films were "specifically French," he insisted. "The best proof of the fact that they are not American is that the Americans do not want them. They do not understand my films, the motivations of my characters." Revising his earlier, harsh appraisal, Tavernier echoed this judgment in his recent documentary, *My Journey through French Cinema*: "The waiting and the silences are more emphatic. He is finally closer to Bresson than to Wyler." Far from copying Hollywood film sets, Tavernier added, "he recreated the atmosphere of his studio and bedroom."

On the night of June 29, 1967, Melville's studio and apartment burned down. He had been woken up by one of his cats, and smelled smoke. His archives—thousands of photographs and books, as well as two dozen screenplays—were destroyed. He never complained, except when a rumor spread that he'd set fire to the studio in order to collect insurance. (He'd actually forgotten to renew it.) "Too busy to give himself over to suffering," according to Florence, he went back to work on *Le Samouraï*, the first of three pictures he made with Delon, and perhaps the purest distillation of late Melville.

The men first met at Delon's home in the Twelfth. Delon asked Melville to read aloud from his script. It begins: "A pale gray light coming from two sash windows that cut into a dark wall. We see the rain falling through the windows and reflecting on the ceiling, and the shadows of passing cars." He continued reading until Delon stopped him. "You've been reading for seven and a half minutes, and there's not yet a shadow of dialogue. That's enough for me: I'll make the film. What's it called?" "*Le Samouraï*." Delon led Melville into his bedroom, where there was a leather bed, a spear, a sword—and a samurai dagger.

To the role of Jef Costello—a contract killer on the run from both the police, who want to arrest him, and his employers, who want to kill him before he's arrested—Delon brought a "virility tinged with femininity," as Barny says of her alluring co-worker, Sabine Lévy, in *Léon Morin, prêtre*. Delon's serene fatalism is irresistible. Melville imagined the film as a portrait of a schizophrenic "made by a paranoid, since all creators are paranoids." The second of his films in color, it was shot by Decaë in moody blues and grays. It opens with an epigraph from the bushido that Melville had in fact concocted: "There is no solitude deeper than that of the samurai, except that of the tiger in the jungle, perhaps."

There's a romance, of sorts, in *Le Samouraï*, between Costello and a *métisse* nightclub pianist, played by Cathy Rosier, who passes by him in the corridor just after he has killed the club's owner. Apparently smitten, Costello returns to the scene of the crime to see her again. They drive to her place, a swanky flat that turns out to belong to the man chasing him. When Costello is given a new contract, this time to kill her, he never loads his gun and instead sacrifices himself for her in a hail of police bullets. As Melville put it to Nogueira: "Jef falls in love with his own death. Cathy Rosier, black death dressed in white, possesses the charm to capture him, to captivate him." Melville himself appears to have been captivated by—or was at least possessive of—Rosier, a petite, elegant former model from Martinique. After discovering that she was having an affair with his set designer, François de Lamothe, he asked Lamothe to come for a drink once the shoot was over. Lamothe walked into Melville's office and found it covered wall to wall with images of Rosier. For his next film, Melville decided to hire Lamothe's assistant instead.

Does Jef have an affair with the pianist? I've watched *Le Samouraï* countless times, and I still don't know. Melville doesn't spell things out, and, in any case, the pianist is less a character in a thriller than a beautiful phantom in a Melvillian dream of a thriller. This is the paradox of the films that Melville made after rejecting the New Wave. In his efforts to win over the "grand public," Melville became more, not less, enigmatic and, as de Baecque suggests, drew even closer to Bresson: "The same radical style, the same taste for the pure, the dry, the concise, the same manner of filming faces and glances. The same relationship, from *Pickpocket* to *Le Samouraï*, to filming gestural technique: how do you steal a wallet? How do you start a car that isn't yours? How do you kill a man you don't know?"

Costello doesn't blink when he's asked to kill someone he doesn't know. Nor does Corey, the robber played by Delon in

Le Cercle rouge. Melville's film about the Resistance, *L'Armée des ombres* (1969), begins with a similar situation. Gerbier, the Resistance leader played by Lino Ventura, and his men have a dirty job: to kill an informer, a vulnerable-looking young man with pillowy lips. They're in a semi-derelict room in Marseille that looks like a Blue-Period Picasso and the curtains are drawn, but they can't use a gun to finish him off because the neighbors would hear the shot, so they strangle him instead. It's the first time they have killed someone, and they look ravaged. (Ventura and Melville, who had fallen out while making *Le Deuxième Souffle*, communicated through a third party on the set, a tension that probably improved Ventura's performance.) The date is October 1942, a month before Melville had left Marseille for Spain; there are no more than six hundred *maquisards* and their main struggle is simply to stay alive. We don't see many Nazis in *L'Armée des ombres*, but we know they're there: even before the opening credits, we have seen them marching down the Champs Élysées in front of the Arc de Triomphe—the first time that actors in German uniform had ever been filmed there (Melville hired dancers to get the goose steps right).

Jardie, Gerbier and their comrades "Le Masque" and "Le Bison" ultimately face a moral test more difficult than killing a traitor: killing a friend, Madame Mathilde, played by Simone Signoret. Mathilde, a courageous and resourceful member of their cell, has been arrested with a photograph of her teenage daughter in her wallet; the Germans have released her from custody, but only after threatening to take her daughter to a bordello on the Eastern Front unless she supplies them with names. She ignored Gerbier's warning to get rid of the picture and has now left them all exposed. The film ends with her assassination by her comrades—at once necessary and futile, logical and horrifying.

L'Armée des ombres was based on Joseph Kessel's novel, which Melville read in London in 1943 and considered "the most beautiful and complete document on this tragic period." But it's much more than an adaptation. The film has autobiographical touches, such as a sequence in London where Gerbier and his boss, Luc Jardie (Paul Meurisse), make contact with de Gaulle. Jardie, who is a mathematician in Paris, is composed of several figures, especially the Resistance martyrs Jean Moulin and Jean Cavaillès. When Jardie's younger brother, Jean-François (Jean-Pierre Cassel), joins Gerbier's cell, he doesn't tell him: surely his brother, lost in his equations, would never understand. Later, Jean-François has the honor of rowing "the Leader" to a submarine. But it's too dark for them to see each other, and both will die under torture without knowing of the other's involvement. It's hard not to see a parallel in the lives of the Grumbach brothers: Jacques, the intellectual resistant, and Jean-Pierre, who lost his older brother in the shadows of the Pyrenees.

L'Armée des ombres is Melville's greatest film, fusing the blue-and-gray minimalism of *Le Samouraï* with the anguish of *Le Silence de la mer*. The scenes in prisons and torture chambers are matched only by those in *The Battle of Algiers*. And in the assassination of Madame Mathilde, the film achieves something close to classical tragedy. Like the spurned Barny in *Léon Morin, prêtre*, Mathilde can't sublimate her feelings: the one sacrifice she can't make for the Resistance is to remove her daughter's photograph from her purse. The difference is that her fate becomes a condemnation of the Nazi occupation, and of the moral deformations it imposed on the Resistance, not of the woman herself. Kessel sobbed at the premiere.

Outside Resistance circles, the response was less enthusiastic. Melville's soixante-huitard "apostles" at *Cahiers du cinéma* ridiculed it as Gaullist, as an official work of art. (In his interviews with Nogueira, Melville bemoaned the "dialectical terrorism" of a "certain journal of cinema.") In *The Vichy Syndrome* (1991), Henry Rousso argues that the film arrived "too late," in 1969, just as the Gaullist myth of a nation united in resistance was crumbling under the impact of May 1968; Ophüls's film about Vichy collaboration, *The Sorrow and the Pity*, was released the same year. But for all the Gaullist clichés, particularly in the London sequence, the film portrays France in 1942 as a country of *attentistes* and collaborators—the Resistance is forever lonely. Moreover, as de Baecque writes, the film's style "has nothing to do with official art: the silences, slowness and duration of the scenes . . . de-Gaullise the monument."

After *L'Armée des ombres*, Melville returned to the *policier*, with the virtuosic *Le Cercle rouge* and the fascinating failure *Un Flic*, his last film. In *Le Cercle rouge*, Delon's character, Corey, just out of prison, teams up with an escaped fugitive, Vogel (Gian Maria Volonte), and an ex-cop, Jansen (Yves Montand), to rob a jeweler's on place Vendôme. They are pursued by the soft-spoken, dedicated Commissaire Mattei (André Bourvil), who lives alone with his cats. The film, for which Melville wrote the screenplay, grew out of his desire to explore every possible situation involving police and criminals (he counted nineteen in all). Melville feuded with Volonte, who refused to take direction. He'd had doubts about Montand over his ties to the Communist Party (Melville never forgot the betrayal of the Hitler-Stalin Pact), but put them aside after seeing his powerful performance in *The Confession* (1970), Costa-Gavras's anti-Stalinist film about the show trials in Czechoslovakia. In the end, Volonte's feral energy worked in perfect counterpoint to Delon's self-restraint, while Montand gave one of his finest performances as an alcoholic who overcomes his demons for the sake of the heist—arguably the most brilliantly choreographed robbery in film history. Something of the tenderness in *Bob le flambeur* resurfaced, too. Brought together by fate in "the red circle"—a Buddhist notion invented by Melville—Corey and Vogel become fiercely protective of each other. When Corey leaves Vogel behind to sell the jewels they have stolen to Mattei, disguised as a fellow criminal, we see Vogel at the window, clasping the red rose that Corey received from the barmaid, as if he were waiting for a lover's return.

Writing under the pseudonym "Michel Servet" in a radical journal called *J'accuse*, Godard denounced *Le Cercle rouge* as "rotten," but it proved the biggest hit of Melville's career. He celebrated by buying a Rolls Royce Silver Shadow and tried to repeat the success with *Un Flic*, released in the autumn of 1972. The film was widely mocked, however, since Melville barely concealed the fact that he'd used maquettes for a long, silent sequence in which a helicopter is used to carry out a train robbery. But the obviously fake shot of a helicopter floating over a train at night is poetic in its artificiality, like Japanese puppet theater, while the bloody raid on a bank in a rain-swept seaside town nearly matches the intensity of the place Vendôme heist in *Le Cercle rouge*. There's also a troubled eroticism just under the surface: Catherine Deneuve's character appears to be the mistress of both Simon (Richard Crenna), the gangster behind the raid, and Edouard Coleman (Delon), the policeman pursuing him; Coleman exchanges lengthy, longing glances with one of his informers, a transvestite prostitute who's clearly in love with him, only to inflict an even more brutal rejection than Léon Morin does.

Melville never recovered from the failure of *Un Flic*, and in August 1973, aged fifty-five, he suffered a fatal stroke while having dinner with Philippe Labro. Delon, who was in Nice, immediately drove back to Paris, and broke down in tears when he arrived at Studio Jenner. After Melville's death, the studio was closed, and his films were hardly seen in France for the next fifteen years. During that period, Melville was at best patronizingly praised as a director of sleek *policiers* with a colourful personality—but he was no *auteur*. The rediscovery began abroad, in the places that had inspired him: the US and East Asia. He found other apostles, long after his death, in Michael Mann and Jim Jarmusch, John Woo and Takeshi Kitano, whose stylized noirs not only paid tribute to Melville, but vindicated his judgment that the crime film is a "major genre, but one that's very difficult to pull off." Today, Melville's films feel less time-bound than most of the New Wave's, because they make no effort to capture their era, unfolding instead in a self-enclosed, nocturnal world, as obsessional as the ones of Hitchcock or Buñuel—the world of Studio Jenner. Labro remembers leaving the studio on one occasion after they'd talked all night, Melville standing in a "halo of lampposts on his blue and gray street, contemplating the car as it drives away. It's the final scene of a film that was never made."

{2019}

15

"One day I'll tell you what I think": Jean-Paul Sartre and Arwa Salih

In the spring of 1961, Frantz Fanon wrote to his publisher in Paris to suggest that he ask Jean-Paul Sartre for a preface to his anticolonial manifesto, *The Wretched of the Earth*. "Tell him that every time I sit down at my desk, I think of him." For revolutionary intellectuals in the Third World, Sartre seemed miraculously uncontaminated by the paternalism—and hypocrisy—that gave the white left such a bad reputation. While intellectuals in the orbit of the French Communist Party were vacillating over the Algerian war of independence, he gave his unconditional support to the rebels, a stance that nearly got him killed by an OAS bomb planted outside his flat. He contributed fiery prefaces not only to Fanon's book, but to Léopold Sédar Senghor's anthology of Négritude poets and to Albert Memmi's *Portrait of the Colonizer*. "Your influence in this region is deeper and wider than that of any other writer," the Egyptian writer Ahmad Abbas Salih told him. Fanon, alert to the transformation that had caused Sartre to replace the abstract "self" and "other" of *Being and Nothingness* (1943) with a new understanding of power relations in *Critique of Dialectical Reason* (1960), based in part on the distinction between colonizer and colonized, gave lectures on the *Critique* to Algerian soldiers in training camps in Tunisia.

But Sartre's cachet crumbled in the aftermath of his visit to Egypt and Israel in 1967, when he aligned himself with Israel on the eve of the Six-Day War. "For reasons that we still cannot know for certain," Edward Said would lament, "Sartre did indeed remain constant in his fundamental pro-Zionism. Whether that was because he was afraid of seeming anti-Semitic, or because he felt guilt about the Holocaust, or because he allowed himself no deep appreciation of the Palestinians as victims of and fighters against Israel's injustice, or for some other reason, I shall never know." Yoav Di-Capua, though, suggests that Sartre's actual position on Israel-Palestine was more troubled, and less hostile to the Arabs, than Said's phrase "fundamental pro-Zionism" suggests. In *No Exit*, he provides a thorough account of Sartre's trip to the Middle East, when Arab and Israeli intellectuals fought to win over a single heart and mind—Sartre's own.*

Existentialism had been in vogue in the Arab world since the mid-1940s, when the philosopher Abd al-Rahman Badawi wrote his doctoral dissertation on "existential time." Sartre's thinking, according to Di-Capua, commanded such a strong interest because it spoke to a hunger for freedom from both colonialism and the fetters of piety and patriarchy. It also provoked a vibrant and specifically Arab response: a movement known as *iltizam*, or "commitment." Di-Capua's readings of this tradition provide a glimpse of a vanished world, as intellectuals gathered in cafés in Beirut, Damascus, Cairo and Baghdad to argue over the meaning of freedom, authenticity and—the most enchanting mirage of the 1950s and 1960s—the "new man" who would transform their traditional societies.

But the man was perhaps more important than his ideas. For the Arabs, Sartre represented the "universal intellectual" who spoke truth to imperial power. His approval was all the more eagerly sought because he had yet to state his views on what, since the decolonization of Algeria, had become the Arabs' most sacred cause: the liberation of Palestine. Had he been silent because of his well-known sympathy for Jews in the face of anti-Semitic persecution, the subject of his book *Antisemite and Jew* (1946)? This was one theory to explain what struck the Arabs

---

* Di-Capua's *No Exit: Arab Existentialism, Jean-Paul Sartre and Decolonization* was published by University of Chicago Press in 2018.

as a maddening enigma: How could the defender of colonized Africans and Algerians not also be a champion of the Palestinians whose lands had been confiscated by Zionist settlers? Another hypothesis was that his views were colored by those of his young Jewish colleague at *Les Temps modernes*, Claude Lanzmann, a fervent Zionist. Sartre's Arab admirers reasoned that if only they could show Sartre the revolution unfolding in Egypt, and the Palestinian refugee camps in the Gaza Strip, he would come to embrace the only authentically Sartrean position: solidarity with the Arabs in their struggle with the colonial-settler state.

Di-Capua's story begins in the late 1950s, when a young Egyptian called Ali al-Samman arrived in Paris to enroll in a doctoral program in political science. Al-Samman established the Association des étudiants Arabes en France and became an eloquent spokesman for the Arab cause. A graduate student without title, he operated, in effect, as Nasser's man in Paris, reportedly delivering messages from the Egyptians to de Gaulle during the Evian negotiations between France and the Algerian National Liberation Front. Nasser couldn't have had a better emissary on the Left Bank: al-Samman, one of whose mentors was a former Resistance fighter who had survived Mauthausen, was unusually sensitive to the legacy of the Holocaust in France, and fought against anti-Semitism inside the ranks of the Arab student movement. But at the same time he tried to persuade "the French left, which always protected oppressed peoples, to protect the Palestinians as well."

Here, he had his work cut out for him. Barely a decade had passed since the war, and Vichy had not covered the French—or its intellectuals—in glory. For most French intellectuals on the left, Israel was a sanctuary for the survivors: they thought no more of the Palestinians driven out to make room for a Jewish state than they did of the Sudeten Germans displaced at the end of the war. Israel, with its kibbutzes and Marxist intellectuals, was also widely seen as a socialist country. After all, it had won its independence with the support of the Soviet Union, and prevailed against the Arabs in the 1948 war thanks in part to a delivery of Czech arms. Only a handful of writers—notably the Arabist

Jacques Berque, and Maxime Rodinson, a Marxist Jewish scholar
of Islam who had lost much of his family in the camps—were
even aware of the Palestinian catastrophe. Most people found it
hard to distinguish Arab opposition to Israel from anti-Jewish
hostility. The often bellicose rhetoric of Arab nationalism—not
least on Egypt's official radio station, Voice of the Arabs, with its
calls to liberate Palestine from *el-Yahud*, "the Jews"—didn't help.

By coincidence, al-Samman was a neighbor of Sartre's on the
rue Bonaparte, and in 1965 Sartre sought him out to learn more
about the Arab-Israeli conflict and the possibility of "fighting
racism" on both sides. Before long they were meeting every
Sunday at Le Dôme Café. Al-Samman tried to persuade him of
the virtue of Nasser's revolution, describing Egypt as a country
on the road to socialism, an unswerving friend to Algerians,
Congolese and Vietnamese in their struggles against imperialism. Sartre was skeptical. Egypt, he said, was a "country which
eliminates freedom": in 1959, as part of a mass arrest of the left
opposition, Nasser had jailed his friend Lutfi al-Khuli, an Egyptian Marxist journalist. But he told al-Samman that he wanted
to see both Egypt and Israel for himself, so through the offices of
the Egyptian embassy al-Samman arranged to have Sartre hosted
by the newspaper *Al-Ahram*. The announcement of Sartre's visit
led to more than a year of negotiations. He would be arriving
with Simone de Beauvoir, a feminist to whom he was not married,
and—a much more delicate matter—with her lover Lanzmann,
whose pro-Israel sympathies were no secret to Arab intellectuals.
(In the Arabic translation of Beauvoir's 1963 memoir, *La Force
des choses*, the passages about her relationship with Lanzmann
were deleted.) There was no question of leaving him in Paris. "I
cannot move without Lanzmann," Sartre told al-Samman, who
prevailed on the Egyptians to invite him along, explaining that a
distinction had to be made between Jews and Israelis.

In an interview in *Al-Ahram* in December 1965, shortly after
the announcement of his impending visit, Sartre said that he had
supported Egypt since the 1956 Suez War but insisted on his
neutrality in the Arab-Israeli conflict. While he had backed the
Zionist struggle against the British, he said that he didn't consider

Israel to be the only place where Jews could live an authentic life, and emphasized his commitment to Algerian independence. A friend of the Jews and the Arabs, he felt "torn between contradictory friendships and loyalties," and experienced the Arab-Israeli conflict as if it were a "personal tragedy."

As Di-Capua puts it, Sartre was leaving himself "ample space for ambiguity." This ambiguity would come to infuriate his Arab friends, but in the months before his arrival in Cairo they heard only what they wanted to hear. The day after the interview, Lutfi al-Khuli, who was no longer in prison and had since made his peace with Nasser, published an article titled "Beginning a Dialogue with Sartre," in which he predicted that Sartre would see that Arab opposition to Israel "had absolutely no relation to the Jewish question." The Israelis were warier, but unlike the Arabs they had allies who could scarcely have been closer to Sartre: Beauvoir and Lanzmann, who were soon engaged in their own private talks with Sartre's sponsors. In March 1966, Beauvoir visited Simha Flapan, a Polish-born Jew who—as the representative in Paris of the Marxist-Zionist party Mapam and editor of the peacenik journal *New Outlook*—was organizing the Israeli leg of the trip, to reassure him that during his visit to Egypt Sartre would not respond to any question that would compel him to criticize Israel. Flapan sent a report back to his boss: "Simone was charming," he said. The Israeli embassy in Paris was less sanguine but conceded to Sartre's appearance in Israel after being assured that he would be met not only by Mapam but by members of a bipartisan public committee.

Sartre, Beauvoir and Lanzmann arrived in Cairo on February 25, 1967. Sartre was welcomed by an editorial in *Al-Ahram*, and treated as a foreign dignitary. "The enthusiasm that the Cairo population seems to feel for Sartre," according to one newspaper, "is very similar to what the Paris population has shown at the Tutankhamun exhibition." He spent three hours with Nasser, urging him to release a group of communist prisoners; they were freed a few days later. He met writers, students and artists, and attended a local production of *No Exit*. He couldn't restrain himself from occasionally correcting what he saw as misinterpretations of his philosophy. In a lecture at Cairo University he asked: "Have you all read my work? I do not think so. I am nothing but a fashion to you." Committed literature, he said, was not a matter of writing "politically oriented texts"—as many Egyptian intellectuals had understood it—but of exploring the "totality" of the writer's "existence in the world . . . When I called for committed literature I did not mean propaganda." One night he drank so much that al-Samman and Lanzmann had to carry him back to his hotel. They were "queers," he shouted, and as such "the prime examples of how to resolve the conflict." Al-Samman was shocked, but not Lanzmann.

"I have come to learn, not to teach," Sartre told his Egyptian interlocutors. In Kamshish, a village in the Egyptian delta, Sartre and Lutfi al-Khuli took part in a Q&A before an audience of peasants. One by one, the audience members asked startlingly erudite questions about existential philosophy and the nature of commitment: it turned out that these peasant philosophers had been coached. Still, Sartre was stirred by the stories they shared of their battles with landlords, and impressed by Nasser's land reforms. On his visit to the Gaza Strip, he asked Palestinian refugees in the camps whether they were waiting to be freed by Arab armies or if they intended to fight Israel themselves. The latter, they replied. Moved by their suffering, Sartre declared his support for "the national right of all Palestinian refugees to return to their country," an apparent endorsement of the right of return; but he also asked why the Arab states had done so little to help the refugees in the meantime. Things started getting tense. When a group of journalists photographed Sartre with a child who was carrying a Palestinian flag, Lanzmann asked them to destroy the film. Any such picture, he said, would jeopardize Sartre's commitment to neutrality. At this point, the refugees physically attacked their guests. As al-Samman put it, "Some of the Palestinian leaders in the camps . . . were not politically suitable for this kind of a meeting."

Events like this hardened Beauvoir's already frosty view of the Arabs, which had been shaped by her conversations with Lanzmann. Although she had been struck by Nasser's "melancholy

charm" and encouraged by his campaign against female circumcision, she was repelled by the "life of repetition" to which
Egyptian women seemed condemned and didn't try to ingrati-
ate herself. As she wrote in her account of the trip, "I accused
Egyptian men of behaving like feudalists, colonialists and racists
toward women." She feuded, too, with her friend Liliane al-Khuli,
Lutfi's wife, who told her "the Jews should have stayed in their
'own countries' after the war." Liliane, she wrote, "knew nothing
whatsoever about the Jewish question as it existed in the West."

Beauvoir wasn't wrong about Liliane al-Khuli: returning to
their "own countries" was not an option for Jewish survivors. But
the real question was whether the European Jewish catastrophe
should determine one's stance toward the catastrophe suffered
by the Palestinians, who bore no responsibility for the genocide and had lost their homeland because of it. Everywhere
he went in Egypt, Sartre found himself confronted by people
whose perspective on Israel had been shaped by the history of
Western colonialism, not the Holocaust. Many were disappointed
admirers. "How," one asked him, "do you, the protector of
freedom, disagree with Israel on its position toward Vietnam,
Cuba, Algeria and Africa yet, at the same time, agree that the
abusive Israeli entity is legitimate?"

How moved was Sartre by these arguments? Moved enough
that Lanzmann began to worry, especially when he noticed that
Sartre had been reading *Fin du peuple juif?*, by the anti-Zionist
Jewish writer Georges Philippe Friedmann. There were other
signs of a shift in Sartre's sympathies. As he left Egypt on March
13, he gave an interview to the Lebanese daily *Al-Nahar*, in
which he promised that "one day I will tell you what I think of
the Palestine problem." Even before his plane landed in Tel Aviv,
Israeli newspapers, enraged by his "flagrant tactlessness," were
declaring his visit a disaster: "Sartre declared his position on
the refugees without even hearing our views." Lanzmann was
preparing for the worst. "The fate of the Jewish people," he told
Simha Flapan, "is dependent on the success of this visit."

In Israel, Sartre seemed aloof, even when asked about his
writing. Israelis were no less excited by his work than the

Egyptians had been, but they too disappointed him. As Annie Cohen-Solal writes in her biography of Sartre, philosophers in Israel were still preoccupied by the "question of concrete relations with the Other" in *Being and Nothingness*, but as Sartre told one audience, "that search is over . . . It no longer interests me." Sartre talked to the Israeli prime minister, Levi Eshkol, for an hour and a quarter—less than half the time he spent with Nasser. He visited the former general Yigal Alon, Eshkol's labor minister, at his home in a kibbutz, and declared him "the most sympathetic fascist I ever met." He canceled a meeting with Yitzhak Rabin, then the army chief of staff, protesting that "I came to meet the people, the left and civil society, not the military. Besides, I had already spent an excellent evening with this fascist general!" He even stood up David Ben-Gurion, the founder of the state, while missing none of his appointments with Palestinian citizens of Israel. When Meir Ya'ari, the Mapam party leader, asked him about his remarks in Cairo on the right of return, Sartre said: "It is impossible to justify the Jewish right of return after two thousand years and to deny the same right to the Arabs after only twenty years . . . The refugee camps that I just saw in Gaza last week are realities that weigh very heavily on the future of Israel."

From Israel's perspective, Sartre's visit went so badly that his Mapam party sponsors were assailed for organizing an "unpatriotic" tour. At his final press conference, he offered muted praise of Israel, but, Di-Capua writes, "his gestures, body language and overall condescending attitude betrayed a profound aversion to Zionism." To his Israeli hosts, he appeared as "a committed Arab philosopher and as a dangerous antagonist." Lanzmann was devastated, feeling that Sartre's coolness toward Israel was a repudiation of his own Jewish identity.

Barely two months later, however, it was the Arabs' turn to be devastated. A report in *Le Monde* gave the impression that during his trip Sartre had endorsed Zionism—Sartre thought the article was "an obvious act of sabotage whose sole purpose is to create a crisis of trust" with the Arabs. The Egyptians didn't mind too much: Sartre had after all embraced their leader and their revolution. But the Palestinians were furious, and the Syrian daily *Al-Thawra* thundered: "Is it possible that every tragedy Europe inflicted on the Jews would become a justification for the occupation and deportation of another people?" In response to these attacks, Sartre expressed his conviction that "the state of Israel must remain open to any Jew who would like to live in it but it cannot request all the Jews to settle there. I therefore reject Ben-Gurion's approach of 'maximal Zionism.'" He also declared his support of the right of Palestinian refugees to "the entire land of Palestine." Lanzmann, disconcerted by the binationalist implications of Sartre's text, which juggled support for a Jewish homeland with support for the Palestinian right of return, showed it to Flapan. "Kudos to Lanzmann who is taking care of our interests," Flapan wrote to his boss. As Di-Capua notes, "no one in Sartre's circle was looking after Palestinian interests."

Ever since he began his conversations with Ali al-Samman, Sartre had been planning a special issue of *Les Temps modernes* on the Israeli-Arab conflict. Negotiations had been complex: Fayiz Sayigh, a member of the PLO executive committee, had flown over from Beirut to discuss it, and the Egyptian embassy in Paris had given its blessing on the condition that Arab contributions would appear separately, rather than in dialogue with those of the Israelis, to avoid any appearance of "normalization" with the enemy. Now that the issue was approaching publication, Lanzmann and Flapan persuaded Sartre that it would be a violation of the journal's neutrality—which they had no scruples violating themselves in their private communications—to publish a statement on Zionism. Instead, Flapan would write a letter on Sartre's behalf to *Le Monde* to make it clear that he had not expressed "any position" on Zionism, which he saw as "an internal business of the Jewish people." This clarification offered cold comfort to Palestinians, for whom Zionism had been anything but the internal business of the Jewish people.

It was just the beginning of Sartre's crisis with the Arabs. On May 27, he began writing his introduction to the special issue, again affirming his "neutrality—or if you will—absence." But his commitment to neutrality had already been severely tested by Nasser's show of force in the Sinai. "The Jews threaten war,"

Nasser declared from an air force base, "and we say welcome, we are ready!" The chorus of fear was led by Lanzmann. "If Israel were destroyed," he told *Le Monde*, "it would be far more serious than the Nazi Holocaust." He said he was ready to "shout long live Johnson because America is the only force that can save Israel." Johnson, in fact, was convinced that the Israelis would "whip the hell" out of the Arabs in a war, and urged them not to fire the first shot—a warning seconded by de Gaulle, Israel's main arms supplier at the time. But the French intellectual class rallied overwhelmingly in Israel's defense. Lanzmann organized a petition in support of Israel, and arrived, paper in hand, on Sartre's doorstep; Sartre grudgingly signed, and on May 30 the letter appeared in *Le Monde*. Jean Genet, who never forgave Sartre, reported that Lanzmann had threatened to throw himself out of a window if Sartre sided with the Arabs.

The special issue of *Les Temps modernes* was published on June 4, the day before Israel launched its offensive. Sartre was not the only left-wing luminary to have signed the petition—or to regret it—but he paid the steepest price because of his standing in the Arab world. In Algiers his books were burned—an auto-da-fé gleefully noted by the CIA. Josie Fanon, Frantz's widow, accused him of having chosen the "camp of murderers, the camp that kills in Vietnam, the Middle East, Africa and Latin America," and asked the publisher to remove Sartre's preface from *The Wretched of the Earth*. Suhayl Idris, his Lebanese translator, cabled the Iraqi government in support of its ban of Sartre's books.

Sartre protested that he had been misunderstood and tried in vain to persuade his friends Lutfi and Liliane al-Khuli over lunch in Paris that he remained a friend of the Arabs. "All I did was to take a principled stand against war," he said. "I did not change my support for the Arab and Palestinian struggle for freedom and progress." They were unpersuaded but agreed to meet again. At their second lunch, Sartre explained that he supported Israel's existence "not because it is a solution to the Jewish problem but because it is an existing human fact which includes men, women and children . . . and these children have no understanding of this problem. From this perspective the talk about the destruction of Israel generates nothing but pain. Once again I do not think that Israel is the solution to the Jewish problem."

Sartre's actual position on how the conflict might be resolved wasn't so different from the views of Maxime Rodinson, the historian of Islam, who considered Israel an expansionist colonial-settler state but also believed that its existence was an irreversible fact and that any lasting settlement would have to accommodate the national aspirations of both Israeli Jews and Palestinian Arabs. But Sartre continued to see Israel through the prism of the Holocaust and European responsibility, while Rodinson emphasized the injustices that Israel had visited on the Palestinians and firmly aligned himself with the Palestinian camp, notably refusing to sign Lanzmann's petition. For their comparative reputations in the Arab world, that distinction made all the difference.

In his few public statements on Israel-Palestine before his death in 1980, Sartre tried to balance his belief that Israel had a right to exist and his belief that the Palestinians had a right to take up arms against their occupiers. But he did his best to avoid the topic, and when he bothered to address it he seemed incoherent: justifying the Black September attack at the 1972 Munich Olympics as "terrible" but "necessary," then assailing UNESCO for withdrawing funds from Israel. It's possible that Sartre's feeling of being caught between his Arab and Jewish friends left him incapable of committing to either Israel or the Palestinians. He wasn't the only French writer to experience the conflict as a "personal tragedy": so too did Pierre Vidal-Naquet, a son of Holocaust victims who had helped lead the campaign against torture in Algeria, Jean Daniel of *Le Nouvel Observateur* and Eric Rouleau of *Le Monde*—to say nothing of Jewish radicals like Rodinson and the Trotskyists Marcel Liebman and Daniel Ben Saïd. But unlike Sartre, they all became critics, with varying degrees of vehemence, of Israel's occupation.

Neutrality in one of the last struggles of national liberation was a peculiar stance for the philosopher of commitment. Arabs construed Sartre's position as pro-Zionist, much as Camus's

silence on Algeria, which had enraged Sartre, had been interpreted as implicit support for the French army. Sartre's fall from
grace, Di-Capua argues, led to the sad demise of "Arab existentialism." I'm not sure Sartre had much to do with it. Much of the
writing Di-Capua excavates appears to have been an unstable,
superficial compound of nationalist mysticism and Heideggerian
jargon, and, as he himself concedes, the Arab version of "committed literature" was often closer to didactic writing on behalf
of the "masses" than the engagement with the world Sartre had
meant it to be. So, too, with Sartrean categories such as freedom,
alienation and authenticity, which had barely arrived in the
Levant before they were given a nationalist, Baathist or Marxist-
Leninist gloss. And the appeal of these concepts may have owed
less to their explanatory power than to the seductive fragrance
they emitted of Paris after Liberation. In a wry remembrance
of his literary peers in the early 1950s, Jabra Ibrahim Jabra, a
Palestinian writer exiled in Baghdad, writes that "few of them
could distinguish" Sartre from Camus, and

> fewer still realized that Albert Camus was not an existentialist
> in the sense that Sartre meant. Most of them liked to understand
> existentialism as a new bohemianism, philosophized this time in
> the cafés of Saint-Germain in Paris. For some it meant commit-
> ment as the left in those days understood it. There were some who
> saw in its logic something exactly the opposite, namely, a sort of
> nihilism that allowed the individual to go beyond all values and
> all political philosophies.

Intellectual fashions come and go, and Sartre was swept away
by the next wave of French thinkers—including Michel Foucault,
whose even greater sympathy toward Israel was never an obstacle
to his appeal among Arab thinkers. The hopes that Sartre raised
by visiting the Middle East had as much to do with philosophy
as Noam Chomsky's celebrity in the global South has to do with
linguistics.

If any system of thought suffered a blow in 1967, it wasn't
Sartrean existentialism: it was the secular Arab nationalism that

had led to what Nasser called the *Naksa*, the setback. In the days after the defeat, Arab leftists who had piggybacked on the Nasser project began to express their doubts, though still mostly in whispers. But even these were heard by the regime. Shortly after their lunch in Paris with Sartre, Lutfi and Liliane al-Khuli were arrested in Cairo: the secret police had been bugging their conversations. Liliane was soon released, but Lutfi was freed only after Nasser's death in 1970. Death spared Nasser from having to take the blame for the "setback." But the promise of his ideology began to fade as Sadat, his handpicked successor, steered Egypt into an alliance with the United States and Israel. In the early years of the Sadat era, the radical left seemed on the march on Egyptian campuses. But they were no match for the growing Islamist movement, which had stronger links both to the poor and to the regime. Leftist intellectuals who had made a tactical alliance with Nasser found themselves orphaned in a post-Nasser era. Nasser had been their persecutor, but he was also their father, their sole connection to "the masses," and without him they were lost.

The story of the Egyptian intellectual left's conflicted attachment to Nasser, a bigger and more tragic story than their estrangement from Sartre, isn't told by Di-Capua, but the costs of this relationship are conveyed with unflinching candor in Arwa Salih's essay from 1996, *The Stillborn*, which has just been published in English.* Salih, a leader of the Marxist-Leninist Workers' Party in the early 1970s, reflects on the wreckage of the radical left in 1970s Egypt, the young men and women who had received their education thanks to Nasser, and who had been intoxicated by the Palestinian revolution and the promise it heralded of radical transformation in the Arab world. Her tone is fearless, often furious, as if she were fed up with allowing others—especially insecure and arrogant male comrades who had nervously crowned themselves with "the status of 'leader'"—to tell her what to think. "I no longer believe that the Israeli state is

---

* *The Stillborn: Notebooks of a Woman from the Student-Movement Generation in Egypt* was published by Seagull Books in 2018.

more vicious or more oppressive than its neighbors (and may my comrades forgive me if they can)," she writes. "It is simply the stronger state. Moreover, I confess, with grief, to now believing that a future Palestinian state—if it ever comes into being—will almost certainly also be built on inequality and exploitation."

For Salih, the chief problem that bedeviled Egypt's left was its sanctification of state authority, a weakness she traces to its alienation from the masses. "Incapable of resisting a regime that claimed to be leading the battle against imperialism," intellectuals embraced Nasser's revolution, only to discover that "the intellectual's role was scripted by the Nasser regime: a reasonable prison sentence, discharge, then a job in one of the regime's bustling bureaucracies." After Nasser's death, "there was nothing to clutch at in the darkness but nostalgia . . . The new map moved the masses of the Egyptian people back into the fold of religion while our generation continued to cling to its old faith." That old faith had been exposed, she writes, as little more than a "militant kitsch" that "had no consistent, principled application in the world." For all their praise of the masses, Egyptians were "incapable of thinking about the history of socialism or its future without anchoring it in state power." Nasser "turned himself into an idol raised high above the corpse of the masses who had worshipped him . . . *we* were shamed and disgraced while his image continued to shine in glory."

These sorrowful and defiant words have resonance in an era of counterrevolution and dictatorship in the Arab world. A few months after *The Stillborn* was published, Salih killed herself. She could find no exit from her anguish, but in her writing she helped pave the way for an indigenous and radical Arab existentialism, and for future generations of Arab rebels, who are her children more than they are Nasser's or Sartre's. For all the despair she expresses, her book flickers with the profane illumination that, in the struggle to overcome the weight of the past, father figures usually stand in the way of emancipation.

{2018}

16

Writers or Missionaries?

Time is education, even when they tell you it's sophistication.

—Sly Stone

You have never been to the Middle East and have no personal connection to it. Although Jewish, you have no family in Israel.* Your parents are not Zionists but left-liberals of the civil rights generation; neither has gone to Israel. What sparks your interest in the Middle East is the First Intifada, which breaks out when you are a teenager. You are aghast at the scenes of Israeli soldiers firing rubber bullets at demonstrators and bulldozing homes. Instinctively sympathetic to the uprising by the "children of the stones," you set out to educate yourself about the occupation. You read Noam Chomsky, I. F. Stone and Edward Said, and later Israeli revisionist historians like Simha Flapan, Ilan Pappé and Benny Morris (who has yet to reinvent himself as an apologist for the ethnic cleansing he did so much to expose). In college, you meet left-wing Jews like yourself, as well as progressive Arabs with whom you find you have more in common than you do with the students in Hillel. You go to demonstrations against the first Gulf war and the Israeli occupation, and you rail against America's double standards to anyone who will listen. The tirades come naturally to you. You overflow with righteous indignation; you are exasperating in your certainty.

I was that kid. I didn't know very much about the Middle East, but I had the right attitudes, or so I thought. I also had a sense of mission and the energizing clarity that comes with it.

* This essay originated as a lecture, delivered at Brown University and Harvard University.

If you were a young leftist, it was easy to have a sense of mission during the run-up to the 2003 invasion of Iraq, a time of insidious propaganda and deceit about "weapons of mass destruction" and the threat that Saddam Hussein allegedly posed to "the home-land." The American press was full of Middle East "experts" explaining "why they hate us." These experts invariably started with the writings of Sayyid Qutb, a leader of Egypt's Muslim Brotherhood, who was hanged in 1966 for plotting to overthrow the Nasser regime. The roots of violent anti-Americanism could be traced to the basement of a church in Colorado in the late 1940s, where Qutb had been horrified by the sight of boys and girls dancing together. We were attacked a half-century later not because of what we had done in the Middle East, but because of who we were back home: free, open and tolerant. The *New Yorker*, which had distinguished itself for its opposition to the Vietnam War, was publishing Bernard Lewis on the "rage of Islam" and Jeffrey Goldberg's dispatches from Cairo and Beirut, where everyone he met seemed to be an anti-Semite or a terrorist, or both. Reading the coverage in the *New York Times*, you might have concluded that the Palestinian leadership was entirely to blame for the failure of the Camp David negotiations and for the eruption of the Second Intifada.

One of my first articles about the Arab world was a review of a biography of Frantz Fanon for the *New York Times Book Review*. Shortly after I filed the piece, my editor called me to say that it was fine, except for one thing: I had referred to "Pales-tine," a country that, according to the news desk, did not exist. We changed "Palestine" to "the Middle East." It was just as well. Like most Americans, I saw the Middle East through the prism of the Israel-Palestine conflict, an error that I would discover only much later.

I felt strangely empowered by this brush with censorship. It was proof that I was expressing things, naming things, that were forbidden by the paper of record; that I was speaking truth to power. My task, I believed, was to unmask the rhetoric used to justify America's war in Iraq, Israel's repression in the Occupied Territories and other imperial misdeeds. And there was plenty of such rhetoric to keep me busy, about "humanitarian warfare," "terrorism" and our unbreakable alliance with "the Middle East's only democracy."

I still stand by most of the positions that I took when I was starting out. But when I reread the articles I published then, I find the tone jarring, the confidence unearned, the lack of humility suspect. I have the same reaction when I read a self-consciously committed journalist like Robert Fisk, who seems never to doubt his own thunderous convictions. I recently reread *Pity the Nation*, his tome about the Lebanese civil war, and I was struck by how little Fisk tells us about the Lebanese, a people he has lived among since the mid-1970s.* For all his emoting about the Lebanese, *their* voices are never allowed to interrupt his sermonizing. That I agree with parts of the sermon doesn't mean I have the patience to sit through it. Fisk's book, which once so impressed me, now strikes me as a wasted opportunity, unless journalism is understood as a narrowly prosecutorial endeavor, beginning and ending with the description of crimes and the naming (and shaming) of perpetrators. And yet Fisk's example is instructive, in a cautionary way. It reminds us that immersion in the region isn't enough: it's how you process the experience, the traces that it leaves on the page. The Fiskian *cri de coeur* substitutes rage for understanding, hand-wringing for analysis.

Just to be clear: I'm not saying that one shouldn't take positions or make political arguments in writing about the Middle East. It would be very hard not to. And part of what drives me is anger over injustice, and the hope that I might persuade readers to think more critically about American policy in the region. But developing friendships with Middle Eastern writers and traveling to the region very much changed the way that I understand my work. Two Arab writers have been particularly important in shaping my understanding. One is the former FLN leader turned historian Mohammed Harbi, whose books on the Algerian independence movement are a model of critical history, and who has patiently guided me through the maze of contemporary Algerian

---

* Fisk died in 2020, six years after the publication of this essay.

politics whenever I have seen him in Paris. The other is Raja Shehadeh, the founder of the Palestinian human rights organization Al Haq, a lawyer and writer in Ramallah who has taught me what Zionism has meant—legally, politically and psychologically —for the Palestinians. Anguished and somewhat fragile, he is a man who, in spite of his understandable bitterness, has continued to dream of a future beyond the occupation, a kind of neo-Ottoman federation where Arabs and Jews would live as equals.

When I finally began to spend time in the place about which I had pontificated for so long, I discovered that I was much more interested in what the people I met had to say than in my own views. It dawned on me that I could only be a good writer on the Middle East to the extent that I was a good listener. I realized how insufficient it was to have the right attitudes; they would provide me with little more than an I. The brash young man I was could write with a sense of mission in large part because he had never spent any time in the region; he was intoxicated by the sound of his own voice, the power that he felt it gave him.

Shortly after September 11, I interviewed V. S. Naipaul about his views on Islam for the *New York Times Magazine*. Much of what he said was predictably ugly, a provocation calculated to offend liberal sensibilities. "Non-fundamentalist Islam," he told me, is "a contradiction." September 11 had no cause other than "religious hate." But Naipaul said something else that I will never forget: that ultimately, you have to make a choice—are you a writer, or are you a missionary? At the time, this remark struck me as glib, even dishonest. If anyone was a missionary, wasn't it Naipaul, with his crude attacks on Muslims, his extreme Hindu nationalism and his snobbery, all of it dressed up as devotion to the noble calling of writing and art?

Still, the remark stayed with me. I couldn't dismiss it; I have since seen its wisdom, although I am no fonder of Naipaul's views now than I was then. Naipaul was evoking the tension between the writer, who describes things as he or she sees them, and the missionary or the advocate, who describes things as he or she wishes they might be under the influence of a party, movement or cause. The contrast is not as stark as Naipaul suggests, but it exists, and the more closely you analyze a society, the more you allow yourself to see and to hear, the more you experience this tension.

In *Finding the Center*, Naipaul writes that travel "became a necessary stimulus for me. It broadened my worldview; it showed me a changing world and took me out of my own colonial shell . . . My uncertainty about my role withered; a role was not necessary. I recognized my own instincts as a traveler and was content to be myself, to be what I had always been, a looker. And I learned to look in my own way." He continues:

> To arrive in a place without knowing anyone there, and sometimes without an introduction; to learn how to move among strangers for the short time one could afford to be among them; to hold oneself in constant readiness for adventure or revelation; to allow oneself to be carried along, up to a point, by accidents; and consciously to follow up other impulses—that could be as creative and imaginative a procedure as the writing that came after. Travel of this sort became an intense experience for me. It used all the sides of my personality; I was always wound up . . . There was always the possibility of failure—of not finding anything, not getting started on the chain of accidents and encounters. This gave a gambler's excitement to every arrival. My luck held; perhaps I made it hold.

In this passage, Naipaul captures some of the most crucial aspects of reporting: an alert or receptive passivity; a willingness to expose oneself to unfamiliar and even unsettling experiences and people, to give up control and to get lost. This is not as easy as it sounds. That "readiness for adventure or revelation" has to be cultivated. As Walter Benjamin writes in his memoir *Berlin Childhood Around 1900*, "not to find one's way around a city does not mean much. But to lose one's way in a city, as one loses one's way in a forest, requires some schooling."

Losing one's way is exhilarating, but it can also be destabilizing, even frightening. You may end up asking yourself the question

Bruce Chatwin made famous: *What am I doing here?* I remember asking myself this early one morning last summer in Jenin, when I was awakened by the call of the *muezzin*, my head throbbing from jet lag. I had spent the previous day interviewing a group of activists working at the Jenin Freedom Theater, each more earnest than the last. I wondered if I would ever get closer to the truth of what had happened to Juliano Mer-Khamis, the head of the theater, who had been murdered there two years earlier. I thought of declaring defeat and leaving until a close friend of mine, a French-Moroccan woman living in Jerusalem, told me to get over myself and to press on. And I did. I needed to trust the gambler's luck that Naipaul invoked; I needed to let go. This was not a matter of finding the story, but of allowing the story to find me.

This is the experience I've had almost every time I've reported, but the most memorable of these experiences took place in Algeria in late 2002, on one of my first long reporting trips. It happened almost by accident. I had been writing about the memory of the Algerian war of independence in contemporary France, where the controversy about torture by the French army had been reignited by an interview in *Le Monde* with a former FLN militant, Louisette Ighilahriz, who described her ghastly experiences in a French prison cell and her rescue by a man she knew only as "Dr. Richaud," whom she was desperate to thank after all these years. After Ighilahriz's interview, an even more explosive interview appeared in *Le Monde* with a one-eyed octogenarian general named Paul Aussaresses, who emerged from retirement to give an unapologetic account of carrying out a series of murders, disguised as suicides, of leading nationalists during the Battle of Algiers. Algeria was not my only interest in telling this story. Writing about the French-Algerian war, a story of settler colonialism, guerrilla warfare, torture and repression, was my indirect way of commenting on Israel's response to the Second Intifada. Like the French during the Battle of Algiers, the Israeli government claimed that it was merely fighting "terrorism" in the Occupied Territories, rather than a nationalist insurgency with popular backing. The French, I noted, won the Battle of Algiers, but this turned out to be a Pyrrhic victory.

After my article on the Aussaresses affair was published, I met a group of Algerians visiting New York City, headed by one of the FLN's historic "chiefs," Hocine Aït-Ahmed, the longstanding leader of a Kabyle Berber opposition party. One of the Algerians at that discussion was an intense young woman named Daikha Dridi, a reporter for the *Quotidien d'Oran*. Daikha told me about the war between the security services and Islamic rebels that had claimed more than 100,000 lives; about the machinations of the so-called *pouvoir*, the dominant military-industrial clique that ruled Algeria; about the country's still-traumatic relationship with France, its former colonial master. She urged me to visit: How, having written on France's repression of the Algerian independence movement, could I not care about the fate of the independent Algeria? She was right. Not long after that meeting, I booked a flight to Algiers.

When I arrived there, a city I knew mostly from Gillo Pontecorvo's film, the civil war had been over for about a year, but no one quite believed it: no one had been punished for their crimes, and attacks at fake checkpoints were still common. My editor probably expected me to write about Algeria's history and possible future in a tone—or at least an impression, an impersonation—of authority. Authority, however, was not what I felt, walking through Algiers and in the dilapidated Kabyle town of Tizi Ouzou, where alienated young Berbers were in revolt against the central government. What I felt was the utter strangeness and futility of trying to explain Algeria, a notoriously opaque country. I was often followed, particularly when I went to Internet cafés, by the secret police. One agent, a fresh-faced man with reddish hair, saw that I was typing a message in English and asked if I was from Texas, "like President Bush."

I stayed in a dingy hotel; the only other guests were a group of German tourists on their way to an expedition in the Sahara. I was incredibly free and incredibly alone. I'd return to my room each night too tired to even read my notes; there was so little hot water I didn't have the relief of a decent bath. So I turned on the TV. Every night the same movie was playing on the state channel, Marcel Carné's adaptation of the Georges Simenon novel *Trois chambres à Manhattan,* the story of a love affair between two French expats in New York, a depressed actor and a woman fleeing her marriage. When they're not in bed—or driving each other to tears—they're at a club where the house pianist is Mal Waldron, who performs with his usual sorrowful elegance. He looks as if he's always at the club—as if the club exists so that he might play there. I would drift off to sleep as Waldron played his trance-inducing, darker-than-blue blues, a cigarette dangling from his lips.

My fixer in Algiers, Farès, was a hard-drinking man in his mid-fifties whose candy factory had been burned down by Islamist insurgents. He seemed pleased to have someone like me to drive around, a Westerner who paid him well, listened to his stories and spoke passable French. He wasn't much interested in talking about the present—it was shit, he said, though I sensed he supported the *éradicateurs,* the hardliners who promised to wipe out the Islamist rebels and restore security. I could understand that, even if I didn't share his sympathies for the army: if the Islamists hadn't destroyed his livelihood, he wouldn't have been driving a taxi.

Farès became my guide to Algiers. Whenever we ran into people he knew, he introduced me as a friend from Tizi Ouzou, a Kabyle city. He said I could pass for a Berber; so long as I only murmured a few words in French, no one would ask any questions. He wasn't worried about walking around with an American, but he enjoyed fooling people. We wandered through the Casbah and the slums of Bab El-Oued, where the FIS leader Ali Belhaj had preached jihad against the "impious" regime at the al-Sunna mosque; we went to nightclubs and bars pulsing with strobe lights and frequented by wealthy Algerians and Arab businessmen; we drove through the neighborhoods in the hills where the leaders of the FLN settled after independence. We ate piles of golden fried sardines at long, wooden communal tables, where men (only men) watched football on television, and told the latest jokes about "Boutef"—President Abdelaziz Bouteflika —and Khalida Messaoudi, the fetching minister of culture he was said to be sleeping with.

One day, Farès told me about a novel he was writing, about his childhood during the Battle of Algiers. It revolved around the stories of three friends—a Kabyle Berber, a Jew and a *pied-noir*— growing up in the Casbah. Algeria, Farès said, had lost something in 1962; the country's radical decolonization had sapped it of the diversity that had been a great source of vitality. The Algeria he knew and loved had disappeared, and he wanted to recreate it in his novel. Farès blamed the French for causing the exodus of *pieds-noirs* to the *métropole*; Algerians and the "historic FLN," he insisted, never wanted them to go.

France's ultimate responsibility for everything that had gone wrong in Algeria, I found, was about the only thing Algerians agreed on. I interviewed dozens of people, from high-ranking officials to Islamist sympathizers; from mothers of the disap- peared to hard-line generals; from Berber activists to human rights campaigners. Each claimed to be a critic of *le pouvoir*, including those who were plainly its beneficiaries. Each expressed disappointment in the post-independence era. Each claimed unimpeachable nationalist credentials and believed that his or her views were faithful to the "historic FLN," the leadership that had lost out to those who had "confiscated" the revolu- tion. What no one seemed to agree on was what the Algerian nation actually was. One man, a former member of the *maquis* who fought in the Aurès Mountains during the independence struggle, insisted that Algeria was not an Arab country like Egypt; it had more in common with Mediterranean countries like Italy, Spain and Greece. A Kabyle activist told me, no less passionately, that Algeria was a Berber country, and that its true character had been perverted by state-led Arabization. Others told me that Algeria was profoundly Arab and Muslim in its identity, and that anyone who told me otherwise was self-hating, a victim of a colonial complex. Algerians had been having this argument for years. The feud had started before the war of independence, when "assimilated" Muslims, populists, Islamists and communists quarreled over Algeria's identity, and it continued after independence was achieved. To be an Algerian was, in a sense, to participate in this debate, to have a stake in it. The fact that it remained so alive and so fraught after four decades of "liberation" led me to a realization that applies with equal force to the Middle East: *nothing that is solid melts into air.*

Algeria had been the prism through which I understood the Israel-Palestine tragedy and, to some extent, the rise of an insurgency in Iraq. Now Algeria helped me to develop a more nuanced understanding of power and identity in the region. The Algerian story was, in part, the story of a military government that refused to hand over power to civilians; but to tell that story was barely to scratch the surface. The obsession with France and with French plots, real and imagined, also suggested to me that the French-Algerian story had never really ended with the rupture that decolonization had brought about in 1962: independence was but a new and more subtle chapter in a history of unequal relations between the two countries, the two peoples. Every morning outside the French consulate in Algiers, there was a line of Algerians requesting visas, hoping to get into the country they at once hated and needed. There was no "solution" to France's influence over Algeria; it was too late for solutions.

Algeria made a mockery of my nostalgia for the heroic certainties of anticolonialism and cured me of my lingering Third World–ism. The problems of post-independence Algeria could not be divorced from the history of colonization, but the failures were also homegrown, and they could not all be laid at the foot of France, the native bourgeoisie or even *le pouvoir*. And what was *le pouvoir* anyway? As one friend of mine put it, "*Le pouvoir, c'est nous.*" Algerians deserved better than a regime that had kept itself in power by distributing rents from natural gas. They had suffered terribly, and the world had largely ignored them in the darkest hours of the civil war. I wanted to give an account of their suffering, but I had to do so with a measure of humility, without pretending that I knew more than I did—or, more to the point, more than they did. Algerians were at once impressively informed about their country and stunned by what had happened to it during the civil war. Reporting on Algeria, I was forced to own up to my own uncertainty and to make it a part of my writing.

This is easier said than done: readers want to be informed, not given a lecture on the limits of knowledge. I don't claim to have a method, but admitting to the murkiness is a start.

I wish I could say that I always adhered to the uncertainty principle and listened to my own advice, but I didn't. Algeria changed me, but it took a while for these changes to inform my writing. And the closer I got to the Israel-Palestine conflict, the more of a missionary—a Fiskian—I became. This is, as it were, an occupational hazard, the "Jerusalem syndrome" of journalists, whatever their ideological bent.

I was reminded of this a few years ago, when a mysterious man living in Damascus was killed in a car bombing. Imad Mughniyeh was one of the founders of Hezbollah and the architect of some of its most spectacular "operations," from the 1983 bombings in Beirut to the attacks in Argentina in the early 1990s. Sometime in the 1990s, Mughniyeh went underground, and he was never mentioned by Hezbollah again until he met his fate in February 2008.

In 2004, several years before his assassination, I spent a few weeks in Lebanon reporting on Hezbollah's "Lebanonization" under the leadership of Sayyid Hassan Nasrallah. While Israel and its spokesmen in the press continued to denounce Hezbollah as a "terrorist" outfit, Hezbollah appeared to have evolved into a more pragmatic political organization, moderating its rhetoric and entering Lebanese politics—including the confessional system that it had excoriated in its founding manifesto. It no longer seemed fair, or accurate, to describe Hezbollah merely as a proxy of the Islamic Republic of Iran or as an unreconstructed global "terrorist" organization, as Jeffrey Goldberg had argued in an alarmist series for the *New Yorker*. Goldberg's articles on Hezbollah read as if they had been written by committee at the Washington Institute for Near East Policy; he even predicted that Hezbollah, a Shia organization, might attack the United States in solidarity with Saddam Hussein, the great persecutor of the Shia, a modern-day Yazid.

The fact that Hezbollah is a social movement and not just a militia or a pro-Iranian proxy is widely accepted today, but at the time it was a highly controversial thesis. My article came close to being killed. A platoon of fact-checkers spent nearly half a year investigating my claims. The excerpts from my interview with Nasrallah, with whom I had met for more than an hour at the party's headquarters in the southern suburbs, were severely cut for reasons that were never explained. I had asked Nasrallah why the movement hadn't laid down its arms after Israel's withdrawal from southern Lebanon in 2000. Wasn't Hezbollah handing Israel a pretext to attack again? Israel, he replied, has never needed a pretext to attack Lebanon. He pointed out that when Israel invaded Lebanon in order to destroy Arafat's PLO, it claimed to be responding to the shooting of Shlomo Argov, the Israeli ambassador in London, even though the shooting was carried out by the renegade Abu Nidal, an enemy of Arafat. Nasrallah's argument was self-serving, to be sure, but he was right about the Argov pretext, and I succeeded in getting this passage restored.

Still, in my zeal to present a corrective to Goldberg's take on Hezbollah, I made errors of my own. When I asked Nasrallah about Mughniyeh, who Goldberg claimed was still deeply involved in Hezbollah, he played with his prayer beads and told me that Mughniyeh was no longer in the organization and that his whereabouts were unknown. I was not fooled, but I didn't push him further; I did not want to be shown the door, and I was willing to entertain the possibility that Mughniyeh had offered his services to the Iranian Revolutionary Guard. Was I flattered by Nasrallah's generosity and politeness? Was the Mughniyeh relationship simply inconvenient for the case I was building about Hezbollah's evolution? Whatever the case, I remembered these conversations when Mughniyeh was assassinated in Damascus. After Hezbollah staged an enormous funeral procession for him, the world learned not only that he had never strayed from Hezbollah, but that he had directed the 2006 war. His image was revealed for the first time in years and is now a fixture of Hezbollah iconography. I don't blame Nasrallah for lying to me when he denied knowledge of Mughniyeh's activities: he was merely doing his job. But I wasn't doing mine.

Mughniyeh was, for Hezbollah, a heroic figure in what they call "the resistance." No word is more sacred for Hezbollah, which has sought to portray itself as a "national resistance" rather than another sectarian militia. When I started out in journalism, I was more willing to use this word without quotation marks; it seemed preferable, after all, to the alternative, "terrorism." Today, I am more skeptical of terms like "resistance," "armed struggle" and "solidarity." When I read these words, I want to ask: What do they actually mean, and what do they conceal? What do the people who use these words actually do? What does the word "resistance" mean if it can describe a Sunni-based insurgency against Bashar al-Assad and the Shiite-based insurgency in Lebanon that is fighting to crush that uprising? What ambitions, what goals, lie behind floating signifiers like "resistance"? What do those who hold up its banner hope to achieve? Mouloud Feraoun, an Algerian novelist who kept an extraordinary diary of the Algerian war before he was murdered by the OAS in 1962, put it well when he stated: "Sometimes you start asking yourself about the value of words, words that no longer make any sense. What is liberty, or dignity, or independence? Where is the truth, where is the lie, where is the solution?"

A writer's job, I believe, is to ask these questions, even when—especially when—they are inconvenient. And the answers lie in the *verbs*, not the *nouns*. They lie in the distance, sometimes the chasm, between words and deeds.

The aura of the "resistance," of course, is not universal. I remember sitting in a café in Beirut with the writer Samir Kassir. He had devoted himself to Palestine but had grown increasingly alarmed by Syria's meddling in Lebanon, and by Hezbollah's efforts, through its television station Al-Manar, to Islamize the Palestinian struggle. Israel's occupation, he said, was not the first, or even the second, target of "the resistance." This was, above all, a power play inside Lebanon. I remarked that the disaster of America's war in Iraq had only heightened the prestige of Hezbollah's resistance model. To my surprise, he replied, "I'm less worried about the fact that America is here than that it doesn't know what it's doing."

Kassir was no fan of the American war, but he was a hard-headed analyst, unwilling to take refuge in comforting ideological formulas. He was not persuaded that the presence of Syrian troops in Lebanon was an essential component in the struggle to liberate Palestine: Lebanon, he believed, deserved to breathe again, free of Syria's corrupting influence. He made this argument in writing, over and again, and paid the ultimate price. Two years after our conversation, he was killed in a car bomb attack, most likely by pro-Syrian agents. Though I did not share all of Kassir's analysis, I had great respect for his integrity, and I paid him tribute in the *Nation*. In the eyes of the blogger Asad Abu-Khalil, who calls himself the "Angry Arab," I had revealed myself to be an Orientalist for praising Kassir, an opponent of "the resistance." This was a first: I was used to being attacked as a self-hating Jew!

Identity: you can't get around it when you write on the Middle East. I consider myself a New Yorker first, an American second; although I have a certain private connection to Jewish culture and humor, I don't go to temple, I don't believe in God, and I am not a Zionist. My "Judaism," such as it is, is not political. The trouble is that, in the Middle East, the idea of a nonpolitical or non-Zionist Judaism is virtually unintelligible. I have never written as a Jew, much less tried to prove to others that there are anti-occupation Jews like me, an effort that I find silly, if not offensive. So the question has always been: How candid should I be about something that matters to me, but not in a way that most people in the region would ever understand? Would I be opening up the possibility for serious misunderstandings? Isn't it better just to shut up rather than shut down the conversation? After all, I'm here to report the story, not to be the story.

The problem is that sometimes, without your wanting it, you *are* the story: the fact of your presence is news. So while I usually keep my Jewish identity to myself, if asked whether I'm Jewish, I don't lie. And sometimes, if I'm lucky, I can use it to my advantage. Not in the sense of opening doors, but in the sense of opening up the conversation in surprising ways. I think, for example, about the albino Palestinian woman I met in Jenin who, when she discovered I was Jewish, asked me, "Were you in the

Holocaust?" and began to chuckle. Fortunately not, I replied, laughing at the absurdity of her question. This led to one of the most fascinating conversations I had in Palestine, a conversation about the oppressions of occupation, gender and, in her case, colorlessness.

I also think of the conversation I had in Nablus with Ghada, a local PFLP leader who had spent much of her adulthood in Israeli prisons. I liked her immediately. She was as playful as she was fiery, with a disarming, throaty laugh. Before we began our interview, I asked her if she had any questions about me. I usually do this—if people want to have a better sense of who I am, I want to give them the opportunity to ask. Their questions can deepen the conversation and help me to formulate my own. She paused, took a drag of her cigarette and said: "If you are Israeli, or related to Israelis, or even if you are just a Jew, I cannot speak to you. Do you understand?" Abed, my fixer, sat there waiting, nervously, while I came up with a reply. I said: "Really, you wouldn't talk to Noam Chomsky? You wouldn't talk to a Jewish critic of the occupation?" She replied that a French-Jewish journalist who had interviewed her recently had written that she supported a two-state settlement when, in fact, she wanted to liberate Palestine from the river to the sea. A Jew had betrayed her; how could I be trusted?

I said, a bit desperately: "If you read my work, I believe that you will see that I am progressive, and honest. Now, you can decide not to speak with me because I'm Jewish. That's your right. I can't force you to talk to me. But I think you'd be making a mistake not to." She looked at Abed; he looked at her. "Because I love Abed, because I trust Abed, I will speak to you, with total frankness." And she did. She gave me great material.

When we left her office, Abed said, "You never told me you were Jewish!" I said I assumed he knew. He said, "What you don't understand is that for Ghada, your kind of Jew is not really a Jew."

What did I learn from this encounter, besides the fact that in the Nablus offices of the Popular Front, I don't quite count as a Jew? I learned that having a trusted fixer makes a huge difference. And I realized that, in some cases, you can create intimacy by showing your cards, by not being sheepish about your identity, by owning up to your discomfort. I could have lied to Ghada, but if I had lied to her, I would have shown her less respect, and showing respect, I believe, is the yeast of any successful interview.

When I started out, I didn't have the confidence about my identity that I displayed that day with Ghada. And I had not yet learned to listen; I still took words, ideological formulas, slogans at face value. Around the time that I met Ghada, I interviewed Hussam Khader, a Fatah leader in the Balata refugee camp. Hussam, like Ghada, had spent a number of years in Israeli prisons. He told me that he was sure that in time—maybe twenty years, maybe fifty, maybe a hundred—they, the Jews, would all go back to wherever they came from, and all of Palestine would be free. A few minutes later, he spoke of his hopes for coexistence and offered, as proof, the example of his own friendships with members of the Knesset. What did Khader actually believe? Does it matter? Aren't we all contradictory in our aspirations and beliefs—particularly if, as in Khader's case, an ocean lies between our desires and our power to fulfill them? Doesn't this paradox, this floating between the dream of recovering historical Palestine and the dreary and corrupt business of "peace processing" under occupation, tell you more about the Palestinian predicament than any speech, than any declaration of principles?

Words are all we have, but silences are sometimes more meaningful. In *Prisoner of Love*, Jean Genet writes:

> if the reality of time spent among—not with—the Palestinians existed anywhere, it would survive between all the words that claim to give an account of it. They claim to give an account of it, but in fact it buries itself, slots itself exactly into the spaces, recorded there rather than in the words that serve only to blot it out. Another way of putting it: the space between the words contains more reality than does the time it takes to read them.

How do we reach the space between the words, when our only way of doing so is through words? I'm not sure, but I would suggest it is largely a matter of listening, observing and describing —with a sense of history, and without false consolations. It also requires resistance, not only to the clichés and stereotypes that are often pilloried as "Orientalist," but also to the missionary temptation to mistake one's hopes for realities. When the uprising in Egypt broke out, I succumbed, like many, to the latter temptation, when I wrote that Islamists and secular opponents of Mubarak appeared to have laid aside their differences in the interest of national unity. I had written about these divisions only six months before the uprising, in an article called "Mubarak's Last Breath"; but during the early days of Tahrir Square, I allowed myself to forget just how deeply the fear and distrust run, and how easily these emotions can be manipulated by the army. I succumbed to this temptation again after Israel's most recent war in the Gaza Strip, when I argued that Israel's strategic position had been weakened by the emergence of a Muslim Brotherhood–led Egypt allied with Hamas and Erdoğan's Turkey. That article, which felt so good to write, could not seem more dated. Mohammed Morsi is in prison along with thousands of Muslim Brothers; Erdoğan, having revealed himself to be a thug rather than a visionary Islamic democrat, is embroiled in several scandals; Hamas is scrambling to repair ties with Iran; and Israel is deepening its colonization of East Jerusalem and the West Bank and, once again, launching an offensive in Gaza—only this time without much protest from Cairo.

Edward Said was fond of quoting Raymond Williams's argument about the struggle, in any society, between dominant, residual and emergent forces. But the Middle East severely tests the teleological assumptions, or wishes, of Williams's formulation. "Emergent" forces like the progressive youth movements in Egypt are not destined to win, however much we admire them and hope for their success. And what about jihadi organizations like the Islamic State of Iraq and Syria, a Sunni Islamist group so extreme that it was excommunicated by Ayman Zawahiri of Al Qaeda? Is ISIS, which captured several major Iraqi cities and declared a new caliphate, an "emergent" force or a "residual" one, or some combination of the two?

The Middle East is the graveyard of predictions. Just after the uprisings, the so-called experts declared that Al Qaeda had died in Tahrir Square. But these days Tahrir Square seems moribund, while Al Qaeda is resurgent and facing competition from still more radical offshoots. A military dictatorship even harsher than Mubarak's rule has returned to Egypt, and Assad appears to be winning in Syria, thanks not only to his horrifying tactics, but also to the fragmentation and brutality of the insurgents. Nine million Syrians have been internally displaced, and more than 2 million have gone into exile; more than 100,000 have been killed. Meanwhile, a highly sectarian government in Iraq has been fighting against an extremist insurgency. The Arab uprisings brought about an end to the political stagnation that had characterized the military dictatorships of the region during the Cold War, but except in Tunisia, they failed to deliver on their promise of establishing more democratic systems of governance. The result, for now, is a deepening sectarian struggle throughout the region and, in Syria, a vicious proxy war that has produced a Nakba on a scale that, in numbers of dead and displaced, dwarfs the Nakba of 1948. There is no obvious solution to this crisis, and it seems all but inevitable that Syria—and perhaps Iraq as well—will be dismembered under any transition.

Writing about the region, never an easy undertaking, is likely to become still more difficult. I am not sure whether the most influential current of oppositional thinking about the Middle East is equipped to deal with the changes the region is undergoing. I am referring to the critique of Orientalism that Edward Said initiated. This style of thinking was formative for me, but I fear that it has congealed into an orthodoxy; and, as George Orwell wrote, "orthodoxy, of whatever color, seems to demand a lifeless, imitative style." That we are now able to have a more open conversation about Palestine, that students are mobilizing against the occupation, is welcome; but Palestine is not the Middle East, and it seems peculiar, if not myopic, to talk about Palestine as if it were insulated from the rest of the region. And while it is understandable that young American students are particularly concerned about their government's policies in the region, these policies do not wholly determine its shape and direction. America's power in the Middle East has weakened, though not in favor of forces that most of us would consider progressive. Today, we are witnessing a tacit alliance of Israel, the military regime in Egypt and the Gulf states—particularly Saudi Arabia—against Iran, with which the United States, in conflict with its own regional allies, is seeking rapprochement. The latest Israeli offensive in Gaza is a measure of how marginal Palestine has become to the agenda of Arab states.

But to quote a poster I recently saw in the home of a solidarity activist, isn't Palestine still *the* question? That "still," you'll note, qualifies the confident "the": it suggests an anxious insistence, perhaps a fear, that Palestine might *not* be the only, or central, question in the contemporary Middle East—especially now that much of the region is preoccupied with other matters, like the wars in Iraq and Syria, Iran's overture to the West and the re-emergence of military rule in Egypt. It is, of course, only natural that Palestinians would consider the question of Palestine to be *the* question; they experience the daily humiliations of occupation and the sorrows of exile, the ongoing and, it seems, ever-deepening results of the 1948 catastrophe. It is only natural that Arabs and Muslims, for national and religious reasons, see Palestine as a sacred cause. For them, Palestine is not just a national struggle but a metaphor for suffering and redemption, exile and return, dispossession and justice. But that does not explain why Palestine is seen on the Western left as *the* question, the key that opens all doors in the region, not just those to the homes from which Palestinians were driven in 1948.

"Do you know why we are so famous?" Mahmoud Darwish asks the Israeli writer Helit Yeshurun in *Palestine as Metaphor*. "It's because you are our enemy. The interest in the Palestinian question flows from the interest in the Jewish question . . . It's you they're interested in, not me! . . . So we have the misfortune of having an enemy, Israel, with so many sympathizers in the world, and we have the good fortune that our enemy is Israel, since Jews are the center of the world. You have given us our defeat, our weakness, our renown." As Darwish suggests, this concern for the Palestinians is not a matter of anti-Semitism, as Israel supporters claim, so much as it is a reflection of self-absorption: the Palestinians are important to the West because, through their oppression by Israeli Jews, they have become characters in a Western narrative.

I thought of Darwish's remark when I saw a poster in the Balata refugee camp declaring, in English, "Our existence is resistance," as if opposition to oppression were a way of life. "A gift from our foreign guests," the Fatah leader Hussam Khader explained to me, unable to suppress a smile.

In an essay on French opposition to the war in Algeria, Pierre Vidal-Naquet observed that for a small but influential current of French dissidents, identification with the FLN's struggle was a kind of surrogate religion; for these so-called Third World–ists, "Algeria represented the suffering just man and thus a Christ-like figure . . . the symbol of a humanity to be redeemed, if not a redemptive humanity." The most devout Third World–ists, he noted, believed that Algeria's liberation might awaken the dormant French working class, spark a revolution in France and rescue the West from its spiritual decadence. Vidal-Naquet, a scholar of classical Greece who lost his parents in the Holocaust as well as an independent socialist who campaigned tirelessly against torture during the war, saw this faith for what it was: part of France's conversation with itself. The Algerian struggle, he understood, was a struggle for national self-determination, not for humanity as a whole, and Algerian nationalists were themselves profoundly divided, not some unified subject of history who could replace the proletariat. Today, it seems to me, Palestinians are for the radical Western left what Algerians were for Third World–ists in Vidal-Naquet's day: natural-born resisters, fighting not only Israel but its imperial patrons, as much on our behalf as theirs. That is the role assigned to them in the revolutionary imagination. Like the *keffiyeh* worn by antiglobalization protesters, this Palestine is little more than a metaphor. Palestine is still "*the* question" because it holds up a mirror to us. "Too many people want to save Palestine," one activist said to me. But it could just as well be said that too many people want to be saved *by* Palestine.

I understand this Palestine-centrism and have felt its gravitational pull. Israel's occupation, now nearly a half-century old, is the longest in modern history. It is subsidized by US tax dollars and maintained by a state that claims to speak not only in the name of the Jewish people but, more obscenely, in the name of those who perished in the Holocaust. I have witnessed the occupation's horrors firsthand: the subjugation of an entire people through a system of pervasive control and countless petty humiliations, always backed by the threat of violence; the confiscation not only of that people's land, but of its future. I have been shamed, as well as touched, by the hospitality for which Palestinians are rightly famous. While traveling in other Arab countries, I have seen the poisonous effect that the occupation has had on the perception of the United States, the well of resentment, suspicion and rage it has bred. Still, I am not sure that the Palestinians benefit when their struggle—an anticolonial, nationalist struggle like that of Algeria, no more, no less—becomes a matter of metaphysics rather than politics; when their suffering is romanticized, even sanctified. Palestinians need friends, not missionaries or fellow travelers.

When Gershom Scholem scolded Hannah Arendt for showing no love of the Jewish people in her book on Eichmann, Arendt replied that she could not love a people, only friends. Her point was overdrawn for dramatic effect; our political positions are almost always influenced by the bonds we form. I would be the first to admit that my own hatred of the occupation has been deepened by spending time in Palestine with friends like Raja Shehadeh, a man who embodies *sumud*—steadfastness in the face of a system of oppression as absurd as it is cruel. But, as Arendt warned, too strong a bond with one people can lead to a contraction of empathy for others: the case of Israel illustrates this all too well. Love of a people in particular can lead us to engage in moral calculations that betray the principles we claim to hold, even to

defend the indefensible. Now we are told, by some who call themselves friends of Palestine, that we shouldn't concern ourselves
too much with war crimes in Syria, unless they are committed by
jihadists in the opposition; that, all things considered, perhaps
Assad, the butcher of Yarmouk, deserves our "critical" support,
since he is a leader of the resistance front, in the cross hairs of
the West and the Gulf states. I have seen this argument made
privately by one well-known champion of Palestinian rights; this
person is a Quaker, but then so was Richard Nixon. According to
Amal Saad Ghorayeb, writing in the Lebanese paper *Al-Akhbar*,
support for Assad is a litmus test of support for Palestine. How
different, morally, is this from saying, as Benjamin Netanyahu
has done, that Israel is better off if its Arab neighbors remain
dictatorships? Can Palestinian emancipation be served by such
vulgar anti-imperialism?

As the regional balance of power has shifted and American
dominance wanes, I have begun to worry that an all-consuming
preoccupation with America and Israel leads progressive writers
to become strangely incurious about the crimes for which the
West can't be blamed and the developments, such as the politici-
zation of sectarian identity, that are shaking the region far more
profoundly than the Israeli-Palestinian arena. This paradigm also
leads them to belittle, or simply to overlook, what academics
call "agency": the fact that people *act* in this region, and are not
merely acted upon by more powerful external forces. And it has
increasingly been my sense that much of the work Said inspired
fails to examine the lived experience of people in the region; it
often relegates much of that experience to silence, as if it were
unworthy of attention or politically inconvenient.

Enormously liberating when it was developed, the critique of
Orientalism has often resulted in a set of taboos and restrictions
that inhibit critical thinking. They pre-emptively tell us to stop
noticing things that are right under our noses, particularly the
profound cleavages in Middle Eastern societies—struggles over
class and sect, the place of religion in politics, the relationship
between men and women; struggles that are only partly related
to their confrontation with the West and with Israel. Indeed,

it is sometimes only in those moments of confrontation that these very divided societies achieve a fleeting sense of unity. The theoretical intricacy of academic anti-Orientalism, its hermetic and sophisticated language, sometimes conceals an attempt to wish away the region's dizzying complexity in favor of the old, comforting logic of anticolonial struggle. Anti-Orientalism will continue to provide a set of critical tools and a moral compass, so long as it is understood as a point of departure, not a destination. Like all old maps, it has begun to yellow. It no longer quite describes the region, the upender of all expectations, the destroyer of all missionary dreams.

{2014}

Epilogue:
Kitchen Confidential

Twice a month, when my daughter, Ella, spends the weekend with me, my apartment turns into a cooking school. Ella is thirteen and started to make cookies and scones a few years ago. She moved on to tarts, fresh tagliatelle and, lately, croissants. Early on Saturdays, before heading to our local greenmarket, we have impassioned conversations about her dinner plans. Pork adobo with citrus and coriander, she asks me, or red lentils simmered Ethiopian-style, with fresh tomatoes and *berbere*? And then she's sure to ask if she can bake. I'm already thinking of the scabs of flour I'll be scraping off my counter on Monday morning, and of how much pâtisserie I'll have consumed, but I give in. I love watching the skill and authority of her fingers in a bowl of flour, eggs, butter and chocolate; her intensity as she pipes ganache from a pastry bag or dusts éclairs with finely ground pistachios.

When she's not cooking, she often watches shows like *Chef's Table*, the sumptuously produced Netflix series featuring somber, admiring portraits of culinary stars. With painterly cinematography and introspective voice-overs, *Chef's Table* pays professional cooks the kind of homage once reserved for artists. Most of the dishes are impossible to replicate in a home kitchen—who has the time to make Enrique Olvera's thousand-day mole, or even find all the ingredients?—but Ella doesn't watch the show for recipes. She watches it for the spectacle of mastery, much as other teens hang out on YouTube watching Lionel Messi's greatest goals or Yuja Wang playing "Flight of the Bumblebee."

The show's self-serious musings on the mysteries of food make me cringe a bit, but I was once fluent in that idiom. From the time I was nine until well into my teens, I was determined to be a chef. I ran a catering business out of my parents' house, in Longmeadow, Massachusetts, and did apprenticeships with notable chefs. So when I watch *Chef's Table* I can't help experiencing the slight pang you get from seeing someone living the life you chose not to live. *Could I have been a contender?* When I was cooking, food was everything to me; I haven't known as consuming a passion since. The kitchen is where I learned the only foreign language I speak: *brunoise, pâte feuilletée* and *demi-glace* were among the first French words I knew, and they retain an incantatory power.

I started to cook after my friends—at least, I thought they were friends—began to bully me for being overweight and Jewish. "Pudgy" was my nickname, and as they threw change at me in the hall I learned that to be a Jew was to love money. I punched one boy in the neck when he called me a dirty Jew, and felt very pleased as he fell to the ground. But the problem of my weight couldn't be handled by vigilante justice. I wasn't ashamed to be Jewish, but I was embarrassed to be plump. While vacationing at the Jersey Shore with my family, I began to hide food, furtively removing items from my plate and placing them in a napkin. I would bury much of my dinner in the sand outside the house my parents had rented. I counted calories, and spent hours appraising myself in the mirror, measuring my progress.

This wasn't much fun. For one thing, I was depriving myself of the pleasures of my mother's cooking. Some families are brought together by faith; we were brought together by food. By secretly not eating, I was isolating myself. As I grew thinner, I felt both proud and terribly lonely. Toward the end of the summer, my parents became aware that I wasn't myself; in photos from that time I look gaunt and unhealthy. When we returned home from the shore, my parents took me to a child psychologist, Sidney Hyman. Dr. Hyman was in his late fifties, wore a bow tie and liked to crack silly jokes. He didn't ask many questions, but I remember playing a lot of board games with him. I'd become very serious, and I think he wanted me to rediscover what it was like to have fun. Trying to have fun is what started me cooking. I opened a cupboard, found some chocolate—I'd hardly touched any since becoming obsessed with my weight—and decided to make what I called fudge. I put the chocolate in a plastic container and placed it in the toaster oven. The container melted a bit, but the warm, liquefied chocolate was delicious, and the fact that I'd melted it myself was exciting: I had transformed something.

The next thing I made was a simple chocolate cake. It came out well, and I even treated myself to a slice, although I was still carefully counting calories. Before long, I was spending all my free time in the kitchen. I worked my way up to more elaborate confections, like *dacquoise*, a hazelnut meringue layered with buttercream frosting, and then to making savory dishes. I especially liked sauces, which, in their textural variety—thick or thin, translucent or cloudy, syrupy or velvety—taught me the subtle poetry of haute cuisine. I became fascinated by emulsions, the mixing of liquids that happens in fancy sauces like beurre blanc and hollandaise but also in the simplest vinaigrette. I pored over my mother's cookbooks and magazines, reading about the great chefs who had defined what it meant to cook seriously. On weekends, friends would come over to sample new dishes. I became a connoisseur of local food shops and butchers. I ordered *magret de canard* from a supplier in the Hudson Valley. Each month, I would prepare a dinner for my family, which I would "advertise" a few weeks in advance by tucking a menu under my mother's pillow.

When I was eleven, I launched a catering company, Adam's Edibles, leaving xeroxed copies of a handwritten menu outside our neighbors' doors. I started with desserts and pastries, but a year later I expanded my repertoire:

Dr. Mr. or Ms.,
My name is Adam Shatz. Last year I ran a successful dessert business. This summer I'm adding appetizers and soups to the menu. My food is delicious and not too complicated. All the

ingredients I use are fresh . . . I live on 106 Morningside Drive, Longmeadow, Mass. I have the only red house on the street. I know you'll love my food!

The menu included *gougères* ($3.50 for twelve), ravioli ($8 for four servings), and vichyssoise ($4 with onions, $6 with leeks, for four servings). I changed the company's name to Le Trésor— "Shatz" means "treasure" in German—and began to cater multicourse meals, mostly for my parents' friends. This meant that I was now cooking in other people's kitchens. I would shop for ingredients the day before a dinner, arrive at my customer's home the morning of, and spend the entire day cooking. The clients must have found my presence amusing, but to me it was no stunt. I couldn't have been more certain that my future lay in the kitchen. I was already dreaming of going to cooking school, apprenticing in France and opening my own restaurant.

Word of my exploits got around, and my art teacher made a documentary about me for the local cable-access channel. She called it *Adam Cooks*, and that's pretty much what you see: a nerdy, bespectacled twelve-year-old in a chef's uniform making a baked-goat-cheese salad, a chicken ragout with watercress cream sauce and morels, and a raspberry crème brûlée. Later, he pontificates on his culinary influences, against a musical backdrop of classical guitar. At one point, you see him apologizing for no apparent reason. The reason was that I'd just screamed "Fuck!" in front of the film crew, after burning myself on a hot pot.

The cable-access channel had very little content, and so *Adam Cooks* was shown on a virtually continuous loop for a couple of years. People assumed it was a weekly show, rather than a one-off, and I became a local celebrity. "Garbed in a chef's hat and cooking jacket, Adam rattled off the names of his favorite chefs, debated the influence of famed female and male chefs, and the offerings of exclusive restaurants in America and Europe," the Longmeadow *News* reported. In that article, I discussed "the cooking philosophies of Escoffier and Fernand Point," my preference for gas stoves, and sexism in professional kitchens: "Men are afraid to let women cook."

The same year, I had a more bruising encounter with the media, after my uncle, for my thirteenth birthday, scored me an invitation to a conference in Boston on wine and gastronomy. There I met Ruth Reichl, who was then a food writer for the *Los Angeles Times*. That's where she wrote a short profile of me, under the headline "tyke with a toque":

> "The most important thing in cooking is to have your own style," Adam Shatz, 13, is saying, when his mother taps him on the shoulder. "Look Adam," says Adam's Mother, "it's Michael McCarty." She turns so he can see the great chef. Adam squares his shoulders and walks manfully over.

Reichl described a boy with "extraordinary poise," who boasts that he "never cooks a dish more than once," and says "airily" that he charges "about $25 a person." I was devastated. And I'd got off easy compared with my parents, who'd done nothing more than take me to the event:

> Adam's father snaps a picture . . . Before long there are four chefs surrounding the young prodigy. His proud papa is still snapping away . . . Stage mothers were once all the rage, but now it's time to bid farewell to the movie mama as we make room for the latest breed of pushy progenitor—the stove-top parent.

In fact, my parents tried to protect me from the media. When ABC television approached them about making a movie based on my life as a child chef, they immediately rejected the idea.

Still, Reichl was right about one thing: I was awfully serious. But cooking, far from being an expression of my "extraordinary poise," was a refuge from the world of my peers. True, I had a new circle of friends, who appreciated my cooking and didn't taunt me, and I was no longer seeing Dr. Hyman. Yet I still kept fastidious track of what I consumed and felt terribly uncomfortable in my body. Giving shape to food, turning it into something artful, was an escape, and the kitchen became a laboratory in which I could lose myself in experimentation.

And I had so much to learn. Cooking was not just a skill but a practice with a remarkable history, requiring absolute devotion. My parents encouraged my ambition, buying me equipment, taking me to restaurants and coming home with menus signed by chefs I followed in the food press. I read everything I could find on pioneers of the "New American cuisine," such as Jeremiah Tower, the brilliant, bitchy Harvard-educated architect who created Stars, a dazzling brasserie in San Francisco; and Alice Waters, the owner of Chez Panisse, in Berkeley, where Tower had got his start before the two became bitter enemies over who invented the Chez Panisse style. Once, I got to dine at the Campton Place Hotel, in San Francisco, where Bradley Ogden was developing a style based on local ingredients and regional recipes. "You seem to have a deep appreciation and dedication for this business, but don't take it too seriously," Ogden wrote afterward. Good advice that I wasn't ready to hear; wasn't taking it seriously the whole point?

Besides, my real heroes weren't American but French: Paul Bocuse, the visionary of Lyon; the formidably articulate Joël Robuchon; the Troisgros brothers, renowned for their salmon with sorrel sauce; Michel Guérard, the inventor of *cuisine minceur*, a low-calorie version of nouvelle cuisine. I was fascinated by Bernard Loiseau, the moody creator of *cuisine à l'eau*, a style built around water-based sauces. (He later killed himself, fearing that he was about to lose his third Michelin star.) But the chef who most seized my imagination was Alain Senderens, a bearded, bespectacled intellectual who looked more like a poststructuralist theorist or a Kabbalah scholar than like a cook. At L'Archestrate, in Paris, he made daring adaptations of recipes he excavated from ancient Roman cookbooks, and shocked the culinary establishment with wonderfully mad flavor combinations, like lobster with vanilla sauce.

I was in awe of Senderens. Not that I'd ever tasted his food—I hadn't even been to Paris—but merely to *read* about Senderens was to know that he was a genius. I discovered him thanks to my favorite food critics, Henri Gault and Christian Millau, who ran an opinionated, witty, literary rival to the staid Michelin Guide.

They declared Senderens "the Picasso of French cooking." He was certainly my Picasso, a bold and uncompromising revolutionary who'd reinvented the language of food.

My own cooking was more cautious. I was attached to traditional forms and intent on pleasing. I recently unearthed the menu for a dinner party I catered when I was maybe fourteen. The dishes—"Fricassée of Mussels with Yellow Pepper Cream and Spinach" or "Summer Fruits with a Sabayon Sauce Flavored with Framboise"—show that I was more interested in absorbing the great tradition of French cooking than in disrupting it. How could I break with a tradition if I hadn't properly learned its techniques? Boning poultry, cutting perfect julienned carrots, peeling and dicing a tomato unblemished by skin or seeds, making a lumpless roux for béchamel, caramelizing onions without burning them, whisking pieces of butter into a wine reduction without curdling the sauce: such skills had to become second nature, like tying one's shoes or swimming breaststroke.

These are physical as much as intellectual forms of knowledge. How do you know that a steak, or a piece of salmon, has been cooked to your liking? Not by a timer, or even by looking, but by the feel of its flesh when you press it, and the indentation left by your finger. I began to keep a food diary, charting my progress and recording my innermost thoughts about cooking. I was interested in its relationship to art and politics, both growing enthusiasms, and to sex, an unknown terrain that I was impatient to explore. (One of my friends came across a cassette I had made, full of poetic confessions about food and sensuality; after enduring hours of ridicule, I destroyed it.)

In the kitchen, I sought out meats that I'd never eaten—rabbit, quail, pigeon—and discovered the voluptuous frisson of offal, on the delicate line between succulent and repellent. There were a few disasters. Once, I made pasta with chanterelles that had been picked in a forest in Maine by a family friend, an old Russian Jew who claimed to be a mycologist. Suddenly, my grandmother said she felt sick and started to panic. Everyone put their forks down. The mushrooms turned out to be fine. While my parents made sure that I hadn't poisoned my grandmother, I went back to the kitchen and whipped up a simple *spaghetti aglio e olio*, which I secretly preferred to chanterelles.

Not long after Reichl's profile appeared, I found a French culinary mentor, Gérard Pangaud. In Paris, he'd become, at twenty-seven, the youngest chef ever to receive two Michelin stars. Then Joe Baum, the themed-restaurant pioneer, persuaded him to come to New York and head the kitchen at Aurora, on East Forty-ninth Street. The restaurant was a chic and dreamy midtown oasis in muted shades of blue and pink. Bryan Miller, the restaurant critic for the *Times*, called it "the Versailles in Joe Baum's impressive collection of culinary chateaus."

I first went there for lunch with my grandmother, after writing Pangaud a fan letter. He was waiting when we arrived. For the next few hours, we ate rounds of lobster tail in a tangy, buttery sauce of Sauternes, lime and fresh ginger, on a bed of spinach; a ragout of periwinkles, briny as the sea; and slices of grilled, rosy-pink pigeon breast with olives, tomato and lemon confit, in a rich, somber sauce that haunted the tongue. Pangaud wasn't a revolutionary like Senderens, but he had a grippingly visceral imagination, an intuition for unusual combinations of flavor and texture, and an earthy elegance. After lunch, he invited me to study with him.

There was nothing unusual about a chef asking a teenager if he'd like to work in the kitchen. In France, culinary training is based on what's known as the *stage*, an unpaid apprenticeship that all chefs pass through, beginning with the lowliest of activities and gradually rising to more complex tasks. French kitchens are deeply hierarchical institutions, run along essentially military lines. My studies with Pangaud weren't quite a *stage*—living in Massachusetts, I could train for only a few days every couple of months—but my education there lasted several years. The days began at dawn and ended well past midnight, and I made the most of them. I usually worked in garde-manger, preparing salads and chopping vegetables, but I was occasionally allowed to work on the line, searing steaks, duck breasts and thick slabs of foie gras.

Restaurant kitchens are enclosed worlds, and now that I was inside one I wanted to know who its players were and how they operated. The chefs on the line were mostly blue-collar white guys, though there were a few women. The only thing the line chefs talked about—other than food, keeping up with their orders and who had screwed something up—was fucking, and I guessed that some of that was happening downstairs, in the basement kitchen, where the meat was stored. The prep cooks chopping vegetables in garde-manger were mostly East Asian and Central American immigrants. Once they graduated to the line, they adopted the brassier, saltier argot that cooking in conditions of extreme heat and pressure seemed to require. The intensity of the kitchen—the speed, the insults, the burns from hot oil splashing—was frightening at first, but soon I was intoxicated. And it was satisfying to be welcomed as one of the team. Some of the cooks referred to me teasingly as the Kid. But I *was* a kid, and I didn't know a luckier one.

In the summer of 1987, just before I turned fifteen, I went to France for the first time, with my family. The highlight of the trip was a visit to Lameloise, a Michelin three-star restaurant and hotel in Chagny, a small industrial town in Burgundy. I'd written to Jacques Lameloise, the chef and owner, before we set out, and Pangaud had sent a letter of recommendation, too. Lameloise greeted us warmly, and I spent the next day in the kitchen. Afterward, he asked if I wanted to come back to do a *stage* there. My parents said I could, provided that I covered my living expenses, which meant that I needed to get a job back home.

So, when I wasn't in school, I started working in a very different kind of kitchen, at the Student Prince, in Springfield. Known to its regulars as the Fort, it was an old-school German restaurant, whose owner, Rupprecht Scherff, had fled the Nazis. The dining room was a festive place, but the kitchen was almost Dickensian in its sordidness and gloom. Whereas Aurora's employees were ambitious and obsessed with the art of food, no one at the Fort imagined that they were doing much more than punching a time card. Many of the waitstaff seemed to be on chemical mood enhancers. The Polish woman who chopped lettuce and placed it in bins the size of garbage cans wore gloves because she had severe eczema. If working at Aurora was an apprenticeship in haute cuisine, working at the Fort was an education in injuries of class that are invisible from the dining room. In school, I'd been reading *The Jungle*, Upton Sinclair's novel exposing exploitation in the meatpacking industry. Soon I understood Sinclair's fury that readers had been more alarmed by the book's food-hygiene implications than by its indictment of working conditions.

The kitchen was on two floors. I worked downstairs, in a basement that looked as if it hadn't been cleaned since the place opened. In the morning, I pounded veal cutlets for schnitzel; in the afternoon, I put scraps of pork through an electric meat grinder for bratwurst. One day, the grinder blew up. Sparks flew, and my face was pelted with bits of ground pork and slicked with brine. The only other person downstairs was Walter, a man in his sixties who bore a passing resemblance to Elijah Muhammad. He had recently returned to the Fort from a long leave of absence after being convicted of stabbing a fellow employee; Rupprecht hired him back as soon as he was out of prison. Walter didn't talk much and had a way of chuckling to himself. I didn't think much about him, until one day he grabbed my meat tenderizer and chased me through the basement. He cornered me, and I pleaded with him. He broke out laughing, as if my terror was the funniest thing he'd ever seen. After that, we got along beautifully.

In school, meanwhile, I was channeling my food obsession into writing. I contributed restaurant reviews to the school newspaper, closely mimicking the style of Gault and Millau. I was also writing about politics and culture: editorials denouncing Reagan's support for the Nicaraguan Contras, essays on contemporary cinema. Reading *The Autobiography of Malcolm X* and Claude Brown's Harlem memoir, *Manchild in the Promised Land*, I was discovering a New York very far from the exclusive restaurants I expected to make a career in—closer, in a way, to the basement at the Fort. New interests were taking hold of my imagination. I immersed myself in French literature, dressed all in black, and thought of myself as an existentialist, although I couldn't have said what that meant. I looked forward to my adult life in New York, the only place in America where one could be an authentic existentialist.

In the summer of 1988, taking the money I had made at the Fort, I set off for France, and stepped into a gleaming modern kitchen where more than a dozen young chefs—mostly French, but also a few Japanese—worked with utter absorption, fired up by the idea that they, too, would one day run an establishment like Lameloise. I spent hours at a time paring turnips, trimming haricots verts and shaving potatoes for potato tartlets; occasionally, I was permitted to sauté pieces of duck foie gras, which were then nestled on top of mâche dressed in sherry vinaigrette.

I became very efficient at my tasks—the whole point of being a *stagiaire*—but the kitchen was monastically quiet, and I missed the banter of the cooks at Aurora, their pleasure in conversational combat, their improvisatory élan. If Pangaud's kitchen was a jazz band of many voices, Lameloise's was a symphony orchestra performing high-fidelity versions of the classic repertoire. Lameloise's food was traditional Burgundian haute cuisine updated with nouvelle touches. I wondered what Alain Senderens would say, and was pretty sure that he would disapprove. One young chef, who had worked at L'Espérance, a three-star place an hour and a half's drive away, glumly admitted that Lameloise was a letdown. Soon after, while we were in the middle of some task or other, I asked, "Is this how they do it at L'Espérance?" imagining he'd appreciate my sarcasm. With sudden vehemence, he told me never to mention L'Espérance again. He left before the summer was over.

Jacques Lameloise's son, Armand, was only a few months older than me but seemed vastly more sophisticated, especially about girls, who frightened me. A self-styled intellectual who worshiped New Wave cinema, he adored his mother, a reader of classical French literature with whom he would linger for hours in the morning over café au lait, croissants and cigarettes. His father, who had probably never opened a book that wasn't about food, was the odd man out in his own home. He was a kind, doting father, but Armand considered him a fool and believed himself to be cut out for grander things than inheriting the family restaurant, however many *étoiles* the Michelin inspectors had awarded it. I still wasn't sure there were grander things than running a three-star, but I was becoming bored in the kitchen, so, whenever I could, I started joining Armand on excursions he took with his friends.

Our first trip was to Noyon, a hundred kilometers north of Paris, where Armand's friend Jérémie, an actor-comedian, was throwing a Bastille Day party. Noyon had seen its share of luminaries—Charlemagne was crowned co-king of the Franks at its cathedral in 768, Calvin was born there, and through the centuries the town had fallen to Vikings, Habsburgs and Nazis—but now it was a backwater. There were no adults in sight, and I watched a teenage bacchanal unfold with fear and fascination. A group was roasting suckling pigs over a fire and opening bottles of beer and champagne; couples cavorted in the grass. Someone poured me a glass of punch. It went down easily, and I drank another. Next thing I knew, I had thrown a bottle into a wall and collapsed on the floor of someone's bedroom. A couple came in and began to have sex on the floor next to me. "What's wrong with the American?" the woman asked. "Oh, it's just the jet lag, I hear he flew in today from California." They continued their business and I passed out.

A few weeks later, in the Jura, Armand's friends and I sped through a field on bicycles to a discothèque, and danced till early in the morning. When we left, a group of skinheads attacked us with baseball bats and stole our bikes. We spent the rest of the morning filing a report in a police station. Then we made fondue, smoked and listened to Serge Gainsbourg, Sade and the Cure. I had just read Camus's *L'Étranger*, but I'd never heard the Cure's song based on it, "Killing an Arab." I was stunned by its blunt, angry insistence on the identity of the man Meursault had killed. Later that summer, I found myself in a car with a group of middle-aged friends of Jacques's, who were joking about "the Arabs" (no one said "Muslims" then). It was Eid al-Fitr, and the men were talking about the blood that flowed when the Arabs sacrificed their sheep. They seemed to relish the image of Arab "savages." Only a quarter century had passed since the liberation of Algeria from French rule, and some of these men had probably served in the army there. I sat in silence, understanding almost nothing, and yet understanding everything I needed to know.

The most important things I learned that summer were outside the kitchen. I still enjoyed cooking, but the idea of a life of eighteen-hour days at the stove had started to seem less enthralling. Perhaps cooking had achieved its unconscious purpose: although I didn't exactly *like* my body, I was no longer counting calories or scrutinizing myself in the mirror. Finding a refuge from the world seemed less necessary, too—indeed, I was impatient to plunge in and make a difference in its conflicts. At one of my last stints at Aurora, I showed up wearing a "U.S. out of Central America" pin; one of the chefs said that I should probably take it off when I was in the dining room, since many customers were Reagan supporters. He was teasing me, but I knew that he was right. Cook for imperialists? For a teenage radical, it was unthinkable.

During my last two years of high school, I stopped working in restaurants, aside from a summer job at a McDonald's in Enfield, Connecticut. The owner praised my skill at frying fish fillets and said I had a great future in his establishment. I discouraged customers from ordering Coke, because the company refused to divest from South Africa, and I came home every day smelling like cooking oil. I worked one final time with Pangaud, on the opening night of the Rainbow Room, where he was an adviser, an experience that felt like a beautiful last dance in haute cuisine. By then, Pangaud knew that I wasn't planning a culinary career, but he was fond of me, and said that I was always welcome in his kitchen.

The last time I worked in a restaurant kitchen was in 1994, when I needed a job after college. I wrote to the chef of an acclaimed New American restaurant on the Upper East Side about my food experiences. He invited me to spend a few days in the kitchen on a trial basis. My immediate supervisor was in his fifties and had studied comparative literature under the Palestinian-American literary critic Edward Said, one of my heroes at Columbia, where I had just got my bachelor's degree. "I didn't realize they had a cooking school at Columbia," one of the other chefs said when he heard I'd gone there. They didn't.

I was assigned to the garde-manger, where I chopped carrots, cleaned buckets of squid and fixed the occasional salad. But my skills, especially my knife skills, were rusty, and my supervisor wasn't fooled. He needed a trained chef, not a former child prodigy. After a few days, he took me aside, and said he didn't think he could hire me: "You obviously have a real passion for food, and for cooking, but your skills aren't where they need to be to work here." If I was serious about a career, he said, I could work in a lesser establishment, improving my technique, or I could go to cooking school. And if I wasn't serious? I asked.

"You might give some thought to graduate school."

I lost touch with most of the people I knew in my cooking years. Armand became a filmmaker, and his parents sold Lameloise. Jérémie, the host of the party in Noyon, killed himself. Rupprecht and Walter died, and the Fort was sold to new owners. Pangaud left New York to open a restaurant in Washington, and then became a private chef and a teacher. Ruth Reichl, of course, went on to become the chief restaurant critic for the *New York Times* and then the editor of *Gourmet*. I wrote to her when she was at *Gourmet*, reminding her of the "tyke with a toque" and suggesting that we meet, since I'd joined her profession rather than becoming a chef. She never replied.

Restaurant culture has changed profoundly since the eighties. Food is glitzier and more international but also more politically conscious—militantly organic and swirling with debates about cultural appropriation. It's arguably more democratic, too. Celebrity chefs, competitive cooking shows and the collapse of French hegemony have made haute cuisine seem like a relic of the past. My daughter is less interested in the French sauces I revered than in berbere, za'atar and dried rose petals. Perhaps one day we'll see the reign of haute cuisine as yet another Eurocentric fable that propped up unthinking assertions of cultural superiority. The preparation of high-end restaurant food hasn't been entirely democratized, but the best chefs today often come from countries in Asia and the Global South. An increasing number of them are women, and #MeToo has begun to challenge a culture of sexual predation that was widespread in the restaurant industry. Restaurant culture is more worldly, and more reflective of the revolutionary turbulence of our world, than it's ever been.

The notion that food can be art no longer raises any eyebrows. When I was spending all my free time in kitchens, chefs could be artistic, but they couldn't be full-fledged artists, partly because their "work" was, literally, consumed. Today, this fact is no strike against them; on the contrary, chefs are the signature artists of Western consumer society, in which what you eat and where are defining marks of what the sociologist Pierre Bourdieu called "social capital." In 2007, the contemporary art show Documenta featured the "molecular gastronomy" of Ferran Adrià, the most innovative of today's cooks. At his restaurant El Bulli, in Catalonia, Adrià had devised novel scientific techniques to produce a "deconstructivist" cuisine that centers on foams.

I don't even know how to make a foam, and so far I've resisted buying a blowtorch, which Ella wants for making s'mores and crème brûlée. The food I make these days—like seemingly everyone in the age of Ottolenghi—is Mediterranean, a mélange of Italian, North African and Middle Eastern influences. The French technique I absorbed during my culinary education still comes in handy: I can chop onions with a precision and speed that occasionally impresses friends who don't have a culinary background. I know exactly when egg yolks have reached the perfect texture for a sabayon, or egg whites for a soufflé; I can whisk butter into a reduction sauce in a way that imparts just the right sheen. Small things, but I am very glad to have remembered them.

Ella is not particularly interested in my tales of the kitchen, and she loves to remind me of one awful dish I prepared for her: a botched experiment of roasted salmon flavored with honey. But, watching me when we're at the stove, she has refined her skills, and taught herself new ones. Her fresh pasta is enviably delicate, her pastry crusts a sublime balance of firmness and crumbliness. I'm still alarmed when I see how rapidly she chops vegetables, until I remind myself that she's just doing what I've taught her, and won't cut herself. She has the "poise" that I was mostly feigning and is a much more relaxed and patient cook than I was. For her, cooking isn't a professional ambition but simply a pleasure, and a way of sharing her pleasure with others.

Recently, Ella made croissants for the third time. Croissants are notoriously difficult: if you're not careful as you fold the butter into the dough, you can easily end up with something stiff and hard, rather than a flaky, airy, multilayered marvel. As Ella rolled the dough after completing the first "turn," I thought I saw butter oozing. When I started to speak up, she said I had to leave the room, and I did as I was told. Whatever she ended up doing, the croissants were the finest she'd made. I'm learning that the best thing I can do to encourage her in the kitchen is to stay out of the way. Becoming a cook is about achieving mastery, independence and, if you're lucky, originality. My role these days, when Ella puts on my old toque, is to step aside, taste something if she asks, and wash the dishes.

Acknowledgments

I have benefited enormously from the sensitivity, refinement and wise counsel of the editors who shepherded these essays to publication: Mary-Kay Wilmers, Alice Spawls, Jean McNicol, Daniel Soar, Christian Lorentzen and Paul Myerscough, my brilliant colleagues at the *London Review of Books*; Ian Buruma at the *New York Review of Books*; Edwin Frank at New York Review Books Classics (who commissioned the essay on William Gardner Smith as a foreword to the republication of *The Stone Face*); Luke Mitchell at the *New York Times Magazine*; David Remnick and Leo Carey at the *New Yorker*; and Roane Carey and John Palattella at the *Nation*. I am also grateful to John Merrick, Nicole Aschoff and Andy Hsiao at Verso for suggesting this collection of pieces. And thanks to Sara Roy and Elias Muhanna, who hosted my talk, "Writers or Missionaries," at, respectively, the Harvard Center for Middle East Studies and Brown University.

Thanks to Sarah Chalfant at the Wylie Agency, an unswerving supporter of my work and a wise (and patient) adviser.

My thinking about the ideas in this book has been greatly enriched by conversations with (among others) Sasha Abramsky, Ratik Asokan, Caroline Abu Sada, Eric Banks, Leonard Benardo, Carl Bromley, Rony Brauman, Daikha Dridi, Dominique Eddé, Brent Hayes Edwards, Barbara Jeanne Fields, Paul Gilroy, Vivian Gornick, Ricky Goldstein, Mohamed Harbi, Tobi Haslett, Jeremy Harding, Brent Hayes Edwards, Stephen Holmes, Andreas Huyssen, Arun Kapil, Kiana Karimi, Randall Kennedy, Tammy Kim, Leela Jacinto, Sean Jacobs, Amber Joseph, Jake Lamar, James Lasdun, Jessica Loudis, Jordan Mintzer, Pankaj Mishra,

Brian Morton, Michaël Neuman, Darryl Pinckney, Eyal Press, David Rieff, Joe Sacco, Joan Wallach Scott, Nermeen Shaikh, Scott Sherman, Christine Smallwood, Clifford Thompson, Joëlle Touma, Enzo Traverso and Kelvin Williams.

Thanks to my family: Stephen and Leslie Shatz, my parents, who have always been my most devoted and thoughtful readers; my sister, Sarah Shatz, a gifted photographer who is always there to remind me that I am not, in fact, a native of New York City; and my daughter Ella, a budding ceramic artist and baker whose intellectual and creative passions rekindle my own.

Thanks especially to Sayeeda Moreno, whose love (and affectionate mockery) keeps me sane.

Index